Music Publishing and Patronage

C F Peters: 1800 to the Holocaust

Music Publishing and Patronage

C F Peters: 1800 to the Holocaust

Irene Lawford-Hinrichsen

EDITION PRESS

Dedication

This book is dedicated in loving memory
to Martha and Henri Hinrichsen
the grandparents I never knew

The Families of Martha (Née Bendix) and Henri Hinrichsen

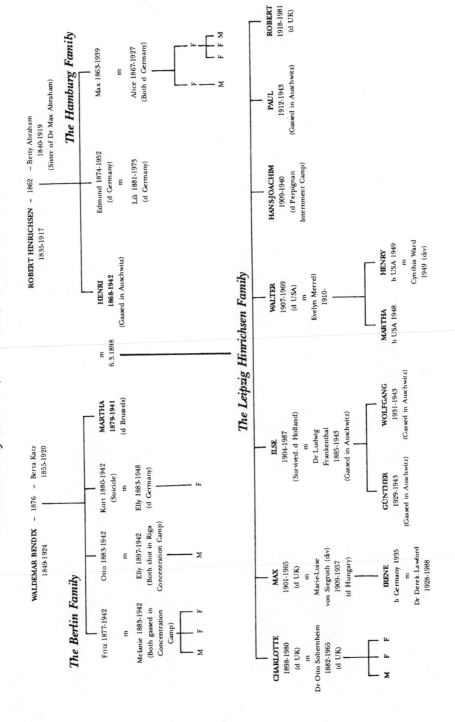

Contents

List of Illustrations

All illustrations are from the collection of the author.

Foreword

by

Lord Menuhin, OM, KBE

This is an unusual book as it relates to a hereditary line of music publishers - the great C F Peters Editions - and traces world history through the experiences of a most important publishing house and through people I knew well over these horrendous decades, which both Max and his brother Walter Hinrichsen and their father's publishing house survived.

We know of composers and performers, but not so much of the institutions, commercial and distinguished, which supported and promoted these great musical figures of our era.

I am sure this book will provide enlightening reading not only to all people associated with music, but also to the general reader who wants to know how destiny and history impinge on the human being.

Yehudi Menuhin
3rd October 1997

Acknowledgements

First and foremost I wish to thank Annerose and Horst Kemp of Leipzig who, since the day we first met in November 1991, have been dear friends to me and helpful in so many ways, especially with research about the Henriette Goldschmidt Schule. I am immensely grateful to the manager of C F Peters, Leipzig, Norbert Molkenbur, who has been a great help in imparting and locating information and documents about the company. I owe a big debt of thanks to Peter Krause, librarian of the Music Library of the City of Leipzig, which incorporates the Peters Music Library, for his patient and profusely informative replies to so many of my queries.

In Great Britain I wish to thank above all, Professor Brian Groombridge, for his editorial help and enlightening comments. His unfailing encouragement throughout the writing of this book, when he read and made suggestions on each chapter as it was written, was of immeasurable help to me.

Others in Leipzig whom I wish to thank for information and answers to my queries include: Bernd Pachnike, former manager of C F Peters, Leipzig and Franziska Weismann, daughter of the late Wilhelm Weismann, who made her father's recorded 'memories' available to me. Professor Dr Hella Brock for information about Nina Grieg. Dr phil. Hans-Martin Pleßke for archival help. Professor Manfred Unger, retired Director of the Sächsisches Staatsarchiv Leipzig for historical information. Dr Winfried Schrammek, retired Director of the Music Instruments Museum. Herbert Kästner for his notes about the Leipziger Bibliophilen Abend; Frau Brigitte Richter of the *Stadtgeschichtliches* Museum for information on Henri Hinrichsen's gifts; Dr Thomas Schinköth for information about music in Nazi Germany. Dr Michael Märker for information on the Music Instruments Museum. Bernd-Lutz Lange, journalist, for information. Steffen Poser for information on the *Völkerschlachtdenkmal.* The archivist of the Gewandhaus zu Leipzig for a Grieg photo. Dr Gerald Wiemers, archivist of the University of Leipzig. Hubert Lang, solicitor. The *Jüdische Gemeinde* (Jewish Community), Leipzig. The *Rat der Stadt Leipzig* (Leipzig City Council) for accommodation in the City guest house. The staffs of the Music Instruments Museum; of the *Deutsche Bücherei*; of the *Sächsisches Staatsarchiv Leipzig (StAL)*; of the *Stadtarchiv Leipzig*; of the *Museum der bildenden Künste.*

There were also people who helped me from elsewhere to whom I wish to extend my gratitude and they include: C F Peters Frankfurt for permission to use the correspondence between Edvard Grieg and C F Peters as published in the book: *Edvard Grieg Briefwechsel mit dem Verlag C.F. Peters 1863-1907* and for permission to quote from correspondence in the Bestand C F Peters in the *Sächsisches Staatsarchiv Leipzig*. Dr Susanne Popp and Dr Susanne Shigihara of the Reger Institute Karlsruhe for information and photos on Max Reger and for permission to quote from the correspondence between Max Reger and C F Peters as published in the book: *Max Reger Briefwechsel mit dem Verlag C.F. Peters*. Fred K Prieberg of Diersheim for the results of his researches into the aryanization of C F Peters. Norvall Skreien of Bergen, Norway, Editor of *Amoroso,* for information. Dr Hans Schneider, Music Antiquarian of Tutzing for providing a photocopy of the *Jubilee Book* for Henri Hinrichsen and allowing me to quote from it. Erika Bucholz and Raymond Wolff of Berlin. Elfriede Bannas of Bremen for the return of books belonging to Henri Hinrichsen. The archivist of the Staatsarchiv Bremen.

In England I would like to thank the Newspaper Library of the British Library. Dr Lionel Carley, archivist of the Delius Society. The Karg-Elert Society of Great Britain. Paul Reid for information on Max Friedländer. Professor Peter Gordon of Woburn Press for editorial advice. The late Norman Williams for legal information. The musicologists Felix Aprahamian, Professor Denis Stevens and Dr Stanley Sadie.

I also wish to thank Dr Wolfgang and Dagmar von Kaltenborn-Stachau of Magdeburg for help in transcribing old German script. Dr Carl-August and Hildegard Pauly of Hamburg for information. My cousin Martha Hinrichsen of New York for documents. A cousin in California and several second-cousins who wish to remain un-named, for family memories, photos and documents.

I am grateful to my daughter Julie Lawford for her appreciation and encouragement, which meant a lot to me.

Introduction

Publishing music demands intuition, sensitivity, patience, psychology and a love of music. It is an act of faith. It is also a business. This is the story of a business motivated by humanity. It tells of composers: their personalities, their conflicts and their music. It describes how music is published through the story of two men, Dr Max Abraham and his nephew, Henri Hinrichsen. This story reveals how they developed the small music publishing company: C F Peters Leipzig, Bureau de Musique to achieve world-wide stature. It tells of how these two men turned the profits from their astute business methods to humanitarian purposes, to help and promote musicians and to become major sponsors of several cultural and educational institutions.

The enfolding story will give an insight into the many different aspects of music publishing by this famous firm. It illustrates, often through correspondence, the interaction of the people involved in the publishing house and the wider society around them. Starting in 1800, the early development of the company is outlined, highlighting the publication of music by Beethoven and Louis Spohr and the birth of copyright legislation. The period 1863 to 1900, when Dr Max Abraham became a partner in C F Peters and founded the famous 'Edition Peters' is covered in greater depth. There is a chapter on his remarkable relationship with Edvard Grieg. The main thrust of the book is the period after Dr Abraham's death in 1900, when his nephew, Henri Hinrichsen became sole proprietor. He was in due course joined by his three eldest sons.

The book demonstrates how the complexities of society and politics are juxtaposed with the process of translating a composer's inspiration into the realisation of printed sheet music and musical performance. There are stories about some of the many composers whose music was published and who were befriended and financially supported. Emphasis is given to the relationships between Henri Hinrichsen and Edvard Grieg and Max Reger. There is also a brief exploration of the personalities and creativity of Christian Sinding, Karl Straube, Walter Niemann, Percy Grainger, Hans Pfitzner, Sigfrid Karg-Elert and Richard Strauss and several musicologists. The traumas surrounding the publication of two major works - Schönberg's *Five Orchestral Pieces* and Mahler's Fifth Symphony - are detailed and the negotiations for other publications are revealed. Collaboration with printers and suppliers is covered. Working, social and business conditions as they are affected by political changes are shown.

Henri Hinrichsen was the author's grandfather. His work and life, not only as music publisher and friend of composers, but also as benefactor, patron of the arts and major supporter of Leipzig institutions, are recounted. A firm believer in the importance of education for women, he was the founding benefactor of the first all-women's college in Europe, in Leipzig - the Henriette Goldschmidt School. He financially supported the Peters Music Library which Dr Max Abraham had donated to the City of Leipzig and he donated the Music Instruments Museum to Leipzig. These, along with other important acts of patronage are covered.

Henri Hinrichsen's world and that of his family, was destroyed completely with the election to power of the Nazis, in 1933. The Hinrichsens were a Jewish family and the brutal new laws enacted to deprive the Jews of all their rights are detailed. The tragic consequences for both the firm of C F Peters, which was confiscated in a process called 'Aryanization', and for the family are described.

The story finishes with Henri Hinrichsen's murder in the gas chambers of Auschwitz.

A brief *Afterword* describes how the firm of C F Peters survived both the Second World War and subsequent Soviet occupation.

The Background: The City of Leipzig

The City of Leipzig in the State of Saxony, lies at the cross roads of the main trade routes of Europe. The name Leipzig goes back to the year 1050. An annual trade fair, held since 1160, has been an International Trade Fair - the *Leipziger Messe* - since the fifteenth century. The University of Leipzig was founded in 1490. In the nineteenth century Leipzig was at the centre of the Napoleonic Wars, with the *Völkerschlacht* (Battle of the Nations) taking place in 1813. 1837 saw the publication of the world's first daily newspaper, when the Brockhaus Verlag issued the *Leipziger Allgemeine Zeitung* (Leipzig General Newspaper).

Long a centre for the fur trade, with the opening of the Leipzig-Dresden Railway in 1839, commercial opportunities increased. The population reached the 100,000 mark to transform Leipzig into the eighth largest city in Germany by 1870; the *Deutsches Reichsgericht* (German Supreme Court) was established there in 1879. Between 1902 and 1913 the largest rail terminal in Europe was built in Leipzig . The city became prominent for industrial development and was the cradle of the Workers' Movement.

City of Books

Leipzig became a centre for the book trade as a direct result of the International Trade Fairs, with the printing of the first Trade Fair Catalogue in 1594. The centre of the printing industry, Leipzig saw the flowering of many fine publishing houses. This resulted, in 1825, in the foundation of the *Börsenverein der Deutschen Buchhändler* (The Association for German Book Traders). This organisation's many-sided efforts contributed enormously to the development of the entire German book trade and to its high reputation. The *Börsenverein* is one of the founders of the *Deutsche Bücherei* (the German Library), the foundation stone of which was laid on 18th October 1913. It was, and still is, a reference library in the style of the British Library, not a lending library.

The *Centralverein für das gesammte Buchgewerbe in Leipzig* (Central Association for the entire Book Industry in Leipzig) was founded on 29th October 1884, to encourage excellence in book production and as a Book Museum. Leipzig was the seat of the *Deutsche Buchdruckverein* (German Association of Book Printers), which was founded in Mainz in 1869 and of the *Buchgewerbeverein* (Book Trade Association) founded in 1884, as well as of the *Buchmuseum* (Book Museum). The book trade was supported by such outstanding printers as Johann Gottlob Immanuel Breitkopf, Carl Ernst Poeschel and C G Röder. Many major printing works, producing books in many languages, cartographic institutions, graphic artists, type foundries, manufacturers of printing blocks and allied trades were situated in Leipzig. Before World War I, one in ten Leipzig inhabitants was employed either in the book trade or in the graphic trade.

Leipzig has always been concerned with providing the education to secure the future of the trade and its striving for excellence. The *Kunstakademie* (Art Academy), founded in 1764, became an Academy for Graphic Art and the Book Trade in 1900. There are two different Technical Colleges for Librarians. A special Technical College for the Book and Printing Trade - *Deutsche Buchhändler-Lehranstalt*, was founded in 1853 and was encouraged and supported by the Börsenverein.

City of Music

Leipzig is famous throughout the world for its vibrant musical history, the most important association being with the name of Johann Sebastian Bach. Bach became *Thomaskantor* (Choir Master of the St Thomas Church Choir) in 1723, remaining for twenty-seven years. The famous *Thomanerchor* (Choir of St Thomas Church) is as old as the church, which was consecrated in 1212. The office of *Thomaskantor* was (and still is) of such importance, that it is not the church authorities who choose the incumbent; it is an appointment of the Council of the City of Leipzig itself.

The idea of a permanent orchestra was first mooted by members of one of the many musical circles known as *Collegium Musicum*. With modest beginnings, the Gewandhaus Orchestra, though not yet with that name, was the first concert organisation formed in Germany. Founded in 1743 by a group of sixteen businessmen and sixteen musicians - each businessman sponsoring one of the musicians - in an inn, it was called the *Grosse Concert* (Big Concert). In 1781 the orchestra moved into a hall in the old *Gewandhaus* (Guild of Cloth-makers and Wool Merchants' House) - hence its name. A purpose-built hall - the New Gewandhaus Concert Hall was opened in 1884. (Destroyed by allied bombs in 1944; a new Gewandhaus was opened in 1981.) The heyday of the Gewandhaus Orchestra began when the twenty-six year-old Felix Mendelssohn-Bartholdy became Director in 1835.

Mendelssohn's contributions to the musical life and musical heritage of Leipzig were enormous. He resurrected the memory of Bach, after almost 100 years of oblivion, in the city which owed him so much.

On 26th May 1892 a substantial monument was unveiled in Mendelssohn's honour. In his speech on its inauguration, the director of the Conservatory of Music said: 'The monument is presented to the City of Leipzig. She should take care of it in the gratitude which the city owes to him whose name we speak with love and honour.' A worthy sentiment, but one which was expressed in vain. (The splendid monument was destroyed by the Nazis barely forty-five years later, in 1936. A new statue, by Jo Jastram, was erected in 1993.) Perhaps the most lasting memorial to Mendelssohn though, is the *Hochschule für Musik* (Conservatory of Music), later renamed the *Mendelssohn Akademie*, which he founded in 1843, as the first Conservatory of Music in Germany.

Apart from Bach and Mendelssohn many musicians have been intimately connected with Leipzig. Richard Wagner was born there in 1813 and received early musical training from the Thomaskantor Theodor Weinling. Robert Schumann was active in Leipzig 1830-1844; he founded the *Neue Leipziger Zeitschrift für Musik* (New Leipzig Journal for Music), which appeared twice a week from 3rd April 1843 onwards. Albert Lortzing worked at the Stadttheater (City Theatre) 1833-1845 and composed his operettas *Zar und Zimmermann* (1837), *Der Wildschütz* (1842), and *Undine* (1845) during his tenure.

Music Publishing

Music had been available in published form since the invention of printing. However, it was the invention of engraving and subsequently of lithography, which saw the growth of music publishing and the availability of printed sheet music in large and reasonably priced quantities. Music publishing flourished in four cities, starting with London from around 1700; Paris followed between 1740 and 1760 and Vienna just before 1780. It was not until about 1800, that Leipzig became a major music publishing centre, becoming in due course the greatest.

Leipzig achieved leadership in the music trade through the development of *Notentypendruck* (moveable type), which replaced the hitherto expensive copper engraving. More than half the sheet music of the entire world was printed by Leipzig's music printers, and nine out of ten of all music engravers in Germany worked there.

Between 1800 and 1825, several Music Publishers started up business in Leipzig, by which time Breitkopf and Härtel had already been established some years as an innovative printer and music publisher. The company which forms the subject of this book, C F Peters, was established in 1800, when it was called Bureau de Musique.

Both the Bureau de Musique and Breitkopf & Härtel had employed Friedrich Hofmeister, before he started his own music shop and music publishing business in 1807. He published the *Handbuch der Musikalischen Literatur* (Handbook of Musical Literature) and from 1829, a *Musikalisch-literarischen Monatsbericht neuer Musikalien* (Musical-literary Monthly Report of New Musical Publications), raising his publishing firm to become the centre for musical bibliographical work for Germany. Hofmeister instigated the formation of a copyright association when he called several progressive music publishers together on 23rd May 1828.

Originally called *Verein der Musikverleger gegen musikalischen Nachdruck* (Association of Music Publishers against Musical Reprinting) the aims and purpose of the society were detailed in a *Conventional-Acte* (Constitution), which was subsequently expanded on 12th May 1830. The society which was formed then, exists to this day as the *Deutscher Musikverleger-Verband e.V.* (German Music Publishers Association). The association was significant for music publishers who were then, in 1834, permitted to become members of the all-important *Börsenverein*.

Both Dr Max Abraham and Geheimrat Dr hc. Henri Hinrichsen as well as their predecessors at C F Peters, played an active part in these and other professional associations. The firm of C F Peters was always at the forefront of new developments, both in a regulatory capacity and in the technology of music publishing.

The year 2000 sees the bicentenary of the foundation of C F Peters; the year also marks the centenary of Henri Hinrichsen's assumption as sole proprietor. The continued existence of C F Peters proves that so much that was good about Germany did manage to survive the Nazi regime.

This book should fittingly commemorate a music publishing company, a family and a way of life worthy of being recalled by future generations.

Irene Lawford-Hinrichsen
January 2000

A Note about Money

Henri Hinrichsen was a generous benefactor and throughout the book various large sums in German Marks are mentioned. A valuation in today's terms is difficult. A rough idea of the exchange value at the time, would be that from 1900 to World War I, 20M were equal to about £1.00. By 1920, the exchange had risen to 227M to the £1.00. At the height of inflation, 1923, it had gone up to 449,375,000M. The Mark was stabilised in late 1923 and the rate returned to about 20M to £1.00 in 1930. By 1940 it was about 10M to the £1.00.[1] In order to understand the value in today's terms, it is necessary to multiply the £s by about 300 times. This is a rough, not a precise guide to give some idea of the sums involved. It is based on a comparison of the starting salary of 20M (£1.00) per week, of a twenty-five year old secretary in 1915, which is approximately £300.00 today.

---

1   Based on figures quoted in *The Statistical Yearbook of Germany* published respectively in 1901, 1911, 1921, 1924, 1930, 1940, Statistiches Bundesamt, Wiesbaden.

PART ONE

The First Hundred Years from 1800

CHAPTER ONE

Bureau de Musique
From its Inception in 1800 to 1863

Bureau de Musique Hoffmeister and Kühnel

The music publishing venture which was ultimately to achieve world-wide recognition as 'Edition Peters', passed through a gradual metamorphosis of names before settling for its well-known trade-mark and logo. The **Bureau de Musique** in Leipzig was founded on 1st December, 1800, by two musicians: Franz Anton Hoffmeister born in Rothenburg am Neckar in 1754, and Ambrosius Kühnel born in 1770 [Fig 1]. There is an unsubstantiated suggestion that it may have been developed from the Taunus Verlag which had been founded around 1757. It was fourteen years before the firm acquired the name of C F Peters from the man who owned it for only thirteen years; and sixty-seven years before the famous 'Edition Peters' was launched by Dr Max Abraham.

Hoffmeister was a multi-talented man, being a composer, conductor and a practising lawyer, working in Vienna. After completing his musical studies he took on the post of church music-master in Vienna, whilst at the same time running the book, art and music shop which he had opened in 1784. At this time he also founded a music publishing company there in his own name. This energetic man also opened and ran two further music shops, composed eight operas, many Church music works, several large and small symphonies, quartets, piano pieces, etc., as well as many works with obligato flute – including 156 quartets, 96 duets, 44 trios, 30 concertos and 18 quintets — all this during the course of thirty years, whilst still fulfilling his musical duties in the church.[1] In October 1799 Hoffmeister gave two concerts in the Gewandhaus in Leipzig when he played some of his own compositions to rapturous applause. This was probably the time at which the two musicians, Hoffmeister and Kühnel, met and discussed the foundation of their music publishing house.

Kühnel was a book and art dealer who exercised his musical talents as organist of the Pleissenburg Palace Church, having been appointed to the post of 'Organist and Information Officer at the Electoral Chapel', which had been installed for the Roman Catholic services in the Pleissenburg Palace. He had the reputation of being an outstanding musician who understood all the main instruments and was himself an excellent cellist and quartet player.

Hoffmeister and Kühnel, both being Roman Catholic, the law of the day did not allow them to take Leipzig citizenship and to own a business in the city; it is ironic that the city which rejected the Roman Catholic founders of the firm would, 133 years later, reject its Jewish owners. Hoffmeister and Kühnel were joined by Christian Heinrich Richter, a Protestant businessman of Leipzig. Whilst he became the first signatory to the founding document, he did so in a purely nominal capacity and had no share in the company. The fledgling business, in the Fleischergasse 292, was called **Hoffmeister & Kühnel, Leipzig, Bureau de Musique**. Founded 'through a genuine love of the arts and pure patriotism for the arts', the undertaking comprised a music engraving studio, a printing works, the music publishing business itself and also a shop selling music and musical instruments. Before this time, there were relatively few music publishers. Bach, for example, was often his own publisher and even undertook his own engraving.

Hoffmeister and Kühnel laid the best possible foundation for their new publishing venture. Recognising his musical genius, they approached Beethoven with a view to publishing his works, as soon as they started in business together. Johann Sebastian Bach and Ludwig van Beethoven formed the strong foundations on which the first catalogues were built. The publisher's policy was one of 'quality – not quantity', which policy was maintained by future owners of the business. Amongst the earliest works to be published were complete editions of the String Quartets of Haydn as well as Quartets, Quintets and Piano works of Mozart. Furthering the revival of interest in the music of Johann Sebastian Bach, the first edition of his complete Piano works was issued in fourteen volumes between 1801 and 1803. (A daughter of J S Bach was living in such dire straits, that Hoffmeister and Kühnel used to pay her a monthly allowance, which she came to collect personally.[2])

Ludwig van Beethoven

Beethoven was thrilled about the Bach edition and wrote to Hoffmeister, whom he always addressed as his 'Dearest Brother and Friend', from Vienna, on 15th January, 1801[3]:

...With much pleasure, my dearest Brother and Friend, did I read your letter. I heartily thank you for the good opinion you have of me and my works and hope that I am able to merit that opinion. That you wish to publish the works of Johann Sebastian Bach is something which does my heart, which beats for the exalted art of the great forefather of harmony, good and which I wish to see realised with all speed; I hope from here, as soon as we have heard the Golden Peace announced, to be able to contribute something of my own...

As regards our negotiations proper, I should like to serve you herewith just as you have wanted me to. For the time being I offer you the following items: septet (of which I have already written you and that it can also be arranged for the piano for the purpose of greater dissemination and profit) for twenty ducats; symphony – twenty ducats; concerto – ten ducats; great solo sonata (Allegro, Adagio, Minuetto, Rondo) – twenty ducats. (This sonata, my dearest brother, is something really terrific.)...

The composer followed this up with a long explanation as to how he had arrived at the price for each item, and then continued:

Now that sour business is done. I call it that, because I wish that it could be different in the world. There should in this world be a depository of art, where the artist would deposit his art works and take from it what he needs; as it is, one has to combine being a business man with being an artist, and having to put up with that – oh, dear God – that, I call sour.

The heavens keep you and your associate. I have not been well for some time and it is therefore even a little difficult for me to write notes, and even more, to write letters. I hope that we shall have frequent occasion to give each other assurances of how much you are my friends and how much I am your brother and friend.

Hope for a reply soon – Adieu.

Ludwig van Beethoven

On 22nd April, 1802 the publisher acquired Beethoven's Piano Concerto No 2, in B-major, Op 19; the Septet in E-flat major, Op 20;

the Symphony No 1 in C-major, Op 21 and the Piano Sonata in B-major, Op 22. These were rapidly followed by more compositions by Beethoven. However, on the subject of one particular composition which his publisher had requested, he felt strongly enough to respond, on 8th April, 1802:

> …Are you being completely ridden by the devil, my dear sirs? – to suggest to me that I should write such a Sonata? – At the time of the Revolutionary fever – that would have been something like it, but now, when everything appears to be sliding back onto its old tracks, buonaparte [sic] reaching accord with the Pope – such a sonata? – if it were to be a Missa pro Sancta Maria à tre voci, or a Vesper etc. – for that I would happily immediately take my brush in hand – with great pound notes I would write a Credo in unum, but dear God such a sonata – in these newly beginning Christian times – hoho, – leave me out of it – nothing'll come of it –

In his breathless way, Beethoven moves from his disgust with Napoleon to the question of the commission for a Sonata:

> Now with greatest speed my answer – the lady can have a Sonata from me, and I would even follow your plan aesthetically – and without key signature – to comply – for the price of 5Fl – for this she can keep it for her own enjoyment for one year, during which time neither I nor she can publish it – after the expiry of one year the Sonata is mine – that means – I will and may publish it and she cannot should the need arise – if she thinks to find an honour in it – ask me to dedicate it to her – now let God bless you Sirs.

> My Sonata is well engraved, though it took a long time, please send my Septet into the world a little faster – because Pöbel is waiting for it and you know that the Empress has it – and there'll be a row in the Royal city as well as in the Royal Court – I will not think well of you – therefore make haste. Mr. Mollo has lately edited my Quartets choc full of mistakes and errata in large and small manner, they are teeming like little fishes in water, that means interminably. *Questo è un piacere per un autore* – that's what I call engraving, in truth my skin is full of scratches and little abrasions over the beautiful editions of my quartets – now live well – and think of me as I think of you. Until the death your true – Bthvn.

In all, Beethoven wrote nineteen letters to his publisher between 1800 and 1825. Inexplicably, there was a break in the association for nineteen years between the end of September 1803 and 1822.

The fledgling business had outgrown its premises by 1803 and moved to the Fürstenhaus (Royal House) in the Grimmaische Strasse, where it remained until 1846. There is a document in the archives dated 2nd January, 1805, detailing Hoffmeister's departure from the company.

Departure of Hoffmeister

Having sold his share of the business to Kühnel, Hoffmeister returned to composing, moving back to Vienna where he continued to run his own publishing company which he had never fully given up, until 1807. He died in 1812. In 1806 the new sole owner of the Leipzig company renamed it **Neuer Verlag des Bureau de Musique von A Kühnel in Leipzig**.

The composer E T A Hoffmann almost joined Kühnel's staff. As a young man he had been an official in Warsaw when the French troops entered, and had returned to Germany. Seeking a job he applied for the post of proof-reader with Kühnel's Bureau de Musique. The publisher offered E T A Hoffmann a monthly salary of fourteen Thalers on 4th November, 1807. However, this was not enough for Hoffmann, who turned him down. Kühnel raised his offer a month later, but by then the composer had accepted the invitation from the Imperial Count Julius von Soden, for the musical directorship of the newly-built theatre. Hoffmann was a writer, music critic, composer and conductor, who had music lessons whilst studying law. He went on to compose ballets, symphonies, a mass, piano sonatas and more as well as ten operas, including *Undine*, composed in Berlin in 1816 – about 100 years later, on the suggestion of the composer Hans Pfitzner, the vocal score of Hoffmann's *Undine* was published by C F Peters and the opera received its first performance in Leipzig in 1933. Best known for his humorous tales, he himself is the hero of Offenbach's *Les Contes d'Hoffmann*.

Kühnel developed the business to include works by many composers such as Giacomo Meyerbeer, Daniel Gottlob Türk, Justus Johann Friedrich Dotzauer and others. In his shop, he sold the pianos made by Johann Andreas Streicher. (Goethe visited the Music Instrument shop in 1821 and bought a Streicher piano on which the twelve-year-old Felix Mendelssohn-Bartholdy played him Bach's Fugues.)

The musicologist Johann Nikolaus Forkel , the greatest Bach expert of his time, was selected as Editor-in-Chief for the ambitious project of publishing the complete orchestral works of J S Bach. He was in possession of much valuable material, through his friendship with two of Bach's sons, Wilhelm Friedemann and Carl Philipp Emanuel and in 1806 he began to edit the Complete Organ Works. This first phase of the publication of Bach's works saw the issue of a considerable amount of keyboard works; these volumes are today valued as great rarities.

1806 was also the year in which the great collaboration with Louis Spohr, which was to last for half a century, started.

Louis Spohr (1784-1859)
and Carl Friedrich Peters (1779-1827)

During this prolific partnership and friendship with three proprietors of the company, all the main works of Spohr were published by the Bureau de Musique. A fascinating correspondence of some 158 letters from Spohr (including eight from his brother Ferdinand), written between 1805 and 1856, shows the deep friendship, respect and trust which existed between publisher and composer.

The twenty-six-year-old Spohr was not afraid to pen his views about Beethoven's music when he wrote to Kühnel from Gotha on 24th November, 1810:

> ...I do not yet know Beethoven's newest Quartet. His last three Quartets as well as the newest Symphonies (which do in fact have some lighter points) and especially his Overture to Leonora are for me totally unbearable. They seem to me to be like the Rhapsodies of a madman.

Ambrosius Kühnel died on 18th August, 1813, just two months before the Battle of the Nations. On 1st April, 1814 the business was sold on behalf of the heirs by Johann Georg Mittler, to the book dealer Carl Friedrich Peters, who bestowed on it *the* name by which it is known to this day. It then became **C F Peters, Leipzig, Bureau de Musique**.

Spohr wrote to Carl Friedrich Peters about his collaboration with Kühnel, on 13th September, 1815:

> ...The fact that I far preferred to give my manuscripts to Mr Kühnel than to all other publishers, was through gratitude, because he received me in my debut as an artist in such a friendly manner and accepted my first compositions in his publishing house, without obliging me to buy 100 copies of my own work instead of paying me a fee, as was the condition made upon me with my first concert for Mr Härtel, in spite of the fact that Mr Härtel was very rich and Mr Kühnel was at that time very poor...

Generosity to its composers became the ongoing tradition of this respected firm of music publishers.

The politically traumatic years after the Battle of the Nations were economically catastrophic and people did not have much money to spend on the purchase of sheet music. In spite of the fact that Peters suffered severe financial problems, he nonetheless continued in business and continued to publish works of the best known masters of the day, including Carl Maria von Weber, Johann Nepomuk Hummel, Ferdinand Ries and others, as well as Theodor Körner's *War Songs* and John Field's *Nocturnes*. Field, who was born in Dublin, was by that time very much a 'continental', travelling and performing throughout Europe.

The collaboration with Spohr, publication of his works and the personal friendship continued, as we see from a few extracts from some of Spohr's letters:

Frankfurt, 19.8.1818:...For the engraving of my portrait I would ask you to choose a *talented* artist, so that the many bad portraits of musicians are not augmented by one more. I don't know whether it would be better to print it on a separate page, or whether it should go on the title-page.

Gandersheim, 16.7.1820:...I have just been told by a traveller that Carl Maria von Weber has taken a journey to Copenhagen in order to apply for the vacant position of Director of Music. Is that true? Please be kind enough to write me what you know about it.

Strasburg, 8.2.1821: Dearest Friend!

Please don't be angry that I didn't write to you from Paris; I wanted to do it every day, but it wasn't possible to extract oneself, even for one hour, from the chaos of business and diversions in which we spent the past two months in a complete frenzy. I am very happy with my stay there even though it cost me more than I earned, as all the main goals of the trip have been achieved. I made the personal acquaintance of all the excellent artists, became friends with many of them, let most of them hear my latest compositions, had the pleasure of seeing these received with enthusiasm by them; I then appeared publicly and was received by the public with huge acclaim and, last but not least, I saw and heard everything noteworthy and excellent about Paris...

Throughout the nineteen years of silence between Beethoven and the publishers, both Hoffmeister and Kühnel and then Peters tried through intermediaries and direct letters to Beethoven, to revive the relationship. Finally, Beethoven wrote to Carl Friedrich Peters on 5th June, 1822, expressing as his greatest wish, that Peters should publish his complete works. He also offered 'the largest work that I have written so far, the Great Mass with choirs and four obligato voices and full orchestra' – the *Missa Solemnis*. With regret and after much consideration Peters turned down the request to publish Beethoven's complete works, on account of the enormous cost involved. But he did want to publish the *Missa Solemnis*. This, Beethoven offered him on 26th July, 1822, complete with piano score, for 'FlC.M. 20 Gulden'. However, delivery was delayed and Beethoven had not sent the promised work by February 1823. Peters expressed his indignation and frustration at Beethoven's unreliability in a letter dated 4th March, 1823:

> ...we agreed a contract with you about the following manuscripts:
>
> 1) Concerning four Military Marches,
>
> 2) Three songs with pianoforte accompaniment in the same style as *Adelaide*, hence, not small ones but quite lengthy ones, so that *each one* could be issued separately.
>
> 3) Concerning Bagatelles for pianoforte.
>
> We agreed a price and I paid you, except for the extra which the Songs and Bagatelles might cost; I have thus kept my side of the bargain – you, however, deliver:
>
> 1) Instead of four Marches, only one March and three *Zapfenstreiche* (Tattoos). *Zapfenstreiche* are perhaps popular in Vienna, I, however, cannot use them...
>
> 2) Instead of a series of three lengthy songs with pianoforte, you send me only one *Ariette* and two Songs with orchestral accompaniment as well as with piano. I did not ask for the Songs with orchestra...
>
> ...as what you have sent me is not suitable, I cannot accept it – I, having conscientiously kept my part of the agreement, expected that you would do likewise, because where would it lead if I, with my many connections were not to adhere strictly to my agreements...

> I wrote to you last year that I wanted to publish your Mass…As
> I now see your method of delivering manuscripts and you
> now write to me that two others are asking you for Masses, I
> release you from your agreement with regard to the Mass and
> have no objection if you give it to someone else…

As a direct consequence of this letter, Beethoven's *Missa Solemnis*
was published by B Schott's Söhne, and not C F Peters.

Three weeks after the letter from Peters, Beethoven wrote on 20th
March, 1823, rather frostily starting his letter 'Your Honour', instead
of his customary greeting 'My Dear Good Friend':

> It is only today that the three Marches are being sent, the
> post was missed eight days ago. As untidily as I dealt with you
> this time, it should not appear unnatural to you, if you were
> to be present here and could see my situation…

He then asks whether a Violin Quartet for 50Fl, or a Piano Quartet for
which he would have to charge 70Fl would be required. These were
the subject of his next four letters over the course of two years, but no
manuscripts were ever delivered. Even so, the Catalogue of the Bureau de
Musique published in 1826 shows a large number of Beethoven's works.

Carl Friedrich Peters was in poor health, both physically and
psychologically and Louis Spohr was concerned about his friend's
illness. A typical letter was the one written from Kassel on 24th
December, 1824:

> Dear Friend,
>
> It is with sadness that we learned from your letter that you
> have been unwell for such a long time and we are worried
> about the melancholy tone in which you write. Rouse yourself
> and don't dwell on such bleak thoughts.

Peters' mental condition did not improve and we can see how badly
he upset his friend when we read Spohr's letter of 1st May, 1826:

> Dearest Friend,
>
> I deliberately left your letter for eight days, before answering
> it; because if I had sat down to write about the contents in my
> first anger, I might well have expressed myself in a similar
> tone as that used by you. What sort of an ill mood could
> possibly have allowed you to dictate such a letter to me?…

On 30th June, 1825 Carl Friedrich Peters made his Last Will and Testament, naming his young daughter, Anna, as the heir to his business.

Throughout the period of his illness, Peters continued to publish Spohr's works and to help him in every way he could. When Spohr's talented young student, Ferdinand David and his equally talented sister, the pianist Louise David, wanted to give a concert in Leipzig, Spohr wrote on 16th December, 1825, asking Peters to 'be kind and helpful to the children'.

Peters maintained close relations with all his composers. Johann Nepomuk Hummel, with whom he was particularly friendly, was aware of how indiscreetly he had referred to other people in his letters, when he wrote this final paragraph to a letter dated 22nd May, 1826[4]:

> ...By the way, I would like you to keep my letters, which contain secrets, between ourselves, even to withhold them from your people, in order to prevent any misuse.

Suffering from a deep depression, the roots of which remain unknown, Carl Friedrich Peters died at the age of forty-eight, on 20th September, 1827, in the Home for the Mentally Disturbed on the Sonnenstein. He had headed the company which continued to bear his name, for just thirteen years. On his death, Spohr wrote to the Commissioner, C F Leede, on 13th December, 1827: 'With deepest sadness I have learnt of the early death of Mr Peters. The world loses with him an active and honourable man...'

Commissioner Leede ran the business until its sale on 29th October, 1828. Peters had left it to his daughter, Anna Peters, who was only eleven years old at the time. She was represented by the banker, Georg Wolfgang Schrepffer, and the book dealer, Johann Georg Mittler (who was the guardian of Kühnel's children). The new owner was the tobacco manufacturer, art and music patron, Carl Gotthelf Siegmund Böhme who was a new citizen of Leipzig.

Carl Gotthelf Siegmund Böhme (1785-1855)

Böhme bought it 'with all publishing rights, complete stock of copper and tin plates, sheet music here and elsewhere, utensils, printing works and equipment...' Böhme continued to publish the classical composers and added music by Franz Hünten, Johannes Wenzeslaus Kalliwoda and the *Bolero*, Op 19 by Frédéric Chopin, amongst others.

The collaboration with Louis Spohr carried over to the new owner, the first letter from Spohr to Böhme being dated 23rd January, 1829, when he discussed his manuscripts. The publishing business continued to expand and in 1829 brought out the full scores to Spohr's operas

Faust and *Jessonda,* Schumann's opera *Genoveva* and Gasparo Spontini's *Vestalin.*

There were at that time no legally binding copyright laws, publishers would regularly reprint each other's works. As a result of political events, infringement of publishing rights became rampant. Several unscrupulous publishers reproduced works of their competitors without permission. This caused Böhme to issue a statement at the end of his New Issues list published for the Jubilate Trade Fair: 'I neither accept, nor will I publish, arrangements of original works which do not belong to me. I can therefore rightfully expect that other decent publishers will observe similar considerations as regards myself.'

In order to clarify the uncertainties concerning publishing rights, a group of music publishers, under the chairmanship of Friedrich Hofmeister, signed a declaration, the *Conventional-Akte* dated 23rd May, 1829. Signatories included Johann André, Breitkopf & Härtel, C F Peters, B Schott's Söhne and Nikolaus Simrock. Louis Spohr became very involved and the correspondence between himself and his main publishers, C F Peters, can be seen as a documentation of publishing history. This was published posthumously for the first time, in the *Allgemeine musikalische Zeitung* (General Musical Newspaper), Leipzig in 1867.

Right from the start, it was a policy of the company not to have too many composers, but to select a few of outstanding promise and then to promote their work vigorously. One of those whose talent was fostered, was the pianist and composer Carl Czerny, a pupil of Beethoven, whose Studies are still widely played. The collaboration began with a letter from Czerny to C F Peters, in which he cited Friedrich Wieck (Schumann's father-in-law) as a reference; the fruitful association was continued by Böhme and lead to the publication of many original educational works by Czerny.

The composer was a renowned Bach scholar and when Böhme decided to continue the publication of all Bach's instrumental works he persuaded Czerny to head the editorial team. With this end in view, Czerny commissioned the Bach collector, Franz Hauser, to follow up clues leading to long lost manuscripts in Italy. Between 1837 and 1842, Bach's complete piano works, violin concertos, the Brandenburg Concertos and the Orchestral Suites as well as the *Art of the Fugue,* appeared in print for the first time. The committee of editors included the greatest Bach authorities of the time, the foremost of whom was a pupil of Forkel's, Friedrich Konrad Griepenkerl, as well as Siegfried W Dehn, Ferdinand A Roitzsch and Moritz Hauptman, a former student of Louis Spohr, amongst others.

Böhme also published the complete organ works of Bach in the famous nine volume edition, edited by the renowned organ scholar

Griepenkerl, who had in 1819 edited Bach's *Chromatic Fantasy and Fugue* for C F Peters. The organist's main activity was as Professor at the Carolinium College in Brunswick. In 1842 he wrote *Lehrbuch der Aesthetik* (Instruction Manual of Aesthetic) in which he applied Herbart's philosophical theory to music. Griepenkerl was an avid collector of Bach's manuscripts and Böhme chose well in entrusting him with the tremendous task of assembling and critically reviewing the organ compositions of J S Bach; these were scattered, mostly in manuscript form throughout Germany and elsewhere. The edition is still highly regarded by leading organists.[5]

By 1846 the company had outgrown its premises and moved to the ground floor of 12 Königstrasse [Fig 2], which had been built the year before. Felix Mendelssohn-Bartholdy occupied the first floor apartment for the last two years of his life, 1845-47.

The Leipzig book dealer, August Theodor Whistling, joined the firm on 2nd October, 1852 as General Manager. The following year Böhme decreed in his will that in the event of his death the whole business should devolve into a charitable trust, with his wife Emilie Luise Böhme as his sole heir. He also stipulated that the firm should carry the name of C F Peters in perpetuity. On Böhme's death on 20th July, 1855 Whistling continued to manage the business, working with the same composers, including Louis Spohr, until its sale by the committee of trustees, on 1st January, 1860. The new owner was the book and music dealer Julius Friedländer, in Berlin.

Julius Friedländer

The name became **C F Peters Leipzig und Berlin, Bureau de Musique**. Friedländer's capital was derived from his invention, patented in 1861, of a speed press for printing music which cut the costs of printing sheet music by 800 per cent. Friedländer sold the retail shop to Whistling. Thus the ongoing business became solely a music publisher.

Friedländer met Dr jur. Max Abraham from Danzig, in Berlin in 1862. On 1st April, 1863, he announced that he had made Abraham his partner in the firm. The new partner was well chosen and was soon left in sole charge while Friedländer returned to Berlin, only to pay sporadic visits to the Leipzig office. On 1st April, 1880, Friedländer sold his interest in the business for a huge sum, payable over five years, to Dr Max Abraham. With the departure of Friedländer, the company dropped 'Berlin' from its name and reverted to its earlier one: **C F Peters Leipzig, Bureau de Musique**.

As sole owner, Dr Max Abraham could now proceed to expand the firm in the direction which was to elevate it to the position of international stature, which it has maintained to this day.

1   Hoffmeister's output quoted in *Musikalische Charackterköpfe*, Vol I, Richl, Cotta, 1899.

2   Letter to Dr Forkel in Göttingen, 2nd August, 1802.

3   The letters in this chapter were all translated from the original German by the author. They are taken from: *L van Beethoven, Seine an den Verlag von Hoffmeister und Kühnel, Später C F Peters, Leipzig Gerichteten Briefe. Verzeichnis seiner in der Edition Peters erschienenen Werke*, C F Peters, Leipzig, 1927; *Chronik*; *Zeittafeln*; *'1880-1975 Edition Peters'* and from copies in the author's archive. The original letters should be in the 'Bestand C F Peters Verlag' in the Staatsarchiv Leipzig (StAL).

4   This letter is now in the British Museum.

5   Alfred Riemenschneider's investigations into the history of Bach's original-text editions, in *Musical Yearbook Vol VIII*, Hinrichsen, London, 1956.

CHAPTER TWO

Max Abraham, 'Edition Peters' and the Peters Music Library: 1863-1900

Dr Max Abraham (1831-1900)

The first sixty-three years of the company's existence had seen several different owners and directors. The arrival of Dr jur. Max Abraham [Fig 3] as a partner in the firm of C F Peters Leipzig, Bureau de Musique in 1863, stabilised this unsettled state; henceforth a sense of purpose marked its progress. His was the name of *the* man who was to stamp his personality indelibly over the brilliant future of this publishing house. He brought not only a new spirit into the offices, but also an entirely new tempo into the business. And he ensured a continuity of family ownership.

Kürze ist Würze (Brevity is the essence) was the slogan by which he lived and by which he conducted his business, and that was the attitude he expected those around him to adopt. All his comments and instructions, from meetings and consultations to correspondence, followed this maxim. These few words encompass the character of Dr Abraham, who lived his life by the example which he set: *Sein, nicht Schein* (Reality, not appearance). For him the objective took priority over the person. The publishing house and especially the 'Edition Peters' which he founded, was all.

Born on 3rd July, 1831, Max Abraham was the fifth of seven children of Markus Leiser Abraham, business man and mayor of Danzig, and his wife Henriette. He grew up in a cultured home where he learnt to love music, art and the theatre. After gaining a degree in law at Bonn, he studied banking in Paris and London before going to Berlin. He was working in Berlin, where he took an active part in its thriving musical life, when he met Julius Friedländer. At the age of thirty-two Dr Max Abraham embarked upon the venture which dominated the rest of his life and which was to remain a lasting memorial to his inspiration, making the name of C F Peters synonymous with the concept of excellence in music, long after his death.

His life's work can be encapsulated in two main concepts:

'Edition Peters'

and

'Musikbibliothek Peters' (Peters Music Library)

The first was to make classical music accessible to all, in first-class editions, at reasonable prices. And the second was the unique Music Library which he presented to the City of Leipzig. All his intellectual gifts were concentrated into realising these two entities. Having set his goals he single-mindedly pursued them to achieve results far outshining everything that the firm of C F Peters had accomplished hitherto.

He sought contacts with the famous musicians and composers of the day, amongst whom can be counted Clara Schumann, Johannes Brahms, Hans von Bülow, Franz Liszt, Adolf Jensen, Josef Raff, Richard Wagner and many more. Already as early as 1864 he was negotiating for compositions from Franz Liszt when he wrote on 22nd November, 1864:

F. de Liszt, (le Commandeur), Monte Mario, Parocchia del Rosario.

At the request of Dr v. Bülow, through whose friendly mediation I was so happy to acquire three compositions from you, I permit myself the liberty of asking you, whether you are happy with the titles which you wrote on them:

1) *Alleluja* pour Piano pr. Fr. Liszt.
2) *Ave verum d'Arcadelet* (16. siècle). Transcription pr. Piano p. F.L.
3) *A la Chapelle Sixtine.* Transcription du *Miserere'* *d'Allegri* et de *l'Ave verum corpus* de Mozart pour Piano pr. F.L.

or whether you wish to change them. At the same time, I permit myself to send you the certificate of ownership which, for reasons of ownership reprinting laws may not be dated from Rome, with the respectful plea for your signature and return to me. I have already sent the fee to Mr v Bülow...[1]

The conductor Hans von Bülow was making some arrangements of the Sonatas of Scarlatti and Carl Philip Emanuel Bach for C F Peters, Leipzig during the 1860s.

Max Abraham was a very modest and private person. Apart from music, he was passionately interested in sculpture, being particularly fond of the Greeks. He was a friend of the sculptor and painter, Max Klinger, whose works he collected. One of his many acts of generosity was to present Klinger's magnificent sculpture *Cassandra* to the *Museum der bildenden Künste* (Art Museum) in Leipzig, anonymously, only allowing his name to be released after his death. His only other passion was riding. Every morning one of his horses, *Anitra* or his *Presto*, would take him through the woods of Leipzig. Remaining unmarried, all his attention was directed to his Edition Peters, and he took a fatherly interest in his composers.

The most important composer for Dr Abraham, was the young, unknown Norwegian who had studied at the Leipzig Conservatory of Music, Edvard Grieg. From their first contacts in 1863, they developed a deep and lifelong friendship, such as is rare in music publishing history. C F Peters published virtually all of Grieg's compositions. (Chapter Three describes this moving relationship.)

The business was expanding and in 1867 Dr Abraham took additional accommodation in 12 Königstrasse, moving into the apartment which had belonged to Felix Mendelssohn-Bartholdy, where the firm stayed until 1874.

In 1868 an event happened in Hamburg, which was to have far-reaching effects. Dr Max Abraham's sister Betty, married to Robert Hinrichsen, gave birth to her second son, Henri. Nineteen years later, young Henri Hinrichsen was to join his uncle in Leipzig, and eventually to become his heir.

The music publisher and inventor, Theodor Litolff had, only two years earlier, improved the fast-running printing press, the printing from zinc engravings and the combined printing of music and words. With this advancement in printing technology and improvements to the principle of the speed printing press for sheet music, Max Abraham was able to implement his policy of *gut und billig* (good and cheap). This was also the beginning of the firm of C F Peters' long and fruitful association with the Leipzig sheet music printers, C G Röder, whose progressive ideas had been turned down by other publishers. Max Abraham's trust in Carl Gottlieb Röder and Röder's trust in Abraham laid the solid foundations for a collaboration which was to revolutionise the face of music publishing in Europe.

After ten years' apprenticeship as music engraver and printer with Breitkopf & Härtel, Carl Gottlieb Röder had opened his own music engraving business in Leipzig in 1846. In 1863, after many attempts he succeeded in adapting the lithographic mechanical press built by G Sigl to the printing of music; his subsequent improvements to mechanical music printing processes were used for various musical editions (from 1867) and considerably furthered the development of

German music publishing. The Röder printing works were among the most important of their kind and collaborated with the world's leading music publishers. In the 1870s Röder's two sons-in-law and later their successors ensured the constant expansion of the firm.

Max Abraham now made it his business to know important musicologists and musicians, such as the concert master of the Gewandhaus Orchestra, the violinist Ferdinand David, who had given the first performance of Mendelssohn's Violin Concerto; the pianist Theodor Kullak, founder in 1855 of the *Neue Akademie für Tonkunst* (New Academy for Music) in Berlin; Alfred Dörffel, who was to become an important member of his permanent staff from 1878 onwards; the first cellist of the Gewandhaus Orchestra, Friedrich Grützmacher, a somewhat high-handed editor whom Dr Abraham was constantly reminding to respect the composers' original intention; the world-famous violinist Joseph Joachim, who gave the first performance of his friend Brahms' Violin Concerto and who, as director of the Berlin Music Conservatory, elevated this establishment to a position of renown. These and many more, contributed their expertise to produce first-class editions of the classics. As Abraham wrote to Grützmacher: 'I see it as my holy duty to make sure that the works of the great masters are available in truly legible style.'

C F Peters, Leipzig had agents throughout the world. Perhaps the most mutually rewarding relationship was that with the firm of Augener Ltd, in London, which Dr Max Abraham forged with George Augener in 1873. This was another close friendship which expressed itself in family visits and tokens of a personal nature, as well as being a successful business collaboration.

Edition Peters

The acclaimed Editions Peters, new editions of the Classics, prepared by the finest editors of the day, was launched in 1867. The editor of EP numbers 1 and 2, J S Bach's *The Well-tempered Piano*, Carl Czerny, was already dead; however, his association with the publisher went back a long way.

From 9th November onwards, in quick succession, the following first works were issued:

EP 1, 2:   J S Bach, *The Well-tempered Piano*, Vols I and II. (Czerny).

EP 1a, 2a: J S Bach, *The Well-tempered Piano*, Vols I and II. New critical edition (Franz Kroll).

EP 3:   Beethoven, Sonatas for Piano. Popular Edition in one volume.

EP 4:   Handel, Compositions for Piano (Köhler).
EP 5:   Mozart, Complete Sonatas for Piano (Köhler).
EP 6:   Mozart, Pieces for Piano (Köhler).
EP 7:   Schubert, Compositions for Piano (Köhler).

This then was the beginning of the musical *Universalbibliothek* (universal library) Editions Peters; a new era in the history of this publishing house. For the first time, sheet music became marketable on a larger scale, giving affordable access to music, to many more people.

These new editions received immediate popular and professional acclaim. Amongst many admirers, Clara Schumann wrote: 'They are absolutely excellent, sensitive and playable, and I prefer them to all others which I know.'

The success of these and the following works, was phenomenal; and why? Because people recognised the quality of the engraving, the print, the paper, the format, and the incredibly cheap price, as being something hitherto unobtainable. With the economic expansion of the 1870s, the green covers (copyright free works) and the pink covers (original C F Peters copyright works) with their composers' names in large capital letters, soon became known, admired and purchased, the world over [Fig 4].

All this was possible through Max Abraham's mission to provide 'the best' at the lowest prices. His excellent relationship with C G Röder almost came to a parting of the ways when the old man's sons in-law came into partnership and wanted to raise all the printing prices. In his usual terse manner, Abraham said to Röder at a meeting: 'We will not be seeing each other again.' 'Nothing will come of it, we will stay together,' replied his old friend, and the printing prices were not raised.

As important as the printing, is the quality of paper used and here C F Peters was well served by the firm of Ferdinand Flinsch whose paper was consistently better than that from any other company. A close friendship was forged between Abraham and Flinsch. The creation of bound volumes demands an equally strong collaboration between publisher and binder, and this was carried out by the firm of E A Enders. Here the relationship was so close that for many years, from its construction in 1874 onwards, Enders had their workshop in the basement of the new Peters offices in the Talstrasse.

Talstrasse 10

By 1873 C F Peters business had grown to such an extent, that new premises were desperately needed. Dr Abraham commissioned Otto Brückewald, the architect who also designed Wagner's Bayreuth Festival

House, to build him a suitable property, in classic style. In August 1874 C F Peters, Leipzig moved into its final home: number 29a, Talstrasse (Valley Street), which was subsequently re-numbered when it became number 10 Talstrasse – famously known as Talstrasse 10 [Fig 5]. The inauguration of the house was celebrated two months later with a grand ball, which was preceded by a performance of Schumann's *Die Rose Pilgerfahrt.*

Victory seemed to be assured for Germany in the Franco-Prussian War by December 1870, and Abraham wrote to Richard Wagner in Lucerne, asking him whether the great event might inspire him to write a work for the coronation of the Kaiser, for which he offered 1500 Francs.

Richard Wagner (1813-1883)

Wagner accepted, and in 1871 sent a piece for publication. Wagner agreed with the publisher's suggestion of naming the work the *Kaisermarsch.* Abraham followed this up by suggesting to Wagner on 8th April, 1874, that he compose an overture based on some of his *Nibelungen* themes, for which he offered 5,000M. Wagner composed the work, but negotiated a higher fee with another publisher. When Abraham questioned this, Wagner wrote that he was under a contractual obligation to the publisher for life. Abraham consulted lawyers and wrote to Wagner explaining that the composer was permitted to have his work published by another publisher if he so wished. He raised his own offer for the work to 9,000M (3,000 Thaler), explaining that it was not the anticipated profit of the work which interested him so much as the honour and personal pleasure of publishing the new creation. Wagner did not relent.

In 1877 Wagner, through his wife Cosima, offered Abraham five compositions including an Overture and a Piano Sonata as well as the *Siegfried Idyll.* But Dr Abraham considered the fee demanded for the collection to be too high to make the project worthwhile. He offered 6,000M for the *Siegfried Idyll* alone, which was not acceptable to Wagner.

It is interesting to note that for all his alleged anti-Semitism, Wagner was not averse to negotiating publication of his works with a Jewish publisher, though with little result. Brahms was another contemporary composer whose works were poorly represented in the Edition Peters.

Johannes Brahms (1833-1897)

Max Abraham very much wanted to publish some works by Brahms, but to the composer's regret, he was tied up in a contract with the firm of Simrock, though he did promise to send a number of works. In fact, only one important work, *Nänie*, and a few smaller works and arrangements were published by C F Peters. Brahms wrote, in one of his twenty letters to Abraham: '...I feel like the donkey between two rose bushes...'

In spite of the fact that Abraham suggested he were willing to pay whatever price Brahms asked, nothing further but promises was forthcoming.

By that time the copyright law was fully operational and a composer's music was protected until thirty years after his death; this meant that no publisher could reproduce music published by another, without first getting his permission. Anticipating which top selling compositions would be profitable, Max Abraham always had new editions of the most important works prepared and ready to issue as soon as they were in the public domain; sometimes on the actual date, thirty years after the composer's death. Thus C F Peters published the complete works of Mendelssohn in 1878, those of Chopin in 1880 and in 1887, those of Schumann.

The Expiry of Copyright on Robert Schumann (1810-1856)

C F Peters was so well prepared for the release of Schumann's works that almost one hundred works were available for sale on the day that the copyright was lifted. Anybody was now permitted to publish Schumann's works without payment of a copyright fee, and his widow Clara was not entitled to any further payment. However, Max Abraham appreciated the fact that he would probably make a handsome profit and he had always had a great admiration for the composer's creative output. He wrote Clara Schumann a warm and respectful letter, expressing his delight at finally being able to publish more of Schumann's works than he had hitherto been able to do. With the letter, he sent her a totally unexpected and very generous ex-gratia payment of 3,000M.

In order to accommodate all the Schumann sheet music being published and to make room for planned new orchestral material, a new stock room was needed. Hence, the basement which had been at the disposal of the Enders bindery for thirteen years was converted to stock room use. As Enders' business had also expanded, he too needed larger premises; the working relationship between the two companies continued to thrive as before.

With the increase in new publications a new reader and music editor, Alfred Dörffell [Fig 6], joined the firm in 1878; far-reaching results were to come from his employment.

Alfred Dörffel (1821-1905)

One-time student of Felix Mendelssohn-Bartholdy, Dörffell was a musicologist whose strength lay in his meticulous attention to editorial detail and in proof-reading. He worked on the huge Bach edition, as well as on collections of German Folk Songs and Lieder, Schumann's works and other collections. He compiled thematic catalogues of the works of Bach and Schumann; translated Berlioz' *Treatise on Instrumentation* from the French into German and wrote several books. In 1881 he wrote a commemorative publication celebrating the centenary of the Gewandhaus in Leipzig, which he followed up in 1884 with a book on the history of the Gewandhaus concerts. For this Dörffel received an Honorary Doctorate from the University of Leipzig in 1885. His weakness lay in his unsympathetic attitude towards *avant garde* music, which sometimes resulted in C F Peters turning down modern works which were then accepted by other publishers and subsequently became successful. His antagonism towards the music of Max Reger was an unfortunate consequence of this blind spot. Another composer whose music didn't appeal to Dörffel was Anton Bruckner, a frequent visitor to Leipzig.

Anton Bruckner (1824-1896)

Bruckner was a friend of Arthur Nikisch, Director of the Gewandhaus Orchestra, an admirer who made it his business to promote the composer's music. Nikisch conducted the first performance of the Seventh Symphony at the Gewandhaus on 30th December, 1884, and naturally wanted to find a publisher for the work in Leipzig. He invited the two main publishers to attend the concert, Breitkopf & Härtel and C F Peters, hoping that at least one of them would want to publish this masterpiece. Dr Max Abraham attended the performance with Dr Alfred Dörffel, who also studied the score. But Dörffel was too old to accept this modern music, he found the last movement too complicated and advised Abraham against publishing the symphony.

Bruckner, somewhat uncouth in his speech, said to Dörffel in his broad Austrian dialect: 'Look Sir, tha's wha' they said in Vienna when Beethoven performed 'is firs' symphony – the swine!' Bruckner was no luckier with Breitkopf & Härtel. As a parting shot he is alleged to have said: 'You print so much muck, you could jus' as well tek mah manure too!'[2] Bruckner's Seventh Symphony was published in 1885 by Gutmann. It has become a major element of the standard repertoire of the Leipzig Gewandhaus Orchestra, as well as being regularly performed by orchestras the world over.

Publishers are not always infallible!

By the time that the thirty-year period of copyright following the composer's death expired, Bruckner's work had become universally acclaimed. Thus in 1927 C F Peters was able to compensate to a small degree for its earlier rejection of the composer by publishing scores and piano arrangements of his symphonies.

Dr Abraham was a good employer who chose his staff well and who exercised the most advanced ideas for their welfare.

Working Conditions and Contemporary Music

Abraham introduced a compulsory savings scheme to which he contributed generously. He insured his staff's lifelong loyalty by instigating a pension scheme at the company's expense and contributed towards his staff's tax payments. In the 1880s he was one of the first employers in Leipzig to instigate holidays: three days per year; unaccustomed to such free days, the employees were initially quite unhappy at the idea! At Christmas he gave a bonus and for any member of the staff suffering hardship he provided financial benefit for coal and potatoes. He was serving a double purpose: he wanted to instigate a sense of financial responsibility into his staff and, at a time when there were no sickness benefits or old age pensions, he wanted to cover his staff, and indirectly himself, against any possible future needs. In the early 1870s there were three employees; however, the success of the new Edition Peters led to an increase in staff, until by 1900 there were seventeen.

Max Abraham finally paid off his debt to his partner Julius Friedländer in Berlin and became the sole owner of C F Peters on 1st April, 1880. The company name at that time was **C F Peters, Leipzig, Bureau de Musique**. He was then able to extend his policy of acquiring other publishing firms which the owners wanted to sell. On 15th May, 1876 Dr Abraham bought the music publishing firm of Gustav Heinze, which also included the Whistling Publishing Company which Heinze had taken over in 1858 and works from the Bernhard Friedel Publishing Company. On 1st January, 1886 he bought the firm of G W Korner of Erfurt and in 1893 the firm of F Whistling's widow.

After almost fourteen years of publishing classical works in the Edition Peters, Abraham was prepared to accept the risk of publishing more modern works, being especially interested in orchestral and chamber music.[3]

More contemporary music was published and also many popular works in arrangements for various combinations of instruments; for example arrangements for piano of the classical symphonies for two, four or eight hands, which were played by many music-lovers in their own homes. A lot of educational material was published as well as choral arrangements of folk songs and piano scores of operas. Along with the classical composers, works by contemporary composers including d'Albert, Brahms, Bruch, Busoni, Dvorak, Flotow, Franz, Goldmark, Gade, Edvard Grieg, Herzogenberg, Hiller, Jensen, Kiel, Kirchner, Liszt, Loewe, Lortzing, Marschner, Meyerbeer, Moszkowski, Prinz Reuss, Raff, Reinecke, Rubinstein, Sinding, Smetana, Svendsen, Taubert, Vieuxtemps and Wagner were published before the turn of the century. The first opera published by C F Peters was *Boabdil*, by Moszkowski.

Moritz Moszkowski (1854-1925)

Boabdil (the last King the Moors) was premièred on 21st April, 1892 in the Royal Opera House in Berlin. There were just twenty-five performances, and those probably due only to the popularity of the ballerina dell 'Era, before the opera disappeared from the programme for ever. It made brief appearances in Prague and London the following year, but was not successful. Henri Hinrichsen wrote about it in his *Chronik* in 1933:

> It was not only the somewhat undramatic music which was responsible for this unpopularity with the public, but the fault lay largely with the text by Karl Witkowski who, at the height of the Italian *verismo* was still anchored in the passé historisizing style of a Meyerbeer libretto. With the exception of the Overture, the two Marches and the successful ballet music from Act II, C F Peters had neither acquired the stage rights nor had published the orchestral material, so the financial 'fiasco' of *Boabdil* was of no consequence to the company.

Though Moszkowski had a certain amount of success with his lighter works, like most composers, he largely earned his living by teaching and as a pianist and conductor. He lived in Berlin and taught the piano at Kullak's Academy. He was well-known as a pianist, touring widely, and was popular in England as a conductor and pianist. He retired to Paris in 1897.

Over 300 letters written between 1886 and 1914 attest to the close friendship and collaboration enjoyed by Moszkowski and Dr Max Abraham which, like the friendship with Edvard Grieg, also carried over to Henri Hinrichsen who wrote further:

> Apart from that, many piano pieces by Moszkowski were published, amongst which *Gondoliera* and *Guitarre*, *Jogleurin* and *Liebeswalzer*, which was long popular in France because it

was used in a play, but not as popular as the *Spanish Dances* which were acquired by C F Peters through a special agreement with the publisher Carl Simon of Berlin during the '80s. In 1909 they were completely taken over by C F Peters, along with Op 1, 4, 6 and others by Moszkowski. The price was agreed at 100,000M, of which (at the express wish of Carl Simon) 10,000M should be paid to the composer who, as a twenty-year old had only received 150M for his *Spanish Dances*. Simon, who was more of an idealist than a business-man, was so delighted that he presented Mrs Martha Hinrichsen with a model harmonium by Balthasar Florence of Namur.

Whilst Moszkowski was a German of Polish descent, it is as a composer of 'Spanish' type music that his reputation was built. His two books of *Spanish Dances*, Op 12 have remained popular.

There were times when, like any other publisher, Abraham would turn down compositions which were offered to him. He may have considered them to be unsaleable because people were not buying that type of music, or perhaps because one of his advisers felt that the work was not well written or that it would not fit in within the scope of the catalogue. Another reason might be that the composer was asking a fee which the publisher felt was too high for the work. Whatever the grounds were, on which he rejected a work for publication, Abraham was always courteous and never wanted to be hurtful, trying where possible, to encourage a composer. An example of this tact is shown in his letters to the young Frederick Delius,

Frederick Delius (1862-1934)

Delius was introduced to Abraham by Edvard Grieg, who suggested he submit some of his songs. After due consideration, Max Abraham wrote politely to Delius on 2nd February, 1891:[4]

> ...It is extremely difficult, even impossible, to be able to succeed with songs, of which more than 1000 are published every year in Germany. Whilst returning your manuscript which you were kind enough to send me, I would suggest that you steer clear of songs for the time being. When you have first made a name for yourself with other works – piano pieces or short chamber music works, that would be the time to introduce your songs, but to make your debut with songs does not seem to me to be a practical idea. What I am telling you here, so frankly and honestly, I would not normally say to

a composer, but as I have the honour of knowing you personally, I feel am able to do so...

Two years later Delius sent Abraham a sonata which he once again, with his letter of 28th February, 1893, but very kindly, rejected.

Henri Hinrichsen joins his Uncle

Dr Max Abraham's nineteen-year-old nephew from Hamburg, Henri Hinrichsen, arrived in Leipzig to take up his apprenticeship in music publishing in his uncle's firm in 1887. He was granted power of attorney in 1891 and became an equal partner with his uncle in 1894, the year that Dr Max Abraham opened the Peters Music Library.

The Peters Music Library: 1894

Leipzig had been acknowledged as a centre of musical life in Germany since the beginning of the eighteenth century. It could boast the Gewandhaus Orchestra, the St Thomas Church and its world-famous choir, its Music Conservatory and its strong connections with several composers. The city was the heart of the music publishing industry and of the book and printing trades. However, for all of its many musical attributes, Leipzig was lacking one vital element – a really comprehensive and freely accessible Music Library.

From about the middle of the nineteenth century there were a number of so-called *Musikalienleihanstalten* (Musical Loan Institutions) which were valuable educational institutions from which one could borrow sheet music or musical encyclopaedias against a fee. In addition to the private loan institutes, such as the Dörffel Library, the Music Department of the City of Leipzig Library was formed in 1856. However, these musical loan centres were, owing to a paucity of materials, totally inadequate for the demands of the times.

Dr Max Abraham was well aware of these shortcomings and had long wanted to improve the situation. When the splendid private musical library assembled by the musicologist Dr Alfred Dörffel came up for sale in 1891, it was suggested that this would be ideal for the Music Department of the *Stadtbibliothek zu Leipzig* (Library of the City of Leipzig). Negotiations were protracted and the City Council could not find enough money. A suggestion from a nephew of Abraham's, Privy Councillor Dr Edgar von Ubisch, director of the Berlin Armoury, generated the idea of the *Musikbibliothek Peters* (The Peters Music Library).

Alfred Dörffel specialised in his great love – Bach and the composers of the Classical and Romantic periods. Dörffel had been curator of the

Music Department of the City Library for some years. A lifelong lover of books, he had assembled a valuable collection of musical literature which included music newspapers and magazines and full scores which were organised to provide a lending library. This was the library which Dr Max Abraham purchased in 1893, and which formed the foundation for the Peters Music Library. The section of opera scores was considerably enlarged to include many first editions from the seventeenth and eighteenth centuries. Dörffel became Honorary Librarian and received an annual pension until his death.

Dr Abraham was particularly keen on filling the library with books and sheet music which would be difficult and too expensive for most people to acquire for themselves; hence the emphasis on full scores. The City of Leipzig was to become the beneficiary of this, the finest music library in Germany at that time.

In 1872 Max Abraham had purchased a house: 26 Königstrasse (now Goldschmidt Strasse) which was to house the library [Fig 7]. The festive opening of the Peters Music Library took place on 2nd January, 1894 in the presence of the *Oberbürgermeister* (Mayor) Dr Georgi, the violinist Joseph Joachim and many representatives of Leipzig's cultural institutions as well as musicians and music publishers. In his speech, Dr Abraham, the founding benefactor, said that: 'the new institute should, in contrast with the State or City libraries, promote the study of music from the classics onwards. It should thus take into consideration new musical works through a study of which an understanding of contemporary music and current musical trends could be acquired.'

The Peters Music Library was to be a free Reference Library open to all; i.e. a public library. The opening of the Peters Music Library caused a sensation both in Germany and throughout the world. It was the first Public Library accessible to all, even to women, which at the time was not a matter of course. In view of the valuable contents of the collection it was not a loan, but a reference library. Some eight to nine thousand volumes, comprising musical encyclopaedia, reference works original scores and sheet music, could be viewed in the reading room from the outset.

As well as books, Dr Abraham, and later Henri Hinrichsen, loaned valuable original manuscripts and pictures from his own personal collection. Manuscripts of J S Bach, Handel, Gluck, W F Bach, Beethoven, Weber, Schubert, Spohr, Chopin, Wagner and others, the silver-point drawing of Mozart by Doris Stock (Vienna 1789), the portrait of Beethoven – a pencil drawing – by August Kloeber (Mödling 1817), a pastel portrait of Joseph Haydn attributed to the Dresden painter Joh Carl Roessler, but possibly by Anton Grafft. Max Klinger was commissioned to design a bookplate for the Peters Music Library which was eventually only used for the private library as Dr Abraham did not like it. (A reproduction was used on the reverse of the title-page of the Pauer edition of Beethoven Piano Sonatas. Unfortunately the original block was accidentally destroyed.)

From the second year of the existence of the Peters Music Library the *Jahrbuch der Musikbibliothek Peters* (Yearbook of the Peters Music Library), edited by the current head librarian, was issued annually almost without a break from 1894 until 1941. (The only exceptions were the war-time 1914/1915 issue, which actually came out in 1916; and the issues for 1921-1923, of which 1921 appeared in two parts, part II being a commemorative publication in honour of Max Friedländer on the occasion of his seventieth birthday; 1922/1923 was affected by the inflation and did not appear until 1924.)

These large, sought after volumes contained not only the annual reports of the Peters Music Library, covering new acquisitions and reader usage, but also an international bibliography of studies published by leading musicologists. These were further enhanced by learned articles written by the foremost musicologists of the day – professors of Music from Leipzig and Berlin, one of the most notable of these being Hermann Kretzschmar, who contributed regularly almost every year. The *Yearbook* grew in scope and research to achieve world-wide recognition as a valuable source document for research into musical life and publishing life from the turn of the century until 1941. (After the DDR authorities incorporated the Peters Music Library into the Music Department of the Leipzig City Library in 1954 the appearance of the *Peters Music Library Yearbooks*, under other names, was sporadic.)

Dr Emil Vogel, whose musicological work on Monteverdi (1887) and Marco Giuliano (1889) as well as books on musical manuscripts of 1500-1700, was the first librarian and immediately started on the preparation of the first *Yearbook* which was issued in 1895. In its structure and high standard of research it became a benchmark for future issues. Unfortunately Vogel became seriously ill in the winter of 1899 with a softening of the brain. With his characteristic generosity, Dr Max Abraham retired him in 1900 on a full pension until his death in 1908 and, on the death of Dörffell in 1905, named him as Honorary Librarian.

During Vogel's illness, his one-time student friend Rudolf Schwartz [Fig 8] took over his job, becoming Librarian in 1900. Originally a student of philosophy he subsequently studied musicology and specialised in music of the fifteenth century. He issued a complete catalogue of the contents of the Peters Music Library in 1910 and continued to edit the *Yearbooks*. In 1907, on the suggestion of Henri Hinrichsen he was awarded a Royal Prussian Professorship. He retired as Librarian at the age of seventy-one in 1930 and received a pension from Henri Hinrichsen which, on his death in 1935, was paid to his widow.

The musicologist Kurt Taut became the next Librarian, editing the *Yearbook* from 1929 onwards. He was also consultant for bibliography and librarianship for the *Deutsche Musikgesellschaft* (German Music Association) and edited the first Handel Bibliography for the Handel *Yearbook* of 1934. He remained Librarian until his death in 1939, when Eugen Schmitz was appointed.

When building up the stock of the library these men put great stress on the acquisition of books on music in all languages, which were published during the nineteenth and early part of the twentieth centuries. They underlined the importance of collecting most of the works by composers of this period as well as Complete Editions and *Denkmäler der Tonkunst* (Monuments of Music). Works on the theory and practice of music from the sixteenth, seventeenth and eighteenth centuries enlarge the stock. There are long runs of music periodicals from the time when this type of literature was first being published. Between 200 and 300 items were added every year.

The Peters Music Library became the Mecca for professors and students of the Leipzig Music Conservatory and of the music faculties of the Universities of Leipzig and of Halle. It quickly gained respect and already during the first year 5,000 people consulted about 9,400 volumes. International standards for music librarianship were set through this exciting new Library. The *London Musical Standard* [5] wrote:

> A generous music-lover has just done for Leipzig what sooner or later should be done for London. At first sight of the room, which is decorated with portraits and busts of famous composers, one is immediately struck by the impression that here is a place which beckons the music-lover to a rich and fruitful hour. Superfluous to say that such a library is of incalculable value for countless professional musicians and music-lovers; on the one hand for those who seek references in the catalogues, and on the other hand for those whose financial means prohibit them from acquiring valuable works, and lastly for the many amateurs who would like to take a peek into composers' original scores which would otherwise be out of their reach. One can imagine the sensation caused in Leipzig by this private creation.

The Leipzig *Musikalisches Wochenblatt* (Musical Weekly) of 18th January, 1894 wrote a glowing report, which ended with the following words: '…In every respect, the City of Leipzig can be proud of a fellow citizen who, from pure interest in the Arts, has enriched the city's musical institutions by such a treasure.'

Looking through the Guest Book of the Peters Music Library we find that the first signature, on 1st January, 1894 is that of the violinist Joseph Joachim, who was then at the height of his career and world famous. This is closely followed by Edvard Grieg and his wife Nina on 30th January, 1894. Johannes Brahms came on 1st February, 1895, Max Reger on 21st November, 1904. Gustav Mahler, Richard Strauss, the virtuoso pianist Wilhelm Backhaus, as a student at the Leipzig Conservatory and many more came over the years, were impressed and signed the visitors' book making a few comments.

The shelves of the library were stocked with specialist literature in many languages, music magazines, the complete works of the great masters, manuscripts and first editions of early music as well as editions of contemporary music. In the autograph collection the reader could study valuable original manuscripts by Bach, Handel, Mozart, Beethoven, Mendelssohn-Bartholdy, Weber, Schubert, Schumann and more. Apart from the valuable collection of paintings and drawings, many photographs were also added to the collection.

Dr Max Abraham willed that at his death the Peters Music Library would be left in Trust to the City of Leipzig. He provided for a capital of 400,000M, the interest on which was to pay for the upkeep of the Library, for new acquisitions, for the payment of employees' salaries and for the publication of the *Yearbook*. The building, 26 Königstrasse, was to form a part of the Trust and the City of Leipzig was to continue to make the upper three floors available rent-free to the *Frauen Gewerbeverein* (Women's Trade Association) which Dr Abraham had founded.

After Dr Abraham's death, his nephew and heir, Henri Hinrichsen, made a contract with the City of Leipzig in 1901, effecting the *Stiftung Musikbibliothek Peters* (Peters Music Library Trust), providing a sum of 400,000 gold marks for the maintenance and enlargement of the library's holdings, and the salary of the Librarian and Assistant Librarian. He supplemented this with a further agreement in 1929. There were to be three trustees: the proprietor of C F Peters (Henri Hinrichsen); a member of the *Börsenverein* (Book and Music Trades Association) and a representative from the Culture Department of Leipzig City Council. The appointment of Head Librarian was in the hands of the proprietor of C F Peters.

The Peters Music Library was considerably enlarged when the splendid Bach collection of Georg Gottlieb Schreibner was purchased in 1902, and that of Mempell-Preller in 1904. By 1913 the Library had grown to 17,000 titles. In 1917 Henri Hinrichsen also bought the Rudorff collection of Berlin for 30,000M, which greatly enriched the

Library. This comprised musicological books, sheet music and autograph manuscripts including some prized pieces of J S Bach, C M von Weber, Felix Mendelssohn-Bartholdy, Otto Nicolai, Niels W Gade, Max Bruch and Johannes Brahms. The musicologist Max Friedländer was employed to find important manuscripts to purchase for the Library. Amongst the many treasures in the library were the original manuscripts of four Cantatas by J S Bach, a Cantata by Wilhelm Friedmann Bach, Weber's *Aufforderung zum Tanz* (Invitation to the Dance), Schubert's *Heidenröslein* and all fourteen Lieder of his *Schwanengesang*, two Polonaises and a Mazurka by Chopin, as well as manuscripts of Schumann, Wagner, Hugo Wolf and the full orchestral score of Beethoven's Violin Romance in G-major, Op 40.

Amongst those items which were borrowed the most during the first few years were books by Nietzsche on Wagner, books written by Wagner himself, and several different collections of writings edited by Hanslick. Of the many musical scores borrowed, the most popular were the works of Richard Strauss and Richard Wagner. Both Nietzsche and Wagner's writings had fallen from popularity by 1902 but Wagner and Strauss continued to head the lists of most popular scores for many years. Between 1894 and 1909, the first fifteen years of the existence of the Peters Music Library, the collection of opera scores grew from 134 to 304 and of orchestral scores from 250 to 354.

Although he was a very private man, Dr Abraham played an important role in the business world and in the community. He was a member of various committees on which he played an active part, including such as the committee of the German Music Dealers Association and he was an important benefactor, especially in his concern for the education of women.

The Social Benefactor

Whilst music publishing was his overriding obsession, he was a pioneer for the betterment of women's position in society. In support of his ideals for the education of women, Dr Abraham made the three upper floors of the house at 26, Königstrasse available rent-free to Frau Hauptmann Anna Schmidt, for the *Frauen Gewerbeverein* (Women's Trade Association) which he also supported financially. This remarkable association offered education and training to working-class women at a time when this was unheard of. They were instructed in various trades, as well as being given a basic education. They also learnt cooking, sewing and housekeeping, and their spiritual needs were catered to in the form of lectures, music making and play-reading amongst other activities which included outings. One floor of the house became a hostel for poor single women.[6]

Max Abraham supported many musicians through the *Holstein-Stift* (Holstein Trust) founded in Leipzig in 1878 in memory of the officer, poet and composer Franz von Holstein who had died that year. Holstein was the co-founder and Chairman of the *Bach-Verein* (Bach Association) and had lived in Leipzig since 1853. After retirement from the army, he studied with Hauptmann at the Leipzig Conservatory of Music. A relatively wealthy music-lover, he had provided a home in his house for seven impecunious students of the Leipzig Conservatory. The Holstein Trust was started after his death to perpetuate his good work; Max Abraham was its major benefactor.

Abraham further granted scholarships to music students at the Leipzig Conservatory, and at the *Leipziger Lehranstalt für Buchhandlungsgehilfen* (College for Students in the Book Trade) to which institute he also made regular generous contributions. He made allowances to various deserving people individually and to many good causes, being a major contributor to the Organisation in Support of the Poor. In celebration of the centenary of C F Peters in 1900, he made a contribution of 15,000M towards the building of a *Musikerheim* (Home for Musicians) in Jena.

As Max Abraham's wealth increased, so did his generosity, but he preferred not to let it be known publicly. He financially supported the singer, Dr Max Friedländer, over several years, throughout his researches into Schubert's songs, enabling him to present each song as Schubert had originally intended without any of the many later additions and alterations. Friedländer had been a successful Lieder and Oratorio baritone when Dr Max Abraham persuaded him to make the change from practical to theoretical work.

[7]Max Friedländer (1852-1934) and the Schubert Song Albums

Only 172 of Schubert's songs appeared in print during the composer's lifetime, although a further sixty-seven songs appeared from various publishers in the years immediately after his death in 1828. Between 1830 and 1851 Diabelli published 126 songs in serial volumes, known collectively as *Nachlass*, although these editions frequently suffered from editorial accretions. J P Gotthard, who had acquired the manuscripts from Diabelli's successors, published forty songs during 1872. More than 250 songs, extant in manuscripts or contemporary copies, still remained unpublished, twenty-five years after Schubert's death.[8]

The first six volumes of the celebrated seven-volume edition of Schubert Songs were published by C F Peters in 1871-3, containing songs which had been published previously, although Friedländer went back to autograph scores wherever possible, and tried to present an authentic text. He had by then begun his own collection of Schubert manuscripts and turned his attention to the unpublished songs, producing a collection of twenty songs, which was published by C F Peters in 1885, with the title *Nachgelassene (bisher ungedruckte) Lieder für eine Singstimme mit Pianofortebegleitung* (posthumous, previously unprinted, songs for voice with piano accompaniment). The album contained seventeen previously unpublished songs. Volume VII of the *Schubert Album,* which followed in 1887, contained fifty songs. The first twenty songs are reprinted from the 1885 collection described above, and of the remaining songs eighteen were first publications.

When the new edition was published the firm of Litolff, publisher of the previous edition, adopted Friedländer's urtext corrections which now constituted a new copyright edition, without seeking any permission, when they issued their new edition by Benda in the 1890s.

Astoundingly, there were still about 200 songs which had not yet been published, and these appeared in the Breitkopf & Härtel complete edition in 1894-5, edited with great care by Eusebius Mandyczewski.

Friedländer's original seven volumes without alterations, except that the popular *Seligkeit* (D433), was appended to volume VII, have been continually reprinted. The Peters *Schubert Album* has remained the staple diet of Schubertians for more than a century.

With Max Abraham's support, Friedländer went on to study under Spitta and gained his PhD in 1894 with his dissertation, *Beiträge zur Biographie Franz Schuberts* (Contributions to the Biography of Franz Schubert). He qualified as a university lecturer at Berlin University in 1894 and became a full-time musicologist. He maintained his collaboration with C F Peters until his death.

Max Abraham was not only concerned with commemorating the past, he had a great appreciation of new technology and was always in the forefront of technical development.

The Way Forward

Electricity had been introduced at the Paris World Fair of 1889 and in 1896 Dr Abraham was one of the first in Leipzig to get it installed, in the offices of C F Peters. He could see its practical advantages and also felt that it would offer a more pleasant working environment to his staff. A few years earlier, he had been amongst the first to have the newly invented telephone installed. Abraham welcomed the concept of World Trade Fairs and exhibited Edition Peters in Philadelphia in 1876. When he exhibited in Chicago in 1893, he sent his young nephew Henri Hinrichsen to represent the publishing house. At the World Trade Fair in Paris in 1900, Edition Peters was awarded the *Grand Prix.*

It was characteristic of him that he himself lived very modestly, in almost Spartan-like rooms, furnished in great simplicity. Here, in the early years, he enjoyed entertaining young musicians; but this declined as his illness, an advanced asthmatic condition with complications combined with acute eye problems, became more severe, until the only person he welcomed was his nephew Henri Hinrichsen.

1st December, 1900 saw the issue of a new complete Catalogue of all works published by C F Peters, with a foreword by Max Abraham, to celebrate the centenary of the foundation of the company. Dr Abraham was already seriously ill then, but nevertheless took part in the celebrations. Delegates came from the Gewandhaus, the Leipzig Conservatory of Music, the University of Leipzig, the City of Leipzig Council, as well as many professional colleagues, friends and suppliers; messages of congratulations were received from around the world.

A week later, on 8th December, 1900 Dr Max Abraham in his seventieth year, the pain of his illness being insupportable to him, died by his own hand. The official funeral was held at the Leipzig cemetery, but the burial of a suicide was not permitted in consecrated ground, so his remains were transported to Gotha for burial. Some twenty-five years later they were exhumed and re-interred in Leipzig.

The concluding remarks of Dr Abraham's Foreword to the new catalogue were:

> As hitherto, it will be our endeavour to achieve an ever greater perfection with the issues of the Edition Peters and to enrich the name of the publishing house with important contemporary works.

Dr Max Abraham left the imprint of a strong personality and high ideals, which were to be perpetuated in his spirit, by his nephew and heir, Henri Hinrichsen. His relationship with the young Norwegian composer Edvard Grieg, which is related in the next chapter, lasted the entire thirty-seven years during which he directed C F Peters.

1   Copy of letter, author's archive.
2   *Bruckner und Leipzig* by Stephen Lieberwirth, published by C F Peters Leipzig, 1990.
3   Letter to Edvard Grieg of 2nd December 1880.
4   Both letters in the archives of the Delius Society, London.
5   As quoted in German in the *Leipziger Amtsblatt* of 7th February, 1994 and translated by the author. The British Library was unable to trace the original source (Letter dated 27th November, 1996.)
6   *Frauen Gewerbeverein*, from Leipzig newspapers 1902, 1907, 1909, 1910, 1911, 1913.
7   Much of this information on Max Friedländer's Schubert Song Albums was kindly supplied by Paul Reid of the Schubert Institute of the UK.
8   See Maurice Brown: 'The Posthumous Publication of the Songs' in *Essays on Schubert*, Macmillan, 1996.

CHAPTER THREE

The Relationship of Edvard Grieg with his Publisher

Three days before his death, on 5th December, 1900, Dr Max Abraham wrote to Edvard Grieg:

Dear Mr Grieg!

If I have not written to you for a long time it was not only because of my asthmatic attacks, but also because of stress. However, I was delighted to see from your last letter that you are well and that Voksenkollen has proved to be a beneficial sanatorium for you...In the meantime the firm of C F Peters celebrated its centenary on the 1st of this month, but in a relatively modest manner. During the morning people came to congratulate and the next evening the office staff celebrated under the chairmanship of my nephew, as I was too ill. You will have received the Jubilee Catalogue. In this your name of course plays a major role, because the publishing house owes you an enormous debt of gratitude. Almost forty years ago I received your Op 1 and ever since then I have been so happy to be able to publish, with few exceptions, all of your wonderful works. My thanks for this will never be extinguished.

With the wish that your health will remain as good as possible,

With my very best regards,
Max Abraham

This letter crossed with one written to him on the same day by Edvard Grieg:

Dear Dr!

Just by chance I heard today that C F Peters had celebrated its centenary on the 1st of December. I hardly need to tell you how deeply distressed I am that it was not possible for me to be able to express to you my heartiest congratulations on this important day...I can only assure you, that my congratulations *post festum* come as sincerely from the heart, as is the heat of my distress over this apparent negligence. I hope that you were able to enjoy the many proofs of your popularity and the many declarations of love from all sides in relatively bearable health. What concerns my own personal relationship to Edition Peters, enfolds itself on this occasion like a total picture for my inner eye, and this picture shows to me yet again the deep gratitude for the house of C F Peters and its dear proprietor, from which I will be imbued until my dying breath...

In deepest friendship also from my wife,

Your true friend
Edvard Grieg.

Dr Max Abraham did not live to receive the composer's letter and Grieg did not receive his letter until after his publisher's death. Both letters are witness to the mutual gratitude and friendship of two men whose lives had been interdependent for almost forty years:

This unique relationship, forged with the Norwegian composer Edvard Grieg, was the major thread running throughout the thirty-seven years of Dr Max Abraham's directorship of C F Peters. More than the regular interaction between composer and publisher, it was a bond of friendship, support and mutual care, rare in a business relationship.

An idea of its depth can be gleaned from the over four hundred illuminating and personal letters from Grieg to his publishers, Dr Max Abraham and his successor Henri Hinrichsen. Grieg's letters were not only about his compositions, but also about his health, life, problems, concerts on his many tours throughout Europe and his opinions; they are an eloquent testimony to his character.[1]

Illustrated through their correspondence we learn the main themes of the relationship between composer and publisher. Firstly, it is important to note that it went on for a long time. From 1863 until the end of 1900 with Dr Max Abraham and from around 1890 until the composer's death in 1907 with Henri Hinrichsen.

Grieg and Abraham both suffered lung problems. Abraham had severe asthma most of his life and, since the age of seventeen when Grieg survived a long bout of pleurisy, he was able to breathe with one lung only – the right one – for the rest of his life; much of the correspondence is taken up with mutual sympathy and discussion of their ailments and experiences in various sanatoria. Surprisingly, for men in such a position, they both loved hiking in the mountains and Grieg's love of the countryside especially, expressed itself in his music. The main focus of the letters was Grieg's compositions – their creation, publication and popularity. But the two men also shared their interests in politics, philosophy, music, literature, theatre and art. As the relationship deepened over the years, Grieg grew to rely more and more on his publisher for advice, both professional and personal as well as financial assistance. In due course Grieg came to regard Abraham as his 'adoptive father'.

Grieg was only fifteen when he became a student at the Leipzig Music Conservatory in 1858. He returned to his home town of Bergen in Norway in the spring of 1862, after giving a triumphal graduation concert in the Gewandhaus in Leipzig, at which he performed his *Three Piano Pieces*, Opus 1. At his first public appearance in his own country he performed his Opus 1 again, together with his Opus 2, *Four Lieder*. The positive response encouraged him to seek a publisher. The twenty-year-old Grieg's first approach was made to C F Peters, in September 1863 through his piano teacher at the Leipzig Conservatory, Professor Ernst Ferdinand Wenzel. The thirty-two-year-old Dr Max Abraham, who had just been made a partner in the firm and had recently moved to Leipzig, was immediately attracted to the young composer's music. He accepted his Opus 1 and 2 for publication that same year.

Dr Max Abraham was thrilled whenever a new manuscript arrived from Edvard Grieg. He was especially delighted when the composer came as a guest to number 10 Talstrasse, Leipzig – the offices of C F Peters as well as the private home of the proprietors. Whenever Grieg's winter concert tours brought him to Germany, he arranged his time so that he could spend days, weeks or months in what, after Goethe, he called his 'little Paris', in order to devote himself to work. He nearly always travelled with his wife Nina. They stayed in Leipzig as guests of Dr Abraham, usually in Hauffe's Hotel, where the publisher would hire a piano for him for the duration of his stay.

Dr Abraham also provided him with a study, which Grieg called his 'workroom with Cerberus'. Grieg inhabited the most secluded room in the house in Talstrasse in order to work undisturbed. Dr Abraham gave his favourite composer many presents over the course of the years and took him on many holidays. He always paid Grieg generously for his compositions. The composer was immensely grateful for all the help he received from his publisher.

By 1866 Grieg's Opus 6 and 8 had been published by C F Peters and the composer who was in Rome wrote on 18th March: '...A few days ago I received copies of the longed for *Humoresques* and the *Violin Sonata*...Soon my beautiful dream in the South will be over, and then I will have the pleasure of visiting you during the middle or towards the end of April...' He ended the letter with: 'And now live well. See you soon in Leipzig, Your Edvard Grieg', which was an extremely informal way of ending a letter; but Grieg was only twenty-three, and German was a foreign language to him.

The friendship between Edvard and Nina Grieg and Dr Max Abraham deepened during the Griegs' sojourn in Leipzig in early 1875. Subsequent letters from Grieg referred to 'your friendliness in Leipzig' and point to several informal meetings. Abraham was constantly encouraging Grieg to compose and was eager to publish his works. Whilst Grieg's songs were popular in the salons of the day and C F Peters published five albums of these between 1875 and 1885, his piano music was in greater demand.

Sales of Grieg's works were so successful that the publisher sent Grieg an invitation to accompany him to Bayreuth for performances of Wagner's *Ring of the Nibelungen* cycle. It is a mark of Max Abraham's interest in everything new, that he invited his favourite young composer to the first performance of the complete *Ring* at Wagner's newly-built Festival House in Bayreuth. Grieg expressed his delight when he wrote from Bergen on 5th February, 1876:

> Your letter today was a delightful surprise. If you had wanted to do me a favour you could not have chosen better. I am very grateful to you and hope to be able to express my thanks to you personally in the summer. It would be lovely if we could meet in Leipzig and then travel together to Bayreuth...

He also mentioned that he had just completed a new work for piano, the *Ballade,* Op 24. Abraham was very pleased and replied that he would have been happy if Grieg had sent it right away and hoped that he would send it as soon as possible: 'as you know how I love to publish your works.'

Grieg's incidental music to *Peer Gynt* received its première in Kristiania on 24th February, 1876, but he was unable to be present. The young composer first saw a performance of it in November and reported with delight to Dr Abraham from Kristiania on 12th November: 'The day before yesterday I had my first experience of seeing a performance of *Peer Gynt*, and had the honour, in the middle of the piece (after "Solvejg's Song") and at the end, to be stormily applauded. At the end of the performance I had to leave my seat and go up on stage.'

Early 1877 found Grieg lacking in inspiration and doubting his own talent as a composer. Abraham encouraged him with reports of the success of his compositions, gave him friendly advice and invited Grieg and Nina to come and visit him. Turning down his invitation, the composer said he really wanted to bring some worthwhile compositions with him. In his turn he invited Abraham to Hardanger in Norway, writing on 27th May: 'This is one of the loveliest parts of Norway. Do try and see if you can come here. I will receive you with great celebration…'

Grieg remained in Hardanger until the end of the summer, the peace and tranquillity feeding his inspiration. He started his String Quartet, Opus 27 and his *Albums for Male Chorus,* Op 30 amongst other works, all of which Abraham received with delight during the course of 1878. With a travelling grant from the Norwegian government, Grieg left Norway at the end of August, to travel and give concerts, for about two years.

He spent the winter months of 1878/9 as Dr Abraham's guest in Leipzig when his host entertained him to a full programme of operas, concerts and plays in Leipzig. The friendly tone of Abraham's subsequent letters indicates that the months spent together had further deepened the friendship between him and the Grieg couple. Abraham wrote Grieg an encouragingly on 7th April:

Dear Friend!

The beautiful days of Aranjuez are past![2] Since you have been gone, I have heard no music, have eaten no oysters, have seen no Norwegian lady! A new time has started for you, as for me. You will work on the material which you collected here and will make the world happy through new works, from which I fervently hope you will find the same success as with your Violin Sonata, Opus 8. One can but praise this; the whole world is delighted with this as with your piano playing;…

On becoming sole proprietor of C F Peters in December 1880, Max Abraham could concentrate on his goal of publishing more contemporary music. He was particularly keen to publish almost everything that Grieg wrote, not only his piano compositions and songs, but also his chamber music and orchestral works. His letters to Grieg were filled with exhortations to send more manuscripts for publication. The composer completed his *Norwegian Dances,* Opus 5 for piano four hands in Loftus, Hardanger. These proved so popular that Abraham commissioned an arrangement for orchestra some ten years later, which achieved world-wide popularity in concert halls and subsequently in recordings.

Grieg jokingly wrote to Abraham on 22nd August, 1881, that his inspiration to compose would be stimulated if someone were to offer him 1,000M. Abraham immediately reacted by offering him 3,000M for several chamber, orchestral and piano works which Grieg would compose during the coming year.

June 1882 saw performances of all ten of Wagner's operas in Leipzig, to which Abraham invited Grieg, but nothing came of the proposal. Instead, and following many invitations, Max Abraham finally visited Grieg in Norway, where he enjoyed a wonderful holiday with the composer and his wife. It was to be his only visit, as the climate was bad for his asthma.

Abraham made a point of encouraging Grieg, as in this letter of 23rd January, 1883, giving an update on how the composer's works were selling:

> ...I am delighted to be able to tell you that your works, which two years ago were not in great demand by the public, have for the past year been finding greater popularity. This can be partly attributed to the fact that my editions are now being given better publicity than previously in France, where your name has a high reputation. Opus 12, 3 and 6 were played most, then Opus 19 and 28; whilst Opus 24, probably your most important, my favourite piano work after Opus 19, is still neglected. Of the songs, the most often sung are those in Volume II, then those in Volume I; and your fresh, original Violin Sonata is becoming ever more popular...

It must be remembered that at this time it was customary for a composer to sell his works outright to a publisher and he was not entitled to any further payment for the work. But Abraham, with his humanitarian ideals and in a spirit of generosity, wanted to share the profits of successful works with their composers. In this he was anticipating a royalty system. Grieg's works were doing so well, that Abraham sent the composer an ex-gratia fee of 1,000M on 9th May asking him to accept this as his share of the profits, which delighted the composer. When expressing his thanks in a letter from Bergen, dated 23rd May, 1883, he added:

> You have expressed the wish to have all my publishable works for all countries, and even though my circumstances are such

that I cannot commit myself in this respect, I hardly need to tell you that I would infinitely rather be under contract to the firm of Peters and its wonderfully kind director than to all the French and English publishers...

Grieg had often talked about his wish to build himself a villa, but had never managed to save enough money. Max Abraham now enabled him to realise this dream, when he gave Grieg the money with which to buy the land and build his villa at Troldhaugen.

The building of Troldhaugen was proceeding apace and on 24th March, 1885 Grieg wrote:

Dear Doctor, I really do not know these days whether I am a musician or a builder. I go each day by train up to the villa and back. All my ideas are exhausted there, and unborn works are swallowed in quantities in the ground. If ever you come, we only need to dig, and Norwegian Pieces for choir, orchestra and piano will gush forth from the earth! The fact that they look like peas and potatoes and radishes need not disconcert us. For there really is music hidden inside them. But to convince myself that I am really a musician, I gave a concert last week, the programme of which you will find enclosed. You will realise from it that the suite *In Holberg's Time* is actually written for orchestra. I was most eager to hear this periwigged piece, and how pleased I was that it sounded so very well, and that I had to repeat the concert a few days later.

Seven weeks later, on 15th May, 1885, he could write: 'We have now moved in to our little villa *Troldhaugen*. I think you will find the place heavenly. The guest – or rather friends – room is ready (wonderful view). So, a hearty welcome awaits you!' In the meantime Max Abraham had sent Grieg a further ex-gratia payment in recognition of C F Peters' earnings on his music over the past year and they were discussing publishing the orchestral version of the Suite *In Holberg's Time.*

Abraham was concerned about Grieg spending too much on his villa, but the composer assured him that his income was up to his expenses. On 22nd February, 1886, Abraham sent him an extra payment of 3,000M specifically in order to give him something with which to start a savings account, writing: '...I feel a responsibility to do this, in fact I am merely paying a debt, because it does not seem right that you are without a fortune, whilst I live in comfort, which is partly thanks to your compositions...'

From the time when Dr Abraham's nineteen-year-old nephew, Henri Hinrichsen joined him in Leipzig in September 1887, the young man grew naturally into the relationship with the Griegs and learnt to feel the same responsibility and friendship towards them as his uncle.

In response to Grieg's reliance on his advice, Abraham was taking on more and more of the intermediary work and promotion of Grieg's concerts. After the so-called *Holberg Suite* received its very successful first performance in Dresden on 14th January, 1887, Abraham sent the score to Carl Reinecke, the conductor at the Gewandhaus in Leipzig, where it was subsequently performed to great acclaim. He assured the composer that he would promote performances throughout Germany. Grieg was disappointed that just this work, which he felt was not typical of his style, was the first of his orchestral works to be performed at the Gewandhaus. The following year Abraham went to Berlin on Grieg's behalf, to speak to the concert agent who wanted Grieg to conduct in one of the series of Bülow concerts. Abraham did not like the agent Hermann Wolf, of whom he wrote on 10th October, 1888: '...My antipathy towards him was justified, because I found the world's most arrogant fellow...'

Abraham not only personally saw to the laborious arrangements with the concert promoters regarding dates and places of concerts, but also advised Grieg in detail about the selection of the programme and the choice of performers, commissioned the French translations of the texts and booked and paid for Grieg's hotel reservations.

The publisher had been urging Grieg for some years to compose a second Piano Concerto and referred to this again in his letter of 19th May, 1887:

> ...I returned from Naples two weeks ago. It was so nice that my inner soul cries out for a *da capo*, and as I know that you are also drawn to the country where the lemons grow, it would be wonderful if we could meet there next spring. But I hope to see and hear you in Germany before then. Your friends are eagerly awaiting your new compositions, especially the second Piano Concerto, and if you want to give me pleasure, please don't let me wait too long for the manuscripts. I take this opportunity of repeating my plea to allow me the rights to your works for all countries; because I'm really having a very difficult time with Hansen regarding your Opus 3, 12 and 19, which really upsets me and I would rather not have any more to do with the man...

Grieg, who brought new manuscripts with him, spent some months in Leipzig with Nina in the winter of 1887/8 and enjoyed many social and musical occasions together with his host Dr Abraham. When Grieg gave a Christmas Eve party in Leipzig for his musical friends, Sinding,

Halvorsen and Delius, Abraham sent a huge hamper of the highest quality food and all sorts of liqueurs. Nina sang Grieg's songs and Halvorsen played his Violin Sonata.

Max Abraham took the Grieg couple to London on 23rd April, 1888, combining a business trip to his agents with a concert when Grieg performed his Piano Concerto with the Philharmonic Orchestra to resounding applause. Then he took his friends to Ventnor, Isle of Wight for a holiday, by which time Grieg was referring to him as his 'patron angel'.

The composer also worked, completing the revision of four pieces from his music for *Peer Gynt,* which became the *Peer Gynt Suite No 1,* Opus 46. The music was printed within a matter of weeks and the first performance took place in the Gewandhaus in Leipzig under the baton of Carl Reinecke on 1st November, 1888.

There was an epidemic of diphtheria around Troldhaugen and fearing he might succumb to it, Grieg did not want to die without expressing his appreciation to Abraham for everything his friend had done for him. Grieg was 45 at the time and Abraham had been showing his concern for him for twenty-five years. In his letter of 3rd December, 1888 the composer wrote:

> ...I hope we will be spared. But if not — then I will again express, just in case, my deepest thanks — for everything. For the many, many expressions of your good will! You have really lightened the heavy path through life for me so far. Please be assured of my undying gratitude!...

One of the recurring themes in the correspondence is Abraham's generosity to Grieg, not only in the form of innumerable ex-gratia payments, invitations and holidays, but also as presents for special occasions. Both men admired the music of Richard Wagner. As a Christmas present that year Abraham sent his friend a valuable full score of Wagner's *Tannhäuser.* This was the first edition of the full score, produced in an edition of only 100 copies by auto-lithography; this was the only case where Wagner made the lithograph masters himself. It was autographed by the composer and was a present from him to a friend. He had also drawn a picture of himself when young on the title-page.[3] Grieg was thrilled to receive such a unique gift.

One of the major events of Grieg's life was when he and Nina celebrated their Silver Wedding anniversary, surrounded by friends in Troldhaugen, on 11th June, 1892. Dr Abraham sent a magnificent present, which he referred to in his letter of 1st June as a 'sugar basket'. It was a Steinway grand piano.

Max Abraham finally achieved his desire to engage Grieg in an exclusive contract, allowing him to publish all of the composer's works, when Grieg signed the contract on 22nd August, 1889. Both partners were happy with the conditions and with the outcome; Grieg would make about twice as much from his music as he had until then. He had been so well taken care of for so long, that he knew he could place his full trust in Dr Abraham. C F Peters ultimately published all of Grieg's works from Opus 1-74 (with a very few exceptions). Some works had originally been published in Scandinavia and, from 1873 onwards, Max Abraham had gradually been buying the German rights for those works which had not originally been published by C F Peters.

There were over forty-one, mostly very long letters during 1889 between the two men, about Grieg's concerts and about publications of his music; several concerned the preparations for Grieg's concerts in Brussels and Paris and the composer enjoyed sharing his triumphs with Abraham; a typical letter came from Christiania dated 27th October, 1889:

> ...Yesterday evening, after a performance of the scenes from *Olaf Trygvason*, I had an experience which I should not have considered possible. It puts even London completely in the shade. First came the 'calls', I don't know how many, and then the public produced a crescendo of sound that rose to real jubilation. Handkerchiefs were waving in the air, accompanied by hurrahs and bravos. I was cheered first by the public, then by the choir, and finally by Bjoernson, who mounted the conductor's rostrum after I had given him a cheer. Then the handing of bouquets, a wonderful great lyre and a gigantic laurel wreath (not bought by me!) – in short, I really didn't know where I was. But I do know this, that it was much much more than I deserved, and that you simply don't know where you are with national enthusiasm...

Grieg always discussed his problems with his 'adoptive father' and asked his advice. The *Société des Auteurs* (Society of Authors), designed to protect authors' rights and collect performing fees on their behalf, had recently been formed; Grieg was approached to join this new organisation whilst he was in Paris. Being confused about the implications of such a novel idea, he wrote to Dr Abraham on 9th January, 1890, describing the conditions and asking his opinion:

> ...The Society, the result of the Bern Convention[4], was founded some two years ago. Mr Durand told me that Mme Clara Schumann receives a large sum every year, I think he said between 1500-2000 Frs. One does not have to pay any

subscription, the Society is financed through the deductions it makes from the fees: in France fifteen per cent, in other countries (that means in the countries of the Bern Convention) thirty per cent. The Director wrote to me. I spoke to him today, and he couldn't understand why I had allowed so much money to slip away from me over the course of the past two years. Please be kind enough to give me your opinion...

In his reply of 13th January, Abraham counselled caution and gave his reasons:

I have always followed the principle of making performances of works in my editions as easy as possible to realise, whilst the *Société des Auteurs* makes them more difficult to achieve in Germany and England. It is different in France and Belgium. There the concert organisations are accustomed to paying performing fees and do not allow themselves to be deterred from performing a work because of that. You would therefore be best advised to strike out the words: 'and abroad', from the enclosed agreement or, in the event that this is not allowed, not to sign at all for the time being. It really doesn't depend on a mere four weeks, and by the time you arrive here I will have informed myself more precisely about the Society and the consequences of your membership. Please enquire as to whether Brahms is a member...

In order to guard against any misunderstanding I just want to add that the Society is most likely upright, the goals which it sets itself are excellent, and nobody would be happier than I, if you were to receive performing fees for every performance of your works. The question is whether Chappell in London or small German and Austrian concert organisations would include your works in their programmes, if they had to pay performing fees. The Philharmonic Orchestra is planning to perform the *Peer Gynt Suite*, it will however probably not do so if it were even expected to pay the tiniest fee. It is sad but true.

Grieg followed his mentor's advice and signed only for France, the colonies and Belgium. This resulted in an annual income for him from the Society of 800-1400 Frs. He found out that Brahms was not a member, because his publisher in Paris was said to be incompetent. Brahms would have been entitled to about 10,000Frs, which went into the Society's pension fund.

On return from his travels and happily installed in Troldhaugen once more, Grieg yet again invited Abraham to come and visit and this time Abraham accepted his invitation. The composer's delight leapt from the page of his 11th June letter with exclamation marks: 'You're really coming! Bravo! That was really a wonderful surprise!...' Grieg had planned an exciting walking holiday and the party would also include the Russian violinist, Adolf Brodsky, and his wife and probably the English composer, Frederick Delius, and Grieg's Norwegian friend, Frants Beyer. But sadly it was not to be, once again Abraham was prevented from coming through ill-health. Grieg was bitterly disappointed. The holiday did Grieg's health so much good that he was able to send Abraham his fifth album of *Lyric Pieces*, Opus 54.

That year he also completed his *Peer Gynt Suite No II*, Opus 55; he gave it its première in Christiania on 14th November at the jubilee celebrating his twenty-five years as a concert performer in the Norwegian capital. The jubilee concert was followed a few days later by a banquet, which was also attended by Ibsen. Grieg wrote delightedly about both events. He was making so much from concerts that season that he asked Max Abraham to invest his fees for the new compositions in stocks and shares, rather than send him the money. Henri Hinrichsen took care of Grieg's investments. Grieg continued to do so well financially, that various sums were invested in stocks and shares and State Bonds on his behalf over the next few years.

The creation of the *Peer Gynt Suite No II* was not without problems for the composer. It had already been performed a few times in manuscript, but was still the subject of doubts expressed in the correspondence between Grieg and Abraham in early 1892. Abraham felt that a work which lasted only twelve minutes would not readily be performed by major orchestras in the big cities and suggested the addition of the *Arabian Dance* from the *Norwegian Dances*, Op 33. Grieg was having his problems with 'this Mr P Gynt' as he wrote on 12th February. The promoters of a forthcoming performance of Ibsen's play wanted him to write some more incidental music by the end of February, which he was unwilling to do. When they threatened to get another composer to do it, Grieg had to leave everything else he was working on to write the pieces. With regard to Abraham's suggestion he wrote:

> If you really are right in your suggestion that the second *Suite* is too short, then the thing wouldn't work. There are still one or two pieces which could be added, including the "Arabian Dance" which you mentioned. I'll have to work out which of these pieces would be most appropriate to orchestrate and would fit in best. Number two of the *Norwegian Dances* [Op

35] would not do, because the theme is not originally mine, but was borrowed from a folk dance. Everything must be original in *Peer Gynt*. But I'll find something…

By 20th March Grieg had thought the problem over and could write to Abraham from Troldhaugen:

> You spoke of a new *Finale*-piece for the *P G Suite*. The work must at all events end with 'Solvejg's Song'. 'The Arabian Dance' which I am now orchestrating for the *Suite*, ends pianissimo, which of course is also the case with 'Solvejg's Song'. However, I think the work will have greater success if it ends gently with the song. I have thought a great deal about the format, because it wasn't easy to compile something unified from the available material. That is why I tied the two last movements together with an interlude. I readily admit that this results in three movements instead of four, and that therefore a fourth piece would be most appropriate. Before I determine the sequence precisely, I must have the opportunity of hearing the newly orchestrated piece right through. Now that the season is finished, it would probably be better to leave publication of the work until the autumn. I would then be able to hear the whole work in Christiania before it is printed. That is unfortunately not possible here. Then I will appear quite suddenly in Leipzig with a new full score which will hit the nail on the head!?

Abraham was pleased that Grieg would take up his suggestion and asked him to start thinking about making arrangements for piano solo and piano four hands of the *Peer Gynt Suite No II*.

The orchestral work was not completed until early 1893 and in that version it did not include the 'Arabian Dance', though it did end with 'Solvejg's Song' and had the 'Dance of the Mountain King's Daughter' as the second movement. However, at Abraham's request Grieg did include the 'Arabian Dance'. Grieg came to Leipzig to conduct his second *Peer Gynt Suite* and his Piano Concerto on 3rd February, 1893. The *Suite* was published in 1893 as a five movement work, ending with the 'Dance of the Mountain King's Daughter'. But Grieg was still not happy with this version. The final version of the *Peer Gynt Suite No. II* has four movements: 'Ingrid's Lament', 'Arabian Dance', 'Peer Gynt's Homecoming' and 'Solvejg's Song'.

Shortly after the performance Grieg and his wife, together with the composer Christian Sinding, travelled as guests of Dr Abraham on a trip lasting almost three months, to the French Riviera, Italy and South

Tyrol. Grieg completed the outline sketches for his sixth volume of *Lyric Pieces*, Op 57, in Menton.

After returning to Christiania via Leipzig in May, Grieg went to Copenhagen for some months, where his *Vilhelm Krag Lieder*, Op 60 received their première and then went to Leipzig with Nina. He had written to Abraham on 9th December saying that he would like to conduct his orchestral pieces for *Sigurd Jorsalfar* in the Gewandhaus and received an invitation from the Gewandhaus to conduct there on 1st February, 1894. He wrote to Abraham on 1st January: '…You are the almighty God of Leipzig. I hope you will be pleased to see your son…'

Grieg had just heard that Max Abraham had, on 1st January, 1894, made the twenty-six-year-old Henri Hinrichsen, his partner and added his good wishes:

> …That is a very important matter and moreover something for which I wish him from the depths of my heart, much good fortune. Please give him my best wishes and sincerest congratulations. But my wishes for you are that you will remain at his side for many more years. I am looking forward more than ever to seeing you again soon…

Two days before the concert Edvard and Nina Grieg paid their first visit to the newly opened Peters Music Library in Leipzig. From Leipzig he travelled to Munich, where he conducted his best known orchestral works with huge success; the pianist Oscar Meyer played his Piano Concerto [Fig 9]. He travelled continuously, his breathless schedule taking him to Cambridge where he received an honorary doctorate on 10th May. He went on to give a concert with the Philharmonic Society in London on 24th May at which he conducted *Three Orchestral Pieces from Sigurd Jorsalfar*, Op 56.

The two friends were reunited when the Griegs went to Leipzig in October 1895, as guests of Max Abraham for six months. There the composer renewed his friendship with Brahms, whom he met again the following winter in Vienna.

Grieg was always keen to further the interests of younger composers where he felt there was merit in their music. In his birthday 'thank you' letter of 18th June, 1895 he introduced the Norwegian composer Johan Halvorsen, describing his music and his career in detail. He suggested that Abraham should consider publishing Halvorsen's orchestral suite based on his music for the Indian drama *Vasantasena*. He added:

> …However, I want to fulfil my duty as a Norwegian artist and can give you my word: It will give you pleasure. The music is

original, very oriental, excellent for orchestra and at the same time *very* understandable. You see, that is a lot at the same time, but not exaggerated. I have the score at the moment. If you would like to consider it, I would suggest that you do not consult any of the conservative Leipzig musicians such as Richter. It would be best if you had it played to you and made your own decision. You will like it. And if not, then you have surely got a very serious ear infection! However, I hope that the Harzburg air has not been without influence on your spiritual and physical well-being...

Abraham liked Halvorsen's music and agreed to publish it, he sent Grieg a letter to pass on, requesting another composition for 'next year – not 1898 or 99'.

In October and November Grieg gave a series of over-subscribed concerts in Stockholm, writing glowing reports to his friend in Leipzig. He was particularly pleased with their success and wrote on 7th November that he felt that they 'reached beyond the art itself' and fulfilled a 'national mission' during the tense political situation between Norway and Sweden. He then travelled to Christiania, Copenhagen, Berlin and Vienna for more concerts. The strain had been too much and he wrote to Abraham from Vienna on 23rd November: 'Today is the first concert, and I – am ill in bed with influenza!...' Brahms came to enquire after him several times and Grieg was delighted that he came to his concert on 19th December and shared in the celebration afterwards, even though the older German composer was terminally ill.

Grieg had hoped to return home via Leipzig in early December but he remained in Vienna over Christmas. It cost him more than he was earning in Vienna to live there and in desperation he appealed to Abraham to send him some money, which he duly acknowledged on 7th January, 1897, when he wrote: 'Many thanks for the money! Now I am at least saved. But you will be amazed to hear that Vienna is the most expensive city in Europe. In these six weeks I have spent almost my entire fees of 1500 Guilders...' A few days later he did finally travel to Leipzig where he and Nina stayed for four weeks.

In the meantime Grieg's newly published *Lyric Pieces,* volume VIII, Op 65, was enjoying success and Abraham showed a prophetic intuition when he wrote to the composer on 9th March: '...I count this amongst the loveliest you have written, especially the *Wedding Day at Troldhaugen,* a real masterpiece of which one can never tire...'

Grieg had been liberally showered with honours over the years, but he felt that they had their uses. He wrote Abraham on 14th March reporting on his successful concert in the Hague, which had been attended by royalty and where he had been appointed an officer of the Order of Oranien-Nassau: '…If you know me, you will understand how overjoyed I was! Orders are most helpful in one's luggage. The customs officials at the frontier are always very amiable when they see such things…'

When Brahms died in Vienna on 3rd April, 1897 Grieg was in Copenhagen. His outpouring to Max Abraham the following day was very reflective of the state of health of the two of them:

> …Brahms is dead! Now the critical fraternity can start measuring him with their yardsticks. He is fortunate. He has not outlived his creativeness, and died without suffering. When I was a child I was allowed to choose my favourite dish for my birthday. We ought to be able to choose our favourite illness too! But mother nature is not so liberal as that. How poor, musically, Germany is now!…My Dear Dr! Forgive these reflections. The great man who is departed has occasioned them. If I were now in Leipzig I would have called on you to exchange thoughts about him…

In his reply of 6th April, Max Abraham wrote: '…Rarely have I been so overcome by the death of an artist, as with that of Brahms…'

Grieg went to England in October for a strenuous two month tour, during which he and Nina gave ten concerts which were all detailed in letters to his friend in Leipzig. They were accompanied by Johannes Wolf, Grieg's partner on many musical tours, a writer on music who later became the Director of the Prussian State Library. Grieg's letter of 10th December, 1897 gives a lively report of their reception by Queen Victoria at Windsor Castle:

> …Windsor. It was very nice. I must say the Queen is charming, and astonishingly interested. Oh well, it's natural that I find her charming, for her first words were in German – 'I am a great admirer of your compositions.' We – my wife, Johannes Wolf and I – made music for about an hour (all by me) and she wanted to have still more. Then I played the Gavotte from *The Holberg Suite,* a work which, incidentally, is received everywhere here in England with great enthusiasm…

Dr Abraham was always in awe of Grieg's genius. A letter which he wrote to the composer from Harzburg on 25th August, concerning Op 68 and some other works, contained the following remark: 'You may write what you like, I hold everything with love to my fatherly heart.'

Grieg was tremendously politically aware and shared his feelings on
the growing national unrest with Dr Abraham in a letter dated 30th
September, 1898:

> ...I have just read that the old loveable Queen Louise of
> Denmark is dead, a more peaceful death certainly than that
> of the Empress Elizabeth of Austria. What do you say to that?
> It is assuredly more than a way of speaking to say that we are
> dancing on a volcano. What a pity that you cannot read Prince
> Kropotkin's[5] letter to Georg Brandes[6] in *Politiken* in
> Copenhagen. The letter was indeed written in French but,
> alas, translated into Danish. One thing in the letter is worth
> remarking. He says: When the higher and highest strata of
> society have no hesitation in butchering thousands – nay
> hundreds of thousands – of peasants and workers to obtain
> the peaceful and comfortable conditions these highest
> grades of society desire for themselves, how can one wonder
> if this utterly and entirely unenlightened social stratum
> turns the tables and says: 'I do not care whom I strike down
> of the higher grade. That will give people something to
> think of and then perhaps the better conditions we hope
> for will come at last.' Kropotkin considers that the one is as
> bad as the other. But enlightenment must begin some time:
> So first recognised butchery from above must be discontinued.
> Utopia! isn't it? But believe me: Other times *will* come.
> Through blood or intelligence! Through the latter it is to be
> hoped...

Because of Grieg's profound sense of justice, he became
inadvertently involved in what became known as the 'Dreyfus affair'.
In 1893-4 the French Jewish army officer Alfred Dreyfus was falsely
charged with delivering defence secrets to the Germans, court-
martialled and transported to Devil's Island. It became an extreme anti-
Semitic issue after protests from his wife, his friends and Emile Zola
and in 1899 the case was tried again, when Dreyfus was found guilty
but pardoned; the verdict was reversed in 1906. His innocence was not
finally proved until 1930.

Grieg had every reason to be angry about the French action, his
publisher and close friend for over thirty years, Dr Abraham, was a Jew.
When Grieg received an invitation in September 1899 to conduct his
own works in the Châtelet Theatre in Paris he turned down the
invitation, as he wrote to Abraham on 16th September: 'What do you
think of the Dreyfus scandal? I wrote to Colonne who invited me to
conduct, in the heat of indignation, that it would be impossible for me

to enter into any rapport with a public in a country where justice was handled in such defiance of the facts as in France'. In his letter to Colonne Grieg wrote: 'Like all other non-Frenchmen, I am shocked at the injustice in your country and do not feel myself able to enter into any relation whatsoever with the French public.' Grieg was staying with Bjoernson at the time and the writer's son-in-law, Albert Langen, translated the letter into French. Langen asked whether he could publish the letter in a German newspaper to which Grieg hesitatingly agreed. Publication in all the major European newspapers followed, which resulted in official vilification from France being heaped upon the hapless Grieg and with libellous and threatening letters. Grieg did not accept another engagement in France until April 1903.

A lively correspondence continued and this extract from the letter which Grieg wrote to Dr Max Abraham from Troldhaugen on 5th September, 1900, paints a moving picture of his thoughts:

> I have just received your kind letter. I have recently been evolving for myself a philosophy of health, in consequence of which I am trying – like yourself – not to complain any longer. Just as real music requires not only crescendo and fortissimo but also diminuendo, so life shows us the same graduations of tone. We have finished with our crescendo and fortissimo. The diminuendo is now being played. And a diminuendo *can* be actually beautiful. The thought of the pianissimo which is to come is by no means uncongenial to me, but of the unsightliness attendant on the diminuendo (suffering!) I stand in the greatest awe. The good Herzogenberg once said: 'Life is a dinner. I am now at the cheese course, and it tastes quite excellent!' That is what he said then. Whether the cheese tastes quite so good now in Wiesbaden, where he is trundled about in a chair, completely paralysed, is, I should say, a big question. But he is a real philosopher, and it would not be unlike him to be content with his lot.

Heinrich von Herzogenberg, born the same year as Grieg, was an Austrian composer and close friend of Brahms. He died a month later.

Coincidentally, as we saw earlier, Grieg and Abraham wrote to each other on the same day, 5th December, 1900. When Dr Max Abraham died on 8th December, Grieg was shattered at the loss of his dear friend and 'adoptive father'. The gentle soul of the artist comes to the fore in his expression of grief written from the sanatorium at Voksenkollen on 9th December, 1900:

My Dear Mr Hinrichsen,

That was a hard blow! Would that I were in Leipzig, to be able to press his hand once more in parting for the last time! How you must be feeling I know from my own state of mind. He was, in the best sense of the word, a fatherly friend, and he invaded my life with benevolent energy in a way that few have done. When we got to know each other forty years ago, our relationship in the early years was certainly only on a business footing. But underneath the business man I soon discovered the lover of humanity and the personal kindliness, which on my part evoked a sympathy towards him which has never stopped, but on the contrary has always been compelled to increase. I am deeply conscious...

I regret all the more that I had no chance of giving expression to these feelings at the Jubilee. For my letter, which I beg you to open, unfortunately came too late. How empty everything felt yesterday evening, after I had received the news! And now this morning there comes, like a last greeting from the deceased, his last dear letter, in which he expresses his thanks to me! This last greeting is a great, great comfort to me. I would not have missed it for anything.

By that time, Henri Hinrichsen was thirty-two years old, exactly the age Dr Abraham had been when he published Grieg's Opus 1, thirty-seven years earlier. He felt able to take on all the responsibilities he was heir to; which included taking the same father-like interest in Edvard Grieg which his uncle had done.

---

1   The Grieg letters (apart from a few which found their way into other hands) were taken from Leipzig either by Henri Hinrichsen's son Robert in July 1939 (which is unlikely) or by his son Walter between 1945 and 1947. They were kept at Walter Hinrichsen's company, C F Peters Corporation, New York. In 1986 his widow, Evelyn Hinrichsen sold them to the Norwegian State, who presented them to the Grieg Collection in the Bergen Public Library. In 1930 Nina Grieg presented those letters to Grieg which she still had from Dr. Max Abraham and Henri Hinrichsen, to the Bergen Library; the missing letters were lost or destroyed, though copies of many are to be found in the C F Peters Copy Books in the *Sächsische Staatsarchiv Leipzig*. The complete letters along with many replies, in their original German, are published in *Edvard Grieg, Briefwechsel mit dem Verlag C F Peters 1863-1907* (Edvard Grieg, Correspondence with C F Peters Publishers 1863-1907), edited by Finn Benestad and Hella Brock. Published by C F Peters Frankfurt, 1997.

2   Quotation from Freidrich Schiller's drama, *Don Carlos*, spoken by Pater Domingo.

3   From *Grieg and Delius* by Lionel Carley, published by Marion Boyars, 1993.

4   First important international copyright convention, which was concluded in Berne in 1886, and revised in Paris in 1896.

5   Peter Kropotkin (1842-1921), Russian geographer and anarchist.

6   Georg Brandes, Danish literary critic and essayist.

PART II

The New Century to the Great War

CHAPTER FOUR

A New Owner for the New Century

When he died on 8th December, 1900, it was as though the personality and aspirations of Dr Max Abraham passed to his thirty-two-year-old nephew, Henri Hinrichsen. Edvard Grieg put it into so many words, when he wrote to Hinrichsen on 11th December, 1905:

> …You are truly the resurrected Dr Abraham personified!…

Henri Hinrichsen's Background and Entry into C F Peters

The new owner of C F Peters had been born into a well-to-do German business family in Hamburg. His parents were Robert and Betty Hinrichsen. The Hinrichsen family originated in Spain, the name having evolved from the Spanish name Henriques (or Henriquez); they were Sephardic Jews and fled from Spain to Portugal in 1492. 150 years later they emigrated to the newly created town of Glückstadt, on the German-Danish border. There, the first member of the family to take up German citizenship was one Ruben Henriques. His name was entered in the *Bürgerbuch* (Citizen's Register) as Ruben Henrichs, Portuguese national, merchant, on 26th July 1646.[1] He and his descendants were successful business people in many spheres and contributed generously to the well-being of others.

Nine members of the Hinrichsen family, spanning five generations, were active as court financiers for two hundred years. They were the most successful court administrators' family in Mecklenburg. Principally court and state bankers, they supervised the tobacco and timber industries of the state, controlled the lottery, were active as political agents and were regularly leaders of the Jewish Community of Schwerin whose founders they had been. The family officially changed its name to Hinrichsen in 1814.

Abraham (known as Adolph) Hinrichsen, born in 1808 in Schwerin, settled in Hamburg, where there were already members of the extended Hinrichsen family in prominent governing positions in the city. The *Hamburgische Wappenrolle* (The Hamburg Heraldic directory) of 1912 lists four Hinrichs and four Hinrichsen families each having its own coat of arms. There, Adolph Hinrichsen founded a corset factory which, on his death in 1887, passed to his eldest son Robert.

Robert Hinrichsen, born in 1835, was a dour man, though a good business-man. Hamburg was then a commercial centre; its cultural life was not highly developed and he was not interested in the arts. In 1862 he married Betty Abraham from Danzig, five years his junior.

Born in 1840, Betty was the youngest of the seven children of Markus Leiser Abraham and Henriette (born Herrmann). Older than her by nine years, was her brother, Max Abraham, proprietor of C F Peters, Leipzig. Their father was the Mayor of Danzig, which at that time was a flourishing, intellectual and artistic city. Robert and Betty Hinrichsen had three sons: Max, Henri and Edmund. As her sons grew up, Betty instilled in them her love of the classics, literature, art and music, thus showing them a world far removed from the commercial interests of their father.

Henri Hinrichsen was born on 5th February, 1868 in Hamburg. His formative years were spent in his parents' elegant house at Hallerplatz 9. The tone was set by the lively Betty, who entertained with great style, surrounding herself and her family with guests from all walks of life. She was especially happy to entertain intellectuals and people from the world of art and the theatre.

Young Henri first attended a private school run by Dr Otto. He went on to the Realgymnasium des Johanneums (the Johanneum Grammar School). That was where he first met and made friends with Paul Ollendorff, who would in adulthood become his chief assistant. Henri grew up with his two brothers, as the middle child. Though totally different, the three brothers enjoyed a deep friendship and always remained in close touch. The Hinrichsens were a close-knit family. It was said that the young Henri, in contrast to his brothers, was always busy and conscientious.

After leaving school, Henri entered the family firm of Adolph Hinrichsen & Co and undertook a course in business management. However, an effect of all the stimulation offered him by his mother and his own widening outlook, was that he could not settle happily into his father's business. Together with his brothers, he had spent frequent holidays in Leipzig visiting his bachelor uncle Dr Max Abraham. There he had been allowed to ride his uncle's horses. He had been taken to concerts at the Gewandhaus, had glimpsed the world of music publishing and had met some of the famous composers whose music he had heard. The intoxicating aroma of freshly printed sheet music had entered his veins.

Henri's elder brother, Max, had already escaped the paternal factory to study law. He became Chairman of the Senate of the Provincial High

Court and Court of Appeal in the Free City of Hamburg. A portrait of him still hangs in the court room of the Senate.[2]

Robert Hinrichsen had naturally assumed that his second son would feel duty bound to continue the family business. But after only six months, Henri knew that he wanted something more culturally significant to stimulate him; he felt that the world of music publishing was the life he wished to embrace. In the end it was Robert's third and youngest son, Edmund, who was to inherit the mantle of manufacturer of ladies' foundation garments.

And so the nineteen-year-old respectful rebel embarked on his new life. It was to be a life of excitement, achievement, music, social responsibility, education, honour – persecution, tragedy and murder. Henri Hinrichsen could not have imagined, as he boarded the train to Leipzig, on 20th September, 1887, what a profound and far-reaching effect that step was to have – both on himself, and on the city of Leipzig.

The train carried the young man from the commercial Hansa city of Hamburg, to the provincial railway station of Leipzig. Henri Hinrichsen was met by his uncle, Dr Max Abraham, who was to become his guardian, his mentor, his teacher, his role model and ultimately his testator. As he himself wrote in 1933: '…my uncle Dr Max Abraham, who became from that moment onwards the best and kindest teacher, whose influence and impression on me, a nineteen-year-old youth, was to become of utmost importance and supreme value.'

Sound business sense decreed that the inexperienced and untrained young man should not immediately become his uncle's right-hand man. It was, and still is, customary throughout the music publishing world in Germany, that the young heir to a business should first of all follow several different, but allied apprenticeships, before entering his father's company. This not only gave the future proprietor necessary business experience, it also allowed him to get to know and to understand his future clients – the retailers, it acquainted him with methods of publishing and with different types of retailing. It also gave him a good background knowledge of what the different publishers were publishing – what the competition was producing, and gave him the chance of examining various different types of sheet music. Added to that, he was given practical instruction into methods of printing and engraving, and gained an understanding of paper quality and the intricacies of binding.

For young Henri, this term of apprenticeship lasted twenty months, starting just ten days after his arrival in Leipzig. He was sent to Basel, Switzerland to work in the music retail shop of Hug & Co, first as an apprentice, then for the last four months as a sales assistant. He did not feel at ease in the reserved and old-fashioned Swiss town, and was happy when his time there was over and he could leave Basel for Brussels in 1889. He remained there for a year and then spent some months in London, where he learnt English and got an insight into the workings of C F Peters' agent in England from 1873-1937, the music publisher Augener & Co. He also forged lasting friendships with the Augener family – Dr Max Abraham's friend George Augener who came to England from Germany in 1852 and his son William.

During his training he returned to Leipzig to work with his uncle for short periods, and on 15th May, 1891 he finally entered C F Peters, Leipzig, with power of attorney. He took to the business with the enthusiasm of youth, a profound interest and a love of and growing understanding for music.

Dr Max Abraham recognised his nephew's talents and his dedication to the ideals on which he had built the reputation of C F Peters, when he named Henri Hinrichsen his partner and heir only four years later, in 1894. The new heir was granted Leipzig citizenship that year.

By 1895 Abraham was able to leave the young man in sole charge when he went on holiday. Henri kept his uncle fully informed with regular letters: about progress, about people, about the weather – he was concerned that his uncle should wear his winter coat when the weather was cold. He wrote about the condition of Abraham's horses. He was particularly thrilled about the expansion of the business, when he wrote to his uncle on 13th April, 1895:[3]

> …I am absolutely delighted that every day at least one or two export orders are received, up to now not nearly so much was sent to South Africa and South America; the catalogues and conditions which we sent out in the autumn have really proved their worth. On Thursday a case went to South Africa (400M), one to Mexico (800M), today one to South Africa (600M), today Durand sent an order for about 500M for Valparaiso. Now it occurs to me that it might be a good idea if we were to include a poster next time we send out the catalogues. As it would be too complicated to send a large one, would it not be possible to make a smaller one of the same size as the overseas catalogue?
>
> Happy holidays and good weather.
>
> Your Henri

It is interesting to note that as long ago as 1895, so much sheet music was being demanded by people living in countries so far from Europe. Henri had progressive ideas on publicity, which lead to an even greater demand for music from across the world.

Henri Hinrichsen was remembered by one of his nieces as having been a tall, handsome man, of upright posture, proud of having been born a Sephardi, though he was not a practising Jew. With his black hair and beard, and his sparkling dark brown eyes, he grew to have the appearance of a Spanish nobleman. Born in Hamburg, he spoke an educated and attractive Hamburg dialect. He was always well-dressed and in his breast pocket he carried a silver toothpick which he would use after meals. He had been brought up to respect all people and was always courteous and friendly, whilst still maintaining a distinctive formality.

The business continued to expand and it was apparent by 1896 that additional staff would be needed to run C F Peters efficiently. Henri Hinrichsen knew that he would need somebody close to him, on whom he could rely completely, and he thought of his old school friend, Paul Ollendorff.

Employment of Paul Ollendorff

Just six months his junior, Ollendorff was born in Hamburg on 22nd October, 1868 and, after leaving school had completed apprenticeships in the music trade similar to those undertaken by Henri Hinrichsen – in Hamburg and Berlin. He had been employed by C F Peters agent in Berlin from 1891 to 1896. A creative man he had wanted to go on the stage and had produced some youthful compositions, but he had abandoned his original ambitions. Ollendorff accepted the offer of a job with his childhood friend and moved to Leipzig to start work on 15th March, 1896 where he settled in successfully. Of him Hinrichsen wrote in his *Chronik* in 1933:

> Paul Ollendorff was the most faithful and most tireless employee ever at C F Peters. The woes and well-being of the publishing house lay nearer to his heart than did his own. He was unusually intelligent and worked ceaselessly and had acquired in-depth knowledge into various aspects of his profession through self-motivated study. Thanks to his musicality, both Dr Abraham and I would always seek out his advice on artistic and more difficult matters, whilst he was less keen on the business aspects and chose not to involve himself with the accounts. Over the course of the years, he became my right hand as it were.

On Henri Hinrichsen's wedding day Paul Ollendorff was granted power of attorney and effectively took on managerial duties.

Marriage and Family

On 6th March, 1898 Henri Hinrichsen married the charming and intelligent Martha Bendix. Theirs was a love-match which became a happy and rewarding marriage lasting more than forty years; they had seven children – five sons and two daughters, three of the sons following their father into C F Peters.

Martha Bendix was born in Berlin on 2nd March, 1879; with three brothers, she was the second of four children. Their parents were Waldemar and Bertha (born Katz) Bendix. Waldemar, like his father, was a leading member of the executive of the Jewish Reform Community; his wife was the daughter of a banker. Waldemar Bendix had a linen mill, Bendix & Company at Sorau, a hundred or so miles east of Berlin. The Bendix family, of Polish origin, had held German nationality since 1809.

The marriage of Martha Bendix to Henri Hinrichsen in Berlin was the occasion for a great family gathering. There were many Bendix relatives from Berlin. The groom's parents and extended family came from Hamburg, whilst further relatives came from Danzig, and elsewhere. The employees from Bendix & Co came. Waldemar Bendix had not been required to pay a dowry on his daughter's marriage and so he decided to contribute the money thus saved towards the welfare of his employees. He established a fully paid health insurance scheme for them.

Henri Hinrichsen's upbringing, in contrast to his wife's, having been much more relaxed in religious terms, the new Hinrichsen household was not run according to Jewish beliefs. In all things, the Hinrichsen family belonged to the cultured German elite of Leipzig society; they had little contact with the 15,000 strong Jewish Community, whose members were largely of East European origin.

The new couple's first home was an apartment on the second floor of the elegant house, 8 Stephanstrasse in Leipzig, with its beautiful balcony and view over the Johannistal (St John's Valley). Here, their first child, a daughter, Charlotte, was born on 27th December, 1898. In October 1900 the little family moved to live with Dr Max Abraham in the fine C F Peters house, 10 Talstrasse, occupying the second floor apartment.

With the business of C F Peters Henri Hinrichsen also inherited monumental obligations and debts which Dr Max Abraham had run up to finance his huge publishing endeavours and his support of the Peters Music Library and many charitable organisations. It took many years before the new owner could pay off his predecessor's debts, the worry causing him severe nervous problems throughout his life.

Professionally, Henri Hinrichsen, like his uncle before him, was at the forefront of new developments, especially where he saw that they might be of advantage to his composers. He was one of the first members of the *Genossenschaft Deutscher Tonsetzer* (Co-operative of German Composers), referred as the GDT.

Genossenschaft Deutscher Tonsetzer

The GDT was formed by composers, for composers, in order to protect their copyright and founded at the instigation of its first President, Richard Strauss, on 1st July, 1903. It had three main aims:

1) The protection and encouragement of the professional interests of its members;
2) The setting up of institutions for the appraisal of musical copyright;
3) The support of needy members and their dependants, as well as the provision of pensions and help as necessary.

Few music publishers joined the GDT, most did not want to pay a subscription and took the attitude that the society would not work in their best interests. They were against it to the extent that they would only support concert societies who refused to pay fees to the GDT. Henri Hinrichsen felt precisely the opposite; because, as he wrote to the conductor, Dr Georg Göhler, who did so much to promote Mahler's Fifth Symphony: '...I always and always have the wish to make the artist's life in general more agreeable.' This credo he amply demonstrated throughout his more than forty years as a music publisher.

At first the GDT did not work in the best interests of the composers, as it would not allow concert societies who refused to pay a subscription, to perform the works of its members. In 1915 a new society, the GEMA – *Gesellschaft für Musikalische Aufführungs- und Mechanische Verfielfältigungsrechte* (Society for Musical Performing and Mechanical Reproduction Rights), with somewhat similar aims was formed; Henri Hinrichsen was also a founder member of this. There were also other similarly motivated societies. The GDT and all the other societies combined in 1930, which led, in 1933, to the formation of the STAGMA – *Staatlich genehmigte Gesellschaft zur Verwertung musikalische Urheberrechte* (State approved Association for the Utilisation of Musical Copyright). In 1945, after World War II the Allies insisted that the organisation revert to its former name of GEMA.

C F Peters' composers continued to enjoy the cordial relationships established over the years between them and Dr Max Abraham without a break on his death, the new owner accepting all the existing responsibilities. Having known Edvard Grieg for some twelve years, it seemed natural for Henri Hinrichsen to take on the same role as 'adoptive father' and friend as his uncle had done.

Edvard Grieg

Grieg was delighted that the relationship would continue in a similar way. He had been unwell for some time and regretted his own lack of productivity. But Hinrichsen encouraged him as his uncle would have done, when he wrote on 24th June, 1901 giving him some financial advice. He added, in a very understanding manner: 'Of course you cannot compose whilst you are ill, but it seems to me that you are thinking too pessimistically with respect to your future productivity, because I am firmly convinced that as soon as you feel better you will once again feel inspired to compose, as this has been the case so often in the past.' In the same letter, Hinrichsen suggested that 'as a mark of my gratitude' he would be increasing the quarterly retainer paid to Grieg which had been set at 1000M in the contract of 1889, to 1500M and enclosed 500M. This encouragement had the desired effect in raising the composer's 'productivity'.

Grieg's reply from Troldhaugen on 29th June, 1901 shows that he fully accepts Henri Hinrichsen in the role of 'adoptive father' vacated by Max Abraham, even though Hinrichsen is twenty-five years younger than himself:

> ...Whether your extremely kind suggestion really was, in this instance, in the spirit of the dearly departed, I don't know. But that you want to behave towards me in his spirit, that, at one and the same time delights and moves me deeply. Please be assured that I know how to value it. Naturally I accept your kindly suggestion with greatest thanks, even though I cannot lie when I admit to being somewhat embarrassed at having provoked the same. Though you are not nearly old enough to become my 'adoptive father'. (As I always used to call Dr Abraham.) However, I will make sure that I become the obedient adoptive child. Also, as proof that you will not be disappointed in my future production, I will soon send you the tenth *and last* volume of *Lyric Pieces*.

The friendship and confidence between the two men was as sincere as that between Grieg and Dr Abraham. Hinrichsen continued to pay for some of Grieg's holidays, and sometimes to go with him, and presents and financial support were generous. The composer enjoyed his visits to his publisher's house which took on a new dimension, which delighted Edvard and Nina Grieg.

Martha and Henri Hinrichsen's second child and first son Max[4], named after his great-uncle Max Abraham, was born on 6th July, 1901. When Grieg heard the news he sent his congratulations from Troldhaugen on 20th August:

Three cheers for Opus II! My wife and I send our heartiest congratulations. So: a daughter and a son! Very energetic! And at the same time as the deluxe edition! I am sufficiently egoistic to hope that the young siblings will soon be mature enough to play the four-handed *Norwegian Dances*. Then I will come to Leipzig to sit in a quiet corner as audience. You write that the new world citizen was born in the Talstrasse. Have you really moved in? And perhaps even in the old beloved rooms? I didn't know…'

The Grieg's always took a great delight in the children and followed their lives with interest.

Grieg's prolific output of letters continued unabated – there were about 140 to Henri Hinrichsen during the last seven years of the composer's life. They were about compositions and business matters and also many which extended to several descriptive pages about his personal life, progressively worsening state of health and his thoughts and opinions. The tenth and last volume of *Lyric Pieces*, Op 71 was published in November 1901. Grieg had suggested that C F Peters should issue the complete *Lyric Pieces* in one bound volume. To his delight, Hinrichsen took up this suggestion and sent him a beautifully gift-bound copy for his fifty-ninth birthday in June 1902.

Grieg's sixtieth birthday was celebrated in June 1903. Henri Hinrichsen sent a number of presents, one of which was a huge bookcase which the composer had wished for. He also sent a copy of the photograph which had been taken on the Grieg's visit to Leipzig in May, showing Nina and Edvard Grieg together with Martha and Henri Hinrichsen and Paul Ollendorff [Fig 10]. Grieg's reply from Troldhaugen dated 12th June, 1903 indicates the extent of the pre-celebrations for his birthday and the celebrations for his thirty-sixth wedding anniversary, when he was so overwhelmed and exhausted that he completed the report some six weeks later with a further letter:

I should have replied to your friendly letter of the 5th immediately. But it's a bad time for me. The 'pre-celebrations' are in full swing and I am the unhappiest object which is dragged like an idol from temple to temple. Today I will delay no longer. Please accept my sincerest thanks for the various presents…We are actually put to shame and at the same time deeply moved by your magnificent present of the book cupboard. I accept the gift with my heartfelt thanks and look forward to assembling the cupboard.

You should have been here yesterday (it was our thirty-sixth wedding anniversary). I had a small dinner and the pleasure of receiving Bjoernson with wife and son in Troldhaugen, for the first time. Today my friend Julius Röntgen will come from Amsterdam. In the newspapers I read of deputations and presents from all over. Soon I will say as did Tannhäuser: 'Too much, too much!' But still: I don't want to be like Gounod's Faust: 'Nothing!' I hope everything will turn out harmoniously and naturally. I will tell you about the festive programme...

In celebration of Grieg's sixtieth birthday and to create a lasting memorial to the composer, Henri Hinrichsen commissioned the famous German sculptor, Carl Seffner[5], who was very fashionable at the time, to make a marble bust of Grieg, at a cost of 6000M, for the Gewandhaus, Leipzig. Grieg had sat for the sculptor on his visit to his publisher in May 1903 [Fig 11].

Hinrichsen presented the bust to the Gewandhaus in January 1904. As it was a rule of the house that no bust was to be placed in the main foyer whilst the subject was still alive, it was placed in the main stairway instead. (It was lost when the Gewandhaus was destroyed by bombs in 1944.) Grieg was delighted that Hinrichsen had a copy made for him.

This was not the first time that C F Peters had commissioned a portrait of their favourite composer. Franz von Lenbach had previously been commissioned by Dr Max Abraham to paint a portrait of Grieg. However, when Dr Abraham saw the almost completed portrait, he is alleged to have said: 'It is nothing, and it will become nothing.' Lenbach would not alter the painting, and it was never delivered.

Grieg often asked Henri Hinrichsen to liaise with his correspondents, as he did not have the time to answer every query. On 16th September, 1903 he wrote reminding his publisher: 'You know that you are replacing my "adoptive father"', when he asked him to write to a certain Herr von Franquet who wanted to know something about his string quartet. Grieg recounted the story of its gestation as follows:

...I wrote the Quartet during a stay in the wonderful natural surroundings of Hardanger in 1877-78 and it was first performed at the end of '78 to great success, by the Heckmann Quartet in Cologne. However, when it was published by E W Fritzsch in Leipzig, it was so scathingly reviewed by the conservative press after the Heckmann Quartet's performance in the Leipzig Gewandhaus at the beginning of '79, that it remained in the doldrums for a number of years. Later it was published by C F Peters and by then the conservatism in Leipzig had abated under the Gewandhaus management. The

Quartet was discovered by the modern masters of the violin (headed by Brodsky) and has since been performed everywhere by the finest string quartet ensembles...

This story led the publisher to ask Grieg to write down any other such stories as they occurred to him, as he would like to publish a collection of such recollections, though nothing came of this idea. Grieg had been asked to write an autobiographical sketch in 1903, entitled *Mein erster Erfolg*[6] (My First Success) for the American *McLure's Magazine* which however, did not publish it; it did appear in several other magazines. The sketch was published by C F Peters in 1910 as the introduction to *Edvard Grieg: Verzeichnis seiner Werke mit Einleitung: Mein erster Erfolg* (Edvard Grieg: Catalogue of his Works with Introduction: My First Success).

Just as Max Abraham had advised Grieg in 1890 about joining the French *Société des Auteurs*, now in 1903 Henri Hinrichsen advised him about joining the GDT. He explained the details of the contract to the composer and replied to all his questions, as well as taking care of all the tedious details for him.

In his turn Grieg informed his publisher about the agreement achieved between the Americans and the Norwegian Authors' Society, which had been struggling over the constant infringement of copyright of which the Americans were guilty. Like other European publishers, C F Peters had been losing sales to the USA, because the American publishers did not recognise the European copyright agreements and would reprint whatever they wanted, under their own imprint. Hinrichsen's reply of 20th December, 1903 indicates his own frustrations over this question: '...I am eagerly awaiting further news. The possibility of putting the reprint-happy Yankees in their place, does my heart good...'

Appreciative of everything his publisher had done, not only for himself, but for the dissemination of Norwegian music, Grieg was instrumental in achieving official recognition for his friend's support and sponsorship. The St Olav's Order of Chivalry 1st Class (roughly equivalent to a British knighthood) was awarded by King Oskar II of Norway to Henri Hinrichsen on 27th May, 1904. He counted it amongst his most prestigious possessions. He wore it proudly on the occasion of his younger brother, Edmund's wedding in November, when it aroused great interest.

The letter informing the publisher of his award arrived coincidentally with the birth of the Hinrichsens' third child, a daughter, Ilse, in January 1904. Grieg was away from home at the time and it can be seen as a mark of the sincere friendship between composers and publisher, that he learnt the news from his friend and compatriot the composer

Christian Sinding, another C F Peters composer and Hinrichsen family friend.

In his letter of 21st July Grieg described in great detail his visit to Kaiser Wilhelm II in Berlin, a man whom he considered to be most cultured and musical and in every respect surprising. He ended with the remark: '...The Kaiser is definitely an extraordinary man. An incredible mixture of great energy, extreme self-confidence – and of great kindness. He talked about children and animals with delight and with love – I regard that as a meaningful sign...' Hinrichsen, a great admirer of the Kaiser, who bestowed a medal on him three years later, was thrilled over Grieg's very informative description.

In his many letters to Hinrichsen he went into detailed descriptions concerning the political situation in Norway and Sweden and his own views on the events. Grieg was a convinced Republican; but in 1905 he was of the opinion, in view of the tense situation, that the monarchy offered the only viable option of circumventing a difficult political and economic crisis.

Grieg had long been encouraging Henri Hinrichsen to visit him in Norway. His hopes were fulfilled when the publisher and his wife Martha came on 13th November, 1905 for a few days to stay in the hotel in Christiania in which the Griegs were living; it was the Hinrichsens only visit to Grieg in Norway. They missed the celebrations for the dissolution of the Union between Sweden and Norway, by a few days. Bjoernson's play *Sigurd Jorsalfar* with Grieg's music, was performed for the festive entry of the Royal couple – King Haakon VII and Queen Maud – to the capital. A few days later Grieg conducted his *Landerkennung* (Recognition of the Country), Op 31 before the King and Queen.

On 28th November, 1905 Henri Hinrichsen gave 25,000 Norwegian Crowns towards the establishment of a Grieg Museum at Troldhaugen. He intended with this generous gift that Grieg should be able to live in his house at Troldhaugen free of financial worries, to the end of his life and that the villa should then be handed to the Norwegian State in order to create a Grieg Museum or a Home for Musicians. Grieg did not have much confidence in his country's enthusiasm for the enterprise and expressed his doubts from Troldhaugen on 11th December, 1905:

> ...How sensitively you thought the whole thing out! And in addition to which , the more than modest request, to be left out of the game! I hardly need to tell you that both my wife and I are very happy at this further proof of your kindness and support. So, in the name of the Norwegian State, my deepest thanks for the wonderful intention! But now hear what this authority on his people has to say: The concept of piety can hardly be said to exist here. It may be bad for us,

but it is a deeply ingrained condition of our history, which must be reckoned with. Here we have neither memorial plaques nor museums for worthy men of the nation. There is just no interest for that sort of thing. If you want to bequeath 'Troldhaugen' to the Norwegian State after my death, then the State would receive the gift with thanks, but would no doubt, and almost vehemently, feel the same as Dr Abraham said to Anton Rubinstein when the composer demanded newly engraved scores for works which had already been the subject of many alterations: 'You know, dear Mr Rubinstein, for me that would be more an honour than a pleasure!' (A genial reply). In other words: the State would have to undertake the upkeep of the villa and to pay taxes for it...

Whilst Hinrichsen did believe that a Grieg Museum would prove successful, he agreed that Grieg should dispose of Troldhaugen in his will as he wanted. Grieg was tremendously grateful that Hinrichsen had, 'like a second adoptive father' made it possible for him to keep Troldhaugen for the rest of his life.

Though in poor health, Grieg undertook several concert engagements during 1906. In April he went to Leipzig as a guest of the Hinrichsens. There, on 11th April he made a Phonola-System recording of six of his piano pieces on perforated paper rolls at Ludwig Hupfeld's. Six days later he made a further, similar type of recording of three pieces, at Popper & Co, this time on the Welte-Mignon piano. (All these recordings were saved and made available for the first time, on CD, in 1993 – for the 150th anniversary of Grieg's birth.)

Grieg had really looked forward to his return to Troldhaugen in June, but was soon unhappy again; the climate was terrible for his asthma. As he wrote from there on 29th June: 'I keep on repeating the experience that when I return to Bergen, especially to Troldhaugen, my health deteriorates...The delight has gone and an inner voice tells me: go, go from here to the East, to Christiania, where I can at least breathe.' He also discussed the corrections to his Piano Concerto, which were causing him considerable worry: 'I'm really getting fed up with making alterations to the instrumentation in the Piano Concerto and to the bowing in the *Peer Gynt Suite...*' He joked about his visits to the King of England and the King of Norway and gave his opinion of Percy Grainger as an 'inspired pianist' and Hermann Sandby as 'a quite extraordinary cellist'. He ended: 'In my present condition the memory acts like the sun breaking through the clouds.' Grieg composed his final work, the *Four Psalms*, Op 74, for baritone solo and mixed chorus in 1906.

Edvard Grieg had been having premonitions of his death for the past year, however, he still committed himself to the strenuous concert tours which he loved so much. When he gave a concert in Berlin in April 1907, Henri and Martha Hinrichsen were in the audience. Afterwards the Griegs came to Leipzig for a few days, when they delighted in the children, ate their fill of oysters and enjoyed a concert of the St Thomas Choir. It was the composer's last visit to his 'Little Paris'. From Leipzig he returned to Copenhagen via Kiel where he gave a very successful concert – the applause always served to lift his spirits and make him feel better, but only very temporarily; he fell seriously ill again. He described his various ailments in graphic detail in his letter of 2nd June from the Skodsborg Sanatorium near Copenhagen and ended:

> ...Invitations to conduct are coming in from around the whole world! The irony of fate! America wants to turn me into a rich man! I thank. A completely different expression of thanks is the one I owe to you and dear Dr Abraham for the fact that you have made it possible for me to enjoy an old age free from financial worries. My gratitude for this will never cease, as long as I breathe...

Edvard Grieg died in Bergen, on 4th September, 1907 and Nina sent a telegram to Henri Hinrichsen immediately. She followed this up with a long letter from Troldhaugen dated 11th September, 1907:

> Dear Mr Hinrichsen! Please forgive me if I write you a badly phrased letter. Everything that has happened lately is so completely unfathomable to me, that I don't know where to start. This is the first letter I am writing since Grieg departed from me, and you will understand how very difficult it is for me. However, I will not speak of myself, there is no point in it, my purpose with these lines is to thank you with all my heart dear Mr Hinrichsen, for everything you have done for Grieg, in that you took up the inheritance from dear Abraham so completely and were, from beginning to end, a true and devoted friend to my husband.

The letter continued with a detailed description of Grieg's final illness and his death. It ends:

> Dear Mr Hinrichsen, please understand, I cannot think in a foreign language at the present time. Have my deepest thanks, that is all that I can tell you and your dear wife, from the depths of my heart.

As the death of Edvard Grieg ended Henri Hinrichsen's association with the composer, it marked the deepening of his friendship with Nina Grieg, to whom he continued to be adviser, friend and benefactor. They had an ongoing relationship, with visits, presents to Nina, holidays, but most of all with a warm and sincere friendship. Henri Hinrichsen went to Copenhagen for a memorial concert of Grieg's music in January 1908. Their concern for each other is revealed in their many letters, of which there are over 200 from Nina in the archives of C F Peters, expressing her gratitude towards her patron, who not only shielded her and her sister Tonny Hagerup from financial worries, but also advised her on questions of tax, performing rights and many personal worries.

Apart from the substantial income which Nina received from the performance of Grieg's music, Henri Hinrichsen voluntarily paid her a very generous pension of 5,000M to 6,000M every year. And he delighted in sending her luxuries – Grieg had always loved caviar, but Nina let it be known that she preferred oysters and so Hinrichsen sent her this delicacy at regular intervals. Nina had never been a keen housewife, not even in Troldhaugen. After Grieg's death she and her older sister Tonny Hagerup lived in the King of Denmark Hotel, in Copenhagen, where Henri Hinrichsen visited them almost every year.

Nina was constantly longing for 'the lovely old days' when she and Edvard used to visit the Hinrichsens in Leipzig. She was delighted with every new addition to the Hinrichsen's growing family and keenly followed their progress through life. Within three weeks of Grieg's death, on 23rd September, 1907 the Hinrichsen's fourth child, Walter, was born. The fifth child and third son, Hans-Joachim, was born in 1909; he eventually followed his two elder brothers into the family business. Two further sons completed the Hinrichsen family: Paul in 1912 and Robert in 1918.

Henri Hinrichsen still felt convinced that Grieg's villa at Troldhaugen should be preserved as a museum in spite of Grieg's rejection of the idea in 1905, when he had diverted the money which his publisher had sent for the museum, to another purpose. In 1910 he sent Nina another 25,000M to be put towards the anticipated Grieg Museum at Troldhaugen. However, Nina was no more interested in the idea than her husband had been and, some years later, gave the money to a nephew, Joachim Grieg, a ship owner. Time has shown Henri Hinrichsen's belief to have been well founded; the Grieg Museum at Troldhaugen is one of Norway's most popular tourist attractions.

The sense of responsibility and friendship which Henri Hinrichsen displayed towards Nina Grieg was typical of the many acts of kindness, generosity and patronage which marked the guiding principles of his life. He was completely integrated into the civic life of Leipzig, as well as the social and cultural life. He took his responsibilities as citizen seriously, and expressed his sense of belonging to the City of Leipzig with generous sponsorships and gifts to many institutions.

Social Involvement

Like Dr Max Abraham, he had a profoundly developed social conscience, in which he was fully supported by his wife. As he became wealthy through the sound publishing policies which he was following, so he became more involved with the needs of those less fortunate than himself. He was on the committee of several charitable organisations and was a generous supporter of many worthy causes and benefactor to a number of institutions. Whilst Henri and Martha Hinrichsen were definitely a part of the establishment – which in Leipzig was known as the *Bildungsbürgertum* (the educated classes) – and conventional, they were also supportive of feminist ideals.

Henri Hinrichsen became a major benefactor of the city of Leipzig, and established himself as one of the leading citizens. Even before he became father to seven children, he placed a high value on education. He had also inherited Dr Max Abraham's concern for the education of women at a time when this was generally considered to be of little importance. They saw education not only in academic terms but, for the less intellectual, working-class women, the learning of skills. Dr Max Abraham had founded and supported the *Frauen Gewerbeverein* (Women's Trade Association) and Henri Hinrichsen continued to support this fully after his uncle's death. He also sponsored a Kindergarten in the Spittastrasse, a working-class area of Leipzig, which was free of charge – unique at that time in Leipzig.

Martha Hinrichsen, to whom her husband referred as 'the power behind the throne' had a great deal of sympathy with the problems of women's rights and needs. She took her place on the committee of the *Frauen Gewerbeverein* in 1899. Henri Hinrichsen donated a further 100,000M towards the upkeep of the house, 26 Königstrasse, and towards furthering the aims of the Association.

So, from the time of his arrival in Leipzig, when he came under the influence of his uncle, Henri Hinrichsen developed a deep interest in and involvement with the education of women. Though he was a business man and music publisher, he felt equally at home amongst academics and intellectuals. He naturally inclined towards belonging to the bourgeois intelligentsia – people who met to talk about ideas, philosophy, books, art, music, education and social welfare. It was as part of this group, that he first came in contact with Henriette Goldschmidt and became so impressed by her ideas on the education of women.

The Henriette Goldschmidt School, the first All Women's College in Germany: 1911

Henriette Goldschmidt, born in 1825 [Fig 12], with a lifetime of educational involvement behind her, was already eighty-six years old when she saw the realisation of her great dream, the creation of the *Hochschule für Frauen* (College for Women) in Leipzig. She oversaw it for the first ten years of its existence. In 1871 she had inspired the citizens of Leipzig in the foundation of the *Verein für Familien- und Volkserziehung* (Association for Family and National Education), of which she became the President. She worked tirelessly for women's rights and the official recognition of Kindergartens. She acquired a house for her association, with the financial sponsorship of Henri Hinrichsen, which she established as an educational institute for kindergarten teachers and as a kindergarten.

These, very briefly, were the credentials of the woman who inspired Henri Hinrichsen to this generous patronage, which started in 1910 with the purchase of the plot of 18/20 Königstrasse and ultimately lead to the founding of the *Stiftung Hochschule für Frauen* (Trust for the Women's College).

It could be said that the first Women's College in Europe was founded by default! How this happened is best described in Henri Hinrichsen's own enthusiastic words, in the *Chronik* which he wrote in 1933:

> It had been my intention to have a house built on the plot of land, Königstrasse 18/20 with its surrounding garden on the Lindenstrasse, which I had bought from the Felix heirs, which would serve the common good of women's needs. I was thinking in terms of the August Schmidt House which was being planned at the time. One day, quite unannounced, I called at the house in the Fockerstrasse of Frau Hauptmann Schmidt, the originator of this plan, to discuss the idea with her. She was not at home – and thus destiny was influenced. I quickly decided to seek out the originator of another plan: Frau Henriette Goldschmidt, who wanted to create a special establishment for the intellectual education of young women. She was at home, and I discussed my intentions with her, in broad outlines. Frau Dr Goldschmidt was as though in a dream, because it seemed to her, that which she had never dared to contemplate on this scale, had suddenly fallen into her lap. Her plan of a modest, whilst at the same time highly intellectual, educational establishment for young women, in the context of a *Hochschule für Frauen* (College for Women) was to be realised. So I had

the elegant and tasteful building at No. 18/20 Königstrasse built. I dedicated it:

'To the noble strivings of German women'.

We discussed the educational implementation with suitable people, primarily [Leipzig] University professors from the Faculty of Education (Spranger, Volkelt and others)...

In the presence of the eighty-six-year-old founder, Henriette Goldschmidt, the *Oberbürgermeister* (Mayor) Dr Dittrich and the aforementioned professors who had been joined by Albert Köster, Carl Lamprecht and others, the First German College for Women was ceremoniously inaugurated on 29th October, 1911. A large tea party at number 10 Talstrasse, at which Martha Hinrichsen, who had done so much to support the realisation of the plan, presided, rounded off the festivities.

Over and above the regular education offered, it was intended that the college should also be an educational institute for all women – those who were not registered as students were invited to attend lectures. For several years, the lectures (on philosophy, history, art, literature, education, sociology, law, biology and nursing) were extremely well attended; however, the continued existence of the establishment as a College of Further Education as envisaged by Henriette Goldschmidt, was of sadly short duration. The by then only illusory name of College for Women, became the *Sozialpädagogisches Frauenseminar* (Women's Training College for Social Education) in 1920.

The plot of land at 18/20, Königstrasse which Henri Hinrichsen had bought for the construction of the College, was in the same block as his home and the C F Peters' office building at 10 Talstrasse, which was next to the Peters Music Library at 26 Königstrasse. The third street in the block was Lindenstrasse, on which he had built his warehouse in 1905, which is described in the next chapter. Hence, the three adjoining gardens all belonged to the Hinrichsen family.

The aims of the college were high:

1) To give women a thorough grounding in the educational profession of motherhood and
2) To equip women to devote themselves to the many-faceted general duties which they would encounter within the community, the state and society, in the broadest terms and with a full understanding for the requirements of the present.

The college building was extended in 1914 to its present size and there were changes and additions to the curriculum over the next few years. 1916 saw the development of three new departments – an educational one for the training of youth leaders and teachers for Kindergarten seminars, a social and a medical department. The educational format changed to become one dedicated to preparing women for their professional role in society.

Henri Hinrichsen established the Trust for the Women's College on 15th September, 1916, with a sum of 340,000M, which brought his total contribution for the college to that date, up to 900,000M. His support continued with huge financial donations. An agreement was reached in August 1916, whereby the responsibility for the college would be handed to the City of Leipzig. The official ceremony celebrating this event was on 26th October, the fifth anniversary of its establishment, in the presence of many dignitaries from the city and the University of Leipzig. The donor expressed his pleasure at the success of the young educational establishment and of its recognition by the state and hoped that the college would achieve its high aims under the protection of the state and of the city.[7] Up to that point, the state had not given the College any financial support at all, it was entirely supported by voluntary donations. Henri Hinrichsen was thanked and praised for his huge contributions, without which the college would not have been brought into existence. It became recognised as an independent trust under the supervision of the Royal Ministry of Education and the Arts in 1917.

Henri Hinrichsen's involvement with the education of women, was only one expression of his desire to devote the profits from his publications to the betterment of the lives of others. He was as concerned for the interests of composers, as he was for the correct conduct of business. His relationship with Edvard Grieg ran alongside his relationship with other composers, a few of whom will be introduced in the next chapter.

---

1 *Glückstädter Bürgerbuch,* Vol I, 1620-1706.
2 There is a street in Hamburg called 'Hinrichsenstrasse' which is named after a cousin, Siegmund Hinrichsen (1841-1902) who was a banker and President of the Hamburg City Parliament. A marble bust of him is still to be seen in the Town Hall.
3 StAL Bestand, C F Peters, 1381.
4 Max Hinrichsen (1901-1965) – the author's father.
5 Carl Ludwig Seffner (1861-1932), sculptor responsible for statues for Bach, Goethe and many others. One of the leading sculptors of the new wave in Leipzig at the turn of the century, especially famous as a portrait sculptor. Seffner was in Leipzig as esteemed as his contemporary, Max Klinger. But his popularity declined and his death was not mentioned in the local newspaper.
6 Manuscript in the Bergen, Norway, Public Library.
7 *Leipziger Volkszeitung.* 27th October, 1916, Stadtarchiv Leipzig, Kap 35. Nr 64, Bd 2.

CHAPTER FIVE

The New Publisher at Work

Development of the Business

Henri Hinrichsen became a member of the committee of the German Music Publishers' Association and of the German Music Dealers' Association as well as having been the first music publisher to join the GDT, the composers' association. He had long respected the importance of the export market and in April 1909 travelled to the USA to improve C F Peters' representation there.

New additions to the catalogue showed that Max Abraham's publishing policy was being continued by his heir, in that he aimed to make classical music accessible to all, in first-class editions, at reasonable prices. He acquired Tchaikovsky's Violin Concerto, piano and organ works by Max Reger, further compositions by Grieg and Sinding, as well as Lieder cycles by Cornelius and Brahms. Of great importance was the new edition of *Choral Preludes of Old Masters*, as well as other works, edited by the *Thomaskantor* Karl Straube; and Max Reger's arrangement of Bach's *Brandenburg Concertos* for piano four hands. Whilst a considerable quantity of new music was published during the early years of the twentieth century, the main emphasis was on the classics.

The genesis of a publication by C F Peters, reflected the personality of the proprietor, Henri Hinrichsen and this has been very succinctly described by a nephew writing in his eighties, whose memories are vivid after almost sixty years.

> He commanded great respect and some people who did not know him too well were in awe of him. He was very witty and I certainly noticed his great sense of humour. He was a grand seigneur who knew how to enjoy the good things in life and he expressed appreciation in a very gracious way for hospitality. He was certainly a presence when he entered a room. He also was a man who needed privacy. It is evident

that he was immensely fair as a publisher and also very prudent. He was generous, but he set limits, so that many talents could share the privilege of being heard and also being printed. He looked very distinguished, always well-dressed but never ostentatious. His speech had that certain Hamburg accentuation.

Henri Hinrichsen had the dedicated support and encouragement of his wife Martha, and in due course of his three eldest sons: Max, Walter and Hans-Joachim who entered the family business during the 1920s and '30s.

Business was expanding and with the constant addition of new titles and the need for more space to hold the printed stock, a new warehouse was built in 1905. The idea for this had been mooted some years before and the plans had been drawn up in 1896 by Dr Abraham's friend, the architect Clemens Thieme. However, Abraham's health was in a critical state and he did not really want to enlarge the business then. The warehouse was built at 22 Lindenstrasse, which was attached to the main building, 10 Talstrasse. Henri Hinrichsen took advantage of the upheaval for a complete redesign of the Talstrasse building, both the exterior and the interior, to provide a smarter appearance, better office facilities and better living accommodation for his growing family; he had central heating installed (electric light having been in place since 1896). He also commissioned a splendid new wrought iron front door, in 'Florentine' style [Fig 13].

Several composers and musicologists were associated with the company in the early years of the twentieth century, concurrently with Grieg. Whilst the association with Grieg, which became a close family friendship between the Griegs and the Hinrichsens, was quite extraordinary, Henri Hinrichsen's attitude of paternalism and sincere concern for the welfare of others was widespread. The atmosphere of friendship and courtesy, which is touched on briefly in the following pages, was extended to all the composers, arrangers and collaborators. Christian Sinding, Karl Straube, Hans Pfitzner, Sigfrid Karg-Elert, Felix Mottl, Hans-Joachim Moser and Max Friedländer, were amongst many others who benefited from the publisher's kindness and concern. The deep personal involvement between Henri Hinrichsen and Max Reger is described in detail in Chapter Seven.

Christian Sinding (1856-1941)

The relationship with Christian Sinding detailed in over 200 letters from the composer and the replies from the publisher, shows a close and warm collaboration. Like the Norwegian and Danish composers:

Edvard Grieg, Niels Gade and Johann Svendsen, Sinding had studied at the Leipzig Conservatory of Music, where he remained from 1874-78. He felt as much at home in Germany as he did in his native Norway. It soon became apparent that Sinding was to become a composer, rather than a violinist and he thrived under the tuition of Salomon Jadassohn at the Conservatory. C F Peters had strong links to the Leipzig Conservatory. In 1893 the conductor Felix Weingartner, a keen promoter of Sinding's music, persuaded Dr Max Abraham to accept Sinding's Symphony in D-min, Op 21 for publication and he continued to perform it regularly. Shortly after that, the composer signed a contract with C F Peters to publish all his works for several years.

Most of Sinding's works did not see any success and eventually fell into oblivion. However, there was one piano piece, *Frühlingsrauschen* (Rustle of Spring), Op 32 No 3, which appeared in 1896, and became the biggest hit the company was ever to enjoy. Sinding had sent it from Paris, along with twenty-three other pieces. When Dr Abraham had the pieces played through to him by the piano student Anton Förster, a holder of a C F Peters stipendium at the Conservatory, *Frühlingsrauschen* made no particular impression on him amongst all the other pieces. However, that one piece turned out to become what everybody who played the piano wanted to master. Sales reached 20,000 copies every year, for decades. One year in fact 43,000 copies were sold. The pianist Ella Pancera, wife of one of the Leipzig piano manufacturers, Blüthner, made the piece her own. She performed it in many concerts and in the Court of Queen Victoria in England, which probably helped to make the work so well-known. The fee which C F Peters paid Sinding was approximately 200M outright, for each piece. There was no further obligation on the publisher to pay the composer anything. However, Henri Hinrichsen felt it was only right that Sinding should also share in the quite unexpected profits. So, for very many years he sent Sinding an ex-gratia fee of 3,000M per year.

The relationship with Sinding lasted over forty years. He was generously supported with loans from Henri Hinrichsen. A prolific letter-writer, Sinding gave expression to his thoughts and feelings, as is shown below.[1] He wrote from near Christiania (Oslo) on 17th July, 1907 with regard to a loan of 10,000M which Hinrichsen had made him and which was to be repaid in the form of compositions:

Dear Mr Hinrichsen!

I received your valued letter of the 12th and am delighted to learn from it that you still have friendly feelings towards me, whilst I was thinking that you were for some reason displeased with me. Whilst I express my pleasure over this, I must accept that your questions over my plans to fulfil my obligations to you are quite justified.

I had thought to be able to cover a part of this 10,000M with my Symphony. I was informed by a reliable source that this symphony, following the criticisms it received in Berlin, would never be published by C F Peters. The poor criticism did not surprise me, as the first performance of my first symphony had caused similar disapprobation in Berlin. Under the circumstances, there didn't seem to me to be much point in risking the humiliation of a refusal. I thought I would save you this embarrassment. – I have made some thematic sketches of other larger compositions and have partially worked them out in depth – a String Quartet, a piano quartet, a Violin and Piano Sonata and also a third Symphony, which last will need more time. For reasons which you will probably understand, I have been suffering badly from nervous exhaustion, which has distracted me to a great extent from my work. I have also been obliged by frequent travels to break off my work, and have suffered from a bad cold which laid me low for about two months. At last all that is better now and I can promise to send you in my manuscripts by 31st December, 1907, to the value of at least 7,000M, which I am contracted to repay by this date. If you would really like to be so kind as to wait for three years until I repay you the rest of my debt, I would be extremely grateful to you...

From later letters we see that Hinrichsen did see his way to accommodating Sinding, several times. The composer subsequently wrote from Christiania on 22nd October, 1907:

My Dear Mr Hinrichsen,

I hardly need tell you that your very kind lines of the 18th were a great surprise to me; I can only express to you my deepest gratitude. I also hope you will be happy to hear that I will soon be ready with a Piano Trio, which I will be able to send you with a few other manuscripts at the end of November or beginning of December.

Please allow me to assure you of something else: my desire to fulfil my obligations to C F Peters can hardly be greater than it already is, on the contrary it upsets me very much to have found myself in this situation, and nothing would make me happier than to get this settled as soon as possible...

Hinrichsen had a fatherly concern for Sinding and tried in every way he could to help him, both with loans, ex-gratia payments and with advice. He even offered to find Sinding a teaching position, though the composer was not very confident about his abilities as a teacher. He expressed his doubts in this letter sent from Christiania on 3rd December, 1907:

My Dear Mr Hinrichsen,

With apologies for the delay, which was caused by a cold, I send you my deepest thanks for your last letter and for the enclosed 2,000 marks. Please allow me to express to you my deepest gratitude for the friendly attitude which shows through with such sincerity. I have given the greatest consideration to what you suggest; for me, the question is almost to be or not to be. I know that Beethoven and Strauss and Grieg had to teach in order to exist. But I assume that these great geniuses, apart from a gift for creativity, were also gifted teachers and therefore did not expend any creative energy on this. For me on the contrary, it is terribly difficult to teach, and I have to assume that the few students which I had, did not achieve much from their studies with me. If I were now to devote myself to this absolutely unaccustomed work, I fear very much that I would have to lay aside every thought of my own production, and more so now, when the last few years have not passed without leaving their mark on me. I do ask you sincerely not to believe that these my words are not written from a lack of good will...

Sinding went on to ask Hinrichsen for advice as to the kind of position he could expect. Hinrichsen's reply of 13th January was full of advice and suggestions but did not hold out much hope of a job for the composer. Sinding followed this up on 15th January, 1908, explaining his inability to work and asked for a further loan in advance of more proposed compositions. But with his many commitments to other composers and organisations, Hinrichsen expressed his regrets to Sinding turning down the composer's suggestion. The friendship survived and Hinrichsen continued to support Sinding until the composer's fortunes saw an improvement with the advent of sound films, as we will see in due course.

An important association for the firm, which lasted for many years, was that with Karl Straube. Here again was a close friendship, shown through many acts of generosity from the publisher, and extended between both families.

Karl Straube (1873-1950)

The musicologist Karl Straube was of great importance to the company. He never had a formal musical training and became recognised as one of the foremost teachers of organ. He came to Leipzig in 1902 when he took the post of organist at the St Thomas Church, becoming Cantor in 1918 – emulating Bach who was his inspiration. He started teaching organ in 1907 and was soon being referred to as the *Organistmacher* (the maker of organists). His weekly performances of Bach's Motets in the St Thomas Church drew crowds from the whole of Leipzig and the six Bach Festivals which he directed between 1904 and 1923 further served to promote the music of J S Bach, which had been somewhat neglected. Straube, who had students at the Leipzig Conservatory of Music, founded the *Kirchenmusikalisches Institut der Evangelisch-Lutherischen Landeskirchen Sachsen* (the Institute for Church Music of the Evangelical-Lutheran District Churches of Saxony) there in 1919. He merged the Leipzig Bach Choir with the Leipzig Gewandhaus Choir in 1920 and conducted these combined forces until 1932. From 1931 to 1937 he conducted regular performances of all Bach's Cantatas with the *Thomanerchor* accompanied by the Gewandhaus Orchestra. Karl Straube first met his contemporary, Max Reger in 1897, and was tireless in his promotion of his friend's music, both during Reger's life and after his death in 1916. He received an honorary doctorate of arts and divinity from Leipzig University.

Karl Straube's connection with C F Peters and friendship with Henri Hinrichsen started around the time of his arrival in Leipzig in 1902 and he worked for the company for over forty years. He was a composer and arranger, and a valued editor and adviser, giving detailed critical analyses of various types of compositions which were being considered for publication. An example of his thoroughness in this respect is his opinion given in his letter of 8th December, 1910, of Max Reger's Violin Concerto, which Henri Hinrichsen published:

> [2]...Concerning Reger's Concerto, in spite of the poor playing by the orchestra, I took away with me a strong impression. I actually consider it to be Reger's most mature and original work, even in comparison with the *Psalm* and the *Prologue*. But it should not be seen as a Concerto; it is a Symphony with obligato Violin, in the style of Johann Sebastian Bach's *Brandenburg Concertos*. For the audience it will for the time being remain difficult to assimilate. Especially because it is very polyphonicaly written and should be performed quite differently from the way in which it was given last week...

Where Reger becomes popular, as in the finale, the audience seems enthusiastic; however, this remains the weakest part of the work. – The Adagio must be one of the greatest slow movements in the literature. – Whether people aged thirty to eighty have this impression now, is quite immaterial, the younger generation does at least have this impression and that is why Reger's time will come in the future. I can well imagine that it is not pleasant for you to hear nothing but disparagement from all sides, with so little encouragement. The future proprietor of the business will no doubt experience the successful time...

Unlike Dörffel, who had advised against publishing the works of Bruckner and Reger, Straube had a great understanding of the music of his day. There are hundreds of letters from him in the archives, detailing progress on his many arrangements of the music of Max Reger, J S Bach and other composers for the firm. His opinions on concerts and the music of his day are worthy of deeper investigation.

Straube's letters are peppered with literary references. A respected man in his field but, like most musicians, he was usually short of money. He and Henri Hinrichsen were good friends and there are many references in the correspondence to enhanced fees and ex-gratia payments, which Hinrichsen paid him, in order to help him out, for which Straube was always profuse in his thanks. One such letter, which shows his sense of humour and displays his understanding of literature, dates from 26th June, 1908:[3]

Very Honoured Mr Hinrichsen,

What is too much, is too much. A hundred marks for such a little thing really is much too much! – How then should a real achievement be paid? – However, as I cannot reciprocate your kindness and friendliness by returning your gift with raw gestures, I have handed on the royal present to my wife – This lady, as indeed would all ladies have done, grabbed the blue bank note with childlike pleasure and secreted it in her money box. How deep the box is, I cannot tell you, because I do not have admittance to the treasury. There the note lies in the depths like the treasure of the Nibelungs in the waves of the Rhine. However, my wife does not incline towards reflection on the justification for ownership! With a few words, she instructed me to send you words of her thanks and she was of the opinion that one should accept kindness where it is offered in friendship. – However not, as in Martin Luther's

Catechism: 'through mistrust, doubt and other great disgrace carry misgivings against the comforts of life.' – I have now expressed to you the appreciation and thanks of my high commander.

I will not say more on the subject; I am not completely opportunistic and remain of the opinion that the trivialities of personal kindness stand apart from the mammonistic power of the fee. I am not of the stature of a Richard Strauss, either as a musician or in any other way.

With friendly greetings

Your true,
Karl Straube

In February 1910 C F Peters announced the publication of a new edition of the Organ Works of J S Bach by Professor Karl Straube, to be published in nine bound volumes over the course of three years, at a cost of 6M each. A cheaper edition, in eighteen instalments at 2.50M each was also offered. Proud of their initiative and mindful of the huge investment such an undertaking would entail, massive world-wide publicity to launch this ambitious project was undertaken. However, Straube was not able to devote sufficient time to this huge project and only managed to complete Volume II.

The same year, 1902, that Karl Straube started working for C F Peters marked the beginning of the firm's association with Richard Strauss.

Richard Strauss (1864-1949)

Strauss made his first approach to C F Peters as an unknown young composer, with the first of many letters, on 13th May, 1890. His handwritten letters show that there was a good business relationship over the course of the years. In this first letter he offered his tone poem *Macbeth* to Dr Max Abraham for 1500M, but no contract was reached. Ten years later, by which time he had achieved a respectable reputation as a composer and conductor, Henri Hinrichsen approached him with an invitation to prepare a revision of the famous *Treatise on Instrumentation* by Berlioz. The edition which Alfred Dörfel had prepared some years earlier was felt to need updating. In accepting, on 13th August, 1902, Strauss stressed that he would not allow himself to be pushed:[4] '...I am one of those people who cannot compel myself to any work, but must always await the right mood and a desire to work...' He completed the revision in three weeks, assisted by his friend

Otto Singer, who wrote down what Strauss dictated. Otto Singer was by training a violinist, pupil of Joachim and Léonard, but he made his name with his excellent piano scores of operas, especially those of Richard Strauss. He worked as a freelance arranger for C F Peters over the course of twenty years, from 1901 until 1922, specialising in arrangements for piano solo and for two pianos, especially of symphonies. Henri Hinrichsen wrote about this revision in 1933:

> Paul Schäfer, our proof-reader at that time, and Paul Ollendorff corrected and honed various details to produce the final result. This reworking, which is more than a mere revision, is excellent and has become indispensable to every professional. The full score examples which were detailed separately in the earlier version available in Germany, published by Gustav Heinze (later C F Peters), have been integrated with the text in the new Strauss edition and have been added to with examples from contemporary literature.

Paul Schäfer was praised by Strauss and Mahler. He retired due to eye-strain and received a pension from the company.

Strauss offered Hinrichsen *Two Military Marches,* Op 57 for orchestra which the publisher accepted because he did not wish to offend the composer, though he did not think them worthwhile. Hinrichsen would very much have liked to publish a more substantial work by Strauss and negotiated for his *Sinfonia Domestica,* Op 53, in 1904, agreeing a fee of 30,000M. However, Strauss secretly negotiated a higher fee and sold it to Bote & Bock for 36,000M. (In later years Hinrichsen was not too perturbed about this as he felt it was not such a good work as the Symphonic Poems which he acquired in 1932 from Universal Edition.)

In his letter of 25th January, 1904, apologising for the fact that he had sold his *Sinfonia Domestica* to Bote & Bock, Strauss expressed his delight that Hinrichsen had acquired the new symphony composed by his friend, Gustav Mahler. He was referring to the Fifth Symphony.

Some ten years later Strauss wanted to atone for having sold his *Sinfonia Domestica* to another publisher and offered C F Peters his *Alpen Symphonie* (Alpine Symphony), Op 64, for the exorbitant sum of 100,000M, to which he also attached the condition that the score should be returned to him and that he should receive 40,000M immediately upon signing the contract. Hinrichsen felt that this was really too much. It also appeared to be too much for other publishers, because the *Alpen Symphonie* eventually went to the publisher Leuckart for half the original asking price – 50,000M. The première took place in Berlin and the final, public rehearsal, on 27th October, 1915, was given before an invited audience comprising all the 'musical heads' of Germany as well

as several VIPs from abroad. Strauss wrote to Hinrichsen that this would
be his last major symphonic work, as indeed it was. The correspondence
between Richard Strauss and C F Peters, about compositions and
arrangements continued until 1917; then there was a break. It was taken
up again, but with a different tone, in 1933.

At much the same time as the associations between Straube and
Strauss started with C F Peters, Henri Hinrichsen also established
another long term friendship and collaboration, with the composer
Hans Pfitzner.

Hans Pfitzner (1869-1949)

Pfitzner was already an acknowledged composer, conductor and teacher
in Germany by the time his association with the company started, in
1904. It continued for forty years. This was another of those relationships
which transcended the merely business, to become a personal friendship
between Henri Hinrichsen and Hans Pfitzner. Over the course of the
years C F Peters published a number of his works, including the Piano
Quintet in C-major, Op 23, the riveting Violin Sonata in E-minor, Op
27, *Six Lieder*, Op 40 and *Three Sonnets* for male voice solo and piano,
Op 41. Apart from composing, Pfitzner was involved with organising
concerts, and was also frequently short of money. So the gestation of
his compositions was generally somewhat drawn out.

It was on Pfitzner's suggestion that C F Peters published the vocal
score of E T A Hoffmann's 'magic' opera *Undine*, composed in 1816,
and hardly ever performed since. He was very attracted to it and, whilst
working on the vocal score, wanted to put on a performance in Essen,
but the facilities were inadequate, as he wrote to Henri Hinrichsen on
10th June, 1906 from Zurich:[5]

Dear Sir,

It will be quite impossible for the *Allgemeine Deutsche
Musikverein* (General German Music Association) to put on a
performance of *Undine* this year. The facilities in the Essen
theatre are really not up to performing a work satisfactorily
that makes such high demands in terms of soloists, chorus
and elaborate stage settings. The committee of our
association, including myself, is convinced that it would be to
the disadvantage of the work and, at the present time, also
unwise and impossible; it is vitally important that the first
performance of this work should be endowed with the best
possible facilities and should be prepared in a calm and
problem-free atmosphere.

As you can see, I am travelling. I will not be back until the
20th, and have been ill in the meantime, and then I travelled
again unexpectedly; so the work on *Undine* has again been
delayed, however, it will now be my only work on my return
home, and you will surely receive the second act by the end
of January – I am terribly busy.

With respectful greetings, Your devoted

Hans Pfitzner

Pfitzner needed money for his series of concerts in Munich. He had
in the meantime become more friendly with Henri Hinrichsen and
felt that he could ask for an advance on a proposed composition, in
order to finance the concerts. He wrote from Munich on 15th May,
1907:

Dear Mr Hinrichsen,

Following our recent discussion in which I told you about my
Munich concert project, I permit myself to ask you today,
whether you would also like to become a sponsor. You
probably still have the main points in mind, if not, then my
Munich friends can give you more information about the
business details…But they [the concerts] must be produced
in the best possible way, and in tranquillity! That is why I made
so free to ask you, dear Mr Hinrichsen, for your help in making
my venture a success. As security I will offer you my next
chamber music work for publication, which you can take into
account to cover any possible deficit to yourself from these
concerts. I would like to make a commitment to deliver you
the work by such and such a date, but as I am dependent
upon my inspiration, I do not want to find myself in the
embarrassing position of not being able to keep my promise.
Or to write something unworthy. I would be very grateful to
receive your answer at the earliest possible moment and to
be able to assure myself of your interest.

With Kindest Regards, also to your wife, Your devoted

Hans Pfitzner.

Henri Hinrichsen agreed to support Hans Pfitzner's series of
Munich concerts, and waited patiently for the composer's inspiration

to flower. But he understood composers well enough, to know that it could not be hurried. In the meantime Pfitzner had been appointed director of the Conservatory and conductor of the Symphony Orchestra in Strasbourg; in 1910 he was made director of the opera as well. Hinrichsen was able to tell the composer about a proposed production of *Undine* at the Court Opera in Vienna. Pfitzner, who was friendly with Felix Weingartner, who took up the post of conductor at the Court Opera in Vienna on Mahler's departure in 1908, expressed his delight when he wrote to the publisher from Munich on 31st December, 1907, adding:

> ...Now I have something to tell you – I hope something good will come of it. You may remember our agreement with regard to the Munich concerts. Well, I have long had the desired chamber music work in my head; it will be a piano quintet in four movements. I started writing the first movement in the summer, then so much work came between – the concerts, moving house, etc., and now finally the position in Strasbourg. So of course everything had to be left in abeyance. Heaven knows when I will find the time for composition again. In the meantime, please keep this information to yourself; apart from my wife, I have told nobody about this new work and do not want it spoken about until it is finished.

Pfitzner then went on to ask for advance payment of the agreed sum of 2,000M, merely for the idea of a composition, without being able to offer any sort of completion date. He promised that if the composition were not forthcoming, then he would regard the payment as a loan. His letter was immediately acknowledged and he received his 2,000M by 3rd January, 1908.

The Quintet was duly completed as Pfitzner's Op 23 and was published in 1908. Though Henri Hinrichsen wanted to publish another chamber music work by Pfitzner, this was a long time in its gestation. Hence, when the composer wrote to him ten years later, on 10th January, 1918, announcing that inspiration was once more flowing, in the form of a Sonata for Violin and Piano, he was delighted. Hinrichsen had rather prompted the inspiration, by sending the composer a complimentary copy of the new complete C F Peters catalogue, to remind him that he was still hoping for another work from the pen of the master. Pfitzner, profuse in his thanks, was pleased to hear from the publisher again and wrote:

> ...I will use this opportunity to advise you that I am once again, for the first time since finishing my Quartet, engaged in

> composing a chamber music work – a violin sonata. Though
> I cannot at the moment say when this will be finished, I would
> not like to miss this opportunity of telling you that I would be
> very happy to see this work published in the Edition Peters.
> In case you should share this wish, please would you let me
> know. Please don't forget that I am a member of the
> *Genossenschaft deutscher Tonkünstler* (Association of German
> Composers)...

Pfitzner was living in Strasbourg at the time, but travelling widely,
conducting, performing and teaching. On 5th April he wrote to
Hinrichsen again, telling him that he had almost completed the first
movement. He asked the publisher to make him a concrete offer for
the work and to send him a contract which he wanted to discuss with
Hofrat Roesch of the Association, with whom he discussed all his
contracts. In the intervening ten years, Pfitzner's reputation had soared,
and the price agreed for the new work was 10,000M.

Composers are somewhat impatient and Pfitzner was no exception.
Having delayed ten years in writing the work, he now wanted to send
the first movement to be engraved immediately, so that the work could
be published, virtually as soon as it was finished. The Sonata was finished
within a few months and in his letter of 31st May, 1918, Pfitzner was
eagerly awaiting the proofs, which he promised to correct by return of
post. Like Reger, he had already organised performances of the work,
before even having completed it and was eager to share these with the
publisher:

> ...I propose to perform the première with Prof Felix Berber
> in Munich; I will play the piano part myself. Schnabel and
> Flesch want to give the first performance in Berlin. This will
> probably be during their first concert, on 29th October. I am
> planning to perform it in Strasbourg with the orchestral leader
> here, Grevesmühl, on 18th October. So, the first performance
> in Munich will then have to be around the middle of
> September because, at the end of September and beginning
> of October I will be heavily occupied with concerts. We have
> to be very careful that the work is not performed anywhere
> else *before* the Munich première. I would beg you not to let
> the work be sold more than eight days before the Munich
> performance, and only to send copies to the respective
> performers – Schnabel, Flesch, Berber and Grevesmühl –
> binding them to absolute secrecy. I will of course let you have
> the exact details of performance dates, as soon as they are
> fixed. As the work will need careful study, it would be desirable

if the engraving could be carried out as soon as possible, so that at least the whole of the month of August can be used for studying it. I presume that you will send me a number of free copies (ten?) and that the above plans will meet with your approval. I would be grateful, honoured Mr Geheimrat, for a few lines in reply, and remain with friendly greetings and the expression of my delight at being in contact with you again,

Yours very truly, Hans Pfitzner.

Henri Hinrichsen always did his utmost to please his composers and published the Violin Sonata by the beginning of August, when he sent Pfitzner his desired ten free copies and also copies to the performers. He was delighted, but not surprised, that the composer was impressed with the quality of the production and printing of his work. Pfitzner had already interested more performers, and asked Hinrichsen to send copies to Felix Wolfes, leader of the Elberfeld City Theatre orchestra, and to Wilhelm Furtwängler, who had been Pfitzner's predecessor at the Strasbourg Opera, who both wanted to perform the Sonata. Pfitzner's Sonata for Violin and Piano, Op 27, along with his Piano Quintet, is considered to be amongst his finest chamber music works.

The new publisher was open to many other new associations at the beginning of the new century. Like Straube, Sigfrid Karg-Elert also moved to Leipzig as a child with his family and spent almost his entire life there.

Sigfrid Karg-Elert (born Karg) (1877-1933)

Young Sigfrid's musical talent was soon recognised. He was awarded a scholarship to the Leipzig Conservatory of Music in 1896 to study the piano, whilst supporting himself as a café pianist and orchestral musician. (About this time he added his mother's maiden name, Elert, to his father's surname Karg.) Having started on a career as virtuoso pianist, he subsequently returned to the Conservatory to study composition with Teichmüller. In 1902 he was appointed head of the master class at the Magdeburg Conservatory, but only remained for a short while, returning to Leipzig to devote himself to composing.

It was in 1904, on the recommendation of Edvard Grieg, that Sigfrid Karg-Elert made his first approach to C F Peters, offering a manuscript for publication. However, this first youthful work was turned down; though the subsequent good collaboration between Sigfrid Karg-Elert and Henri Hinrichsen proved rewarding for both, for almost thirty years. He had a high reputation as an organist and harmonium player, though he never achieved a position as organist in Leipzig.

Sigfrid Karg-Elert is best known for his harmonium and organ compositions. He made the harmonium his own speciality, producing over 100 pieces for the instrument between 1903 and 1915. Many of these were published by C F Peters, who employed him regularly from about 1910 onwards, to make arrangements of works for harmonium with, and without, piano and or organ. He made three volumes each of Wagner arrangements for harmonium alone, and for harmonium and piano. Though published by several publishers, he valued his contacts with C F Peters highly, and wrote to Henri Hinrichsen on 9th November, 1910: '…The relationship with your publishing house is, however, so extremely valuable and I rate it so highly, that the question of the fee needs no further discussion.'

Karg-Elert was a busy musician who was prone to bouts of depression and frequently suffered from ill-health; he was also a heavy smoker. Much of his correspondence was conducted by his sister, Anna Marie Karg, who acted as his secretary. However, on matters which he considered to be important, he would write his own letters. Karg-Elert had completed many arrangements of works for harmonium satisfactorily for C F Peters and several of his own compositions had been published by other publishers. He was about to be called up for military service at the front, when he offered Henri Hinrichsen his Trio Studies with a letter dated 22nd April, 1915:[6]

Highly Honoured Mr Kommerzienrat!

As you know, during all the years of our collaboration, I have never offered you a work of my own. If I am today offering you the enclosed educational work it is for the reason that I would like to offer you first refusal, before all other publishing houses, for a work which I consider will be a most successful publishing venture from a business point of view.

The Trio Studies were originally intended for England and were to have served as a recognition of my appointment as a foreign Honorary Member of the Royal College of Organists. It was anticipated that Novello would publish them. The work is the result of many years of intensive study of all the specialised literature, and I may, of course without any arrogance, say that it is the best, most demanding and musicological method for Trio playing. It extends well beyond the expectation suggested by the title: there are also fingering exercises, which are so very important but which are not included in any other instructive work (with the exception perhaps of the Italian Organ Method of Bossi and its

Hungarian imitation by Des Antalfi). Further, there are tone-colour studies of a quite innovatory nature; they will arouse great interest for this reason especially.

Divisions and page-turns have been marked.

In view of my military call-up and my imminent departure for the front, I would be grateful to you for a speedy reply.

With the expression of my extreme respects, I sign

Yours truly
Sigfrid Karg-Elert

Hinrichsen replied, accepting the work, as soon as he received Karg-Elert's letter. The composer wrote again on 27th April, saying that he was: ' filled with happy pride to be able to assume from your valued letter of the 26th, that you were interested in my manuscript and that you would like to buy my studies...'; he then went into great detail discussing the price.

In 1919, after the war and having completed his military service – which he accomplished in the regimental band, Karg-Elert accepted the post vacated by his staunch supporter and adviser, Max Reger, teaching theory and composition at the Leipzig Conservatory. He was a frequent and welcome visitor to the Hinrichsen's home, when he enjoyed being involved with the growing Hinrichsen family and he continued to make arrangements for harmonium and compose works for organ which were published by C F Peters. His fame as an organist grew and he was recognised throughout the world.

The harmonium was popular as a means of making music at home. A more widely disseminated form of music making in Germany was the tradition of choral singing, folk songs being particularly popular. Henri Hinrichsen was proud to be involved in the publication of a major work in this category.

Volksliederbuch (Folksong Book)

One of Henri Hinrichsen's early, and most prestigious publications was the *Volksliederbuch für Männerchor* (Folksong Book for Male Voice Choir). This was commissioned by Kaiser Wilhelm II[7] and is also known as the *Kaiserliederbuch* (Emperor's Song Book). It represented a huge financial investment for C F Peters, but with its publication, Henri Hinrichsen was demonstrating his confidence in the German nation. The commission for this massive work came through the scholar and writer Freiherr Rochus von Liliencron, Prior of the Order of St John in

Schleswig. Liliencron was one of the most important German musicologists of his day. In 1858 the historical commission of the Royal Bavarian Academy of Sciences had commissioned him to collect German folksongs, which resulted in the publication of *Die historischen Volkslieder der Deutschen* (The historical Folksongs of the Germans) (1865-9). Holder of many distinctions he also supervised the publication of forty-five volumes of *Denkmäler deutscher Tonkunst* (Monuments of German Composition). He was related to the Empress and thus had influence over the Emperor.

Baron von Liliencron, a lifelong musician, had always preferred to use the music published by C F Peters, rather than that brought out by other music publishers, so it was natural that he should approach his favourite publisher; a contact which subsequently lead to his being invited to contribute to the Peters Music Library *Yearbook*. There was a special 'Commission for the Folksong Book' comprising twenty worthy members, mostly professors of music, or musicians; Max Friedländer, the Schubert specialist, who edited the Folksong Book for C F Peters, was the deputy leader under Baron von Liliencron. The volume contained a very detailed ten page Introduction by Baron von Liliencron, outlining the aims and goals of the Commission in selecting the songs which were included.

The book was superbly produced in the Edition Peters and available at a very reasonable price, which probably helped lead to its enormous popularity. It was so successful that, over the years, one and a half million copies were sold. The *Volksliederbuch für Männerchor* appeared on 6th February, 1907 and was presented to the Kaiser at a special celebration in the Palace in Berlin, by seven of the gentlemen of the Commission for the Folksong Book.

As the publisher and investor, Henri Hinrichsen had been invited to the Royal Palace in Berlin to take part in the presentation ceremony. He in his turn was presented with a medal by the Kaiser – the *Kronenorden* (Order of the Crown) IIIrd Class. Full of the excitement of the event he immediately telephoned his wife Martha in Leipzig. Fortunately for posterity, she was not satisfied with his telephonic description and asked him to write it all down in a letter, which he did:[8]

> ...So, at eleven o'clock I arrived at the Ministry to speak to Eilsberger about the deluxe volumes...First we were taken to Sturt and presented to him and received our instructions where we had to go, though he said nothing about removal of pince-nez. So I kept it on and am glad that I did, because the Kaiser looked at me several times so directly, that I became aware of it and I believe that it was because of the pince-nez; though two other gentlemen were also wearing one. At 12.30

ten of us gentlemen arrived at the Palace, first floor in a huge hall, where there were many models of ships. We stood there and after a while the Kaiser appeared, made his bows and we made our bows. Sturt called our names. Wilhelm II gave everybody a hefty handshake and looked at us very astutely. Then Liliencron made a short speech in which he said that the *Kaiserliederbuch* was completed etc., etc.

The letter then described the twenty-minute speech given by the Kaiser, saying that for him music was the highest and noblest of the arts and that he noticed to his regret in Frankfurt, that the ability to read music was diminishing and he was afraid that folk songs would become completely forgotten. This was the reason for which he had commissioned this book. He lavished especial praise on the Male Voice Choruses of Essen and of Vienna. Then he gave his opinion that the attraction to alcohol would be reduced through singing, if people had sung for three hours, however, they could certainly be rewarded with a few glasses of wine. He suggested an Anthem for the City State of Hamburg, composed after the famous Störtbeker Poem. Henri Hinrichsen continued with an account of the presentation:

Finally, a privy councillor asked whether he would like to look at the books, whereupon Wilhelm II asked whether the Song Book was to be presented to him. That was the signal for me. I approached the Kaiser uninvited and said that 10,000 copies and 2,500 scores had been ordered by the despatch department; well, that's a pretty good result, he said, and asked whether anything like it had ever been available. Whereupon I replied that there had been nothing published up to now at such a cheap price. After the Kaiser had spoken for about another ten minutes, he bestowed the medals and the pictures and shook everybody individually vigorously by the hand once more, then he bowed and we remained in the room and soon afterwards departed. The impression on me was an indelible one, he is certainly the most interesting monarch alive at this present time and one of the mightiest. His eye lights up marvellously, I have never before seen anybody who can look at somebody so astutely, yet in such a friendly manner...

After Liliencron's death in 1912, Max Friedländer became the head of the Commission for the Folksong Book. The *Volksliederbuch für Gemischten Chor* (Folksong Book for Mixed Choir) which the Kaiser had requested in 1907, and which Baron von Liliencron had also wanted to produce, was edited by Max Friedländer and issued by C F Peters in

1915. This volume for mixed choir was even more highly rated than the edition for male voice choir, perhaps because it appeared in the middle of the war, and mixed choirs everywhere wanted to express their patriotic fervour!

During the War a special *Feldausgabe* ('Field' edition) of the *Kaiserliederbuch* for male voice choir was issued which contained ninety-one choruses. Issued in a one-off edition of 24,000 copies, it was compiled by Professor Fritz Stein. A conductor and musicologist, Stein had studied under Nikisch and Straube in Leipzig and had been a pupil of Max Reger, whose works he particularly promoted; he was also a specialist for the works of Johann Christian Bach. Stein himself, who lead the choir of the Feldgrauen Regiment in Laon, made especial use of the 'Field' edition of the *Kaiserliederbuch.*

In recognition of his considerable financial contribution to the production of the Folksong Book for Male Voice choir and for his charitable work in many spheres, Henri Hinrichsen was honoured with the title of *Kommerzienrat*, on 29th May, 1911. This title was elevated to that of *Geheimer Kommerzienrat* (Privy Councillor), generally shortened to *Geheimrat*, on 26th October, 1916. These titles were conferred on distinguished businessmen, financiers and industrialists in Germany, by the Kaiser. They were no longer awarded after the Kaiser's abdication in 1918. Those men who carried the title were always referred to as *Herr Kommerzienrat* or *Herr Geheimrat.*

Henri Hinrichsen was an admirer of the Kaiser, the Emperor Wilhelm II and was thrilled when they met again some six years after he had been awarded the Order of the Crown IIIrd Class. The occasion was the unveiling of the *Völkerschlachtdenkmal,* the Memorial to the Battle of the Nations, which took place on 18th October, 1913 and which the Kaiser attended with King Friedrich August III. As a member of the Leipzig Town Council Henri Hinrichsen took part in the memorable festivities which lasted several days. He was proud to have been a part of this grand patriotic venture to which he had contributed financially, his name figuring as number 941 on one of the engraved plaques. Dr Max Abraham had also contributed as a member of the Masonic 'Apollo' Lodge, shown as number one.

His feeling of patriotism did not end there. He was able to combine this with his lifelong interest in art, some years later, when he bought two paintings at auction which he presented to the *Stadtgeschichtliches Museum* (City History Museum) of Leipzig in 1927.

> An aquarel by C G H Geissler: *The Last Battles of the Völkerschlacht.*[9]
>
> An oil painting by E W Strassberger: *Flight of the French from Leipzig in 1813.*[10]

In keeping with his policy of commemorating noteworthy events and people, Henri Hinrichsen made a major contribution towards the purchase and preservation of the Bach House in Eisenach.

The Bach House, Eisenach

C F Peters had published various editions of the complete works of Johann Sebastian Bach since 1800 and Reger's Bach arrangements were part of this ongoing policy. The company supported the *Neue Bach Gesellschaft* (The New Bach Society) which was formed on 27th January, 1900 on the dissolution of the original *Bach Gesellschaft*, whose objective of publishing the complete works of Bach, had been fulfilled. The new society was created to popularise the music of Johann Sebastian Bach, by publishing it in practical form (which was done by Breitkopf & Härtel, Leipzig) and performing it at Bach Festivals throughout Germany.

The New Bach Society was also responsible for the foundation of a Bach Museum in the Bach House in Eisenach, where the composer was born. The house came on the market for sale at 26,000M in 1904 when an appeal was launched, inviting contributions towards the purchase. About sixty firms, mostly music related of which about half were in Leipzig, and half a dozen individuals contributed. From Great Britain, the music publishers Augener & Co of London sent a donation, as did the director of the Queen's Hall Orchestra – Henry J Wood, and the music publishers G Schirmer of New York also contributed. Henri Hinrichsen believed strongly in the need to preserve the memory of the greatest German composer in this way; his donation of 10,000M was the largest. Kaiser Wilhelm II donated 8,000M and Breitkopf & Härtel, 5,000M.[11] Hinrichsen also provided a large stock of music published by C F Peters. The purchase was completed on 1st January, 1906, but major repairs and restoration had to be carried out before the Bach Museum was opened in 1907.

Henri Hinrichsen was happy to be involved in this undertaking and wrote to Edvard Grieg about the opening of the Bach House in his letter of 6th June, 1907:

> Two weeks ago I attended the Bach Festival in Eisenach and was involved in the opening of the Bach House. Apart from a wonderful service, in the style of the time of Bach, there was a concert. But the highlight was the performance by the Choir of St Thomas directed by Schreck; the critics and the public were in agreement that the cantata *Singet dem Herren* (Sing Praise to the Lord) was beautifully sung. Schreck told me again what an honour and pleasure it had been that the young choristers had been allowed to sing to you and your wife.

Schreck was referring to Grieg's visit to Leipzig in April, when the composer had enjoyed a concert of the Choir of St Thomas. The guiding light of the *Neue Bach Gesellschaft*, Hermann Kretzschmar, was a major music historian and conductor. Edvard Grieg's great admiration for him, caused him to dedicate his *Slåtter* for Violin Solo to Kretzschmar, in 1903.

Hermann Kretzschmar (1848-1924)

Kretzschmar succeeded Joachim as Director of the Berlin Conservatory of Music, succeeded Liliencron as general editor of the *Denkmäler der Deutschen Tonkunst* and became Director of the Institute of Church Music in Berlin. He had a working relationship of some years standing with C F Peters. The firm had published his fundamental and epoch-making book *Musikalische Zeitfragen* (Musical Time Questions) in 1902. In this book he confirmed his status as one of the founding fathers of modern musicology.

Kretzschmar's contributions to the Peters Music Library *Yearbooks* were of such outstanding and wide-ranging significance, that they were published in 1911 as a complete book, under the title of *Gesammelte Aufsätze aus den Jahrbüchern der Musikbibliothek Peters* (Collected Essays from the *Yearbooks* of the Peters Music Library). Hermann Kretzschmar was revered by many people and was influential in many spheres. An essay by him in the Peters Music Library *Yearbook* of 1898 fired Henri Hinrichsen's desire to publish the Lieder of Hugo Wolf. In 1918, C F Peters published a 184-page commemorative book containing sixty-five contributions, in honour of the seventieth birthday of Hermann Kretzschmar.

The composers Sinding, Straube, Strauss, Pfitzner and Karg-Elert, as well as the production of the *Folksong Book* and Henri Hinrichsen's sponsorship of the Bach House, were not the only musical promotions Henri Hinrichsen was involved with during the early years of the century. Preceding the publication of *The Folk Song Book* by two years, the first publication which he negotiated and produced on his own initiative after becoming proprietor of C F Peters, was the score of a popular opera – Georges Bizet's *Carmen*.

---

1 Sinding letters in StAL Bestand, C F Peters, File 2531.
2 Letter in StAL Bestand, C F Peters, File 2151.
3 Letter in StAL Bestand, C F Peters, No 2510.
4 Letter quoted in *Der Bestand Musikverlag C F Peters Im Staatsarchiv Leipzig,* by Hans-Martin Plesske, Leipzig 1970.
5 All Pfitzner letters quoted: StAL Bestand, C F Peters, No 2012.

6 StAL Bestand, C F Peters, No 1479.
7 Kaiser Wilhelm II (1858-1941). Third German Emperor 1888-1918 when he was forced to abdicate.
8 7th February, 1907 letter from Henri Hinrichsen to his wife Martha Hinrichsen, in the author's archive.
9 Stöpel-Auction No 564.
10 Stöpel-Auction No 568.
11 Figures quoted in *Fünfzig Jahre Bachhaus*, Conrad Freyse, 1956.

CHAPTER SIX

The Business of Publishing, including Gustav Mahler's Fifth Symphony

The Score to Bizet's *Carmen*

Ever since the full score to Bizet's opera *Carmen* had been published by the French publisher, P Choudens, musicians had complained of the poor quality of the editing and of its high price. Whilst the thirty-year copyright period for the music ended in 1905, the text remained in copyright until 1938. Henri Hinrichsen was keen to publish a better edition of this popular opera and in 1905 he obtained a licence from the publisher. He published the full orchestral score, as well as a vocal score and a piano solo version with text. This was a major publishing success due to the excellent editing and printing and the very reasonable price at which C F Peters could sell the music, as a result of their advanced production technology. Hinrichsen proudly sent complimentary copies of the score to a number of musicians, and especially conductors; he was rewarded by their glowing enthusiasm and appreciation. Edvard Grieg wrote to him on 26th September, 1905:

> Most especially I would like to thank you for the *Carmen* score. A true work of art has been created! I cannot bear to let the work out of my hand. What a masterpiece! What clarity and lucidity to be admired every time one studies the score! If only I had had this thirty years earlier...

Operas, especially those by Richard Wagner, were particularly popular. But a visit to the opera was a rare occasion for most people. The only sort of music which was generally available was what they themselves performed; so there was a tremendous demand for arrangements and compilations. These were amongst C F Peters' most popular publications.

The Operas of Richard Wagner

Henri Hinrichsen formulated an ambitious plan as early as 1906, in anticipation of Wagner's works being freely available after 1914. He had known the Bayreuth conductor Felix Mottl since 1896 when Mottl had offered C F Peters some works by Gluck, which he had orchestrated for concert use. The arrangements were successful so Dr Max Abraham had commissioned him to orchestrate further works by early composers: the Belgian André Ernst Modeste Grétry, and the French Jean-Babtiste Lully and Jean-Philippe Rameau.

Mottl had studied at the Vienna Conservatory in Bruckner's theory class. As a young musician he was appointed co-répétiteur at the opera house and conductor of the Academic Wagner Society in Vienna, where he had played in the orchestra for performances of *Lohengrin* and *Tannhäuser*, conducted by Wagner. With Hans Richter's help he was enlisted at Bayreuth to prepare for the first Wagner Festival in 1876, when he played in *The Ring, Tristan and Isolde* and *Parsifal* under Wagner's baton. He had noted down all Wagner's stage directions and details of tempo in his personal score. Mottl conducted for the first time himself in Bayreuth in 1886, when he was jointly in charge of *Tristan and Isolde* and *Parsifal.* Henri Hinrichsen commissioned Mottl to prepare vocal scores of all Wagner's operas. He was chosen because, more than anybody else, he was a witness to Wagner's true intention and musical tradition.

In the Foreword to his Vocal Scores of Wagner Operas for Edition Peters, Felix Mottl emphasised the authenticity of the stage directions which he had noted down from Wagner himself in 1876, all of which he incorporated into his new vocal scores:

> I had the good luck to be present at many rehearsals and performances of *Tannhäuser* and *Lohengrin* which Richard Wagner rehearsed in Vienna in 1875 (he had even conducted *Lohengrin* there personally once). Further, I worked as stage hand at all rehearsals and performances of *The Ring* in Bayreuth in 1876 and finally I experienced a great many of the performances of *Parsifal* in Bayreuth in 1882. On all these occasions I made copious and detailed notes of all the Master's instructions and can, as a result of my stage experience, incorporate these in the Vocal Scores of Edition Peters. I will vouch for the authenticity of these additions. These records will become highly valued by serious people, when authentic conceptions become truly appreciated.

Felix Mottl knew Henri Hinrichsen for a friend, though their letters were normally couched in somewhat formal tones and generally only concerned the work he was carrying out for C F Peters. When he found himself in severe financial difficulties shortly after embarking upon the project, he turned to his publisher. In his letter dated 7th January, 1907[1] from Munich, he asks for a substantial loan of 5,000M, adding: '...I repeat that it is not my fault that I have arrived at this embarrassing position; this letter does not come from a habitual debtor!...I do not need to ask for your discretion! I have an income of over 30,000M and nobody could imagine how it is that I find myself in this difficult position!...' Hinrichsen helped many musicians with scholarships and gifts. He trusted the unfortunate man, whom he admired for his musicological gifts, and immediately sent the money to cover his debts. Mottl was able to reply from Vienna on 10th January, 1907 expressing his gratitude and giving a progress report on the work in hand:

> ...*Tannhäuser*! I have so far completed the new arrangement in the manner in which you asked me to – the new passages marked as appendixes I, II, III, IV and the passages where the Bear edition begins and ends in the old vocal score, with marks which refer to the appendix. Tomorrow I will send you these four additions to have a look at. If you want two entirely separate excerpts, this can still be accommodated. In the meantime, please look through the enclosures and write to me in Munich and let me know how you would like to have it treated. Please also let me know if the pages have arrived safely...

Mottl made good progress with his arrangements of the Wagner operas and kept the publisher fully informed. He was as good as his word and repaid the 5,000M as arranged. But barely was his debt cleared, when his problems resurfaced and he was desperate for money once more. This time he confided fully in Henri Hinrichsen when he wrote less than two years later, on 29th November, 1908 from Munich, begging for a further loan. He explained that the fault was his wife's, who was an 'irresponsible spendthrift' who had run up debts of 25,000M the first time and that he was now faced with a further debt of 15,000M, which he felt obliged to pay. Again the publisher helped his friend.

Sadly, Mottl was only able to complete eight vocal scores. He collapsed whilst conducting *Tristan and Isolde* in Munich and died, at the age of fifty-five, on 2nd July, 1911. His wife, the soprano Zdenka Fassbender was singing the part of Isolde. In his *Chronik*, Hinrichsen mentioned nothing of the help he had given Mottl, though we can see that he had little sympathy with Mottl's wife:

> Five days after Mottl's death in 1911, his widow, the soprano Zdenka Fassbender (later Mrs Edgar Hanfstaengl) demanded

in an extremely rude manner, that her husband's *Tristan* score, with all his annotations, should be given to her. Offended by her tone, I refused, because I felt that this score would be best accommodated in the Peters Music library.

Singers were thrilled with the excellent editing of the new Wagner vocal scores. The soprano Lilli Lehmann, who had made some arrangements of songs published by C F Peters and had prepared a singing manual: *Meine Gesangskunst* (My Art of Singing), wrote to Henri Hinrichsen to express her delight on 13th January, 1914:

Highly Honoured Sir,

At last my long-held wish to do Mottl justice has been fulfilled with the issue of the new Edition Peters vocal scores for Wagner, in which he has achieved something which should have been done long ago. I welcome the publication of the works wholeheartedly and rejoice with the artists who will find a guide within these pages, the like of which I could only imagine in my wildest dreams.

Many, many thanks and greetings...Lilli Lehmann

It was reactions like this which pleased Henri Hinrichsen so much and encouraged him in his pursuit of excellence. Not only was he supplying a long felt need, he was also helping a talented musician and, as a business man, he was making the profits which could be ploughed back into supporting less profitable, but infinitely worthwhile projects, such as Gustav Mahler's Fifth Symphony.

The vocal score of *Tristan* was eventually completed by Gustav Kogel who, over the course of almost forty years from 1878 onwards, was a 'specialist' at C F Peters for vocal scores. He edited the scores of Spohr's *Jesonda*, Nicolai's *Lustige Weiber*, Lortzing's *Zar und Zimmermann* and Marschner's *Hans Heilig*. He also gave his detailed assessment of works submitted to him, in a professional capacity.

Gustav Kogel, a graduate of the Leipzig Conservatory of Music, was an opera conductor in various cities before becoming conductor of the Berlin Philharmonic Orchestra in 1887. He composed a few piano works, but was best known as an editor of opera vocal scores and full scores, his many years of experience in the opera house giving him the necessary insight and understanding. As a young man, during the 1870s Kogel had teamed up with Salomon Jadassohn and under the pseudonyms of 'd'Avenal' and 'Ollivier', had edited hundreds of opera transcriptions and potpourris for C F Peters, which were in due course all pulped.

Rienzi was obtained from the publisher Fürstner in Berlin.

The Flying Dutchman was completed by the composer and conductor Gustav Brecher, another musician whose collaboration with the house of C F Peters spanned many years. Brecher first became known when Richard Strauss conducted his symphonic poem *Rosmersholm*, in 1896. Aged nineteen he became coach in the Leipzig City Theatre in 1898 and studied with Jadassohn in Leipzig. He was welcomed in 10 Talstrasse and impressed Henri Hinrichsen with his profound musical understanding. The two young men formed a lasting friendship and Brecher worked for the publisher on a freelance basis, as arranger and adviser.

Brecher became assistant to Mahler at the Vienna Court Opera in the 1901/2 season and subsequently directed the Hamburg City Theatre and the Cologne Opera Orchestra until 1923. He directed several other orchestras and taught conducting at the Stern Conservatory in Berlin. He became director of Leipzig Opera in 1923, responsible for several modern operas as well as the world première, on 9th March, 1930, of Brecht/Weill's *Aufstieg und Fall der Stadt Mahagonny* (Rise and Fall of the City of Mahagonny). Gustav Brecher fell victim to anti-Semitic persecution and was sacked from his post in 1933. He fled to Belgium, where he and his wife committed suicide on the German invasion in 1940.

It was Gustav Brecher, who introduced Gustav Mahler to Henri Hinrichsen. He had met Bruno Walter, who told him that Mahler had had a disagreement with his Viennese publisher and was now able to place his compositions with whichever publisher he chose. Brecher wrote to Henri Hinrichsen on 23rd July, 1903 suggesting that he should consider offering to publish Mahler's Fifth Symphony.

The Story behind Gustav Mahler's Fifth Symphony

Gustav Mahler was conductor at the Neues Stadttheater in Leipzig, from 1886 to 1888. He first offered his works to C F Peters in 1897, but was turned down by Dr Max Abraham who did not want to take on new composers at that time. Mahler was then about to take up his post at the Hofoper (Court Opera) in Vienna.

Hinrichsen followed up Brecher's suggestion immediately[2], writing to Mahler to ask him what his conditions would be for the publication of his Fifth Symphony.

This was to be the prelude of arguably the most complicated, expensive and exasperating publishing venture Henri Hinrichsen ever embarked upon. It was to tax to the limits his patience, forbearance and faith in the work of a composer in whose genius he believed. It was a supreme example of several – of Henri Hinrichsen's supportive role

Franz Anton Hoffmeister   Carl Gottlob Siegmund Böhme
1754-1812   1785-1855

Ambrosius Kühnel   Carl Friedrich Peters   Julius Friedländer
1770-1813   1779-1827

Max Hinrichsen   Dr Max Abraham   Dr Henri Hinrichsen
1901-1965   1831-1900   1868-1942

Figure 1 – **The proprietors of C F Peters, Leipzig.**

Figure 2, above – c 1900: Königstrass‍
12. Felix Mendelsohn-Bartholdy's
home 1845-47. C F Peters moved in‍
the ground floor in 1846 and into
Mendelssohn's flat on the first floo‍
in 1867, staying till 1874.

Figure 3, above opposite – Dr Max
Abraham (1831-1900). Originator o‍
the 'Edition Peters' and Founder o‍
the Peters Music Library.

Figure 4, left – The ornate two colou‍
C F Peters cover design. This one f‍
Edvard Grieg's *Norwegian Dances* O‍
35.

Figure 5, below opposite – c 1900:
Talstrasse 10. Designed by Otto
Brückewald (architect of the
Bayreuth Festspielhaus) for Dr Max‍
Abraham. Business premises of C F‍
Peters from 1874 and home of the
Hinrichsen Family.

Figure 6, above opposite – c 1900: lfred Dörffel (1821-1905). Long ime Reader and Music Editor at . F. Peters. Working in the room n Talstrasse 10, in which Edvard rieg always worked when he was in Leipzig.

Figure 7, above – 1893: Königstrasse 26, Leipzig. ome of the Peters Music Library and the *Frauen Gewerbeverein*.

Figure 8, below, opposite – c 1915: he Peters Music Library, opened n 1894. Seated behind the desk, the Head Librarian, Rudolf Schwartz (1859-1935).

gure 9, below right – 1894: Dr Max raham, Oscar Meyer, a German ianist who played Grieg's Piano Concerto under the composer's irection in Munich, Nina Grieg, Edvard Grieg.

Figure 11, above – 1903: Bust of Edvard Grieg by Carl Seffner. Presented to the Gewandhaus. Leipzig by Henri Hinrichsen.

Figure 12, below left – 1919: Henriette Goldschmidt (1825-1920). Founder of the first Womens' College in Germany, for which Henri Hinrichsen w the financial sponsor in 1911.

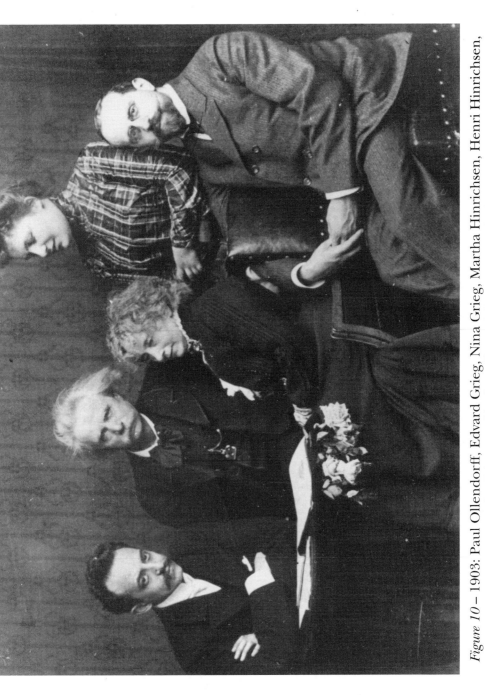

Figure 10 – 1903: Paul Ollendorff, Edvard Grieg, Nina Grieg, Martha Hinrichsen, Henri Hinrichsen, in Talstrasse 10, the offices of C F Peters, Leipzig

Figure 13, right – 1905: New 'Florentine' door commissioned by Henri Hinrichsen for the front of Talstrasse 10.

Figure 14, below – 1920: Willem Mengelberg (1871-1951). Conducted Mahler's Fifth Symphony at the Mahler Festival in Amsterdam, 6th-21st May 1920, which celebrated his own twenty-five years as conductor of the Concertgebau Orchestra.

WILLEM MENGELBERG

Ter herinnering aan zijn 25-jarig Jubileum
Mahler Feesten te Amsterdam
6-21 Mei 1920.

as a publisher to the creative and often unworldly spirit of the composer.
He had to display encouragement and understanding for the unending
corrections, alterations and improvements the composer was to insist
upon making until the end of his life, some eight years later, which
were to cause the publisher enormous expense.

Mahler replied from Vienna on 30th September, 1903:

> Highly Honoured Sir!
>
> I would like to reply to your repeated kind invitation to be
> advised of the conditions for the acquisition of my Vth
> Symphony.
>
> I require a one off payment of 10,000fl (ten thousand guilders)
> for the surrender of the complete publishing rights for this
> symphony. I hardly need to say how happy I would be to release
> my work to a publisher of your standing.
>
> I would be grateful for a speedy reply,
>
> Respectfully,
> Gustav Mahler

Hinrichsen accepted: 'Even though I am surprised at the amount of
the fee'.[3] The contract was agreed in 1904 and was followed by copious
correspondence discussing various matters relevant to the production
of the Fifth Symphony. There are fifty-three communications from
Mahler in the archives of C F Peters dating from 1897 to 1911. They
offer a deep insight into the finest details concerning the purchase of
the Fifth Symphony, its publication and the various proofing problems.
Occasionally the composer would voice his own doubts and insecurities
and ask Hinrichsen for his advice, as in this letter written from Vienna
in November 1903:

> ...Concerning the première, I would like to ask you for your
> advice! – I shy away from the big city press, who usually dig
> up a catchphrase on such occasions, which then gets
> thoughtlessly repeated a thousand fold. Hence for years I
> could not recover from the misunderstanding about me,
> emanating from the Berlin press, which was spread about the
> world. So what do you think would be the most advantageous
> for both you and I, bearing in mind the complications? I must
> point out that a première in Vienna would be out of the
> question, bearing in mind my position here...

The Fifth Symphony was premièred at a Gürzenich concert in Cologne on 18th October, 1904. Already before the first performance Mahler decided to re-score the work. The final, public rehearsal took place on 17th October and Mahler wrote to his wife Alma the following day:[4]

> ...Excellent performance! Audience absolutely thrilled and attentive – in spite of all displeasure in the first bars! There was even some hissing after the Scherzo – Adagietto and Rondo seem to have come through. Many musicians, conductors, etc. came from elsewhere. Hinrichsen is *delighted* and has secured for himself my VIth with great excitement. He added jokingly – Please do not raise the price though – which I certainly do not want to do, because he is such a nice chap...

Henri Hinrichsen was delighted to hear from his friend Gustav Brecher, who was conducting at the Hamburg Opera at the time and read all the newspaper reviews, and wrote to him on 22nd October, 1904:[5]

> Allow me to congratulate you on the success of your new publishing child, the Fifth by Mahler; one can see from all the newspaper reviews, despite the apparent divided opinions, that the work made a great impression – it was the success of an original and deeply meaningful creation. I wish you much pleasure and honour from it...

Apart from the orchestral score and parts, Hinrichsen also wanted to issue a version of Mahler's Fifth Symphony for piano four hands. The musician who made many piano arrangements, particularly of symphonies, for C F Peters over the course of some twenty years, was Otto Singer. Originally a violinist and student of Joachim, Singer made his name through his piano arrangements, which included the operas of Richard Strauss. Singer had assisted Strauss with a new edition of Berlioz' *Treatise on Instrumentation* for C F Peters in 1902. He agreed to prepare the arrangement of Mahler's Fifth Symphony in January 1904. However, the undertaking was fraught with problems, not the least of which were caused by Mahler himself. A number of letters were exchanged, Mahler kept making changes to the manuscript and then, when the composer saw Singer's meticulously prepared, completed piano score, he wanted more changes made. Singer vented his exasperation in a letter to Henri Hinrichsen from Munich, dated 8th July, 1904:[6]

It's really a calamity with Mahler – he has changed his mind about the required alterations from one day to the next and finally agreed to retain what he wanted to throw out in the first place, without according it the deep thought with which I approached every bar. He accepted that each note of the last two bars was in its correct place, what on earth has he now disturbed again? I once retracted my name from an arrangement, because I didn't want it to be misused to cover up a parody which a young composer had superimposed on my work. Will it really be necessary for me to do the same in this case?…

The publisher managed to placate the irate arranger and the piano four handed edition of Mahler's Fifth Symphony was issued in September that year.

Composers and musicians where always happy to be invited to the Hinrichsen's comfortable home and Mahler came to dinner whilst on a visit to Leipzig in connection with a performance of his Third Symphony on 24th November, 1904. Mahler reported on the visit to Alma in his letter of 29th November, 1904:[7]

…In the afternoon I went to Stägemann! They were as always charming to me and invited me to dinner; but I had to turn them down, because Hinrichsen had already invited me to dinner. As I arrived (he had asked me by telephone whether he could pick me up) he was just sitting in front of a piano duet version of a Bruckner symphony and was drumming the second. I sat down and played the entire piano score through with him – secretly it seemed to me like a sacrifice and tax in gratitude for his generosity and a way in which I could to a certain extent work off the costs which the chap had incurred through the failed Fifth Symphony.

Then a charming and famous musician joined us, the local Musical Director, Karl Straube, who is an avid admirer of mine…

Henri Hinrichsen expressed his delight at having acquired Mahler's Fifth Symphony in a letter to Edvard Grieg dated 23rd February, 1905:

…The Fifth Symphony by Mahler, whose happy publisher I am, is slowly making its rounds through the concert halls; that is, with greater or lesser success, as is always the case with important works. In April the Symphony will even be performed in Moscow, that is, if the nihilists have left enough of the orchestral players alive. It really looks horrific in the Tsarist State and everybody asks themselves how it will end...

With his undoubted success, Mahler decided to raise the price for his next symphony, having received a higher offer from the publisher C F Kahnt of Leipzig. He was now faced with a dilemma and wrote to Hinrichsen from Vienna on 7th June, 1905:

> ...Thank you so much for honouring me with your offer to publish my new symphony and for the unceasing trust which you place in my works. Please permit me to put to you an open question concerning the matter. Could you see your way to paying me a fee of 15,000fl, which sum I have been offered from another publisher, for my new work?

> It would be my greatest wish to know that my VIth Symphony were also to be published by your firm. You have treated me in every respect with such huge generosity, that I would on my part like to take into account such extensive kindness. However, you will understand that I (who am not wealthy) must plan for my future and must make full use of every advantage whilst I am still able to produce and am in full command of all my faculties. I would ask you for a perfectly honest opinion which I will in no event misunderstand...

Hinrichsen employed his strict personal code to stick by whatever price he had originally agreed; if the composer asked for more, after a price had been agreed, he would not bargain. Neither would he offer to pay more than he thought a work was worth. Thus he turned down the offer two days later[8] giving as his reasons that the fee demanded was higher than that for the Fifth Symphony, which had only received a few performances. The Sixth Symphony was published by C F Kahnt, Leipzig, in 1906 and taken up by Universal Edition in Vienna in 1909.

Symphonies numbers One to Five, together with all of Bruckner's symphonies, were offered to C F Peters by the original publisher in Vienna, in 1906. The price asked, 160,000M, was considered to be too high, so Hinrichsen, to his subsequent regret, turned the offer down.

The friendship was unaffected and on 13th June, 1906 Mahler wrote Hinrichsen a long letter offering him his arrangement of *Figaro*, but this was rejected. He was keen to have his Seventh Symphony published by C F Peters and wrote to Hinrichsen on 5th December, 1907, shortly before departure for New York: '...I am thinking of publishing my VIIth

Symphony. Before I solicit any other offers I would like to ask whether in principle you would like to consider this, my new work…'

Again Hinrichsen declined, but was pleased that he should be the first publisher to whom Mahler offered his new symphony.[9] That three Leipzig music publishers had published three of Mahler's symphonies, points to the great interest that was evident around the turn of the century, in the music publishing centre of Germany, for the works of the controversial Austrian composer.

Mahler had never been happy with his original version of the Fifth Symphony and had constantly and relentlessly made revisions and alterations to his score for every performance of the work. He wrote to Hinrichsen from Vienna on 1st June, 1910 saying that he regarded it 'as essential, in the interests of the work, to prepare a new edition of the work.' He offered to pay for the new engraving himself and urgently requested a score and parts which he could alter for the performance due the next season. The performance was not to be realised and the project remained uncompleted by the time Mahler died on 18th May, 1911, though he did write to the conductor George Göhler at the beginning of 1911: 'I have finished the fifth!'[10]

Hinrichsen debated whether he should 'make the sacrifice' and scrap all the printed material and issue a completely new version. However, he was unwilling to invest a further large sum for this; Mahler had then reached a verbal agreement with him that he himself would pay the costs. After his death, this was no longer possible. Hinrichsen had already spent a considerable amount on having the engraved plates of the full score and study score, the orchestral parts and the version for piano four hands altered to Mahler's specifications on several occasions.[11]

Publishers must combine aesthetic with commercial judgement and Hinrichsen was disappointed with the lack of expected success with the Symphony which had only seen a few performances. The hand-engraving of large and complex scores on many plates, as well as the instrumental parts, added to the fee originally paid to Mahler, had cost him much more than he felt he was ever likely to see returned. In January 1912, less than a year after Mahler's death, he asked Arnold Schönberg for his opinion of Mahler and confided his lack of confidence that the Fifth Symphony would ever be a success. He wondered whether he shouldn't just melt down the plates. Schönberg was stunned and sang Mahler's praises, saying that Mahler's time would soon come and that even today, young people held him for a God.

The composer and conductor Georg (Karl) Göhler who championed the symphonies of Mahler and Bruckner, was keen to perform the new version of Mahler's Fifth Symphony. He wrote to Alma Mahler asking for the composer's revised score. Hinrichsen made the condition for producing the new edition that he should be allowed to keep this autographed score. The material, altered by hand, was ready and printed by December 1913 and the first performance of the new version was given on 9th January, 1914 in Leipzig.

There continued to be confusion about the work and whilst some conductors were keen to promote it, few concert organisers wanted to pay the costs. One keen supporter of Mahler's symphonies was Fritz Busch, who had recently been appointed music director of the Stuttgart Opera. Like many concert organisers after the war, he lacked funds. He wrote to Hinrichsen on 2nd May, 1919:[12]

> I am hoping to perform Mahler's Fifth Symphony during the coming winter season, if the price of the material – either to purchase or to hire – falls within my budget. This is somewhat limited, as the concert is in aid of the orchestra's pension fund. I would also like to perform the work in my first concert in the Berlin Philharmonie (October this year), but am not myself in the position of being able to obtain the material a second time. As I assume that it is also in the interest of the publisher, that this important and insufficiently performed work should receive as many as possible, and good, performances, I hope I can count on your friendly accommodation and look forward to your early reply.

Henri Hinrichsen was obliged to express his 'friendly accommodation' in many ways as a consequence of World War I and the resulting cataclysmic social changes, which also seriously affected the world of music. In Part Three, we will see how C F Peters revised the way in which its publications were promoted and marketed to accommodate the severe financial shortages, to help people and to survive the crisis.

A revised, newly engraved full score and study score of Mahler's Fifth Symphony were eventually issued in 1920, following suggestions from Rudolf Mengelberg, nephew of the conductor Willem Mengelberg.

One of Mahler's great supporters was the conductor of the Amsterdam Concertgebouw Orchestra, Willem Mengelberg, who did all the preparation for Mahler's concerts with the orchestra from 1903. He had a particular sympathy and understanding for the music through his long association with the composer. To mark Mengelberg's twenty-fifth year with the orchestra in 1920, a Mahler Festival was organised at which all the composer's works would be performed in nine concerts [Fig 14]. The artistic manager appointed to the orchestra in 1917, was Mengelberg's nephew, Dr Curt Rudolf Mengelberg, who was responsible for the organisation of the Festival. A musicologist and composer

himself, he expressed his understanding about the importance of
Mahler's own changes to the score of the Fifth Symphony, in a letter to
Henri Hinrichsen dated 3rd August, 1919:[13]

Dear Sir,

I have studied the alterations to Mahler's Fifth Symphony very
precisely and can only confirm to you, that whilst they are
intervenient, they really are *improvements*. With Mahler's
intensive method of working and his incredibly strong
tendency towards self-criticism, that is hardly surprising. In
fact, I find that the comparison of both versions is a very
fruitful form of *study*, in that it permits a peep into the
workroom of the *greatest* modern master of orchestration –
an occasion which one unfortunately finds only too rarely.

We could not possibly undertake a further performance in
the old version, as Mahler himself used many of the alterations
– *improvements*, in his performances there, in, I believe, 1905.
It is to be highly recommended that in a new printing of the
work your corrected copy of the score should be compared
with the score privately owned by Willem Mengelberg, which
Mahler used at the time, so that the new edition should be as
authentic as possible.

Yours sincerely,
C Rudolf Mengelberg

Hundreds of plates had to be scrapped and new ones engraved.
There was confusion resulting from all the alterations on the various
scores and parts. It was not clear which was Mahler's final version.
Because of the complications, the firm of Röder had underestimated
the cost, which produced acrimony between publisher and engraver.
The whole venture was ultimately to cost the publisher a huge sum,
more than double the original estimate. And still it was not entirely
correct, because not all the alterations on the various scores had been
taken into consideration! Because of its complexity, delivery was delayed
until April 1920.

Hinrichsen continued to have faith in Mahler's Fifth Symphony in
spite of its huge cost and in October 1920 he wrote to Otto Singer
asking him whether he would like to make an arrangement of the work
for piano solo. On 4th November, he wrote to Hermann Behn inviting
him to make an arrangement for two pianos four hands. Behn turned
down the commission on 7th November, saying that he was involved

with the gigantic task of making arrangements of Wagner's operas for two pianos, which would take him years. Apart from which, he had already had experience of the complexities of Mahler's scores and at the age of sixty-one, felt he could not devote the necessary six months to the task.[14]

In 1921, Alma Mahler wrote to Henri Hinrichsen expressing her regret over the fact that the one-off fee which Mahler had agreed for his Fifth Symphony, meant that she received no income from the many performances.[15] Hinrichsen, the owner of the copyright, was under no obligation to her. Having bought the symphony outright from Mahler and having invested a fortune in its production, he was still running at a considerable loss. However, he displayed his extraordinary generosity and sent her an ex-gratia fee of 5,000M. In 1930 there was a successful performance in Leipzig conducted by Bruno Walter, who was planning to conduct it the following year in Vienna. From 1933 the Nazis banned performances of Mahler's works.

Under new regulations which came into force in 1911, the period during which a work was copyright had been extended from thirty years to fifty years after the death of the composer. It was not until 1964 that most of the mistakes were corrected with the publication of the *First Edition of the Definitive Version of Gustav Mahler's Fifth Symphony*, included in the *Critical Complete Edition* of Mahler's Works published by the *Internationale Gustav Mahler Gesellschaft*, Vienna.

Publishing Mahler's Fifth Symphony was a huge venture. Not much less protracted and complicated, was the acquisition of the Lieder of Hugo Wolf.

Purchase of the Lieder of Hugo Wolf (1860-1903)

Henri Hinrichsen had enjoyed the Lieder of Hugo Wolf, since his interest had been aroused by an article by Hermann Kretzschmar in the *Peters Music Library Year Book*. He had long wanted to acquire the rights to them for C F Peters.

The negotiations were protracted and complicated, owing to Wolf's mental illness from tertiary syphilis during the last five years of his life. The publisher Heckel was selling Wolf's Lieder under an agreement with B Schott's Söhne, Mainz, who had acquired them in the 1880s but had then handed the plates over to Heckel with the understanding of the composer. This was because Wolf had complained bitterly that, after a few years, his share of the proceeds was so small. Hinrichsen's negotiations with Heckel in 1901, to acquire the *Selected Lieder of Hugo Wolf* proved fruitless. It was not until after the composer's death that C F Peters was able to purchase the rights to the Lieder and obtained fifty-three *Mörike Lieder*, forty-six songs of the *Italian Lieder Book*, forty-eight *Goethe Lieder* and three *Michelangelo Lieder*, for the price of 153,975M.

Edvard Grieg was interested in Hinrichsen's acquisition and welcomed the publisher's offer to send him copies for himself and Nina. As he wrote on 12th January, 1904: 'I know some of his work which I admire greatly.' In his reply of 22nd January Hinrichsen expressed his views as a publisher: 'The acquisition of the Wolf Lieder was a great coup, even though it is more or less the music of the future.'

A further contract was agreed with Heckel in 1905 for rights to the thirty-four Lieder of the *Spanish Lieder Book* and twenty *Eichendorf Lieder*, which had first been published by Lacom in Vienna. Hinrichsen was so enamoured of the Lieder of Hugo Wolf, that he travelled to Stuttgart in October 1906, where he attended recitals devoted to the Lieder on three consecutive evenings. In December 1907 he was able to obtain the twenty-three *Lieder by Various Poets* for 70,000M through personal negotiation. C F Peters had finally acquired copyright to all the Lieder by Hugo Wolf with the exception of the *12 Lieder of Youth* which were published by Lauterbach and Kuhn (later Bote & Bock).

Hinrichsen was keen to acquire all the vocal works of Wolf and in 1919, after many years of verbal and postal negotiation with Hugo Wolf's heirs, was able to purchase the vocal score to his opera *Corregidor* for 10,000M. He also obtained the complete scores and parts for *Feuerreiter* (The Fire Rider) for choir and orchestra; for the *Frühlingschor* (Spring Chorus) from the opera fragment *Manuel Venegas* and for the hymn *Dem Vaterland* (The Fatherland) for choir and orchestra. In 1927 he acquired the right to publish the seven Lieder of Heine's *Liederstrauss* from Tischer & Jagenberg, Cologne, but these proved to be less popular.

It could be said that Henri Hinrichsen was somewhat obsessive about the works and personality of Hugo Wolf. Not only did he seek to acquire the copyright to Hugo Wolf's compositions, but he purchased the letters of the composer whenever they were offered for sale, either at auction or privately, especially during the inflationary years after World War I.

Music publishing relies on a good understanding and sympathy between publisher and composer or arranger; on the ability to negotiate contracts which are advantageous to both parties and on persuasive powers of salesmanship – to retailers, performers and concert organisers. But all this would be without value if the all-important relationship between publisher and contractor were unsatisfactory.

Production

Like Dr Max Abraham before him, who had built up an excellent relationship with the printer, Carl Gottlieb Röder, Henri Hinrichsen now enjoyed a similar collaboration with Röder's heirs, his two sons-in-law; the high standard of printing was maintained.

He similarly strove for loyalty and the highest degree of excellence between himself and all his contractors. It is a mark of the mutual respect between the suppliers – the printers and engravers, the paper suppliers and the binders – and the publisher, that contracts between the various firms who worked for C F Peters continued for decades. Each supplier was eager to provide the best service and the best product, in order to come within the orbit of this fine music publishing company, whose reputation for excellence at reasonable prices, was acknowledged the world over. As important as the printer, is the binder.

E A Enders Bindery

The firm of E A Enders had been the bindery [Fig 15] for almost all the 'Edition Peters' works, including the fine bound volumes, published by C F Peters since 1863 and there had been a close personal friendship between the two firms all those years. In December 1913, on the occasion of the celebration of their fifty years' collaboration, Max Enders presented Henri Hinrichsen with a fine illuminated document[16], drawn by R Glauser, in appreciation of this association. The text shows the extent to which first Emil Alexander Enders and then his son, valued their association with Dr Max Abraham and Henri Hinrichsen. This glowing testimonial, flowery and exaggerated though it may seem to modern eyes, is an indication of the appreciation Enders felt for the confidence placed in his company by the proprietors of C F Peters, and of the close collaboration between the two firms, as well as the friendship between two generations of their proprietors.

Highly Honoured Mr. Kommerzienrat!

By the time a firm comes of age it has many memories and jubilees to look back on, and each of these backward glances gives further stimulus for greater achievement in the future.

It has been given to your house to reach incomparable heights and at the turn of the century to have been able to celebrate its centenary to its own satisfaction, to the delight of contemporaries and not least to the good fortune of those who can, with pride, count themselves amongst your colleagues. A great power has it within itself to include many smaller powers in its orbit, to allow them to develop and to flower. Your house is like a gigantic tree, spreading its blossoming branches like an umbrella over the saplings which

> delight in a strong life under its protective crown. My company
> too feels itself as such a sapling, over which the leaves of this
> tree bend with compassion...

The document continued with a résumé of the expanding association between the two companies over the course of fifty years.

The world-wide reputation of the 'Edition Peters' was so high that it attracted imitators, both in the use of its name and in the copying of its cover and title-page designs. Whilst the first titles were produced in 1867, it was not until 1901 that the name was patented, thus protecting the integrity of its reputation. (The firm's name remained C F Peters, Leipzig, Bureau de Musique.) The classic and tasteful cover design was copied by several music publishers and the engraved baroque design of the title-page was imitated repeatedly. Designed by E Baumgarten, the title-page, like the music, was printed by C G Röder. Until almost the end of World War I, the engraved frame design was printed in red, with the title appearing in black. This was expensive to produce and after the War the whole title-page was printed in black. Further economies were made during the 1920s, when the engraved frame was abandoned in favour of a simpler design.

Henri Hinrichsen counted many publishers, both of music and of books, amongst his friends. He was deeply interested in all aspects of book production – the printing, typography, design, illustration and the binding; he was also a voracious reader. In pursuit of his interest he was amongst the founder members of the Leipzig Bibliophiles Association.

The Ninetyniners – The Bibliophiles Association of Leipzig

There had long been collectors of valuable books, however it was not until the 1890s that bibliophiles in Germany started gathering together in so-called *Bibliophilen Abende* (Bibliophile's Evenings).

The *Leipziger Bibliophilen Abend* (Leipzig Bibliophile's Evening) – LBA – was founded in 1904. Started by the scholar, Georg Witkowski, and Johannes Baensch-Drugulin, proprietor of a printing works, it was somewhat akin to a masonic lodge in character. Witkowski was a major figure in literary scholarship in Leipzig and throughout Germany: a professor emeritus, teacher of several well-known writers, researcher and author of over 700 titles, he was asked to retain his post after retirement. But after 1933 Witkowski was persecuted as a 'non-Aryan' and his lectures derided by the state; he was deprived of his pension. He escaped to Holland in 1939 and died of bronchitis within four months. His co-founder, Johannes Baensch-Drugulin was a leading printer of books of the late nineteenth/early twentieth century, praised for the variety of his oriental fonts. He was the printer of the magazines *Pan* (1895-1900), *Zeitschrift für Bücherfreunde* (Magazine for Book Friends) (from 1897) and *Die Insel* (The Island) (1899-1902).

Henri Hinrichsen, one of the first to join, may have been at the inaugural meeting of seventeen founder members who met on 17th February, 1904 in Baarmanns Restaurant. His name is shown on a list of members published in the first LBA publication: *Sperontes. Singende Muse an der Pleisse* (Sperontes. Singing Muse on the River Pleisse), on 25th February, 1905. The constitution of the society limited the number of members to ninety-nine – hence its nickname of 'The Ninetyniners'.

This was the first local bibliophiles' society in Germany and it became the model on which all other such societies in Germany were based. There were 'six convivial lecture evenings every year' at which participants were provided with a variety of stimuli, when members were happy to share their expertise in their various bibliophile and literary specialities, with their colleagues. These evenings proved very productive, in view of the fact that two-thirds of the Leipzig Ninetyniners were either publishers, proprietors of printing works, book designers, book dealers and antiquarians, or worked as librarians or professors.

The Bibliophiles Evening and its regular publications were financed through the membership subscriptions. There were also special occasions, such as the Annual General Meeting and the annual banquet, when the members would surprise each-other with limited edition prints, so-called 'gifts' – which they sponsored individually. The edition was usually limited to ninety-nine, plus the requisite copies for the German Library in Leipzig and other libraries. More than 160 such 'gifts' and twenty regular publications over the course of the twenty-nine years of its existence, point to the flourishing publishing activity of the LBA, and to the multiplicity of interests of its members.

Henri Hinrichsen delighted members with the presentation of beautiful editions which he had sponsored on at least four occasions. In 1918 he presented a woodcut selected by the Art Association: *Caricature of Gustav Kirstein* by Hans Alexander Müller. Müller was professor at the Academy for Graphic Arts and Book Production in Leipzig, specialising in book illustration, and a member of the LBA; he was relieved of his post when the National Socialists came to power in 1933 and emigrated to USA.

Gustav Kirstein became business partner with his friend Ernst Elert Artur Seemann the publisher, in 1899. On Artur's death the partnership devolved to his son, Elert Seemann. Kirstein was Chairman of the LBA, for whom he edited the magazine *Zeitschrift der Bücherfreunde* (Magazine for Book Friends) from 1913. In 1933 Elert Seemann joined the Nazi Party and severed relations with his friend and partner. Kirstein, who was a Jew, was obliged to relinquish chairmanship of the LBA. He committed suicide in 1934.

In 1918 Henri Hinrichsen also presented a long drawing: *Moritz von Schwinds Lachner Rolle*, a single sheet facsimile print by Moritz Schwind, showing scenes from the life of the composer Franz Paul Lachner, in the form of a roll, after the original in the Peters Music Library.

Hinrichsen shared his passion for autograph collecting with his friends in the LBA in 1922 when he presented them with: *Henri Hinrichsen: Letters from Famous Musicians from my Autograph Collection.* Facsimile print. (Containing letters from Leopold Mozart (1762), Ludwig van Beethoven (1800), Joseph Haydn (1801), E T A Hoffmann (1818), Richard Wagner (1871), Franz Liszt (1876), Johannes Brahms (1881) and Hugo Wolf (1894).)

As a music publisher, it was only right that he should present something musical. He chose a very appropriate 'gift' for the LBA members in 1929: *Kommerslied der Leipziger Bibliophilen* (Drinking Song of the Leipzig Bibliophiles) by Fedor von Zobeltitz and Paul Graener. Text and music. Fedor von Zobeltitz was a writer and founded the Association of Bibliophiles, of which he was the long time Chairman, in 1899. He was editor of the magazine *Zeitschrift der Bücherfreunde* (Magazine for Book Friends) from 1897 to 1909.

Paul Graener was a composer and conductor who taught composition at the Leipzig Conservatory of Music 1920-1925. He was Director of the Stern Conservatory of Music in Berlin (which had belonged to the Jewish Hollaender family, who emigrated to USA in 1934) from 1930-1933 and held master classes at the Academy of Arts. He became vice president of the Reichsmusikkammer till 1941.

As Leipzig was a world centre for book production, great stress was laid on the design: the care with which the typography was selected and the perfection of the printing, production and binding. The large volume produced for the twenty-fifth anniversary of the LBA in 1929 was particularly successful; it was selected as amongst the fifty most beautiful books produced in Germany that year.

The anniversary marked the high point in the life of the LBA. When the National Socialists came to power they ordered that all 'non-Aryan' members should be dismissed. As this constituted almost half the membership, the remaining 'Aryan' members agreed unanimously to disband the association, rather than be dictated to and allow the entire concept of their organisation to be changed. The LBA met for the last time in May 1933. Henri Hinrichsen was one of the few who had been a member during the entire twenty-nine years of its existence.[17]

Along with his passion for books, Henri Hinrichsen also had a love of paintings. He had grown up surrounded by paintings and had the opportunity of meeting many artists himself. He had learnt to love art through his mother's enthusiasm and knowledge and when he came to Leipzig, he was further encouraged by his uncle.

Collection of Paintings

Whilst Henri Hinrichsen's interest was not exclusive, it centred itself on paintings by German masters of the nineteenth century and he became a discerning collector. He studied auction catalogues and bought wisely, not specifically for investment, but for his own pleasure and embellished his home with masterpieces by such painters as Adolph von Menzel, Adam Friedrich Oeser, Max Klinger, Hans Thoma, Wilhelm Leibl, Joseph Carl Stieler, Karl Spitzweg, Fritz von Uhde, Max Liebermann, Defregger, Feuerbach, Passini, and several others.

There were also paintings by some more widely known painters including *Lucretia* by Lucas Cranach and a small painting by Gustav Courbet.[18] The collection included good portraits of the classical composers which adorned the walls of the music room and Henri Hinrichsen's office, as well as some exquisite engravings and water colours.

When the subject of a painting was one of the composers as closely linked to C F Peters as Ludwig van Beethoven, the publisher could not resist the opportunity to buy it. One particular portrait, however, had an even stronger claim to his interest, owing to a connection with Louis Spohr, whose collaboration with the company spanned some fifty years.

The Beethoven Portrait by Stieler

The portrait of Beethoven painted by Joseph Carl Stieler in 1819-20, is one of the best known of the many portraits which were painted of the composer [Fig 16]. It was acquired by the brother of Louis Spohr at a raffle run by the Art Association of Brunswick. He valued the portrait highly because Stieler had assured him, when they had met at their friend Kaulbach's house in Munich, that he was the only painter to whom Beethoven had allowed sittings – and that, only at the specific wish of the composer's friends and patrons, the Brentanos. It is understood to be a very good likeness; only the hands had to be painted from memory, as Beethoven could not be persuaded to sit any longer.

The Stieler portrait was treasured and well cared for in the Spohr household. Permission for reproductions was not given until thirty years after the painter's death and the firm of Hanfstaengl, who made lithographic reproductions, were not able to produce their 'Aquarel' print until 1907. On Spohr's death, the painting was inherited by his daughter Rosalie, the Countess Sauerma, a well-known harpist. It was through the mediation of the musicologist Max Friedländer, that Henri

Hinrichsen was able to buy it for 25,000M from the Countess Sauerma on 10th February 1909. It had pride of place as a symbol of the C F Peters tradition, in his private music room in 10 Talstrasse.[19] A year later, he had a limited number of reproductions produced for presentation to a few selected friends. One of these was the composer Max Reger, whom he admired tremendously. Henri Hinrichsen was the one person who helped and supported the workaholic composer through many difficulties, as we will see in the next chapter.

---

1 All three letters quoted in Bestand C F Peters, StAL 1884.
2 StAL, C F Peters, Kopierbuch H.
3 *Ibid.*
4 *Gustav Mahler: Briefe.* Published, Verlag Philip Reclam jun. Leipzig. 1981.
5 StAL Bestand. C F Peters, file 319.
6 Letter quoted in *Jahrbuch Peters 1979.* 'Zur Geschichte der Fünften Symphonie von Gustav Mahler'. Edited by Eberhard Klemm, Peters, Leipzig 1979.
7 *Gustav Mahler: Briefe.* Published, Verlag Philip Reclam jun. Leipzig. 1981.
8 StAL, C F Peters Kopierbuch J, 9th June 1905.
9 StAL, C F Peters. Kopierbuch J.
10 *Jahrbuch Peters 1979.* As above.
11 Full details of the various versions of the scores and complexity of the plate engraving can be found in *Jahrbuch Peters 1979* as above.
12 StAL Bestand, C F Peters, file 367.
13 StAL, C F Peters Bestand, file 1837.
14 *Jahrbuch Peters 1979.* As above.
15 StAL, C F Peters Bestand, Alma Mahler file, 10th September and 1st October 1921.
16 Enders document in the archive of the author.
17 All the archives of the '99ers', the original Leipziger Bibliophilen Abend, were lost during WWII. A new LBA. was formed on 8th January 1991. This was founded as an offshoot of the Leipzig Pirckheimer Society. Members are book lovers and collectors, rather than book producers, number more than ninety-nine and include women. The emphasis is on lectures and discussions, not on 'gifts'.
18 The Lucas Cranach painting (the author is not certain whether this was Cranach father or son) was, like the Lachner Rolle and others, confiscated by the Nazis in 1939 (see Chapter Nineteen). The Courbet painting was taken out of Germany by Henri Hinrichsen's son Max in 1937; however, without a certificate of authenticity.
19 Carl Stieler's portrait of Beethoven was rescued from Leipzig in 1945 by Walter Hinrichsen and taken to the USA, where it hung in his office at C F Peters Corporation in New York. A copy was painted to replace it when the original was sold to the Beethoven House in Bonn in 1981, where it now hangs.

CHAPTER SEVEN

Max Reger
His Association with his Patron, 1901 to 1916

Max Reger was unfortunate that his talent was not recognised early enough at C F Peters. The one person in whom he could place his trust, Henri Hinrichsen, came into his life when he had already committed himself to an ill-conceived contract with another publisher. His lack of trust in any one, coupled with the complexities of his character, caused him to have his works published by no fewer than forty publishers. However, it was Henri Hinrichsen who became his benefactor and friend for the last twelve years of his life. Not only over-work, but an overindulgence in good food, fat cigars to keep him awake and a dependence on alcohol contributed to his death at the age of forty-three.

This caring relationship between composer and publisher is outlined in the 460 or so letters and postcards which the composer wrote to Henri Hinrichsen, all of which the publisher kept in his personal autograph collection. Reger was in the habit of throwing away most letters which he received, after replying to them, so there are fewer extant letters from Henri Hinrichsen, or from his manager Paul Ollendorff, though the main details from these were entered in the *Copy Books*.[1]

A small selection of Max Reger's letters was published in 1928.[2] Henri Hinrichsen had hoped to publish the complete collection, but was unable to fulfil this dream. His autograph collection was confiscated by the Nazi authorities in 1939. All the correspondence from Reger to Hinrichsen has since been traced[3], and published in a scholarly book which is dedicated to the memory of Henri Hinrichsen.[4]

From these letters we can see how seriously Reger took himself and what tremendous energy he put into his music and into its promotion. He wanted to be taken seriously by the cognoscenti and to be accepted by posterity as a great composer. We see the gruelling schedule which he set himself with his constant concert tours. As much as anything, we see the immense patience and understanding exercised by Henri Hinrichsen with a composer who was impatient, not always business-like and not sensible about his health, but whom he respected and in whom he had great faith. Hinrichsen is shown as a good friend and a man who is prepared to take the risk of investing considerable sums in publishing 'difficult' music, because he believes it to be of value; if not for the present day, then for posterity. Quotations from a few of these many letters serve to illustrate the relationship.

Max Reger's earlier works were published by Augeners in London, but the company refused to publish any more of his works after 1896. He was twenty-five when he made his first approach to C F Peters on 18th September, 1898, submitting his Opus 20, 22 and 26. At seventy-eight, C F Peters editor at the time, Dr Alfred Dörffel, was unsympathetic to the stormy tones of the music of the future, he recommended rejection. Thus Reger's Opus 19-57, with few exceptions, were published by Aibl in Munich and were taken over in 1900 by Universal Edition.

1901/2

In 1901 a mutual friend effected a new introduction. Henri Hinrichsen then accepted Reger's Organ Pieces, Opus 59 and followed this with the Quintet, Opus 64 and further Organ Pieces, Opus 65.

When sending Reger the proofs of the first volume of Organ Pieces on 8th July, 1902 he wrote that his expert advisers had told him that: '...the works are definitely not easy nor even moderately difficult to play but, in view of your extremely complicated harmonics, demand a player of the highest proficiency. That is a great pity for both of us, as the works will be difficult to introduce...'

In Reger's reply of 18th July he shows his abhorrence of any sort of criticism of his music by so-called 'experts' and justifies his writing of 'difficult' music – a trait of which he was accused by critics and publishers many times during his prolific creative life:

> ...The 'experts' have declared that my Op 65 is too difficult! Well 1) *technically* it is not as difficult as Op 59. 2) Concerning the harmonics: Please believe me, it would serve neither you nor I, if I were to compose in old-fashioned, obsolete ways – then there would be merely a *momentary* success – and **not** a permanent one! Furthermore, please would you be kind enough to imagine for yourself: 'in our times', when we have *acknowledged* and accepted *Tristan and Isolde*, Franz Liszt's works, Richard Wagner's works, etc., it is really *no* mistake, if

I am *new* in my harmonics! Believe me, it would be a sin if I were to go back on my original harmonic conception, *against* my better judgement. The reviews which you have already received about Op 59, have surely given you the proof that I am **not** following the wrong track; Op 65 is of course more *original* than Op 59; that is understandable, because I have matured by one year.

In art, it has *always and always* been the case that progress has been triumphant! I will not give you anything to publish which I cannot justify (**every** note) against the *strongest* criticism and *all* experts.

Be assured; I value my name so much that I take the greatest care not *ever* to publish anything which does not conform to the highest standards of the time...

Reger was hoping for an exclusive contract with C F Peters as he needed to supplement his meagre earnings from concerts when he married Elsa von Bercken, born von Bagenski, on 25th October, 1902. However, it was not C F Peters, but the inexperienced Carl Lauterbach and Max Kuhn who offered the modernist composer a disastrous contract, which he accepted without taking advice from anybody, and which was designed to tie him down until 1914.

1904

Reger's popularity took an upswing when his Violin Sonata, Op 72 was performed at the Frankfurt Tonkünstlerfest in May 1904. It created such a furore that concert agencies in large and small towns eagerly organised 'Reger Evenings'. Reger set out on an unremitting series of concert tours. Interest was awoken in other publishers. Henri Hinrichsen accepted two new works for Organ for publication: Op 80 and Op 85. The composer was giving so many concerts, and was so busy with his teaching at the Munich Academy of Music, that he could barely find the time to complete his *Sinfonietta,* Op 90. However, as he wrote in a letter to Hinrichsen dated 18th July, 1905, his *Sinfonietta* had been booked for performances in forty towns for the coming season 'to be performed by the best orchestras and conductors'. It was performed at least twenty times during its first season, when it was conducted by Mottl, Nikisch, Steinbach, Schalk and Suter amongst others.

Henri Hinrichsen commissioned arrangements of Bach's *Brandenburg Concertos* for Piano four hands from Reger, who did not want to hurry the work because: 'this music is too beautiful for me to do with too great a haste'. These were published in two volumes in 1905 and 1906 respectively. Their popularity was such that they were very soon reprinted. C F Peters also published Reger's arrangement for Piano solo of Hugo Wolf's *Mörike Lieder* in 1905.

Reger's output was phenomenal; in spite of all his concert tours and his teaching engagements he had, by the age of thirty-two, arrived at his Opus 90, several of the numbers comprising fifty-sixty works in each. Reger was his own best publicity agent. He did not neglect his students and was concerned for their welfare. Though he was not in a position to help financially himself, he did not hesitate to turn to his friend Henri Hinrichsen to ask for a grant for a desperately poor student, Jacques Handschin. The publisher provided funds for the young man for two years. There were several other occasions when Reger appealed to his friend, who willingly financially supported several of Reger's musician friends who were in need, or their widows and children.

1906

In 1906 Augener Edition in London offered all Reger's early works for sale and Henri Hinrichsen immediately bought them. Reger was not best pleased at the acquisition by C F Peters of his 'youthful sins' as he called his early works and Hinrichsen was unhappy that, because of Reger's manifold concert engagements, the composer was unable to supply him with any new works.

Henri Hinrichsen's interest in and admiration for the young musician grew. He wrote in his *Chronik*: 'As a pianist, Reger had a uniquely unmechanical touch; his rendition of major works, for example Bach's *Goldberg Variations* at the Leipzig Bach Festival of 1911 had, especially in the slow, very thoughtfully played passages, something quite transcendental about it.' However, he was concerned that the huge number of concerts which Reger was giving served to dissipate his energies and prevent him from giving enough time to composition.

The publisher wanted to enable the young man to be able to devote more time to composing and, with perceptive understanding, he wrote to Reger on 18th December, 1906, with a generous idea. He offered to pay the composer an honorarium of 10,000M if he promised to give not more than ten concerts for one full year. This year's salary was designed to free him from all financial considerations and to enable him to devote more time to his own creative work. Hinrichsen said that Reger was not to feel in any way duty bound to offer the resulting compositions to C F Peters.

Dear Mr Reger,

When I last had the pleasure of seeing you here and, between thunderous applause, had the chance to speak to you, a number of ideas occurred to me which I would like to impart to you in your interest. One likes to imagine the creative artist, far from the hurley-burley of life, lost in the inspiration of his genius, working in peaceful seclusion: – that is all theory. – After a tiring ride on the podium, completion of a long programme, public ovations, – thinking of the next journey whilst playing the final notes: – that is the actuality! – Should we not have learnt any lessons from the traditions of earlier centuries? That you originally had the desire to become better known to an ever increasing circle through your concerts, I can fully understand and I find it correct. Now that you have, in such an incredibly short time succeeded so resoundingly, it seems to me that there can be only one duty for you: to look after yourself both in body and intellectually, so that the high expectations which in these times of paucity of creative artists, are vested in you, can in the broadest sense, be realised! I feel that you should draw a thick line under the giving of concerts, and perhaps with the motivation of composing a major work, should decline everything else, in order to follow your creative work in peace and quiet. That means, that you should not create to commission, nor create in need, but only attempt such works which you feel inspired to create out of an inner need...

Then followed his altruistic and generous offer.

Reger was thrilled by Henri Hinrichsen's generosity. In his letter from Munich dated 26th December, 1906 accepting the offer, he justified his own need to give concerts by emphasising his desire to demonstrate how his music should be performed:

...With regard to my concert-life, which has just this winter taken on huge dimensions, and which will take on ever greater dimensions, you are absolutely right; I am myself very upset by it, that I have this winter – so, *for over half a year*, been *totally unable* to come to any creative work, not even the tiniest bit of composition, because I am always on the train; in some months I have twenty-four concerts! This concert work would increase and increase, as currently all indications are pointing this way! That this cannot continue without my suffering seriously as a composer is self-evident! On the other hand, one should realise that it is precisely the *personal* publicity, insofar as I don't exactly play the piano badly, which is so vitally important and that it has, especially in my case, proved itself to be *so very* important.

As I feel within myself the irresistible urge to work and work, so I permit myself with proper heartfelt and warmest thanks, together with my unqualified and complete admiration for your idealistic conscience, to accept your extremely kind proposal!

He went on to ask permission for twelve concerts (not ten), between 1st April, 1907 and 31st March, 1908, so that he could play his works in Leipzig, Vienna, Frankfurt/M, Bremen, Cologne, Brussels, Cassel, Basel, Zürich, St Petersburg, Moscow, possibly Heidelberg and Dresden where he was already under contract for 1907/8, '...which is of the *greatest* importance! Because, as well as making my own publicity, I must create a tradition, so that all will know, *how* I want my works to be played. And this tradition is *absolutely vital...*' He ended with a PS emphasising the importance of performing his works himself:

Regarding *tradition*, I can tell you that Op 94 was received *excellently* in Berlin and St Petersburg, because I myself played the pieces; *now* the people know how Op 94 is intended.

In fact, Reger was unable to resist the lure of concert engagements, and greatly exceeded the agreed twelve concerts in the one year. Hinrichsen accepted this with understanding and did not withdraw his generous support.

1907

Before the year was up, Reger had been offered the post of teacher of composition at the Leipzig Conservatory of Music and that of Director of Music of the University of Leipzig; he moved from Munich, which he had grown to hate, to Leipzig on 23rd March to take up his post.

Hinrichsen had said that he did not want his name to be mentioned, but the association was obviously strengthened through his totally unexpected and uncalled-for generosity and Reger tried to loosen his ties with Lauterbach & Kuhn. It was whilst Reger was composing his Violin Concerto, which was to be a serious major work, without any 'technical fooling around' that the composer proposed 'a much closer co-operation'. On 8th July, 1907 Reger suggested coming under a permanent contract to C F Peters, as he wanted them to publish all his music. He said that his contract with Lauterbach & Kuhn was merely a verbal one which could be cancelled at any time. Reger's proposition came the day following a major change in his circumstances, when he would have wished to make secure financial provision for his future. The Regers' marriage had remained childless and they had just adopted a two-year-old foundling child, Marie-Marta, called Christa [Fig 17]. A contract was prepared between C F Peters and Max Reger; completed on 17th July, 1907, it was designed to take effect from 1st January, 1908, and to give Reger a guaranteed income until 1911.

Barely was the contract signed, when it became apparent that Reger had 'made a mistake' and that Lauterbach & Kuhn had no intention of foregoing their agreed rights; their contract had been 'for life'. In spite of the fact that collaboration since the composition of the *Sinfonietta* had become somewhat unproductive, with comments from the publishers of unsaleability, and requests that Reger should compose shorter, more saleable piano pieces and simple pieces instead of large symphonic works, they did not want to release the composer from his contract.

Reger had thus formally entered into a contract with two publishers, even though he had no right to be contracted to C F Peters; if his works were published by Lauterbach & Kuhn, then C F Peters could register a protest, and if he gave his works to Peters, then Lauterbach & Kuhn would object. Even the lawyer appointed by Henri Hinrichsen, Felix Zehme, was unable to extricate Reger from his contract with Lauterbach & Kuhn. Reger was unwillingly forced into a new contract with them which bound him until 13th December, 1913.

C F Peters eventually gave in and declared their contract with Reger to be null and void. An agreement was reached with a new contract in December 1907, which obliged Reger to offer C F Peters everything which Lauterbach & Kuhn rejected. Hinrichsen's heartfelt hope, expressed in his letter of 6th September, 1907 to Reger: 'that many large-scale works, written with your heart's-blood (but not to order) will be included', confirms his faith in Reger as a composer of major works.

1908

Before Reger's contract was due to expire, Lauterbach & Kuhn decided to sell their business. It was offered to C F Peters for 400,000M; Hinrichsen countered this with an offer of 230,000M which was turned down on 20th November, 1908. The business was then sold to Bote & Bock of Berlin for 250,000M.

In spite of the legal complications over the contract between Reger and C F Peters, brought about by the sale to Bote & Bock, the friendship between Max Reger and Henri Hinrichsen deepened. The letters and cards show Hinrichsen's generous, altruistic and friendly concern for his frantically driven protégé. Reger had settled into his new post at the Leipzig Conservatory of Music and on 1st October, 1907 he wrote to Henri Hinrichsen:

> I insist upon thanking you once again most warmly for your generous gift...I will *never* forget you for the unselfish, idealistic manner in which you want to insure that I can write my 'Heart's blood' works! So, a thousand warmest, deepest thanks!...

> Concerning the Violin Concerto, of course there will be people who are frightened off by the seriousness of the thing! But one does accustom oneself pretty quickly to artistic seriousness! And above all – we are now living in a Violinists' generation, in which one learns – stimulated by Joachim's immortal example – that virtuoso junk means nothing when compared with *serious* art!...

Reger became involved with Henri Hinrichsen's growing family. He composed a Serenade for Walter, the fourth child and second son, who was born on 23rd September, 1907. Reger had written the beginning of a *Wiegenlied* in Martha Hinrichsen's album in May 1907. Now he sent her the completed version of the *Wiegendlied, Schlaf, Kindlein, balde'* (Cradle Song, Sleep baby, soon), with the dedication: *Frau Martha Hinrichsen für Walter* (Mrs Martha Hinrichsen for Walter). C F Peters published the *Wiegenlied* in 1909 [Fig 18].

A frequent guest in the Hinrichsen's home, Reger was always grateful for Hinrichsen's generosity. He wrote in a letter dated 6th January, 1909 to Adolf Wach:[5] '...Mr. Hinrichsen has always been very decent to me; he has always paid me very well, and my latest agreements with him are such that no other living composer, receives such fantastic honoraria as he pays me...'

The composer knew that his Violin Concerto would be difficult for an audience to assimilate and desperately wanted Henri Hinrichsen, who had had so much faith in him, to try and appreciate its merits. The first performance, with Professor Henri Marteau from Berlin, to whom the Concerto was dedicated, as soloist and Arthur Nikisch conducting the Gewandhaus Orchestra, was due to take place in the Gewandhaus in Leipzig on Thursday 15th October, 1908. Reger urged Hinrichsen to attend the final rehearsal.

Whilst the critics praised Marteau's superb artistry in performance, they were less keen on the Concerto itself. They found it technically difficult, unendurably long, and felt it was absolutely ridiculous to allow a solo instrument to play for such a long stretch alone.

Hinrichsen sent Christmas presents for Reger's children. The composer sent a postcard of profuse thanks – his third communication on 24th December – apologising for the brevity of the note and explaining that he was heavily at work. He could not even tear himself away from his composing on Christmas Eve, such was his addiction to work. However, when he joined Henri Hinrichsen's regular Skat[6] afternoon on the following Sunday, 27th December, along with Karl Straube and others, he brought with him the completed score of his Op 108, the *Symphonic Prologue to a Tragedy*.

1909

Reger's *Symphonic Prologue to a Tragedy*, Op 108 [Fig 19] was published coincidentally with the composer's thirty-sixth birthday. It received its world première, under the baton of Fritz Steinbach in Cologne, on 9th March, 1909. The critics regarded it as a progressive step in Reger's compositional output, though they felt it was somewhat sombre and rather long.

Reger tried several different ways of shortening the work, in different concerts, until he arrived at a definitive version in 1912. However, he made no compromises at the first performance which he conducted in Leipzig on 18th March, 1909, though he did not expect much comprehension from the Leipzig audience.

Max Reger wrote to Henri Hinrichsen frequently during his years in Leipzig. He kept up a veritable bombardment of letters and postcards during the rehearsals of his *Prologue* in Leipzig, sending constant reports of his progress, the orchestra's behaviour and others' opinions of the work, as well as exhortations to come to rehearsals and to come to the artists' room after the performance. The work made a great impression on Karl Straube and on Hermann Roth, a music critic in Leipzig from 1907-1910. He wrote a very instructive Introduction to the *Prologue*, which was published in 1909 by C F Peters under the title of *Max Reger Symphonischer Prolog zu einer Tragödie. Einführung* (Max Reger Symphonic Prologue to a Tragedy. Introduction).

Reger was composing his String Quartet, Op 109 and completing his Clarinet Sonata, Op 107 at this time. He wrote to Henri Hinrichsen on 28th March, 1909 about the success of his *Prologue* in Dresden, which he had attended on 26th March. This was the fifth performance of his new work within three weeks. (In the following season – 1909-10 there were at least thirteen performances.) By 2nd May, Reger had completed the four handed piano score of his *Prologue*.

The composer was still giving his courses at the Conservatory and helping aspiring young composers. After a pleasant evening at the

Hinrichsens, Reger wrote to his publisher the following day, on 24th July, 1909:

> Yesterday evening at your house was so delightful and I feel so well, that I was once more at my desk working, at 8.27 this morning. The Violin Concerto, ordered from Zürich, is brilliant, *especially* because it is once again the *young* who are accepting it.[7] Whether people such as Halir, Moser[8] etc. are interested in my Violin Concerto, is entirely irrelevant; for my works it is the young, or at least those of my age who should commit themselves; that this is the case, is for both of us *you and I* the main thing! In ten years my Violin Concerto will be popular, that means that every decent violinist should play it. Friend Marteau, one year younger than I, will by that time have taught a respectable number of violinists. That is the way; to be connected now with people such as the extremely young Zürich leader, etc. etc....

Holidays for the composer were a time of renewed creative activity and long letters and postcards continued to flow to Henri Hinrichsen from Kolberg on the Baltic Coast, where Reger took his family between 9th August and 20th September, 1909. He detailed his work and demanded proofs to read! He wrote on 17th August, 1909: '...We are sitting at the Baltic Coast; I work and bathe and have a dreadful cold...I am awaiting with greatest longing, the proofs of the *Psalm 100*!!!!...' His publisher obliged by sending them the following day. He completed the corrections, which he returned with a long letter and pages of notation, within three days.

Whilst Reger was on holiday, Henri and Martha Hinrichsen's fifth child – their third son – Hans-Joachim, was born on 22nd August, 1909. The composer responded immediately, by dedicating a second cradle song to the mother. The *Abendlied* (Evening Song), Op 76, No 39, whilst being dedicated to Martha Hinrichsen was included in Volume IV of *Schlichte Weisen* (Simple Tunes) sent to Bote & Bock for publication on 16th July, and which appeared in September. Reger sent the manuscript to the dedicatee after its return to him.

Max Reger's compositions were difficult – difficult to play, difficult to listen to and hence difficult to sell. They were expensive to print, and were also expensive for a publisher to purchase from the composer. By this time, Hinrichsen had made a considerable investment in Reger and was yet to see any tangible return, let alone experience any profit. This subject was discussed during a conversation between Reger and Hinrichsen on 31st October, 1909, and prompted the following letter from the composer on the same day:

Dear Mr Hinrichsen!

Following on from our conversation of today, I would like to ask you not to reproach me for the fact that my works are so rarely bought!

Concerning the Violin Concerto! I believe *you know* me well enough that you should know with how much seriousness and dedication I work, that I am modest in respect of my fees when compared for example to R Strauss, but nothing gets me more worked up or hurts me more than when you tell me, for example, that the sales of my Violin Concerto leave much to be desired. Please don't let me go through all *that* again, which I experienced with Lauterbach & Kuhn, with their endless complaints about the unsaleability of my works. I myself am the *last* not to know precisely that the return on my works does not *yet* immediately cover *all the costs* – but: don't you have the copyright until thirty years after my death?! I am hurt to think that you are making a *sacrifice* for me, a sacrifice for which you may believe that the money is lost. I would then prefer not to compose *anything* any more and to devote myself entirely to a career as a conductor and to playing the piano, whereby I would earn *more* than I do as a composer! That my music is not bad, not *as* bad as Mr Niemann makes out, I know full well – I would not otherwise *daily* receive *orders from all publishers*. Your friendship is so important to me that I do not want this to be in any way impaired through mutual distrust.

With Best Wishes from house to house,

Your very devoted Reger

Hinrichsen's reply on 2nd November, 1909 expresses his regret at having hurt his friend's feelings. He suggested that if in future the composer felt offended at anything, then he should tell him 'by word of mouth'.

1910

Henri Hinrichsen had bought Stieler's portrait of Beethoven in February, 1909. He had had a limited number of reproductions produced which he presented to a few select friends, one of whom was Max Reger. The composer found it on his return from Dresden and wrote to Hinrichsen on 5th February, 1910:

Heavens above: you have surprised me *delightfully, most delightfully*; just returned from the 'Vengeance-music' of *Elektra*, I find Beethoven, working on the *Missa Solemnis*! How else can this sign work on me?! First and foremost, be thanked, be well and truly thanked; I am very, very, very proud to have this excellent reproduction, which is otherwise not obtainable and thank you most sincerely, many times. I have already got the exact place in my study where the picture will hang; it is 'sacred' territory; *Death mask* of Brahms, R Wagner, a splinter from Beethoven's coffin, – that's where the picture, about which I am incredibly happy, will hang!

Please keep **absolutely** silent about the death mask of R Wagner! I have it! But **nobody** is to know!..."

The world première of *Psalm 100,* which Reger conducted in Chemnitz on 23rd February, was received with great acclaim by public and critics. In his letter of congratulation of 25th February, 1910, Hinrichsen told the composer how much he was looking forward to hearing the work in Leipzig.

Apart from Reger's own successful efforts at self-promotion, he had a lot of admirers, friends and sponsors. This enthusiasm lead to the idea of devising a retrospective Reger Festival in Dortmund for the 7th, 8th and 9th of May, 1910. Henri Hinrichsen was one of the major sponsors.

1911

Max Reger knew that his phenomenal creative output was in the best publishing hands with Henri Hinrichsen and was always profuse in his thanks to the publisher for the superb presentation and production of the scores. The Cello Sonata, Op 116 was issued by C F Peters at the beginning of 1911, its popularity proved such that it was reprinted in November the following year. When Reger received the first copy, he expressed his admiration and delight at the quality of the production in an undated letter of about 28th December, 1910, promising that he would promote it with all his energy.

The Cello Sonata was first performed in the Gewandhaus on 3rd April, 1911 by Julius Klengel, to whom the work is dedicated, accompanied by Leonid Kreutzer. Reger included the successful work in his concert tour of October 1911 in several towns, with different partners playing the cello, and retained it in his repertoire until his death. He and Philipp Wolfrum who conducted all of Reger's works composed from 1896 onwards, including many premières, played in sixteen towns to capacity audiences and huge acclaim in November 1911.

Following the success of the Reger Festival in Dortmund the previous year, the Reger Festival of 11th May, 1911 in Darmstadt was an equal triumph for the composer, his *Psalm No 100* having to be repeated twice. Baron Heyl von Herrensheim in Darmstadt hosted a celebratory dinner for eighteen people in Reger's honour to which Henri Hinrichsen was invited, along with the Grand Duke and Grand Duchess of Hessen.

Reger completed his String Quartet, Op 121 for C F Peters on 2nd July, 1911 in spite of a constant schedule of concerts and travels. He dedicated the work to the Bohemian String Quartet of Prague who were to perform it in Leipzig on 29th October; though the première was in Dresden on 11th October.

Reger's time in Leipzig drew to a close with the first performance of his String Quartet. The place which had started so well for him and which had been the site of one of his most productive and satisfying periods creatively, had turned out to be the place in which he considered himself to have been the most greatly despised. Thus his call to direct the orchestra at the Court of Meiningen from 1st December, was timely and welcome; though Hinrichsen could foresee the pressures only too well and advised him to consider all aspects carefully.

1912

Reger continued to make arrangements and to compose for C F Peters and came to Leipzig for his weekly days at the Conservatory of Music when he would often meet Hinrichsen socially, for business discussions, games of Skat and visits to their favourite restaurants. Hinrichsen travelled to performances of those of Reger's works which he had published. He attended the Meiningen performance on 15th October, 1912 of Reger's new work, *An die Hoffnung* (To Hope), Op 124, which he had recently published, even though this entailed a four-hour train journey each way. He also attended the performance of the *Ballet Suite* in Magdeburg amongst others.

When Henri and Martha Hinrichsen's sixth child, Paul, was born on 18th December, 1912. Max Reger wrote on 30th December congratulating the new parents: '...that's marvellous, a son; you see, now the future of the House of Hinrichsen is assured...'

There is no security in hope; Paul was to be hideously murdered in the gas chambers of Auschwitz thirty-one years later.

1914

Reger completed the arrangements of Wagner overtures for two pianos during 1913, and C F Peters published them as soon as the thirty-year copyright period for Wagner's works had expired. Entitled *Auserlesenen Stücke aus Opern* (Selected Pieces from Operas) for two Pianos, he received them in January. In his letter of 23rd January, 1914, thanking Henri Hinrichsen, he mentioned his new contract with Simrock, which he was due to sign the following day, emphasising that he had insisted on a clause allowing him to offer one major work a year to C F Peters.

Reger suffered a nervous breakdown from overwork and decided to give up his Meiningen post; his friend Fritz Stein was to replace him. The old Duke Georg of Meiningen died, aged eighty-eight, on 25th June, 1914. He had been a great patron of the arts and had sponsored the excellent Meiningen Court orchestra. However, his son and heir, Prince Bernhard von Sachsen-Meiningen, lacked the old man's cultural tastes. Shortly after the War started the new Duke disbanded the orchestra and gave all members who were not on the permanent staff notice to leave. Reger was devastated and immediately set to, in order to raise money, by giving concerts for the benefit of the sacked musicians and by asking for donations. As in the past when he had wanted support for somebody, he appealed to Henri Hinrichsen.

Reger knew that his friend and benefactor would not let him down, but, as Hinrichsen had no responsibility whatsoever towards the Meiningen Court Orchestra, he had not anticipated the extent of his friend's support for its players. Hinrichsen sent a cheque for 1000M by return, on 22nd August, 1914 and asked that his name should not be mentioned; Reger should say that the money was sent for distribution by a citizen of Leipzig.

On 6th September Reger sent Henri Hinrichsen his *12 Sacred Songs* for solo voice with piano or organ or harmonium accompaniment, Op 137, with the request that they be immediately engraved. He wrote that Hinrichsen could keep the manuscript after publication. His publisher welcomed the new composition, though he found it difficult to decide about publishing new works to the extent to which he had done during peace time; the music dealers were not interested in anything new. However, for Reger he would make an exception and the work would be issued in September of the following year, hopefully together with Reger's 1915 composition for C F Peters.

1915

The Regers moved happily into their new home in Jena in March 1915. It was the first home Reger had actually owned and he was keen that Martha and Henri Hinrichsen should visit him as soon as possible. He was planning to offer C F Peters another original work during the summer and in the meantime he sent an orchestral arrangement of J S Bach's *Prelude and Fugue* in C minor from the *Well-Tempered Klavier*.

Whilst Hinrichsen accepted the arrangement and paid the fee which Reger asked, he pointed out that as business was poor during the war he did not want to issue any more new arrangements at that time. He never did publish it. However, he would be happy to accept a new original work from Reger for publication, and he and his wife were looking forward to visiting the Regers in their new home in Jena. By the end of April Reger had offered him his Op 141a, *Serenade* (G maj) for flute, violin and viola, and Op 141b *Trio* (B min) for violin, viola and cello – the two works belonging together. Hinrichsen was pleased to accept the works, with the remark that 'it is exactly chamber music works such as these which fit so well into the C F Peters catalogue.' Reger graciously presented his publisher with the manuscripts as was his custom.

By 1st August the impatient composer was demanding proofs of his works for correction, even though they were not due to appear for another year. The patient publisher remind him gently on 3rd August: '...with reference to your remarks, I must mention that war-time conditions reign even amongst engravers, printers and editors and that therefore I will not be able to send you the proofs of your *Bach-Reger Suite*, which, as I wrote you will not be issued until the autumn of 1916...' However, he then asked Reger whether he would like to prepare a new edition of Bach's *Well-Tempered Klavier*. He felt that, even though C F Peters had already published four different editions over the years, an edition by Reger would cause considerable interest in the musical world. Reger accepted the commission with pleasure and promised it for the following May. He never got around to producing the work.

1916

Max Reger forced himself to go through with a strenuous tour of fifty-six concerts throughout Germany and Holland between October 1915 and April 1916. Once back in Jena, he continued to work at his compositions and arrangements as though driven by the need to complete as much as was humanly possible in the little time left to him. He wrote to Hinrichsen on 13th April, 1916: '...I am sitting here 10,000 miles deep in work! Hence please excuse the haste...' Complying with his promise to offer one original composition to C F Peters every year, the work which Reger offered on 7th May, for publication in 1916 was to be an improvement on his overlong Violin Concerto: *Andante and Rondo Capriccioso* for violin with accompaniment of small orchestra (or with piano accompaniment), Op 147. He suggested visiting his publisher: 'next Wednesday, 10th May at 8.00 p.m.; then I must leave at 9.30 p.m.!'

Reger's visit in Leipzig on the evening of Wednesday 10th May, 1916, after taking his usual classes in the Conservatory of Music, was his last visit to C F Peters and his last dinner with Martha and Henri Hinrichsen and their older children, in the Talstrasse. After dinner Max Reger's namesake, the almost fifteen-year-old Max Hinrichsen escorted the composer to meet his friends, Karl Straube and others, at the Café Hannes.

He was apparently excited about showing them his work in progress – the *Andante and Rondo Capriccioso*. His friend Fritz Stein reported that there was nothing in his behaviour to indicate that this was to be his last evening. But, shortly after 11.00 p.m. he began to feel unwell and a doctor was called, who gave him a morphine injection. Straube took him back to the Hotel Hentschel where he was staying, put him to bed and offered to stay the night. But Reger said he would be all right. When the doctor arrived in the morning, he found the composer, having died painlessly from an acute heart attack, sitting up in bed, his glasses perched on his nose, with the bedside light on and with the newspaper propped up in front of him. On the bedside table lay the proofs of his *Sacred Songs*, Op 138 opened at the first choral entry:

> 'Man lives and exists for only a short while, and the whole world dies with all its splendour.'

Max Reger was just forty-three years old when he died.

Henri Hinrichsen mourned with Elsa Reger at her husband's bedside and was close to her over the following days. He wrote to her, in response to her letter, giving expression to his feelings, either on 24th or on 27th May, 1916: (Two copy letters, with slightly different wording and intent are preserved in the copybooks of C F Peters. It is not clear which version was actually sent.)

Dear Mrs Reger,

Today fourteen days have passed, since your dear husband visited me for the last time and on which occasion I had the great pleasure of enjoying a more relaxed conversation with the dear departed Master than had been the case for a long time. This last meeting will remain for ever in my memory, because of the surprisingly sudden, and for the whole music world, deeply painful catastrophe, the thought will always be with me that for me it was a particularly lucky stroke of fate, to have been alone with Reger on the last evening of his life, and in fact to have been the last person to have seen him in full bodily health. In answer to Professor Stein's question, I can tell him that Reger arrived here punctually at 8.00 p.m. and, having eaten his dinner with great pleasure, enjoyed an evening of conversation with me until he left at 9.45 p.m. He said then, that he had arranged to meet some friends in the Café Hannes.

Concerning the remainder of the letter, I can give you the information myself, dear Mrs Reger, that Reger offered me, on 7th May, Op 147 (probably his last work) *Andante & Rondo Capriccioso* for Violin and Orchestra as well as piano accompaniment for a fee of 2,500M, and that I, as you know, accepted it by telegram. He wrote me at the time that the score was completed but that he still had to make the piano accompaniment. If you have nothing against it, I will permit myself to send you the full fee, even though the piano part is missing. As soon as I am in possession of the score, I will have it engraved and then commission the arrangement to be produced.

More difficult, however, is the question of the *Well-tempered Klavier*, about which Reger told me on the last evening, that he still had to revise the first volume, whilst he had not yet started work on the second volume. It is probable that he had intended to complete the second volume in the summer of 1917. I would be very grateful to you if you would ask Professor Stein or Straube to report to me on the *Well-tempered Klavier*, in their customary manner. As the suggestion for this edition came from C F Peters, I am of course interested in its fate...

The copy letter of 27th May states:

...Concerning the remainder of the letter, you will know that C F Peters was offered Op 147 and the edited version of the *Well-tempered Klavier*. I maintain my right to both these works for the time being, until Professors Stein and Straube have given me their report, after which I will permit myself to give you a definitive decision...

Henri Hinrichsen then went on to discuss, in reply to her question, the merits or otherwise of publishing a thematic catalogue of Reger's works so soon after his death.

Elsa Reger was moved to reply on 11th June, 1916:

Dear Mr Hinrichsen!

Very many thanks for your kind letter and for the sheet music. Yes indeed, how much work my husband still had to complete;

how happy he was every time he had a new inspiration. I repeat what I have already told you, *you* never ever gave my husband a difficult hour, and I will never forget that, and will always retain grateful feelings towards your house.

…

I also want to build on the creation of his artistic genius; from 1917 onwards house concerts of Reger's music will be given on two successive afternoons every summer, here, in the Reger House. I will invite all those who loved him and who will grow to love him. And so his word will continue to sound in the house which his diligence built. After my death, his house will be held in trust, like the houses of Bach, Mozart, Beethoven, Liszt. I am sure you will be pleased and interested to hear all this. Like my married life which was consecrated to Reger, so will I dedicate my lonely life to him, only in this way will it be bearable.

With friendliest greetings to you and your loved ones
from your devoted
Elsa Reger

Henri Hinrichsen commissioned the sculptor Carl Seffner to carve a bust of Reger in marble, from his death mask. He continued his friendship and financial support for Elsa Reger for many years, until it became impossible for him to so. She survived her husband by forty years.

Henri Hinrichsen, who remained a firm believer in Reger's genius and never ceased to feel that a time would come when this would be universally recognised, wrote about him in his *Chronik*:

He worked tirelessly until his last day. This explains Reger's prodigious productivity, which borders on the incredible, bearing in mind his strenuous concert/conducting/ and teaching involvements on the one hand, and the subtle variety of his works, especially harmonically, on the other hand. He had an iron determination and barely allowed himself any rest, however much his wife and his friends, who included Duke Georg von Meiningen, asked him to slow down.

---

1   The Copy Books are now in the 'Bestand C F Peters' in the Staatsarchiv Leipzig. Most letters to Reger are in the books of *Internationalen Autorenkorrespondenz* (International Author's Correspondence) 1898-1916/7 (StAL 5032-5036). A few (7) come under *Internationalen Geschäftskorrespondenz* (International Business Correspondence) (StAL 5051, 5052, 5160, 5167, 5170).

2 *Briefe eines deutschen Meisters* (Letters from a German Master), edited by Elsa von
   Hase-Koehler, published by Koehler & Amelang, 1928.
3 Henri Hinrichsen's son, Walter Hinrichsen, apparently took 299 letters to USA
   in 1945. All the letters and cards have now been traced to various libraries: The
   Max-Reger-Institut bought ten letters and one postcard at auction in 1971; in
   1988 the Bayerische Staatsbibliothek bought, also at auction, 235 letters and
   183 postcards. Thirty-two postcards remained in Leipzig and are now in the
   'Bestand C F Peters' in the Staatsarchiv Leipzig (StAL 673); one postcard is in
   the possession of the author.
4 *Max Reger – Briefwechsel mit dem Verlag C F Peters* (Max Reger – Correspondence
   with C F Peters Publishers). Edited by Susanne Popp and Susanne Shigihara in
   a publication of the Max-Reger-Institute, Elsa-Reger-Stiftung, Bonn. Published
   by Ferd. Dümmlers Verlag, Bonn. 1995.
5 Quoted in *Max Reger – Briefe eines deutschen Meisters*. Published by Koehler &
   Amelang, Leipzig, 1928.
6 Skat is a very popular card game.
7 The Dutch violinist Willem de Boer (1885-?), pupil of Carl Flesch, leader of the
   orchestra in Zürich and member of the Zürich String Quartet, had got to know
   Reger when they shared the platform at a concert in Zürich on 13th November
   1908, performed Reger's Violin Concerto under Volkmar Andreae on 17th
   January 1911.
8 Carl Halir (1859-1909) Bohemian violinist and student of Joachim, who had
   earlier performed quite often with Reger to whom Reger had dedicated his
   fourth Sonata for Solo Violin Op 19. Andreas Moser (1859-1925), also student
   of Joachim, taught from 1888-1924 at the Berlin Conservatory.

CHAPTER EIGHT

Arnold Schönberg's Five Orchestral Pieces

Henri Hinrichsen, as we have seen, was prevented from publishing much music by Max Reger and had only been able to publish one work by Gustav Mahler. He needed a recognised contemporary composer to fill the void left by the death of Edvard Grieg in 1907. Mahler had been dead five months when the publisher made his next approach to a major composer, Arnold Schönberg. This letter, dated 12th October, 1911[1], was the beginning of what was to become a copious correspondence which continued until shortly before the outbreak of the Second World War.

Schönberg expressed his delighted surprise when he replied to the publisher's query as to whether he was totally committed to one publisher. In his reply of 19th October, he said that whilst he was tied up with a contract with Universal Edition of Vienna, he felt that he was able to offer a number of works to C F Peters. He listed six works, one of which was *Orchesterstücke* (Orchestral Pieces) (five short) approximately sixty pages and continued:

> Now I must ask you for something. Perhaps you do not know that my musical notation looks so unusual, that even the best musicians can get no clear idea of the sound and the effect, from looking at it. Even Gustav Mahler said of my IInd Quartet 'that he could not read these *four* lines'. – Naturally, young composers can play my music straight from the sheet. – With this long explanation I only wanted to say to you that (please do not take this as arrogance, I am merely stating a fact), one must acquire my things without looking at them, taking them only on trust from the person who speaks through them, because the opinions of musicians generally fail in this respect. Quite simply: The fewest have, like Mahler, the courage to admit that they cannot read it and misjudge the work which they *do not know.*

I am naturally prepared to send you the respective works on approval. But I only wanted to forestall the situation that, any 'equally good musician' should lose his teeth over it, without even arriving at the kernel.

A rejection of my work by you would do me no good with Universal Edition, who do a lot for me, but who unfortunately are somewhat timid. Therefore, I would rather send you the music first and then approach Universal Edition to ask them to allow me to give it to you.

He went on to ask which works Hinrichsen would like to see. Hinrichsen replied by return, on 23rd October, pointing out that his enquiry had been whether in principle Schönberg was free to let him have any works. He said that there was no hurry, as his new issues generally appeared in September and that, if he heard from Schönberg in the spring, that would be sufficient. He continued by outlining the type of music he was interested in publishing:

I am well aware of the fact that most of our musicians are 'afraid' of your work and mark it with three crosses (but not musical ones), but it doesn't worry me. It is considerably more difficult for me to find works of a sort which are particularly suitable for the Edition Peters. – That means: orchestral music is not my main field – I also do not like publishing songs, as it is almost impossible to sell anything with the wealth of new issues abounding – however, apart from piano music I always welcome chamber music of all sorts (violin and piano, V'cello and piano, trios, piano or string quartets). Hence, from the works which you suggest, I would be interested in the five short orchestral pieces and possibly also the piano works...

Schönberg didn't wait for the spring and replied on 18th January, 1912 enclosing the original manuscript full scores of two works which he was free to offer: *Chamber Symphony* (for fifteen solo instruments) and *Five Orchestral Pieces*. He asked Hinrichsen for a reply within eight days, reminding him that there was no point in asking other musicians for an opinion as to the merits of the works, and that this would only waste time and would not lead to anything. Hinrichsen replied by return, on 20th January, rejecting the *Chamber Symphony* and making his offer for the *Five Orchestral Pieces*:

You give me the manuscript of the *Five Orchestral Pieces* with all rights, except the performing right, which will go to the

Genossenschaft Deutscher Tonkünstler (Society of German Composers) of which I am a member, for a fee of 600M on delivery of the manuscript.

In fixing the fee, I have to take into account the fact that a publication of this sort only has any sense if the score – in a suitable form for study purposes – is well engraved and as cheaply priced as possible, so that all those who should want to master it, can afford to do so. One must be prepared to present the whole material free of charge for performance to four first-class orchestras and the hand-written parts should be available as cheaply as is feasible, in order to encourage as many orchestras as possible to 'take the risk' of buying it.

The publisher went on to ask whether Schönberg considered it suitable to produce a version for piano solo, or for piano four hands, which would help to make the work better known. He also wanted to know whether the composer had contacts with conductors who might be interested in performing the work if he supplied the material free of charge.

Whilst the thirty-five-year-old Schönberg was disappointed that the fee was not higher, he felt that it was an honour to be published in the Edition Peters. However, he asked in his reply of 21st January, whether he could be granted a percentage of the profits, or some further payment in due course, saying that this was not a condition, but a plea. He was pleased at Hinrichsen's generous offer to give the material free of charge to four orchestras and hoped that soon the work would become so popular that this would no longer be necessary. He pointed out that his works were now being performed by a number of conductors and orchestras including Koussevitzky. He went on to discuss details about possible piano arrangements and to suggest various conductors.

On 22nd January Hinrichsen sent Schönberg the agreed fee and said that it was his principle never to pay a percentage, as this was always open to disagreement. He appreciated Schönberg's business-like attitude and said he would pay him a repeat of the full fee of 600M if the orchestral material were ordered fifteen times within the next five years. He wanted Schönberg to give the work an Opus number and an overall title, and asked him to consider giving titles to the five separate pieces; this would look better in the catalogue, and was more likely to encourage interest. He rejected the arrangement for piano eight hands but would consider an arrangement for two pianos four hands, for which he offered 200M.

Schönberg's reply of 24th January gave the *Five Orchestral Pieces* the Opus number 16. He did not want to give each individual piece a title. He would consider an arrangement for two pianos which he would either do himself, or ask another composer to do and he suggested four conductors to whom Hinrichsen could send the orchestral material.

In his reply of 26th January Hinrichsen announced his visit to Berlin on the 31st, and invited the composer for a rendezvous at Habel, Unter den Linden between 5.30 and seven p.m. He regretted that Schönberg felt unable to suggest titles for the five pieces. His long years of experience in publishing had shown him that compositions which went under the title of *Stück* (Piece), were virtually unsaleable; works by Reger and Sinding without title, compared to those with title, were never ordered. He continued:

> Conductors as well as audience, need to be aroused to some anticipation of the music, apart from the name of the composer, through its title, which should give some form of suggestion as to the type of response they might expect to make. The title does not need to give a programme – but still something more than 'Five Orchestral Pieces Number 3'. You will not find such descriptions either in the music of the classical composers or with modern composers. So please think it over again whether it is not possible to give some sort of general title such as Cheerful, Serious Thoughts, – Episodes, Elegiac Tunes or something similar. You can be assured that such a 'concession' would also be in your interest.

Schönberg did not want to choose an overall title for the *Five Orchestral Pieces* and was averse to the idea of titles for the individual pieces, as his diary entry for 27th January shows:

> Letter from Peters in which he gives me a rendezvous for Wednesday, in order to get to know me personally. Wants titles for the *Orchestra Pieces*; for technical reasons of publication. Maybe I will accede as I have found titles which could be possible. On the whole the idea does not appeal to me. Music is wonderful because one can say everything, so that the knowledgeable person understands everything and still one has one's secrets, which one does not admit to oneself, which are not spoken about. Titles chat though. Apart from which: whatever there is to say, has been said by the music. What need therefore of the word? If words were necessary, they would be included. But art says more than words. The titles

which I might give, chat, as they are in part extremely dark, partly technical, they say nothing. They are: I Anticipation (says nothing), II Past (everybody has that), III Piecework Coloration (technical), IV Peripeteia (is generally enough), V The Obligatory (perhaps better the 'executed' or the 'unending') Recitative. Anyway, with a comment that it concerns the publishing technology not the 'poetic' content.

When the two men met, Schönberg was generously entertained with the publisher's favourite luxury – caviar.

In Schönberg's next letter, on 11th March, 1912, he apologised for not yet having made the arrangement for two pianos, of his *Five Orchestral Pieces*. He explained that as he himself was not actually a pianist, he would like to ask his student, Dr Anton von Webern, whom he highly recommended, to take on the commission. He asked for four proof copies of the score to be sent to him as soon as possible: one for Dr Webern and three for himself, on which he wished to mark the corrections and various instructions to the engraver. Schönberg was fully aware of the difficulties posed by his music, not only to the performers, but also to the engraver and copyist when he wrote:

> As these pieces are difficult I would prefer, in the hope that you will not begrudge the slight additional expense, to have the parts produced in the way they were done for my second Quartet where (in the 3rd and 4th movement) each part carries an uninterrupted, miniaturised notation of what the rest of the orchestra is playing, over its own line. In this way, the player is able to read along, thus simplifying his own entrances and the organisation of the difficult rhythms. This method has proven very valuable to me and to several other younger composers. Please let me know whether you are in agreement with this.
>
> If not, then my markings will only indicate to the copyist how many cues and how many bars he must write for each instrument. I regard this as too important to be left to the copyist. They never do it to my satisfaction.

He asked what Hinrichsen had thought of the titles which he had recently suggested. The publisher did not like them, having hoped for something more down-to-earth and colloquial and decided not to use them. But he was agreeable to Webern making the arrangement for two pianos. The engraving of the score was carried out within a month and Schönberg was pleased with the result. He was also delighted that

Hinrichsen had set the price of the study score extremely low and had printed it in almost as large a format as the full score. He was unhappy with the look of the parts, as there was not enough room left for his cues and he gave copious instructions as to how they were to be presented. His wishes were scrupulously carried out.

Webern had sent two trial pages of the piano arrangements to Schönberg, who was disappointed with them. He wrote to Hinrichsen on 11th June:

Dear Sir,

Dr Webern sent me two trial pages, which look extremely bewildering. However, he assured me that these were the most complicated bars. I can't really judge that without seeing the music. If everything, or at least most of it looks like this, then that does not auger well. Against that though, we must consider that the instrumental instructions are not here to pander to curiosity, but are instructions for performance. Because the p of a flute or the p of a bassoon need a different description. I reckon therefore (and leave it up to you to decide):

That if a substantial number of places like that shown on the sample pages should become apparent, then it would be best to leave the instrumental instructions *out altogether*. However, if the picture only looks so complicated in a few places, then they can be left in. In any case, however: there is no point in removing them only partially. Because they are not superfluous only where there is not enough space, and more necessary where there is enough space. Anyway, I would ask you to tell me and Dr von Webern your decision…

As there was not enought space on the pages, the printer was instructed to engrave the piano arrangement without instrumental instructions.

Schönberg was working hard to try and get performances of his *Five Orchestral Pieces* and on 20th June he wrote to Henri Hinrichsen asking him to send free copies of the full score to seven different conductors, starting with Richard Strauss in Garmisch; he was not keen to perform the work.

The score was sent to Alexander Zemlinsky at the Deutsches Landestheater in Prague; Oskar Fried in Berlin; Arthur Bodanzky, Hofkapellmeister in Mannheim; Oskar Nedbal, Tonkünstler Orchester in Vienna, who had conducted Mahler's First, Third and Fourth symphonies with that orchestra; Siegmund von Hausegger conductor of the Philharmonic Concerts in Hamburg and the concerts of the Blüthner Orchestra in Berlin; and Gustav Brecher. These were conductors of about the same age as Schönberg, in their thirties.

Siegmund von Hausegger was totally bewildered by the work. He admitted in his letter of 29th October, 1912 that the *Pieces* were 'a foreign world' to him. Gustav Brecher felt much the same, when he returned the score on 26th April.

The score was also sent to Max von Schillings who studied it diligently, and was thrilled with it. In his position as Kapellmeister of the Royal Court Theatre in Stuttgart, he wrote to the publisher on 23rd September, 1912: '…This music, which has only for briefest moments, the faintest relationship to previously existing music, is of greatest artistic interest to me…' He borrowed the parts to try out with his orchestra. However, though von Schillings was thrilled with the music, he felt that he would not be doing the composer a service if he were to perform it. His orchestra had no understanding of it and he felt that his audience would certainly not accept it.

Schönberg found some mistakes in the printed score and immediately asked for corrections to be made to the engraved plates. But Hinrichsen's experience told him that composers would continually find cause to want corrections to the music which they themselves had passed for printing, as had so often been the case with Mahler's Fifth Symphony. Any alteration to the plates was a costly business and so he counselled the composer to start a sheet for corrections and to send it to him in another year. C F Peters started doing serious publicity for the work in September 1912, at which time the two-piano-version by Anton von Webern was also available. Scores and parts were sent to a number of conductors.

The world première of Schönberg's *Five Orchestral Pieces* came as a surprise to the composer, who only became aware of the intention through an unflattering announcement printed in *The Daily Telegraph* of 31st August, 1912. He sent this, together with a very irate letter, to the publisher on 4th September:

> I have just learnt from the enclosed newspaper clipping that the performance of my *Orchestral Pieces* will take place in London this week. I am very surprised and concerned that this is the *première* (!) and that nobody asked me whether I was agreeable to a première taking place in *London without my presence (!)* It is *almost impossible* that such a performance can succeed. I myself have never heard the pieces and do not know whether small alterations (etc.!) will be necessary. And now I don't even know who is to perform it; I don't know

whether the orchestra or the conductor will be good enough!!
Apart from that: I would have liked to have heard it myself!
Please will you therefore tell me the following:

   i   Who will perform it? Which orchestra, which
       conductor?
   ii Have these people received the right from you for
       the *first* performance?
  iii Were conditions set with regard to the minimum
       number of rehearsals? (Because this work cannot be
       performed without at least five rehearsals!)

I must say: whoever it is who is going to perform my *Pieces* in
London: it is quite wrong that I was not even asked by these
people. A lot will have been confusing to them with regard to
the tempi and the character of the *Pieces*. And it would be fair
to expect that an author would like to hear his works and
could expect to be invited. I must say, I find this performance
to be a malicious violation. Because it cuts deep into my
inalienable *artistic* interests.

Schönberg had never previously mentioned his interest in the first
performance; he may have assumed that it would be one of his European
conductor friends who would première the work and rehearse it in
full consultation with himself. Hinrichsen's reply to Schönberg's
outburst, of 5th September, was a generous expression of tact and
understanding, born of years of experience of placating temperamental
composers:

Dear Sir,

I regret to note from your letter of yesterday, that the London
performance of your *Five Orchestral Pieces* has caused you
frustration. – With symphonies and large orchestral works,
first performances play an important part and are generally
carried out in accordance with the composer's wishes, –
however, with smaller orchestral works this is rarely the case.
I was unaware that you laid especial importance on the first
performance, as you had never mentioned this in our
correspondence. My willingness to supply the orchestral
material free of charge to several orchestras gave you the
opportunity to control the first performance. I also permitted
myself to tell you on 26th August that the material had been
delivered to London and it would have been my pleasure to

have invited you to attend the concert at my expense, if you had expressed any fear, *by return of post*, that the performance without your presence would be a disaster. – I do not know the date of the concert, I only know that Henry Wood, the most important conductor in England, intended to perform the work (with large orchestra at that) – I therefore thought that Wood had a special interest in your works, if not a personal acquaintance with you.

He then pointed out that one does not give a specific right of performance and that whoever purchases the material, and pays the due fee to the *Genossenschaft* has the right to perform it. He felt that it would be impossible to impose a minimum number of rehearsals, and that the author, like the publisher should be happy if any performances take place. He continued:

I hope that your fears prove to be groundless and that Wood can perform the *Pieces* satisfactorily, in spite of their great difficulty. As an intervention on your part in London would now be too late, it seems to me that we should try and get a performance in Germany which would met with your intentions, as soon as possible and I look forward – with reference to my previous letter – to hearing your wishes in this respect.

Yours Sincerely, C F Peters

The first performance of Arnold Schönberg's *Five Orchestral Pieces*, Opus 16, took place on 3rd September, 1912 at a Promenade Concert in London, conducted by Sir Henry Wood. The critics, published in the papers of 4th September, were scathing:

The Times: 'It was like a Tibetan prayer; not a single soul in the hall could have understood it at first hearing.'

Daily Telegraph: 'New Work Hissed…Well put together music, form and contrast – two important things – are there, a richness of 'ugliness', 'beauty' died of starvation; pure, unexaggerated technical mastery.'

The Globe: 'Fantastic Novelty at Queen's Hall…The music was akin to the complaints of a martyred soul and reminded one of nothing more than the crazy delusions of delirium or the terrible fears of a hyper-nervous infant.'

Schönberg was not surprised at the audience's response which he commented upon in his letter to Hinrichsen on 7th September: '...In the meantime I have received the reviews from England, from which I see that the work made a great impression and had the usual success for my works: hearty booing and equally hearty applause...'

Hinrichsen told the composer that he thought that another performance was in preparation in London. He felt that a concerted effort to introduce the work should now be undertaken and arranged for his manager, Paul Ollendorff, to meet Schönberg in Berlin at the end of September, to discuss the question and work out a plan. So many study scores were sent to conductors, but to little avail, that a new printing was necessary and Hinrichsen asked Schönberg on 12th December to send him a list of any corrections – but only of mistakes in the engraving, so that the new edition would be correct.

In returning the corrected score to the publisher on 13th December, Schönberg wrote reassuringly:

> ...Do not be put out by the fact that there is no performance of the *Five Orchestral Pieces* in view. I profoundly hope that I can supersede the number of fifteen performances over the course of the next five years. The best example of this is my Symphonic Poem, *Pelleas and Melisande* which has so far received six performances...

In July 1913 Schönberg discussed with Hinrichsen the possibility of his conducting the new version of Mahler's Fifth Symphony in Austria. The publisher sent him the piano four hands arrangement which he had requested for study purposes. Nothing came of the proposed performance. He also asked for permission to make orchestral arrangements of some of Hugo Wolf's Lieder for a concert he was planning with the Dutch Lieder singer, Julia Culp.

In the meantime, there had still not been a second performance of the *Five Orchestral Pieces* and Schönberg decided to make even greater efforts to secure performances. He asked the publisher on 21st August, to send him a set of the parts for his personal use, which he intended to mark up with his corrections and use for all his future performances. He also requested that the score to be sent to Hermann Scherchen who might perform it in Berlin and asked about details of forthcoming performances of the work which he had heard about, which were proposed for Amsterdam and London. As before, he expressed his willingness to conduct it himself. The London concert, again organised by Henry Wood, was to take place in January 1914 and Wood invited Schönberg to conduct the work himself.

Schönberg came to Leipzig in March, when he was entertained by

Henri and Martha Hinrichsen at home. He conducted a performance of his *Gurrelieder* in the Gewandhaus on 6th March, which was rapturously received by an enthusiastic audience. This performance had been made possible through the initiative of his friend, Albertine Zehme, who took the part of the Speaker, and under the patronage of a committee of important people in the musical world, which included Henri Hinrichsen.

Schönberg went to Amsterdam a few days later, where his *Five Orchestral Pieces* were performed. He had his titles for the individual Pieces, slightly altered from his original ideas, noted in the programme, though, because of the publisher's objection, the titles had not been printed on the music. Titles were subsequently printed in the C F Peters catalogue as I: 'Vorgefühle' (Anticipations), II 'Vergangenes' (The Past), III 'Farben' (Colours), IV 'Peripetie' (Peripeteia), V 'Das Obligate Rezitativ' (The Obligatory Recitative) as Hinrichsen felt that even these titles were better than none at all, from the point of view of selling the work. However, in time, Schönberg altered some of these again.

The Amsterdam public was understandably confused by the work, though it appreciated the expertise of the orchestration and the first-class playing of their orchestra. A long review of the concert appeared in the *Leipziger Tageblatt* (Leipzig Daily Paper) of 16th March, 1914, an extract from which describes the audience's response: 'It is hardly surprising that after a first hearing, a greater success was not to be expected, because Schönberg appeared here as an original, totally eccentric innovator, whom it was absolutely impossible to follow.'

Though audiences were confused and the music was difficult, a few performances had taken place during the two years since its publication. Henri Hinrichsen still maintained a faith in this music, and in its composer, to whom he wrote on 19th March, 1914 with a generous indication of his confidence:

Dear Mr. Schönberg!

The Leipzig newspaper brought a report of the performance in Amsterdam, of your *Five Orchestral Pieces* which, understandably does not speak of as great an enthusiasm as your *Gurrelieder* enjoyed here. It none the less sounds sufficiently positive to give me pleasure. I am using this Major key to send you, already today – even though the orchestral material of your Opus 16 has only been requested six times – the remaining fee of 600M...

This was a considerable act of faith on the part of the publisher. He had invested a lot of money in the production of the work and in its publicity, for which he would not see a profit for a long time – if at all.

He had originally proposed to Schönberg to pay him a further 600M if the work were performed fifteen times within five years of publication. Now, after very few performances, and only two years, he was generously helping and encouraging the composer, who was overjoyed and wrote back immediately, on 20th March:

Dear Mr Hinrichsen,

Your noblesse gave me extreme pleasure. I am really very happy that I can at last make willing and participating friends happy through my music, and I am glad at last to have achieved recognition. And I regard it as a happy symbol that you, the one who likes it, feels inclined to give me pleasure. I feel like the words written in George's wonderful poem 'Entrückung' (Ecstasy) (which forms the basis for the fourth movement of my IInd Quartet):

'Ich bin der Funke nur vom heiligen Feuer,
ich bin ein Dröhnen nur der heiligen Stimme...'
(I am the spark only from the holy fire,
I am a roaring only of the holy voice...)

I want to tell all people who want to believe it, about the holy fire and if you greet me through friendship and participation, I want to take it impersonally and want to refer it to the object itself; I would like to wish that one could see something in me; the thing which I strive for: *to be a sounding expression of the human soul and its longing for God.*

It is in this sense that I am happy over recognition and friendship which is given to me: it belongs to the object.

Let me thank you once again most warmly and express the wish that you too will soon experience artistic pleasure from this work.

In deepest gratitude, I am, most respectfully,

Your,
Arnold Schönberg

In January 1915 Schönberg sent corrections which were to be incorporated in future editions of the work. However, at that time the work had still not achieved any sort of popularity. Due partly to conditions prevailing during the Great War, demand for it was virtually non-existent and no reprint was needed.

The harmonium player and composer Sigfrid Karg-Elert had edited an album of modern pieces for Harmonium for C F Peters in which he had included an arrangement of the second of Schönberg's *Orchestral Pieces*, leaving out the middle part. Before sending this to the engraver, Hinrichsen asked Schönberg whether he had any objection to the arrangement. Indeed the composer had the strongest objections as this extract from his letter dated 14th January, 1915 shows:

> I *cannot possibly give you my agreement* for the publication of the arrangement for harmonium of the second Orchestral Piece without the middle part. I cannot understand how Mr Karg-Elert, who is a first rate musician, could arrive at such an idea. It is a mutilation in extremely bad taste; a wartime idea! That's the kind of havoc the Russians wreak in East Prussia! No, please do not be upset with me, but that is *absolutely* impossible. Either complete, or not at all. One cannot take parts out of an artistic creation; if it is not feasible complete, then not at all. Surely you wouldn't think of publishing *Götterdämmerung* arranged for guitar and leaving out the 'difficult' bits.
>
> What is a person of artistic feelings and sensitivity for shape to think when he hears such a piece? That doesn't make any sense any more! He would obviously receive a completely wrong impression of the work...

Schönberg's outburst carried echoes of Beethoven's somewhat similar outburst of some hundred years earlier. When the collection was published, the arrangement was not included in it.

In October 1916, Schönberg was called up for military service. During this time he was involved in a legal wrangle with his publishers in Berlin, the Dreililien Verlag (later taken over by Richard Birnbach, Berlin). The matter was handled by Dr H Kirchberger, a partner in a firm of lawyers in Leipzig, who turned to Henri Hinrichsen in March 1918 for advice on publishing matters. Hinrichsen was eager to help Schönberg. The composer had moved from Berlin to Mödling, near Vienna and sent a prospectus for a series of open rehearsals which he was planning for his 'Chamber' Symphony. He wrote that he was hoping to undertake the same type of enterprise for the *Five Orchestral Pieces* the following year. Nothing came of this second plan.

In November 1918 Schönberg founded the *Verein für musikalische Privataufführungen* (Society for Private Musical Performances); music critics were excluded from attending its concerts, in order to get an unbiased hearing for new music. He was planning to promote his *Five Orchestral Pieces* amongst other compositions and asked Hinrichsen for the orchestral material to those and other works, including Max Reger's Violin Concerto.

By 1922 the *Five Orchestral Pieces* were finally accepted. They were being performed in Vienna, Amsterdam and London, amongst other places, to critical acclaim. At last, after ten years, the publisher could begin to see a return on his investment. He had bought the work outright from the composer, and had even paid him a repeat of the 600M originally agreed; he certainly owed him nothing more. But Hinrichsen laid great value on creative genius and felt that it should be continually rewarded. On 22nd February, 1922, he sent Schönberg a cheque with the following letter:

> Dear Mr Schönberg,
>
> Since your *Five Orchestral Pieces* have been performed several times recently, and I am personally convinced that they will become part of the backbone of the classical repertory, and they have already become a worthy addition to the Edition Peters, I permit myself to send you an honorarium as an expression of my pleasure and enclose a cheque in the sum of 3,000M. I ask you to accept it in as friendly a manner as I send it to you.
>
> With Warmest Greetings,
>
> Henri Hinrichsen

Schönberg's gratitude and happiness for Hinrichen's generosity was expressed in his letter of 1st March:

> Dear Mr Hinrichsen,
>
> You have given me a truly great pleasure with your letter and the honorarium which you sent me. Not only is it agreeable to hear something favourable and flattering about my *Orchestral Pieces,* but more than that, I am delighted with the tone of real genuine warmth which speaks from your letter. Your letter is as warm as your intention and so it is with all good and beautiful deeds...

The composer went on to tell Hinrichsen that he intended to put on a performance of Max Reger's Violin Concerto published by C F Peters, on 9th March, in an arrangement which he had made for chamber orchestra and with his student, Rudolf Kolisch, as soloist. Rudolf Kolisch was one of the most important musicians in Schönberg's *Verein für musikalische Aufführungen.* (Schönberg married his sister Gertrud in 1924). In 1922 he formed the Kolisch Quartet and toured the world, settling in USA in 1935. Hinrichsen was very interested in Schönberg's arrangement of Reger's Violin Concerto, especially as he realised that Schönberg held the concerto in such high esteem. He offered to consider it for publication. Schönberg regarded Reger as a genius and he was the composer most performed in the *Verein* concerts. By 1924, twenty-four performances of his works had taken place.

After ten years, stocks of the score of the *Five Orchestral Pieces* were finally getting low and Hinrichsen had to consider a new printing in the autumn of 1922. Until this time he had not had the opportunity of incorporating the corrections which Schönberg had sent him some years before. Now he returned the marked score to the composer asking him whether these corrections were still necessary, or whether he wanted to make any more alterations.

Schönberg was quite definite in his reply of 7th September, that these corrections were vital:

> ...The corrections are a matter of life and death for this work. They are truly improvements, which have become evident from experience. As you have so far shown so much friendly understanding for my work, so I would sincerely ask you to implement these corrections. I am in fact surprised that this has not yet been carried out...

He went on to make a number of suggestions regarding the corrections in both the score and in the orchestral parts, and the issuing of a catalogue of corrections. He continued:

> VI: I would be very happy if the publisher would send a copy of this catalogue to all previous purchasers, without it being requested, because I am interested in the quality of every single performance and am already turning in my future grave, when I think that everything which I have written will be badly performed...

Hinrichsen maintained his faith in the work and was prepared to invest even more money in it, as he assured the composer in his letter dated 13th September, 1922:

Dear Mr Schönberg,

I have received your friendly letter of the 7th together with
the correction copy of the *Five Orchestral Pieces* and will make
every effort to conform with your wishes. My interest in this
epoch-making work will remain till my dying breath, the same
as it has been up to now, and I assure you that I will shy away
neither from effort nor expense on its behalf.

He assured Schönberg that he would incorporate all the corrections
into the new printing and that he would produce the catalogue of
corrections and have it distributed to all those who had already bought
the music, and to all those who would still be buying the original printing
of the parts. A week later he sent Schönberg a proof copy of the
catalogue, prepared by his best editor. It comprised a list of 110
corrections and improvements, with great emphasis on new tempo
markings and dynamic markings.

Schönberg was grateful for all Hinrichsen's understanding and
congratulated the editor on his excellent compilation. In his letter of
29th September he wrote:

Dear Mr Hinrichsen, the way you are doing it is all very good
indeed and I am extremely satisfied. What is being dealt with,
is not actual mistakes, but with improvements which will lead
to a better understanding of the work. I am immensely grateful
to you that you are so enthusiastic and are willing not to shy
away from this great expense in these difficult times...

By Christmas 1922 the revised score had been printed and the
publisher was delighted to be able to send the first copy to the composer.
He also announced that the new score was used by Furtwängler for
performances at the Gewandhaus in Leipzig and Berlin. He was
genuinely proud of having published this work.

In 1924 Felix Greissle, a student who later became Schönberg's son-
in-law, made an arrangement of the *Five Orchestral Pieces* for a chamber
orchestra of eight-ten instruments. Hinrichsen accepted the new score
and paid Greissle 500 gold Marks in Austrian Crowns for it, hoping it
would serve to make the work more accessible. 200 copies were printed
in 1925. (A reprint was not necessary until 1959, when 300 copies were
printed.)

Schönberg celebrated his fiftieth birthday on 13th September, 1924
and Hinrichsen wrote him a warm and friendly letter in congratulation
two days before. He added that he would very much like to publish

another work by Schönberg: '...I deeply regret that Edition Peters has so far been the publisher of your work on only one occasion. Since I have learnt that you are not exclusively contracted to Universal Edition, I would like to ask you whether you would entrust me with another work to publish...'

Schönberg did not respond to this invitation until 2nd February, 1927 when he offered Hinrichsen a number of works. However, it was not clear to Hinrichsen whether in fact Schönberg was at liberty to offer him the works, or whether he had to obtain permission from Universal Edition. He wanted to know whether these were recent compositions, or whether they were earlier works, and what kind of music they constituted. On 5th February he made the following offers:

> I might be prepared to lay out a fee of 3,000 marks for the String Quartet; however, the possibility of regaining the costs on a work of Variations for orchestra is negligible. Orchestras have been paying badly for some time; the members of the bands, soloists, performance fees and other expenses swallow up so very much, that the associations do not want to lay out any money for the material. However, I might be prepared to come to the following understanding: To pay 2,000 Marks on delivery of the manuscript and, after the first twenty-five performances, a further 2,000 Marks...

In spite of all Hinrichsen's past generosity towards him, Schönberg chose not to accept his judgement as a publisher, and asked for a higher fee than that offered. Once again, as with Mahler's Sixth Symphony, Henri Hinrichsen exercised his principle never to bargain about fees.

Schönberg sent no further compositions. His health was not good and as a Jew he had been made to suffer the effects of anti-Semitism since the early 1920s. In 1933 he was dismissed from his teaching post in Berlin and in 1934 he moved to the USA.

Henri Hinrichsen ultimately felt that his faith in the *Five Orchestral Pieces* had been vindicated. In his *Chronik* of 1933 he wrote:

> A 'risky' and therefore even more important action, was the acquisition of the *Five Orchestral Pieces*, Op 16 by Arnold Schönberg (born in Vienna in 1874). At the time of their publication in 1912 this music, with its provocative expansion of musical boundaries, suggested weather flashes and indications of forthcoming battles and imminent overthrow. The musical world, and especially musical youth, tired of post-Wagnerism and post-Romanticism, reached greedily for the new, the unheard and the yet-to-be-heard. Hence, Schönberg's

Op 16 appeared on every orchestral programme of importance (approximately fifty orchestral institutions performed the work), and every performance resulted in, what was so unusual in Germany then, the rare spectacle of a sharp division between those in favour and those against the innovator. Now it has become markedly quieter around the 'bourgeoisised' Schönberg. It will remain the job of musical history and critical style to uncover the reasons for this phenomenon.

When he published Schönberg's *Five Orchestral Pieces* in 1912, Henri Hinrichsen made the comment: 'My grandchildren will be the first to reap the benefit from this seed.' A prophetic thought, as a new revised edition was published by C F Peters Corporation in New York in 1997, where a granddaughter was an Executive.

---

1   Published in *Der Briefwechsel zwischen Arnold Schönberg und dem Verlag C F Peters*, edited by Eberhard Klemm, in *Deutsches Jahrbuch der Musikwissenschaft für 1970*, Edition Peters, Leipzig 1971. Most of the thirty-eight, hand-written, letters and postcards from Schönberg are in the Staatsarchiv Leipzig, C F Peters Bestand, Schönberg file. The thirty-eight replies from the publisher are in the Copy Books (K: August 1908-November 1911, L: November 1911-December 1915, o.Bez.: 5.VII 1915-December 1920, M: December 1920-April 1925, N: April 1925-August 1927.)

PART III

Inflation to National Socialism

CHAPTER NINE

World War I, Inflation and Music Publishing

The First Female Employee

One change brought about by the First World War was that nationalistic fervour caused the company to drop its French subtitle: Bureau de Musique, so that in 1915 the name officially became **C F Peters, Leipzig**. Another was the need to employ women, many of the male staff having been called up for military duty. By 1915 there were only eleven elderly men remaining from a pre-war staff of eighteen. A notice was sent to the Association of Office Workers in September 1915, which resulted in the employment of the first female employee:

> Young lady of good family with neat handwriting, good speaker, perfect in shorthand and typing, required immediately.

Fräulein Gertrud Hopfe was twenty-five when she took up her post as office girl on 11th October, 1915, with a weekly wage of 20M. (She remained until her retirement well after the Second World War, and beyond, when she inhabited a flat in the attic of 10 Talstrasse until 1989, dying in a retirement home one year later.) In December 1915 she decided to keep an occasional diary, noting down the important events of her professional life. She described her employment, which reminded her somewhat of Gustav Freytag's *Soll und Haben* (Debit and Credit)[1], and the offices of C F Peters, Leipzig thus:[2]

> ...Three large double high desks with their swivel chairs and at the front a simple high desk with two seats stood in front of three of the large windows...a forty watt bulb hung below a green-white shade above each working unit [Fig 20]. Small telephones on each desk connected with the stockroom...The small passageway to the door served as reception area: a small

table and two wickerwork chairs as well as a high, narrow safe. Many of the Peters' contemporary composers, whose photos with names or autographed signatures protected by thick glass decorated the walls, looked down on visitors. On the hallway side hung the life-size portraits of the first three proprietors of the company – Hoffmeister, Böhme, Peters. Below, in front of a green wall-screen and on a wooden pedestal was a bust of Max Abraham. On the right, by the fourth window of the large main office a small room had been built of light-coloured wood panels and fluted glass: the office of the attorney [manager] Paul Ollendorff, right next to the beautiful wood-panelled private office of Geheimrat Hinrichsen, with its built-in cupboards...

She went on to describe the stockroom which was through a folding door and past the telephone cabin. The regular stockroom was to the left and stretched as far as the entrance in the Lindenstrasse, whilst the trade hall with wardrobe cupboards was on the right and up to the main entrance. A recessed door in the entrance hall formed a kind of loading ramp from which the parcels – hundreds every day – were placed directly onto the shoulders of the delivery men. The diary continues:

The new employee, generally called *das Fräulein* (the Miss), sat at the single desk. As the youngest, when the telephone rang she had to hurry through the office, through the folding door and to the telephone cabin to answer it and to put the caller through. She also had to connect the many calls made by Mr Ollendorff, because at that time one could not dial for oneself but had to wait patiently until the main telephone switchboard responded. I must mention the Peters' typewriter, a 'New Century Calligraph' with cursive typeface and covered carriage and a whole box full of bits which had fallen off and little screws – but it worked. This artistic writer of the new century was banned from the office, because its tapping was very disturbing. Its place was far away, at the window by the entrance to the stockroom in the Lindenstrasse. The copypress was not so annoying in the main office, but extremely awkward to use – installed beneath the heads of the founders, it was the horror of all those who had to come into contact with it. The copy cloths had to be dampened daily; if this was done early, it was soon possible to copy something onto it, if the script ran out, the cloths remained dry and it was impossible to read anything.

A mark of how the employees shared in the excitement and achievements of the company is shown in a note in Frl Hopfe's diary dated 1st December, 1917:

> It has arrived – our new large catalogue of the Edition Peters! A handsome volume, absolutely worthy of the fiftieth anniversary of the existence of the EP Universal library.
>
> And something else worth noting: Madame told us that her husband had bought a valuable collection of autographs, books and manuscripts in Dresden for the Peters Music Library. Apart from this HH bought the publishing company of Rieter-Biedermann for Peters.

The autograph collection referred to was that compiled by the composer and conductor Ernst Rudorff, which Henri Hinrichsen presented to the Peters Music Library. He purchased J Rieter-Biedermann from his close friend Edmund Astor[3], its proprietor.

J Rieter Biedermann

Edmund Astor had long wanted to unite his company with C F Peters. J Rieter-Biedermann had been founded by Jacob Melchior Rieter-Biedermann, a Swiss music publisher, in 1849. His son-in-law, Edmund Astor, directed the branch established in Leipzig in 1862, which became the headquarters after the original office closed in 1884. Rieter-Biedermann also founded the *Leipziger Allgemeine musikalische Zeitung* (The Leipzig General Music Newspaper), which his firm published from 1866-1882.

Edmund Astor's son, Robert, was killed in the war in April 1917, and when Henri Hinrichsen went to pay his condolences the older man begged Hinrichsen: 'Please take my business.' However, Hinrichsen felt that this was not the right moment and so waited four months before discussing the question with him. They came to a speedy and friendly verbal agreement and on 1st October Hinrichsen paid 400,000M for the J Rieter-Biedermann music publishing company. Astor's godsons, the Linnemanns, were disappointed over the agreement, having themselves hoped to inherit their godfather's business.

In this way C F Peters added a number of useful works to its catalogue. These included, along with several volumes of European Folk Songs and music and art books, important works by Brahms (*A German Requiem*, Op 45; the Piano Concerto, Op 15; the *Magelon Romances*, Op 33; the Piano Quintet, Op 34; the *Schumann Variations*, Op 23; the *Waltzes*, Op 39 and more), thus finally fulfilling Dr Max Abraham's wish of some thirty or so years earlier, to publish more of Brahms'

works. There were also single works by Marco Enrico Bossi, Leopold
Heinrich (Picot de Pecccaduc) Baron of Herzogenberg and Arnold
Mendelssohn, the son of a second cousin of Felix Mendelssohn-
Bartholdy, as well as the latter's new editions of Schütz *Cantatas*, an
unedited edition of Handel's Concerti Grossi and vocal scores of several
of Handel's oratorios with texts translated by Gervinus.

After Edmund Astor's death, Henri Hinrichsen did not lose touch
with his descendants. Shocked when he heard that the money inherited
by Astor's heirs had been completely wiped out during the inflation,
he immediately sent a cheque for 10,000M to Margarete Quarta Astor,
the widow of Robert. On 25th February, 1925, he set up a charitable
trust in the name of Robert Astor, to provide an income for the
dependants of his late friend's dead son. The capital subscribed by
Hinrichsen was sufficiently generous to produce an income which would
provide support for widows and orphans of music dealers who, through
no fault of their own, were suffering hardship. The fund was
administered by the Association of German Music Dealers and was
available to those in need, even if their husbands had not been
members. Further, from 1929 he voluntarily paid Margarete Astor an
annual pension of 2,000M until her death in 1931.

In spite of the War, the fiftieth anniversary of the founding of the
Universal Library – Edition Peters was celebrated on 1st December,
1917 with the issue of a new complete catalogue.

The new Complete Edition Peters Catalogue

The issue of a complete catalogue of Edition Peters was in itself a cause
for celebration. Whilst smaller catalogues were issued on a regular basis,
this large and prestigious hardback cloth-bound volume of over 400
pages, contained full details of all the works published by or taken over
by C F Peters. This was only the third such catalogue ever issued, the
first was in 1888 and the second in 1900 in celebration of the centenary
of the firm.

An extract from the preface to this new volume gives a brief résumé
of some of the company's achievements since the issue of the last
Complete Catalogue:

> The founder of the Edition Peters, the proprietor of the
> business, Dr Max Abraham, died in its Jubilee Year, 1900. It is
> a mark of his extraordinary personality that he is still so widely
> revered in spite of our fast-moving times...
>
> Edvard Grieg, whose name is synonymous with that of the
> Edition Peters, its successes and its blossoming died in 1907.

> The relationship was not merely that between composer and publisher, but was enhanced to become a close friendship between Dr Abraham and the present proprietor of the company, Geheimrat Hinrichsen, and the sensitive and brilliantly witty man and his charming wife; a friendship which still exists between Grieg's widow, who lives in Copenhagen, and the company...

The preface refers to the recent death of Max Reger. Some of the important acquisitions amongst recent additions to the catalogue are highlighted next: The Lieder of Hugo Wolf, works by Reger, Mahler's Fifth Symphony, works by other composers including Brahms, Hans Pfitzner and Richard Strauss. A major contribution to the dissemination of recent writing on music was the *Yearbook of the Peters Music Library* to which the reader's attention is deservedly drawn.

It was a matter of pride, as well as sound business sense, to Henri Hinrichsen, to have popular works which had been published by other publishers, ready for publication in the Edition Peters as soon as their copyright had expired. Some of the major works in this category were deemed to rate a mention. This huge Complete Catalogue of C F Peters made its impact not only in Leipzig and not only in the world of music. Its importance was emphasised throughout Germany, through glowing appreciations in the press, for example in the *Frankfurter Zeitung* No 93 of 4th April, 1918: '...It offers an imposing picture, in its comprehensiveness, of the productivity of German music publishing, amongst whose most respected ranks is the publisher C F Peters...'

The celebration for the issuing of the new Complete Catalogue in December 1917 in a way marked the end of an era for C F Peters. Relations between management and staff had always been good. Employees had shown loyalty in justification for the trust placed in them by the management, who had always given importance to the welfare of their staff. Working hours were similar to those generally prevailing at the time in Germany and wages were agreed between the two parties without outside interference. But that all changed in 1918.

The November Revolution to Inflation

The uprising of the Workers' Movement, with its attendant strikes and demands for better working conditions had far-reaching effects. Whilst Henri Hinrichsen was a good employer within the customs of the time, conditions in general for workers were poor, with long hours and low pay. The so-called November Revolution of 1918 was followed by changes in the relationship between proprietor and staff at C F Peters. Most of the employees joined the Union of Employees in the Book

Trade *Die Eule* (The Owl) and the Transport Workers Union. The introduction of the eight-hour working day lead to the need for more staff, which number in fact doubled during the 1920s, though the turnover decreased. At the end of July 1919 the Union of Employees in the Book Trade called a strike in demand of higher pay. The offices of C F Peters were closed for more than a week until the demands of the staff were met, and all those who had been on strike were promised their jobs back. The final note on the events is best left to Frl Hopfe, who wrote in December 1919:

> Well, that was an exciting year! There were suddenly men in a works committee. Socialists?? The eight-hour day is very pleasant, but did we really have to strike in July and bring the publishing house to a standstill for a week? I didn't go on strike! But – it is very considerate of HH to take back the striking gentlemen and to raise all of our salaries.

Music publishers were all in a similar situation and needed to formulate a strategy for dealing with the new working practices. Henri Hinrichsen took the initiative when he called together a meeting of the leading music publishers in the offices of C F Peters on 21st and 22nd February, 1920. The heads of the following publishers attended: C F Peters, Breitkopf & Härtel, Henry Litolff's Verlag and B Schott's Söhne. They discussed such subjects as export conditions, discounts to music dealers and a proposal put forward by Dr Strecker of B Schott's Söhne, of a 'Union-Edition'. However, this altruistic pipe dream was never realised.

Fräulein Hopfe noted in her diary: 'I've done nothing but brew gallons of coffee over the past two days...Mrs Martha Hinrichsen helped serve it.'

As a result of the shorter working hours the second female employee, Charlotte Kretschmar, joined the company the following month.

The year 1923 saw inflation in the form of hyper-inflation, followed by deflation; unemployment figures in Germany reached many thousands. The currency was valued at:

> 1 billion marks equalled 1 gold mark.
> 1 US $ equalled 4.20 gold marks.

In Leipzig, wages and salaries were paid not only in marks, but also in *Bachmarks*. *Notgeld* (emergency money) was issued by organisations and local institutions throughout Germany and C F Peters issued its own vouchers, *Petersmarks*, based on the value of the sheet music. These vouchers were only for use within the music trade and were designed to protect the retailers from the effects of inflation between the time of ordering and of receiving sheet music.

Fräulein Hopfe noted in her diary for Easter 1923 that she had received eighty billion marks' salary. Her starting salary, less than eight years earlier, had been twenty marks.

These events should be seen against the conditions prevailing in Germany between the outbreak of war in 1914 and the hyper-inflation of 1923 which affected C F Peters, its composers, employees and suppliers, as well as Henri Hinrichsen's family and his sponsorship of charities.

1918-1921 was a period of revolution and counterrevolution, inflation and temporary stability when the immediate consequences of defeat fell upon the German economy. The Kaiser's abdication in November 1918 was followed by the doomed rising of the Spartacists, the reluctant signing by Germany of the Versailles treaty, the abortive Kapp Putsch and the Allied ultimatum on reparations in May 1921. The worst inflation since the beginning of the war was in 1919. The depreciation of the currency was largely induced by domestic factors including the determination of the government to carry out its pledge to introduce the eight-hour day and comprehensive support for the unemployed.

1923 is seen as the definitive year of the German inflation. When the Reichsbank eventually found itself unable to supply all the bank notes needed for the continuation of business, it was compelled to organise the printing of emergency money (*Notgeld*) by local authorities, and the whole monetary structure of the Reich collapsed under a tidal wave of worthless paper. A new currency, the *Rentenmark*, was launched on 5th November, 1923. All credit to the government ceased and the Reichsbank stopped discounting the treasury bills that had been the basis of the nation's finances since 1914. The disintegrating currency brought the first serious unemployment since the end of the war.

By 1924 it was clear that big business was the principal winner in the inflation. The eight-hour day was suspended and rising unemployment strengthened the industrialist's advantage. From 1924-1928 the Weimar government promoted the interests of industry at the expense of the working-class. So ultimately, on the restoration of stabilised monetary conditions, the main burden of reparations fell on the working-classes.

C F Peters survived all the problems brought about by the war and the subsequent inflation thanks to the astute forethought and planning of Henri Hinrichsen. In this he was supported by the collaboration of many of the suppliers discussed earlier, on whom he had to rely for the promotion of his business. One of these was the paper merchant, Gustav Flinsch.

Gustav Flinsch – Paper Merchant

One of Dr Max Abrahams' stipulations in producing the classics cheaply in the Edition Peters, had been that only the best available paper within the price range should be used. The firm of Ferdinand Flinsch, whose standards were as high as those of C F Peters, had been the sole supplier of paper to the publisher for many years. The quality of their paper was consistently much better than any other. There was a good personal and business relationship between the proprietors of C F Peters and the proprietors of Ferdinand Flinsch, Heinrich Flinsch and his successor after 1908, Gustav Flinsch. The collaboration was so close that Flinch, who was courted by Breitkopf & Härtel, refused to sell them any paper, having promised Henri Hinrichsen not to sell to the 'competition'.

Gustav Flinsch, who was until 1932 the Chairman of the Board of Governors of the Leipzig Conservatory of Music, of which Henri Hinrichsen was also a member, always aimed to give C F Peters his best personal service. It was this concern which helped the company to survive the financial crisis between the inflation and the stabilisation to the Rentenmark. Flinsch made it possible for the publisher to buy and print vast quantities of paper, in order to maintain huge stocks of printed music at the most reasonable price. This policy proved to be so successful that it was continued in substantial measure, for the next ten years.

A year after the issue of the new Complete Catalogue, on 1st January, 1919 the firm and family [Fig 21] celebrated the twenty-fifth anniversary of Henri Hinrichsen's partnership with Dr Max Abraham in 1894. To mark this important event in the history of C F Peters, Paul Ollendorff, the general manager, had painstakingly assembled a *Jubilee Book* dedicated to Henri Hinrichsen. Its title was *Stimmen der Freunde, Komponisten und Mitarbeiter zum 1. Januar, 1919* (Voices of Friends, Composers and Colleagues for the 1st of January, 1919).

The *Jubilee Book* 1919

In this unique book of 105 hand-written pages, were contributions from eighty people, including many famous composers and musicians of the day. Some wrote a short greeting, some wrote several pages of appreciation and some contributed musical notation. Arnold Schönberg wrote a few bars of music dedicated to Henri Hinrichsen. The *Jubilee Book* was divided into several sections representing the many faceted interests and involvements of the dedicatee:

'Voices from the Circle of Honorary Activity' came first with fifteen contributors headed by a page of appreciation from the Oberbürgermeister of Leipzig from 1918-30, Dr K Rothe. The philosopher, Georg Witkowski, founder of the Leipzig Bibliophile's Evening included a saying of Goethe's in his appreciation: 'The genuine man's true celebration is the deed!'

Contributions from the senior members of the family came under the heading 'Voices from the Family Circle'. Then came four contributions from very close friends, under the heading of 'Voices from the Circle of Friends'. One of these, the conductor, Professor Otto Lohse, wrote the notation and words, which were by Rudolf Seuberlich, from part of his opera *Prinz wider Willen* (Unwilling Prince), first performed in Riga in 1880: 'He who does good carries the reward in his own heart.' The next section was 'Voices from the Circle of Business Friends'.

This was followed by 'Voices from the Circle of Composers' headed by Dr Max Bruch, who wrote bars from his Violin Concerto, Op 26 in G-minor, published by C F Peters. Nina Grieg wrote that had Grieg been alive he would have written a beautiful and lasting appreciation, she sent her greetings and congratulations and undying thanks for all the friendship she had experienced from him and Dr Abraham. Sigfrid Karg-Elert, Emil Mattiesen and Arnold Mendelssohn wrote warm appreciations. Friedrich Klose wrote the opening bars from the *Andante* of his String Quartet, whilst Walter Niemann wrote a few bars of his piano work *Mit einem Geburtstagsgruss* (With a Birthday Greeting), Op 46 No 6. Hans Pfitzner, Max Reger's widow and Xavier Scharwenka all wrote warm words of gratitude and Christian Sinding wrote several pages in acknowledgement of all that Henri Hinrichsen had done for him.

'Voices from the Circle of Employees' was headed by Paul Ollendorff, with a poem, which was followed by offerings from all the staff. The final section, and the largest, with twenty-three contributors, was 'Voices from the Circle of Musical Colleagues'. This was a series of glowing testimonials and some musical tributes from many of the musicians, conductors, musicologists and editors associated with C F Peters, some of whom are covered in this book.

The Jubilee Book was a unique and irreplaceable collector's piece which took pride of place amongst Henri Hinrichsen's possessions. A crown to his achievements of a quarter of a century.[4]

One of the signatories of the *Jubilee Book* was a one-time student of Hermann Kretzschmar, Hans Joachim Moser.

Hans Joachim Moser (1889-1967)

Moser studied musicology, German philology, history, composition and singing; his prodigious creative personality lead him to correlate elements from many disciplines into his work. Henri Hinrichsen was one of the first to recognise his phenomenal talents when, as a twenty-six-year-old soldier during World War I he approached C F Peters. Folk songs were traditionally hugely popular in Germany and following the success of the *Folk Song Book,* C F Peters was pleased to publish a volume entitled *Alte Meister des deutschen Liedes* (Old Masters of German Song) edited by Hans Joachim Moser, in 1915. Moser's delight at the publication of his first major work was expressed in the following letter which he wrote to Henri Hinrichsen on 2nd November, 1915[5], whilst doing his military service:

> Highly Honoured Mr Kommerzienrat,
>
> Many thanks for sending me my five free copies of *Alte Meister des deutschen Liedes.* I am absolutely delighted at how smart the volumes, with their beautiful print and tasteful presentation, look. I wanted to take the first opportunity to thank you for the fact that you accommodated my intentions so entirely, even though your original plans were quite different. I now hope sincerely that this new publication will be successful and give you much pleasure.
>
> Please would you be so kind as to send me a further five copies? I would like to present them to my own teachers – Kretzschmar, Riemann, Robert Kahn, Felix Schmidt and Max Friedländer for Christmas. It would however be very acceptable to this poor soldier, only earning 1 mark per day, if he could pay the wholesale price instead of the retail price.
>
> With the repeated expression of my gratitude, and in the hope that this will not be my last commission from C F Peters, honoured Mr Kommerzienrat, I remain with sincerest regards,
>
> Your
> Hans Joachim Moser

With his customary generosity, especially to young musicians, Henri Hinrichsen did not ask the young soldier to pay anything at all. Moser went on to become a knowledgeable musicologist with many publications and editions to his credit and became especially revered for his *Musiklexikon* (Music Encyclopaedia) published in Berlin in 1932-5. He was successively reader, professor and director of various institutes and universities, retiring at the age of seventy-one in 1960, as Director of the Berlin Music Conservatory.

Hans Joachim Moser's long association with the firm of C F Peters transcended both the lives of Hermann Kretzschmar and Henri Hinrichsen by many years. During the 1930s when Henri Hinrichsen was being persecuted as a Jew, Hans-Joachim Moser offered his former sponsor the hand of friendship.

Alongside all his publishing commitments and support for various musicians, charitable causes figured high in Henri Hinrichsen's priorities. He was a major benefactor of a charitable foundation, the *Verein für Familien- und Volkserziehung* (Association for Family and National Education) set up by Henriette Goldschmidt in 1871. The committee of the Association, of which Martha Hinrichsen was a member, was headed by Frau Henriette Goldschmidt.

Henri Hinrichsen was already involved in charitable causes as early as 1897, even before he met his wife. Membership cards and receipts for donations held in the files of the Staatsarchiv Leipzig, show details of the many organisations which he supported financially. Amongst his many voluntary offices, he became a judge in trade disputes; he was on the committees of the Leipzig Historical Museum, the Local Transport Association and on the Board of Directors of the Leipzig Conservatory of Music. He was elected to the City of Leipzig Council from 2nd January, 1911 to 15th November, 1918.

The end of the Great War brought cause for celebration to 10 Talstrasse. The Hinrichsen's seventh and last child, Robert – named after Henri Hinrichsen's father, was born in 1918.

---

1   *Soll und Haben*, published in 1855, was Freytag's first important book, becoming a best-seller. It concerns basic civic behaviour and the German work ethic. Freytag was at the centre of a group of politically interested intellectuals in Leipzig, who called themselves "Kitzing."

2   Frl Gertrud Hopfe's diary entry for December 1915, edited by her in October 1974, in the archives of C F Peters, Leipzig.

3   Edmund Astor was a descendant of the Astor family from Mannheim. A Jacob Astor had two sons who were born in Waldorf: George, born c. 1760 went to England, and Jacob, born in 1763 went to USA. They formed an Anglo-American firm of musical instrument makers. Jacob Astor (the son) laid the foundations for the family wealth.

4   The *Jubilee Book* was offered at auction by an untraced vendor during the early 1960s. In the spring of 1966 it was sold at auction in Austria. By the Autumn of 1996 it was being offered for sale by an antiquarian dealer for 30,000 DM (approximately. £12,000). In 1997 the *Jubilee Book* belonged to Hans Schneider, Musikantiquariat, Tützing, Germany.

5   StAL Bestand, C F Peters, No 1878.

CHAPTER TEN

C F Peters 1920s-1930s: 'In these difficult Times'

New Developments

Germany had been through harrowing times during the first quarter of the twentieth century. The Great War, followed by unemployment, inflation and stabilisation in 1923, transformed the way business was run. The old standards had changed for ever and people's lives took on a new pace. C F Peters had survived as a result of astute planning and with the collaboration of their suppliers.

However, most cultural organisations, having no reserves, had less financial flexibility and many people had lost all their money. This and the development of the Workers' Movement and trades unions, led to the adoption of different business attitudes from those employed before the war.

Many people suffered poverty and hardship. Henri Hinrichsen was called upon from all sides – family, friends, musicians, organisations and total strangers – for financial assistance. He helped many, but his resources were not limitless and he had to temper his generosity with common sense. A frequently used phrase was: '...in these difficult times...'

The financial resources of concert organisations were considerably diminished by inflation – often totally absent, making the price of purchasing orchestral material prohibitive. Little new music would be performed and if the new works published by C F Peters were not performed, there would be a loss of performing and copyright fees as well as a loss of sales. There would be no way of recouping the investment that these works had entailed in their production, and hence there would be no income to finance new publications. Orchestral music had to be made available to orchestras at a price which they could afford. This was done at C F Peters by opening a Hire Department in 1924, for orchestral material. The only orchestral music which had previously been available on hire was Edvard Grieg's music for *Peer Gynt*; now a whole catalogue of orchestral music – scores and parts – could be hired by concert organisations at a fraction of the purchase price.

A new forty-eight page Supplement to the large Complete 1917 Catalogue was issued in 1925, showing many new publications, including those by Hans Pfitzner, Walter Niemann and Günther Raphael, a young composer encouraged by Hinrichsen's friend and consultant musicologist, Karl Straube, who introduced him to C F Peters. Raphael became a teacher of composition and theory at the Leipzig Conservatory of Music and at the *Kirchenmusikalisches Institut* (Church Music Institute) in Leipzig in 1926. The first of his works to be published in the Editions Peters, were his *Romantische Tonbilder* (Romantic Tone Pictures) for piano 4 hands, Op 10, and his Trio, Op 11.

Piano transcriptions of orchestral music were still avidly sought. So the catalogue of piano scores was considerable enlarged during the 1920s. Gustav Kogel, who had transcribed many scores for C F Peters, died in 1921 and his place was taken by Kurt Soldan, conductor of the State Opera in Berlin for eight years. A finer musicologist than his predecessor, he had a better understanding of the work. As Henri Hinrichsen always wanted to publish arrangements of the highest standard, he asked Soldan to revise many of Kogel's editions. Through Soldan's work, the catalogue of piano arrangements was considerably enlarged; he also edited albums of arias and extended the orchestral library.

Soldan developed the first Urtext editions to be published by C F Peters with the conductor Ludwig Landshoff, the renowned scholar of vocal music of the seventeenth and eighteenth centuries, and later with Wilhelm Weismann. Henri Hinrichsen regarded Soldan, a teacher of conducting at the Leipzig Music Conservatory, as a friend and a reliable musical adviser.

Several new publications recalled the past. Johann Christian Bach – 'the London Bach' – born in Leipzig in 1735 as the eighteenth child of J S Bach had moved to London, where he died in 1782. A successful musician of his time, his music had almost been forgotten. Ludwig Landshoff had done much research into his music for C F Peters, and, together with the musicologist Fritz Stein, edited the newly discovered piano sonatas and piano concertos of J C Bach. Perhaps Landshoff's most important work for C F Peters was his Urtext edition of J S Bach's *15 Two-part Inventions* and *15 Three-part Symphonies*.

Anton Bruckner had died in October 1896, and whilst C F Peters had been disinclined to publish his Seventh Symphony in 1884, his music had achieved renown since. As soon as the copyright in his works expired in 1927, C F Peters issued full scores and piano arrangements of Bruckner's Symphonies.

1927 also saw the centenary of the death of Ludwig van Beethoven, some of whose works had been amongst the earliest published by the newly formed company – the Bureau de Musique. As a contribution towards the festivities of the 'Beethoven Year' C F Peters published his 'Ode to Joy' in an arrangement for voice and piano, by Professor Max Friedländer. Through Friedländer's influence, there was a huge demand from school boards, town councils and local education authorities throughout Germany. Berlin bought 100,000 copies for the Beethoven celebrations on 26th March, 1927, whilst other towns bought between 1,000 and 17,500, to a total of 232,000. In May, the municipal authorities of Vienna ordered 100,000 copies. Whilst sales were high, profits were minimal; the price had been kept artificially low in order to make the work as widely available as possible. It was also an excellent form of publicity for the company. Further publicity for publications of Beethoven's music was through posters showing Beethoven's death mask [Fig 23] in two different designs. One included portraits of Brahms, Haydn, Reger, Schubert and Hugo Wolf; the other showed facsimile notation of a page of Beethoven's Septet and a few bars from his 9th Symphony.

A further contribution to the centenary celebrations, was the publication of a book of the letters written by Beethoven to the publisher Hoffmeister & Kühnel – later C F Peters, which also contained a catalogue of all of Beethoven's works published in the Edition Peters.[1] C F Peters also published another little book: *Zum 26. März, 1927* (For the 26th of March, 1927) dedicated to the Friends of Edition Peters. It comprised a long article entitled 'Zu Beethoven's Persönlichkeit und Kunst' (Comments on Beethoven's Personality and Art) by Hermann Abert, which was first published in the Peters Library *Yearbook* for 1925.

To mark the centenary of Franz Schubert's death in 1928, the firm published a catalogue of Schubert's works.

Anniversaries always gave rise to many new and revised editions of the music of the composers being commemorated and saw sales increase by upwards of 400 per cent. Amongst the arrangers and editors who worked on these new editions, apart from Ludwig Landshoff and Kurt Soldan, were the musicologists Hans Theodor David, Hermann Keller, Arnold Schering, Helmut Schultz and Fritz Stein, Carl Adolf Martienssen who was a piano teacher at the Leipzig Conservatory of Music, the chorus master Siegfried Ochs, and Wilhelm Weismann.

Three anniversaries were commemorated in 1932 with special editions: the bicentennial of the birth of Haydn, the death centenary of Goethe and the twenty-fifth anniversary of the death of Edvard Grieg. Grieg's anniversary was widely commemorated with many concerts and articles in the musical press. It gave rise to increased sales of his music and C F Peters published a book with a selection from the more than

400 letters which Grieg had written to his publishers between 1866-1907:[2] (The complete collection of the correspondence between Edvard Grieg and Max Abraham and Henri Hinrichsen was published 1997.[3]) The 175th anniversary of the death of Handel was commemorated in 1934 with new editions of some of his works. Grieg was again commemorated in 1937, in memory of the thirtieth anniversary of his death, which was covered by many articles in the press.

Concurrently, the Folksong project was continuing.

Folksong Book for the Young – Max Friedländer

The *Volksliederbuch* (Folksong Book) for Male Voice Chorus issued in 1907, was followed by the version for Mixed Chorus in 1915. The Commission for the Folksong Book, headed by Max Friedländer, was working on a version – *Volksliederbuch für die Jugend* – (Folksong Book for the Young), in three volumes, containing 760 songs. Under the general editorship of Karl Lütge, amongst the editors and arrangers were Paul Hindemith, Ernst Krenek, Günther Raphael, Arnold Schönberg, Armin Knab, Max Butting, Joseph Kaminski, Ernst Toch and others. The first of the proposed three volumes was issued in 1929, after a difficult genesis and made a great contribution to the reform of music in schools at the time.

Henri Hinrichsen and Max Friedländer corresponded about the *Folksong Book for the Young* in 1923, during the height of the inflation, when the Ministry for Culture had no money. Friedländer wrote from Berlin on 30th October, 1923:[4]

> …just now, all the money which you contributed towards the continuation of the work on the *Folksong Book for Schools* has been spent and, for the time being, because of the lamentable finances of the State, there is no clear possibility that more money will be made available. The gentlemen of the Ministry are in a state of total embarrassment.

> In these difficult times we must all hold our heads above water and take heed of Carlyle's words: 'Work and not despair'.

> I think that the most important thing is that one should not allow oneself to become too depressed about all ones cares within the immediate family circle. – When my wife, who has just returned from shopping, occasionally dwells too long at mealtimes about the calamitous prices, I always decide that we should rather be conversing about Hölderlin or Schubert…

Friedländer was enormously appreciative of Hinrichsen's financial support, collaboration and friendship over the years, for himself personally and on behalf of the *Folksong Book*. Wanting to express that appreciation in tangible form, he and some of his colleagues contributed towards a signed presentation volume. Henri Hinrichsen was accustomed to making generous presents to others, but less so to receiving them and he expressed his genuine delight by return, on 2nd November, 1923:

> ...The observation that there are moments in a person's life when one is closer to the world spirit than usual, is one which I have unfortunately never up to now been able to make. However, we do have certain favourable days in our earthly pilgrimage and to these I must most definitely add yesterday, on which I felt myself to have been truly honoured by your wonderful parcel...'

The stabilisation of the currency three days later, did not produce a new supply of money. Friedländer wrote on 22nd November, that the Ministry of Finance was broke. The funds for running the Commission for the Folksong Book and preparing the new album which Hinrichsen had advanced, had run out. There was not even any money to pay the expenses of Friedländer or the members of the Commission. Henri Hinrichsen came to their rescue again, with a subsidy of 1,500 gold marks.

Conditions were so bad, that music shops could not afford to restock their shelves. It was December, and Max Friedländer wanted copies of the book of Christmas Carols which he had edited for C F Peters. He appealed to Henri Hinrichsen. To his appeal he added another request, for a copy of the vocal score of Bizet's *Carmen* published by C F Peters, as a present for his wife. Hinrichsen sent his friend five copies of his Christmas Carols and the *Carmen* score and two bound copies of Friedländer's new edition of *Müllerlieder* (Miller's Songs), for presentation to friends.

Wanting to see the workings of the Commission, Henri Hinrichsen attended their February 1924 meeting. He was so satisfied with their progress and so confident of the future success of the venture, that he advanced a further sum. But the six musicologists who were the Commission for the Folksong Book could not deliver the manuscript by the end of 1927 as they had hoped.

Friedländer was still completely absorbed by his researches into German folksong when he celebrated his seventy-fifth birthday in October. Unable to come to Berlin Henri Hinrichsen expressed his appreciation and friendship with an ex-gratia fee in recognition of Friedländer's more than forty years' association with C F Peters.

The two old friends saw each other on Friedländer's eightieth birthday. Henri and Martha Hinrichsen [Figs 24 and 25] went to Berlin to celebrate the musicologist's jubilee in 1932. They could combine the trip with a visit to Dresden, where Emil Sauer, who had been an arranger and editor with C F Peters for many years, was celebrating his seventieth birthday.

In view of Friedländer's advanced age, the main responsibility for the *Volksliederbuch* was taken over by Karl Lütge. The work had not been completed a year later and there was still no contract between the Ministry and C F Peters. Despite the state of the economy, the promotion of the *Volksliederbuch* was a lucrative contract. Complaints of favouritism were heard from several other publishers, who wanted this for themselves. The agreement for the previous two albums was that C F Peters paid a large percentage of the profits on sales to the ministry, which they had done annually from 1907.

Much acrimonious correspondence had passed between C F Peters and the ministry over three years, about the delay in completing the work and the terms of the contract. Henri Hinrichsen, having paid subsidies to keep the project going, wanted more of the profits than for the previous volumes, as recompense for his high investment in the publication. He asked for sixty per cent, the ministry refused and threatened to terminate negotiations. As termination would have been detrimental to the reputations of Professor Friedländer and the publisher, an agreement was reached.

The *Folksong Book for the Young* was published by C F Peters in 1929 and available in 1930. The whole production had been so protracted that the investment proved a major loss for the publisher. When the National Socialists came to power in 1933 the publication was banned and all copies were ordered to be destroyed.[5] Friedländer died, aged eighty-two, in 1934.

Friedländer was far from being alone as a recipient of Henri Hinrichsen's generosity during 'these difficult times'.

Support for Friends

Business, though not good, was at least turning over and Henri Hinrichsen saw it as his moral duty to offer help to those who were suffering as a result of the inflation, especially those who had in the past had some connection with his company. Often he did not wait to be asked for his help.

Fritz Stein, editor of the *Folksong Book for Male Chorus* for the troops published in 1915, was taken completely by surprise when Henri Hinrichsen sent him an 'honorary fee' in March 1922, having heard that the professor was in need. He was just one of the many people Henri Hinrichsen helped out during 'these difficult times'.

The conductor, Gustav Kogel, who had worked as arranger and adviser for C F Peters on a freelance basis for over forty years, died in 1921. When Hinrichsen heard that his widow had been trying, unsuccessfully, to sell his library during the inflation and that she had no money, he sent her two million Marks on 31st July, 1923, which he said was in recognition of her late husband's work. He wrote:[6]

> ...I had thought that you had sold the library of your late husband and now I hear to my regret, that this is not the case. I must therefore assume that you also, in these difficult times, have to fight to make ends meet. I permit myself, in recognition of the excellent services which your late husband rendered to the firm of C F Peters over the course of many years, to send you the enclosed two million marks as an honorary fee...

He wrote to her again, on 31st December, 1923, after the stabilisation of the currency and sent her a further 100RM, saying: '...that I at least have the knowledge that the beginning of the new year will bring you a little sunshine and be a good omen for the coming days...' He added: 'It will be small consolation to you that you share the lot of other widows of once famous and respected creative artists. I only need to think of the widow of Hans von Bülow and Richard Wagner[7], who is also suffering financially; and things are sadly no better for Mrs Reger either...'

In Memory of Max Reger

After Max Reger's death, Henri Hinrichsen continued his friendship with Elsa Reger, the composer's widow. He supported her financially for many years, paying her a quarterly pension, which increased in line with inflation. He never ceased in his admiration for the music of Max Reger; but when Edith Mendelssohn-Bartholdy wanted to found a Max Reger Society in Leipzig in 1916, shortly after the composer's death, he would not join. Instead, he supported Elsa Reger when she decided to make the last home she and her husband had shared, their house in Jena, into a memorial for her late husband and supported the Reger Festivals which she organised from 1917 onwards. When the Max Reger Society was formally founded in 1919, he refused to join, feeling that he was already doing quite enough by supporting Elsa Reger; he joined it after she became President in 1920.

In spite of all of his other concerns, on the tenth anniversary of Max Reger's death, Henri Hinrichsen found the time to write Elsa Reger a moving letter on 10th May, 1926, expressing the depth of his feelings towards her late husband and herself:[8]

Dear Mrs Reger,

I would not like tomorrow, the tenth anniversary of the death of Reger, to pass without giving you, who stood beside the great master for so many years, through sorrow and pleasure, a sign of life. Much will be written about the so early departed in newspapers and professional journals and you will also read a lot about him during these memorial days, but I am sure you will be pleasantly moved by a few heartfelt words from Reger's most faithful publisher. It still seems to me as though it was just yesterday that we stood together at Reger's bier and that we held each-others hands at his bedside in Hentschel's Hotel where you, dear Mrs Reger, held the wake. It is unforgettable for me how quietly and peacefully the deceased lay there then, with the newspaper in his hand and his spectacles on, as though he had only fallen asleep, not departed into the hereafter.

Whilst there were differences of opinion ten years ago concerning Reger's importance, everybody who counts themselves amongst contemporary thinkers today agrees that a great composer, author of the *100th Psalm* and the *Symphonic Prologue*, has departed; and I am convinced, that the more time which elapses between the living and the dead Reger, the more he will be regarded as a 'classical' composer in the highest sense of the word.

From deep within my soul, I press your hand, dear Mrs Reger, like I did then and remain

With Kindest Regards,

Your faithful
Henri Hinrichsen

In 1928 C F Peters bought all the works of Max Reger which had been published by N Simrock GmbH for 90,000M. Though he had spent a huge sum of money, Henri Hinrichsen was so happy to have succeeded in acquiring all these works by the composer in whom he had such faith, that he wanted to share his happiness with the one person who had shared in the struggle of their creation. He generously sent Mrs Reger a cheque for 1,000M as an honorary fee.

Max Hinrichsen attended the Max Reger Festival in Kassel in June 1933 and the Reger Society meeting, when he learnt that it had debts of 500RM. After discussion with his father, they decided to offer help to offset these debts with a gift of 200RM. Max Hinrichsen outlined their intention in a letter[9] to Professor Karl Straube, then the President of the Society, who wrote a glowing response dated 4th July, 1933, of which the following is a brief extract:

> ...I would like to thank C F Peters and the whole house of Hinrichsen from the bottom of my heart for the so generous and kind help which is being given to the Max Reger Society, the more so because with it the art of a German master who has created great German music like no other, is being promoted...

> With this gift, the house of C F Peters honours a colleague; because it is the glory of the house always to have served German composers with the best possible editions of their works, in order to acknowledge a cultural achievement in an exceptional manner, the value of which can only increase with time...

This letter, written a few months after the Nazis came to power, can be seen as a political gesture in support of a Jewish publisher who was feeling the effects of Nazi persecution.

Publishers are not infallible and sadly, more than eighty years after the composer's death, the music of Max Reger has not achieved the popular appeal which Henri Hinrichsen had been so convinced that it deserved.

Henri Hinrichsen's help for the widow of Max Reger was matched by his continued deep concern for the welfare of the widow of Edvard Grieg, since the composer's death in 1907. She was considered almost a member of the extended Hinrichsen family and interested in all family events; correspondence between them was close and frequent.

Death of Nina Grieg

Nina Grieg enjoyed her visits to Leipzig and Henri Hinrichsen's visits to her; in 1927 he was accompanied by his third son, the eighteen-year-old Hans-Joachim [Fig 26]. He voluntarily paid her a generous pension and sent her frequent gifts.

Nina was always immensely grateful for every attention by the family. In October 1934 she wrote a most moving letter expressing her deepest thanks for the lifelong friendship and support given to her by Henri Hinrichsen and Dr Max Abraham. Such warm appreciation and recognition meant a lot to the elderly Henri Hinrichsen.

Though it presented great difficulties, because of the new laws, Henri Hinrichsen continued to send money to Nina and her sister Tonny. In January 1935 he made provision for the older Tonny, that in case she should outlive Nina, he would continue to pay her an annual pension of 2,000 marks, provided that the foreign exchange regulations permitted it. Nina celebrated her ninetieth birthday in November 1935. Henri Hinrichsen's fourth son, the twenty-three-year-old Paul, studying at agricultural college in Denmark, went to congratulate her. Paul was studying in Denmark because, as a Jew, he was not permitted a place at university in Germany.

When Nina Grieg died about two weeks later, on 9th December, Henri Hinrichsen wrote Tonny a long letter of condolence. His third son, Dr Hans-Joachim, by then twenty-six, travelled to Copenhagen to represent him.

It was a mark of Henri Hinrichsen's deep humanity, that his devotion to the widow of C F Peters' most important composer went far beyond what could normally be expected from a publisher. His generosity towards her and her sister for almost thirty years, must be rare amongst publishers.

Henri Hinrichsen did not forget anybody, at the same time as keeping an observant eye on the anniversaries of his friends and associates, he also kept a compassionate eye on their well-being and on that of their dependants.

Help for Dependents

C F Peters paid regular pensions to several long-term employees after their retirement and after their death, continued paying the pension to their widows.

There were also charitable organisations. *The Hilfsbund für deutsche Musikpflege* (Relief Association for the Care of German Musicians) in Berlin, which supported a number of musicians and was supposed to be funded by the government and by the GEMA, had run out of money. Henri Hinrichsen's response to the situation is shown in a letter dated 27th February, 1926 to the *Hilfsbund*:[10]

> ...It is certainly a good thing that the *Deutsche Volkspartei* (German People's Party) has put in an application to the *Landtag* (State Parliament) to request the *Staatsministerium*

(Ministry of State) to provide immediate funds; hopefully this measure will prove successful and does not come too late for some...

He knew that the wheels of bureaucracy turned slowly. He offered immediate practical help by sending 2,000M to support the eighteen composers who were totally dependent on the fund. As so often, he did not want his generosity to be made public and specifically requested that no mention of his donation should be made in the annual report, saying: 'I do not like such donations, as far as they concern me, to be hung on the big bell.'

The fund was immensely grateful, though for one musician, the son of the violinist and composer Philipp Rüfer, one of whose works had been published by C F Peters, it was too late. He had shot himself. The fund was able to help his poverty-stricken, aged mother. It was some months before a new budget was set, the money coming from the Ministry of Research, Art and National Education, who then referred all needy musicians who came to them for help, to the *Hilfsbund*. The *Hilfsbund* had for some time been pressing Henri Hinrichsen to become Vice President of the Association, but he did not want to take on any further such obligations. On his suggestion, the post was then offered to the violinist, Professor Carl Flesch, who took it up.

Henri Hinrichsen also supported musicians through the Emil and Johanna Sachs Trust, which was administered by the Leipzig City authorities. After a music teacher, a Miss Rieder, to whom he was paying a pension, had died in November 1922, he transferred the pension to a singing teacher and organist by the name of Müller. In 1925 he founded a Trust with 1,000M to issue vouchers to music students to buy music and that year donated 500M to the Leipzig Concert Society. He also supported the Association for Alms for Talented Needy Students, as well as over twenty-five other charities and many individuals who applied to him. He tried not to dismiss anybody empty-handed, even when explaining that his resources were already over-stretched.

Though he had, in 1914, written to Max Reger that he was not then in a position to give scholarships to young musicians, Henri Hinrichsen had long since gone back on that decision, and was supporting several music students at the Leipzig Conservatory. There are many quarterly letters in the archive from grateful students. He was also supporting his cousin, Erich Abraham, a tenor, studying singing at the Conservatory.

The Conservatory of Music

Henri Hinrichsen was on the Board of Governors of the Leipzig Conservatory of Music. Because of his interest in education and his professional and personal interest in music and musicians, he welcomed this way of making his contribution towards the education of musicians. The Chairman of the Board was Gustav Flinsch, paper supplier to C F Peters, and members included Oskar von Hase the proprietor of Breitkopf & Härtel. Their concerns between 1925 and 1927 were typical of those of the country at large.

The annual report[11] read out by the director of the Conservatory, Professor Max Pauer, on 3rd November, 1925 showed that there were 536 students enrolled for the winter term 1925/6, against 497 for the summer term. Generous donations towards scholarships had been received from: the piano manufacturer Blüthner – 2,000M; Römisch – 1,000M; Geheimrat Henri Hinrichsen – 1,000M; the piano manufacturer Grotrian-Steinweg – 420M. The finances of the Conservatory were depleted. Attempts had been made to cover the huge deficit by diverting donations, to pay for the running costs of the Conservatory. After appeal to the Council of the City of Leipzig, emergency help was given, which was followed by further support from the State Parliament of Saxony on 4th January, 1926.

Along with music, books and book production were also a major concern.

Books and Donations

Leipzig was the centre for book production in Germany and had many institutions connected with this. Henri Hinrichsen lent his support to all those which he considered to be worthwhile. Apart from the *Deutsche Bücherei* (German Library) and the *Börsenverein* (Association of Book Dealers), these included the *Buchgewerbeverein* (Book Trade Association), *Deutscher Verein für Buchwesen und Schriften* (German Association for the Book Trade and Writings) and the *Gesellige Verein Leipziger Buchhändler* (Sociable Society of Book Traders in Leipzig).

His interest in books was not merely a passive one, as we saw earlier with regard to his membership of the Leipzig Bibliophiles Association. One of his major concerns was with the *Deutsche Buchhändler Lehranstalt* (College for the Book Trades) in Leipzig. Founded in 1853, it fitted students out with professional qualifications for all aspects of the book trade – printing, typesetting, paper types, binding, publishing, wholesale and retail dealing and allied subjects such as bookkeeping, law, English and French languages, shorthand, German literature, World literature, economics, geography and encyclopaedia; to these were added in due course: sport, social science, music and information retrieval. Dr Max Abraham had annually sponsored a student, covering his entire expenses; this Henri Hinrichsen continued, also making regular donations to the college towards equipment, etc. After the students had graduated, he enjoyed coming into contact with them professionally in the different branches of the book trade in Leipzig in which they were employed.

His support of students and education extended to Jena and Berlin. In Leipzig, apart from the Henriette Goldschmidt School, and the Conservatory of Music, he also supported the Psychological Institute of the University of Leipzig as well as the *Kunstverein* (Art Association) and the *Kunstgewerbeverein* (Art Trade Association), with frequent donations.

In addition to the paintings which Henri Hinrichsen gave to the Leipzig History Museum in 1927, he presented the Museum with a nineteenth century album of valuable hand written entries in 1929. Mrs Liddy Steche, born Angermann, entertained many musicians and composers in her home in Leipzig and her Visitors' book, started in 1850, shows a veritable galaxy of the top musicians of her day. When Henri Hinrichsen saw this album, he decided that he must buy it to present to the Leipzig History Museum where he felt that it belonged.

He saw what was available through the auction houses because he was an avid collector of composers' and musicians' autographs. Whilst Henri Hinrichsen supported many people and institutions 'during these difficult times', there were also certain advantages which came to him as a result of people having to sell some of their treasures, in order to survive. He was able to add considerably to his fine collection of autographed letters. For many years Professor Max Friedländer had been finding choice items for him and as his name as a collector became better known, people would approach him directly to offer him items and he was also on the books of several dealers. So it was that Karl Henrici, a dealer from Berlin, offered him some letters of Hugo Wolf in August 1925, on behalf of a lady in Budapest. He had already been able to take advantage of several such offers and his budget was reaching its limit by the time he wrote to Henrici on 28th August, 1925:[12]

> ...I am very sorry to hear that you find yourself in difficult circumstances – a fate which you share with all too many active business people at this time. I hope with all my heart that things will soon get better for you and that you will soon be able to open a new business.
>
> I will forego the Hugo Wolf letters as I have already acquired quite a number this year, and also the Mahler letter would only be of interest to me if it were really quite unusual.

On occasion Henri Hinrichsen would lend items from his collection for exhibition. To mark the centenary of the death of Franz Schubert in 1928, he lent a valuable letter from Schubert to Schober, to the City Library and Historical Museum in Vienna for an exhibition in May 1928. In March he was approached[13] by the Leipzig Male Voice Choir to become a member of the committee for a new Schubert Memorial; he declined, because he had stopped accepting honorary offices on principle after his sixtieth birthday in February of that year.

Amongst the composer societies which he was supporting during the 1920s were: The Max Reger Society, The German Brahms Society; The Robert Schumann Society; The Hans Pfitzner Society for German Composition and others. And his huge financial commitment to the Henriette Goldschmidt School continued unabated.

The Henriette Goldschmidt School

Both of Henri and Martha Hinrichsen's daughters attended the *Hochschule für Frauen* – the Henriette Goldschmidt School, when they were eighteen – Lotte in 1917 and Ilse in 1922. Henri Hinrichsen, the founding benefactor in 1911, and his wife had devoted a great deal of time and money and had collaborated extensively in the foundation and development of the college. However, changes were taking place within the college and within the curriculum. Society's needs were changing. Henriette Goldschmidt's idea of a '...general higher education of women for their destiny in the care of mankind...' was no longer viable at a time of severe economic crisis. Many women had to equip themselves for professions by which they could earn a living. And so the original brief for the College for Women was superseded and eventually forgotten.

Henriette Goldschmidt died, aged ninety-five, on 30th January, 1920, after a lifetime devoted to the betterment of women's education and the fight for women's rights. A year later, 'The Association for Family and National Education' which she had founded in 1871, having fulfilled its purpose, was wound up. Its buildings and assets, largely donated by Henri Hinrichsen, became a part of the 'Henri Hinrichsen Trust for the Women's College'. On 1st October, 1921, the Trust, together with all buildings and installations, was taken over by the City of Leipzig, when the *Hochschule für Frauen* was renamed, to become the *Sozialpädagogisches Frauenseminar* (Women's College of Social Education). Courses were now run to prepare women for various professions, with qualifications recognised by the State – kindergarten teachers, youth leaders, social welfare workers, as well as social administrators, matrons, technical assistants or nannies. The then director of the college, Dr Hildegard Meister-Trescher, still tried to uphold the ideals of Henriette Goldschmidt within the new context.

Henri Hinrichsen donated a further 100,000M for the creation of a students' home next door to Henriette Goldschmidt's house in the Weststrasse. However, in February 1922, the Froebel Foundation which Henriette Goldschmidt had founded, suffered a complete loss of capital and found itself deeply in debt. It had to sell its property in the Marienstrasse and Hinrichsen agreed to his money being used to buy and convert this property instead. In April, the Kindergartens of the Froebel Foundation became absorbed into the *Sozialpädagogisches Frauenseminar*, which was now the responsibility of the City of Leipzig, though in the Henri Hinrichsen Trust. In May, Hinrichsen donated a further 25,000M to equip the students' home.

Martha and Henri Hinrichsen were actively involved in all aspects of the Trust and the College and Hinrichsen attended many of the lectures and all of the committee meetings. The students' home was to a certain extent financed through the room rents paid by the students. But there were shortages of both money and food.[14] The authorities were asked to pay for this but the home promised to repay the debt when the room rents were paid. The Education Ministry insisted that in view of inflation, the rents would have to be raised. They had been charged on a quarterly basis until September 1923 when a bed in a three-bed room cost 15,000M per quarter. By November, the charge was 175 thousand millions (175 billions) M per week.

Devolution and stabilisation of the currency was in place by December 1923.

Changes had to be made to the constitution of the College, to bring it more in line with the requirements of the day, and ever further from the original, idealistic intentions of Henriette Goldschmidt. Henri Hinrichsen, like several other members of the Board did not favour the changes, but there was no viable alternative.

In 1922, the City of Leipzig had not had enough money to build a much needed new Girls' School and asked Henri Hinrichsen for permission[15] to extend and adapt the splendid building at 18/20 Königstrasse to house this new school. After months of discussions he gave expression to his disapproval in a letter to the director of the College, Dr Prüfer, dated 30th November, 1923:[16]

> ...I have studied your latest memorandum regarding the transformation of the College at 18/20 Königstrasse...I know that with these proposed reforms, the *Sozialpädagogisches Frauenseminar* will cease to exist and that everything which the late Dr Henriette Goldschmidt created with selfless enthusiasm and careful planning during the course of a lifetime, will be completely annihilated only three years after her death. It would seem to be a mockery that she should be

immortalised merely with a statue in the stairwell of the College.

As I was permitted to collaborate to such a major extent, not only financially, in the work of Frau Dr Goldschmidt, I find it impossible to agree to its destruction. It would be a sign of acquiescence if I were to be present at the board meeting at which such a decision, which I am not in a position to gainsay, is to be reached. I would be grateful if you would bring this letter to the attention of the board at the next sitting…

The college was closely linked to the Second High School for Girls and the director of the college wanted to give all the valuable equipment in its photographic laboratory to the school. This had been a gift from Henri Hinrichsen who said that he had no objection, provided that the Education Ministry would reimburse the college with the full value and that this should be used for the purchase of teaching materials for the college. These should henceforth be administered separately as the *Henri Hinrichsen Lehrmittelstiftung* (Henri Hinrichsen Teaching Materials Gift). By June 1925 the 'Gift' comprised a large quantity of books, a projector, slides and further equipment, wall decorations, a violin, sheet music, technical equipment, Kindergarten teaching materials and ex-libris labels with which to mark all the materials. More items were purchased in due course.

The ministry and the college authorities were constantly asking him for financial help. In April 1926, after currency revaluation from the millions of eighteen months earlier, he was persuaded to give a further donation of 612RM, which was intended to fund a salary increase for a teacher. However, he ultimately felt they were taking too much advantage of him. The director of the college approached him again a year later: '…On the instructions of Councillor Prof Stahl I once again come to you begging…'[17] The Education Ministry did not have enough money to pay the salary appropriate to a university lecturer and the college did not want to lose the man to whose salary Henri Hinrichsen was contributing. His reply dated 26th April, 1927 was polite, but definite:

Dear Dr Dyck,

I read your friendly letter of the 24th with great interest and am pleased to hear that you have gained a competent and efficient colleague in Professor Volkelt.

However, that does not prevent me from having to turn down your request on this occasion. Even though I have long since drawn a thick line beneath all the heavy disappointments which I have experienced over the past twenty years in the house 18/20 Königstrasse, and which were before your time there, I cannot continue to pay the salary of a teacher employed in your institute on a permanent basis; and that is what it would come to, if I were to pay three-quarters of the salary of Prof Volkelt once again this year.

I take the view that this should be paid for by the city, which demands a huge trade tax, apart from income tax from its citizens, especially where it concerns such an eminently important subject as that which you describe, and for such a lecturer, on whom to a certain extent the future of the institute is dependent.

Otherwise, I need hardly tell you that I am still extremely interested in the development of the college and always will be...

His interest expressed itself in his willingness to finance various different projects for the college.

Henri and Martha Hinrichsen were saddened to see the erosion of the high ideals of Henriette Goldschmidt with which the college had been launched. As the years passed and with the advent of the National Socialists to power, a great deal worse was to happen.

During these traumatic years Martha and Henri Hinrichsen's three eldest sons were growing up. Max, Walter and Hans-Joachim were to enter the family firm, expand its interests and gradually take over responsibility from their father. [Fig 22]

Max Hinrichsen

Born on 6th July, 1901 and named after his great uncle, Max Abraham, Max was the eldest son and grew up with all the traditions of the family business, in the full knowledge that this was to be his destiny. He felt comfortable with this and enjoyed being allowed to meet composers and others from the musical world such as Arthur Nikisch, Bruno Walter, Arnold Schönberg, Gustav Mahler, Hans Pfitzner and many more, who visited 10 Talstrasse. As a young child he sat on the knee of Edvard Grieg and as a fifteen-year-old he went with Max Reger to meet friends after a visit to 10 Talstrasse, on the last night of the composer's life. Max Hinrichsen was educated at the Nicolai Gymnasium (Grammar School) in Leipzig and for light relief his chosen instrument was the flute, which he played in an amateur orchestra.

Before entering C F Peters Max underwent a long period of apprenticeship and training, as was customary at the time, to acquaint himself with all aspects involved with music publishing and concert management. When he was eighteen he went to Berlin to work for the music publisher Bote & Bock, which resulted in a lifelong friendship with Kurt Radecke, the son of the proprietor. From there he transferred to Zürich where he worked for the music publisher and retailer, Hug & Co, until 1922. Then he went to the United States for four years, becoming manager of the US distribution agency for C F Peters in New York from 1924-27. His American experience taught him about the art of advertising and publicity which he was able to apply to great advantage after he joined his father. He would happily have remained in the USA if Henri Hinrichsen had not sent him a telegram urging him to return home and start work properly.

Back in Leipzig, and after having found himself a bachelor apartment, Max became totally involved as his father's right-hand man and took a lot of the work off Henri Hinrichsen's shoulders. On 25th October, 1928 he was officially granted power-of-attorney to act for his father. He also became administrator of the Peters Music Library and helped with the editing of the Peters Music Library *Yearbooks*. Socially, Max's circle of friends comprised the younger generation of publishers – the sons of his father's contemporaries; the friendly collaboration and rivalry which had existed for so long following its natural progression, continued with the next generation. Never a sportsman, Max surprisingly took after his father in that he learnt to enjoy horse riding, even to the extent of having to get up early in the morning to get his ride in before work.

On his thirtieth birthday, 6th July, 1931, Henri Hinrichsen took Max into equal partnership as co-proprietor of C F Peters, Leipzig. By this time his father, who had become Dr Henri Hinrichsen, was sixty-three and in poor health. He gladly entrusted Max with more and more of the day-to-day running of the business and came to rely on him in ever greater measure. Max's partnership, an important event in the music publishing world, was announced in the *Musikhandel*, the German Music Trade paper and congratulations poured in. Just one example, from the music retailer Alberti of Berlin and addressed to Max Hinrichsen, dated 9th July, 1931[18], shows the extent to which C F Peters was respected:

I have just read in the *Musikhandel* that your father, Dr Henri Hinrichsen has taken you into partnership in the firm of C F Peters and J. Rieter-Biedermann.

I would not like to miss this opportunity of congratulating you most sincerely, and I am convinced that the firm of C F

Peters will retain its hitherto leading position and extend it
in the future through your participation…

Max Hinrichsen's business partnership with his father did not,
however, make him his father's sole heir. Under a family agreement,
after Martha and Henri Hinrichsen's death, their children were to
receive equal shares in the business. The second of Martha and Henri
Hinrichsen's five sons, Walter, was born on 23rd September, 1907.

Walter Hinrichsen

Brought up traditionally like his brother, Max; his personality though,
was quite different. Whereas Max was quiet, serious and introspective,
Walter was outgoing, larger than life and always the popular centre of
attention. After leaving school, Walter spent a short while at the Leipzig
Conservatory of Music before starting his years of apprenticeship in
the music publishing business at the age of twenty in 1927. He was not
happy when he wrote to Max, who had recently returned from the
USA. Max was to be his professional mentor and adviser throughout
his life and this was perhaps an early taste of things to come. What
these apprenticeships of the young heirs to their father's music
publishing companies were designed to achieve, can be gleaned from
the twenty-six-year-old Max Hinrichsen's somewhat didactic reply to
his brother, which was dated 19th August, 1927:[19]

Dear Walter,

It was nice of you to have written to tell me of the pleasures
and sorrows of an apprentice music retailer – at least you
can't complain about boredom! I vividly recalled my own early
days as an apprentice. Though I could barely see over the
counter in the Rathausstrasse, I soon worked my way in; but it
was pretty awful. It was different when I got to Raabe and Plothow
in Berlin whose proprietor, Moritz Raabe, who came from the
Bote & Bock school, is amongst the best of all the German music
dealers. He was terribly strict, a formidable disciplinarian and
made all apprentices and younger employees come to him once
or twice a week and put them through a real exam. We were
asked the key signatures of the various Beethoven and Mozart
symphonies and sonatas, names and prices of all music journals
etc. – We really learnt something there.

It is very important for you to know about the works which
are not often asked for. A knowledge of the [musical]

literature, not only of the German but also of international issues is vitally important. Also, you will have ample opportunity there of becoming acquainted with concert music, with the requirements of orchestras both large and small and with the programmes. All of this will be particularly important later on for Peters, as this is a branch which has, up to now, been rather neglected, but must be taken up and promoted in far greater measure in the future. I would recommend you to concentrate particularly on this; make notes for yourself, insofar as this is feasible; follow the programmes, in Germany as well as internationally. Whatever you learn about cinema and café music is also valuable.

As you will have read, it is intended to reorganise the training for music dealers and to complete the two or three year apprenticeship with an exam. That is essential, as positive knowledge is nowadays more important than ever and through this exam the ambition of the young people really to learn something can be increased.

Many thanks again, continue to enjoy yourself in our beautiful home town...

Your Loving Brother Max

Walter was twenty-one when he went to Hamburg to work for the music publisher, Anton J Benjamin, in 1928. Then he spent some months at the music publisher and retailer, Foetisch Frères, in Lausanne, who had refused Henri Hinrichsen's request to accept Max as an apprentice six years earlier, shortly after the war, for political reasons. Walter went on to Tonger in Cologne in 1929. From there he spent a while in Paris, going to Schott Frères in Brussels and Augener & Co in London. On 1st March, 1931 he joined his father and brother in the family business in Leipzig. From August 1933 to the spring of 1934 Walter made a major round-the-world trip – part holiday and part business – introducing himself to music publishers and retailers throughout the world, expanding his horizons and crystallising his ideas for the future. He decided he would emigrate to the USA and start a branch of C F Peters there.

Henri Hinrichsen's two eldest sons' training was to stand them in good stead and would assure the future of C F Peters, though not in the way envisaged at the time. They were soon to be joined by their younger brother, Hans-Joachim.

Hans-Joachim Hinrichsen

Like his two elder brothers, Hans-Joachim, who was born on 22nd August, 1909, attended the Nicolai School in Leipzig where he specialised in classics and from which he graduated in March 1928. He was the most academic and intellectual of the brothers and studied law. His legal studies took him to the Universities of Freiburg im Breisgau, Munich and Leipzig, followed by a period of practical legal instruction in the courts of Leipzig and Grimma. He was awarded a Doctorate of Law from the University of Leipzig on 20th November, 1934. His thesis, which provided him with specialised knowledge of which he made full use in the business, was on 'The Transfer of Musical Copyright to Music Publishers and Authors' and Composer's Societies'. It was discussed and praised in professional journals throughout Europe and parts were translated for a French journal. A detailed reference was published in the *Bulletin of the Permanent Bureau of the International Congress of Editors* and distributed at the London Publishers' Congress.

Having decided that he would make his career in the family business, Hans-Joachim had been actively involved since 1929. As a student in Munich he introduced himself to the music dealers. He started his apprenticeships in 1934 with two companies in Vienna: Friedrich Hofmeister-Figaro Verlag and Ludwig Doblinger (Bernhard Herzmansky) and then, like Walter, went for a few months to Foetisch Frères in Lausanne. He spent some months in 1935 travelling and representing C F Peters throughout Europe, when he was in contact with music publishers, music retailers, conservatories, libraries, concert managements, conductors, radio stations and record companies. After some time in London, he joined the company full-time in October 1935, when he was granted official power of attorney. His speciality was in copyright and law and his work became indispensable over the next few years.

None of the brothers could have anticipated the cataclysmic changes which were to cause their and their parents' well structured plans to be destroyed and their world to be transformed into a nightmare of suffering, sorrow and loss.

In the meantime though, the company developed in different ways in response to post-war demands and the limiting effects of the inflationary years.

---

1   *L van Beethoven. Seine an den Verlag von Hoffmeister und Kühnel, später C F Peters, Leipzig gerichteten Briefe. Verzeichnis seiner in der Edition Peters erchienenen Werke.*
2   *Edvard Grieg. Briefe an die Verleger der Edition Peters 1866-1907.*
3   *Edvard Grieg. Briefwechsel mit dem Verlag,* C F Peters 1863-1907. Edited by Finn Benestad and Hella Brock, C F Peters, Frankfurt, 1997.

4 All letters in this section in StAL Bestand, C F Peters No 2454.

5 A copy of the *Folksong Book for the Young* was found in the Peters Music Library in Leipzig in 1992. The first time any of the songs from it were performed in public was on 22nd November 1992, at a concert in the Musical Instruments Museum in Leipzig, to commemorate the fiftieth anniversary of the death of Henri Hinrichsen.

6 StAL Bestand, C F Peters No 1540.

7 Cosima Wagner (1837-1930), daughter of Franz Liszt and the Countess Marie d'Agoult, married to the conductor and pianist Hans von Bülow (1830-94) and mistress to Richard Wagner (1813-83), whom she bore three children before her divorce from von Bülow and marriage to Wagner in 1870.

8 StAL Bestand, C F Peters No 2524.

9 Max Hinrichsen to Prof Karl Straube, 1st July 1933. StAL Bestand, C F Peters 2152.

10 StAL Bestand, C F Peters No 4560.

11 Report in the Stadtarchiv Leipzig. Akte No 13, Arch. I (Rat der Stadt Leipzig) ab 1925.

12 StAL Bestand, C F Peters No 4558.

13 StAL Bestand, C F Peters No 4571.

14 Correspondence in the archives of the City of Leipzig.

15 Letter of 17th October 1922 from the Mayor of Leipzig. StAL Bestand, C F Peters No 4553.

16 StAL Bestand, C F Peters No 4553.

17 Letter of 24th April from Margarethe Dyck, Sozialpädagogisches Frauenseminar. Stadtarchiv Leipzip SF 5841, N0 4567-4574.

18 StAL Bestand, C F Peters No 3176/680.

19 StAL Bestand, C F Peters No 4443/310

CHAPTER ELEVEN

From Musical Inspiration to Publication – or Not

Many of the composers published by C F Peters were associated with the company for some forty or so years. We have already been introduced to the early years of collaboration between the company and Christian Sinding, Karl Straube, Richard Strauss, Hans Pfitzner and Sigfrid Karg-Elert. Their stories, along with those of Walter Niemann and Percy Grainger, are now taken up again after the War of 1914-1918 and the subsequent inflation, during which time musical tastes had changed.

Christian Sinding

Sinding [Fig 27], who had borrowed heavily from Henri Hinrichsen, eventually worked off his debt in April 1925. He offered some new compositions, which Hinrichsen knew would not sell well as people now preferred Russian, French and atonal music. Whilst he had to consider the business element, he allowed himself to be influenced by his friendship and compassion towards the composer, and accepted them.

The friendly association continued for many years and Sinding went on sending the sort of compositions which were no longer in demand. But the popularity of *Rustle of Spring* never abated and so the profits on this one piano composition alone, covered the losses on all of the composer's other works published by C F Peters. Congratulating Sinding on his seventieth birthday in 1926 Hinrichsen sent him an honorary fee of 2,000 Norwegian Kroner, which he continued to do every birthday, as long as was necessary.

Sound films came in in 1927, which produced a new and unusual source of royalty revenue for many composers. *Rustle of Spring* was used on a number of soundtracks and by 1932, Sinding was receiving regular royalty payments. So the two men agreed amicably that no further honorary fees would be paid. However, Henri Hinrichsen's generosity towards his old friend did not abate and his sons, who had known Sinding all their lives, would always join in congratulating the old man on his birthday, which was shortly after Christmas.

In December 1935 Sinding received a case of wine from Henri Hinrichsen to celebrate his eightieth birthday. This was quickly followed by a letter from Hans-Joachim Hinrichsen, who wished him good health and happiness for himself and his 'dear wife' and also hoped that he would be able to exchange greetings with him on 11th January, 1946 (a hope which tragically could not be realised). Walter wrote a few days later on his return from a journey to South America, saying that he had heard *Rustle of Spring* played everywhere in celebration of Sinding's eightieth birthday.

By 1938, the piece had been used in five films, including films made in Britain and in the USA as well as Germany and Sweden, all of which were being shown and for which the composer earned fifty per cent of the royalty payment. A royalty statement dated 8th January, 1938[1] lists: *Café Colette,* 1936, a spy melodrama written for Garrick by Eric Maschewitz and Val Gielgud; *Mein Boot* (My Boat), produced by Europa-Stockholm; *Personal Property,* 1937, an MGM comedy starring Jean Harlow and Robert Taylor; and a musical, *You can't have Everything,* 1937, with Alice Faye and Don Ameche, produced by 20th Century Fox; as well as an advertising film for ladies' fabrics which was produced by UFA.

In March 1938, the eighty-two-year-old Sinding, making a detour on a trip from Berlin to Dresden, visited the Hinrichsens in Leipzig – a welcome show of support at a most stressful time.

Karl Straube

Henri Hinrichsen had always rated Straube's opinion highly. In payment for his advice and for his work, he would send him not only a generous payment, but also quantities of printed music for which he was always profusely grateful and always modestly insisted that he was being overpaid. Hinrichsen valued his advice highly. Mindful of the fact that the thirty-year copyright period for César Franck would soon be expired, he wanted to know whether it would be worthwhile to publish some of this composer's works in the Edition Peters. He sent Straube some copies of Franck's compositions with a request for his assessment. This was the opinion which Straube sent him on 27th March, 1918:

> …I would publish all the organ works of César Franck, as well as all the chamber music. All these pieces are *very important* and deserve to become well-known and loved in Germany. The following collections should be considered: *Twelve Pieces, Three Pieces, Three Chorales.* I would publish all the pieces, without any alterations, in the original, with the markings for

French organ. A good German organist will be able to understand every technical marking necessary for performance.

The works to publish from amongst the group for chamber music would be: Violin Sonata, Piano Trios, Piano Quintet and String Quartet. Amongst the orchestral works, the wonderful D-minor Symphony and the Symphonic Variations for Piano and Orchestra. Of the choral works, I would suggest you publish a vocal score of the *Seligkeiten* (Salvations). Then of great note are the lovely piano works: *Praeludium, Chorale and Fugue* and *Praeludium, Aria and Finale.*

Beside Berlioz, we can admire César Franck as the greatest French musical genius. Publishing his music in the Edition Peters would be well worthwhile and very desirable for us Germans.

I am delighted that you plan to hear Arnold Mendelssohn's *Das Leiten des Herren* (The Guidance of the Lord) this Thursday. It is a short, but *exquisite* piece, not forceful but deeply sensitive, sincere and true. Apart from this, we will be performing Brahms' *Begräbnisgesang* (Burial Hymn), so that in this Motet the publishing house of C F Peters rules...

Henri Hinrichsen followed Straube's advice and the works by César Franck which he recommended, were duly taken up, re-edited where necessary and published in the Edition Peters from 1920 onwards.

In 1922 Straube, a perfectionist, was asked to prepare a new edition of a collection of early German music for organ. When Henri Hinrichsen complained that the work was taking much longer than he expected, Straube gave him a good reason, explaining that the result would be infinitely better because of the delay. He had discovered a very old, original organ about which he wrote delightedly to Hinrichsen on 1st May, 1923:

...You should be pleased that nothing has yet been engraved, because a major part of the whole work has to be completely re-done, otherwise it will again only be half of something, unfinished and totally frustrating.

In the meantime I have discovered that there is a perfectly preserved organ of exquisite tone, built by Arp Schnittger in 1688/92, in the St Jacob's Church in Hamburg. I must re-

edit everything by Buxtehude, Pachelbel, Lübeck, Weckmann
which is to go into the volume, according to the properties of
this instrument, because these masters knew this instrument
and played on it. The last-named was in fact organist of the St
Jacob's Church in Hamburg in 1668. So, in this organ we
have the sound which the masters after 1650 used; the
compositions of that time should be edited based on this organ
as a model. Then the volume will be something useful,
something not inconsiderable and something of a certain
value. I hope you will be in agreement with this viewpoint in
the interests of the whole. I will go to Hamburg in the week
after Whitsun in order to work there.

Even if the publication of the album has been somewhat
delayed, this can only be seen as a stroke of luck. The
Praetorius organ in Freiburg is definitive for 1550-1650; the
later works belong to the Hamburg organ. In this way we will
get a more precise picture of the true historical development
of the things and an impression of the sound ideal of the
great old masters...

Matthias Weckmann, a composer and organist who probably ranks
first amongst the pupils of Heinrich Schütz, was one of several
seventeenth century German composers to be 'rediscovered' during
the late nineteenth century through the increasing curiosity about the
antecedents of J S Bach.

Henri Hinrichsen was on the Board of the Leipzig Music
Conservatory. In 1924, a new director was being sought and he invited
Straube to consider accepting the post, or to recommend a suitable
candidate. Straube's letter of 23rd February, 1924 gives us some
insight into contemporary opinion:

...Regarding the question of the directorship of the Leipzig
Conservatory, I have reached the following view; above all, it
must be attempted to attract a new, if at all possible important,
personality to Leipzig; the more talented people are
collected here, the better it will be for the Music City of
Leipzig. Only if all possibilities prove to be fruitless, would I
be prepared to serve in the interim. In the meantime, I have
thought of the following people:

Mr Zilcher, director of the State Music College in
Würzburg; Kaspar Schmid, director of the Regional
Conservatory in Karlsruhe; Leonid Kreutzer – Berlin;

Prof. Dr Fritz Stein – Kiel (first-class organiser and
extremely energetic worker!); Edwin Fischer – Berlin;
Egon Petri – Berlin; Dr Egon Wellesz – Vienna.

I would like to emphasise the last two named whom you should
seriously consider. Egon Petri should be known to you by
name, he is a dedicated, first-class person, as well as being
well qualified and very energetic. Worthy of very serious
consideration is the last named, Dr Egon Wellesz – born in
Vienna in 1888, composer and student of Schönberg –
musicologist, student of Guido Adler. An intellectually
important personality of the highest cultural stature, a
dedicated worker and an international name in Paris, London,
Rome where he is as well-known and at home as in Vienna
and Berlin. I know Wellesz personally, he made a very good
impression on me and to attract this man here, would really
be a great gain for Leipzig, we would be richer by a
personality!...

Ultimately, the pianist Professor Max Pauer was appointed director
of the Leipzig Conservatory of Music, which post he held until 1932.
Pauer edited a number of albums for piano for C F Peters, notably
Beethoven's Piano Sonatas.

In 1925, when Straube was giving up conducting, Henri Hinrichsen
renewed his invitation to edit the complete organ works of J S Bach
for publication by C F Peters.

The 5th January, 1928 marked the twenty-fifth anniversary of Karl
Straube's association with C F Peters, Leipzig. Henri Hinrichsen used
the occasion to send him a very welcome cheque and to offer his
congratulations, when he wrote:[2]

...On this day, on which you can look back on twenty-five
years of activity in Leipzig, I do not want the Edition Peters to
be missing from the deluge of congratulations which you will
be receiving. As important and successful as your work as
organist, as Cantor of St Thomas Church, as conductor and
most importantly – as is shown by the huge number of your
delighted students – as teacher is, so, without doubt do the
collections which you have edited for the Edition Peters
belong as prominently to the outline of your creative
personality. I am convinced that your Old Masters, the
Choral Preludes, your edition of the Organ Works of Franz
Liszt and above all the one volume of Bach Organ Works will
prove of lasting value.

The Edition Peters considers it as an honour to see your name represented in this way in its catalogue, and would therefore today like to send you an honorary fee in respect of our past collaboration. Without wishing to influence the use to which it will be put, it would be a particular pleasure to me if you would put it towards a relaxing trip, perhaps to Italy – the land of our longing – or to Bad Gastein, so that you can continue in your creative activity with the same vigour as now, for many more years...

On 4th January, 1933 Hinrichsen congratulated him on his sixtieth birthday, which also marked the thirtieth anniversary of his activity in Leipzig, sending him an honorary fee of 500M and adding: '...Also my company has to thank you for your warm-hearted interest over the course of a whole lifetime...'[3]

In celebration of the 'Bach Year' 1935, the *Peters Nachrichten* (C F Peters Newsletter) No 46 publicised all the compositions and arrangements of the music of J S Bach published in the Edition Peters. It included new Bach editions issued between 1932-1934 and announced that the complete organ works of Bach, edited by Karl Straube, were in preparation. These were never issued, because Straube, the perfectionist, was never satisfied that he could complete them to his own exacting standards.

The friendship and support which Henri Hinrichsen had been offering Straube for years, continued after 1933 when the Nazi persecution of the Jewish publisher began. Straube was still preparing new editions of Reger's music for C F Peters. Though life was difficult for Henri Hinrichsen in 1938, he sent his friend a substantial gift for his sixty-fifth birthday. Straube's letter of 2nd January, 1938[4] expresses the horror of the times: '...The past year has received its crowning through your kind generosity, because generosity and kindness have become something rare in the storm of our times, which makes he who may experience it consider himself very fortunate...'

Straube's new edition of Reger's *Benedictus*, Op 59 No 9 was reviewed in the April 1938 issue of the *Musical Times*. The reviewer, Archibald Farmer, pointed out that this edition by Straube which was in the Syllabus, was the only one which was acceptable by the examiners.

Karl Straube and his wife were amongst those of the Hinrichsens' German friends who continued to correspond with Martha and Henri Hinrichsen after their exile in 1940. Another who gave his moral support was Walter Niemann.

Walter Niemann (1876-1953)

Niemann [Fig 28] was born into a musical family. His father was the composer and pianist Rudolph Niemann, who was also his first teacher. Walter studied at the Leipzig Conservatory of Music and became a teacher, pianist, writer and prolific composer.

Karl Straube's introduction in 1916 of the compositions of Walter Niemann, led to the publication by C F Peters of many of his piano pieces and other compositions. This was not the first collaboration between composer and publisher. After the death of Edvard Grieg in 1907, Henri Hinrichsen had commissioned the Norwegian writer, Gerhard Schjelderup to write a biography of the composer. This encompassed a detailed appreciation of Grieg's works by Walter Niemann and was published in 1908. C F Peters had also published some of his works before 1916. Henri Hinrichsen wrote about Niemann in his *Chronik:*

> ...C F Peters has published many works of the fruitful composer since 1912, of which *Alt-China* (Old China), *Masken* (Masks) and *Hamburg* have enjoyed particular success. The composer himself arranged several of the pieces (in Grieg's style) for string orchestra. Several works of his have also been issued by other publishers, though none outside of Germany.

> Niemann works tremendously hard at promoting the children of his muse, for which one has to give him credit. Last year (1932) he achieved about 500 performances of his music on German radio stations, whilst he himself appeared as pianist in broadcasts in Leipzig, Hamburg and other cities.

There are several hundred letters from Walter Niemann in the archive in Leipzig detailing the progress of the many publications and the development of a sincere friendship between the composer and the entire Hinrichsen family. Henri Hinrichsen expressed his friendship and liking for the man with many generous presents and ex-gratia payments and consideration for the temperament of the creative artist.

Walter Niemann's type of music appealed to popular taste for many years. When tastes changed C F Peters had to turn down some of his numerous piano pieces. During the 1930s Niemann became didactic and demanding in his negotiations with the publisher and found unjustified cause to complain, which Max and Hans-Joachim Hinrichsen accommodated with tact and understanding. On 9th September, 1935[5] Max had to remind him that far from his publishers neglecting him, they had promised him a pension of 600M per year for at least the next three years, on top of all the fees he was getting.

C F Peters did a lot of publicity for Niemann's music, but his gratitude was grudging, though in his letter of 13th May, 1936[6] he did apologise for his unjustified accusation that the firm was not doing enough for him, when he wrote: '...I was not remotely thinking of an "openly expressed reproach" that C F Peters was not doing enough publicity for me! – On the contrary, I am well aware of and grateful for the generous and systematic publicity which its owners and colleagues have always done for "its Walter Niemann"...' He then went on to ask for advice about a recording contract. The firm continued to publicise his music with many advertisements and free copies; his tone became more mellowed and appreciative.

Niemann was well-known as a composer and as a pianist in Germany and his sixtieth birthday on 10th October, 1936, was acknowledged with articles in several newspapers, which Hans-Joachim Hinrichsen made a point of sending him. The *Peters Nachrichten* No 57, which was widely distributed, was devoted to publicity for his music and Niemann received large quantities which he distributed. Henri Hinrichsen presented his old friend with some choice items out of his own autograph collection. C F Peters accepted Niemann's *Ballet Suite* for publication in 1936 and collaboration was back on the old friendly basis. Niemann's birthday was celebrated by the Hinrichsen family in 10 Talstrasse where he was always welcomed. He had known the Hinrichsen sons since they were children.

Walter Niemann's association with the company originated through his appreciation of the works of Edvard Grieg. Another composer, whose association was entirely based on his admiration for Grieg, was Percy Grainger.

Percy Grainger (1882-1961)

Grainger is introduced, not as a composer in his own right, but as an example of the promotion by one composer, of the music of another. The collaboration and effort expended between publisher and musician, in the dissemination of music which they both hold in high esteem is exemplified.

Edvard Grieg first met Percy Grainger in London, in 1906, a year before his death. He regarded the twenty-four-year-old Grainger as an 'inspired pianist'[7] and, so impressed was he that he invited the younger man to visit him in his villa at Troldhaugen in Norway the following summer. There, Grieg played his A minor Piano Concerto for Grainger and persuaded him to play it at the Leeds Festival, with the composer as conductor. Sadly, Grieg's death one month before the Festival meant

that Grainger played the Concerto under another baton. Grainger
thought so highly of Grieg and his music that, from that time on, he
promoted and played it all over the world.

Having studied music in Germany, Grainger was a fluent
correspondent in German. In 1910, Henri Hinrichsen had sent him
some albums of Grieg's music, together with the *Catalogue of Grieg's
Works with Introduction: My First Success* published in 1908. Grainger
was staying in Troldhaugen and, on 12th September, 1910, sent an
autographed postcard portrait of himself, expressing his profuse
thanks.[8] However, it was not until 1925 that the collaboration between
Percy Grainger and C F Peters was really formed. It started with a letter
from Grainger from White Plains, New York, dated 19th December,
1924:

> ...As you probably already know, I was with Grieg in the
> summer of 1907 (I was his last guest), at which time we did a
> great deal of work on his Piano Concerto. I was to play this
> work at the Leeds Festival under his direction. At the time, I
> made many notes of what was most characteristic about his
> performance, which was not indicated on the printed page.
> There were also various technical alterations which I was
> including in my, already frequent, performances at that
> time, of which Grieg approved. He said to me that these
> should be included in the next edition of the Concerto –
> such as a cadenza in the first movement, amongst other
> things.
>
> In 1909, the firm of G Schirmer, Inc. in New York, my
> American publishers since 1914, asked me to revise the Grieg
> Concerto for them. I saw in this the opportunity to transmit
> the knowledge which I had received directly from Grieg, to
> the whole world, and rose to the task with pleasure. However,
> I reserved something for myself in the contract with
> Schirmers – I retained all the European rights, Great Britain,
> Scandinavia, etc. I did this in order to be in the position to be
> able to offer you, as the *Grieg publisher*, the **European** rights to
> my revisions of the Grieg Concerto, free of charge – if you
> would like to make use of it. I do this now and send you a
> copy of my revision of the Concerto.

Grainger elaborated on his revisions and then continued:

> I play the Grieg Concerto several times every season in
> America. This season I will play the work at least ten times

with symphony orchestra in the USA; apart from which I am playing it four times a day with large orchestra, for a whole week in the Fox Theatre in Philadelphia. In 1926 I will play the Grieg Concerto with orchestra in all the large cities in Australia and New Zealand and *maybe* I will have a European tour in 1927.

In his concerts and recitals Grainger was making an especial effort to perform Grieg's lesser-known works and wanted to play his part in making the unknown works for choir better known, primarily the *Album for Male Choir,* Op 30 and the *Psalms* and wrote further:

In April 1924 I conducted two major concerts in New York and in Bridgeport (Conn) when two of the *Psalms* were performed, which made a *fantastic* impression! I enclose a copy of the programme for you. I want to include the *Psalms* in major choral and orchestral concerts which I will be conducting in 1926 and 1927 in Australia, Los Angeles, San Francisco, Portland, Or. and Spokane, Wash. However, there is no edition of the *Psalms* with English text, which makes performance here or in Australia well nigh impossible. As you will see from the programme of April 1924, I have myself translated the texts of two of the *Psalms. I would be prepared to translate all the Psalms into English* and let you have my translations *free of charge*, if you could publish such an edition by September 1925, so that these can be used by the big American and Australian choirs which I will be conducting. In this case, I would not only translate the texts, but I would write them all in below the notes, as they should appear on the vocal score.

Grainger continued to offer his own feelings and attitudes towards the music of Edvard Grieg:

This spring (or next season) I will probably be performing Grieg's *Den Bergtegne* in New York. Grieg really loved this work. I am particularly looking forward to the *Symphonic Dances* which I will be conducting in the USA and Australia. All such Grieg works are far too little known. Grieg is (with right) well-known as a popular composer, but the day must come when his idiosyncratic and most profound sides should become equally well-known, or at least *fairly well-known.* I am very successful as a composer myself – I can live from my royalties. Therefore, I can allow myself to spend some of the

huge amount of money which I earn as a pianist, in his artistic
interest. (I have nine old friends and relatives in Germany,
Australia and so on, who are financially dependent on me.)
I hope I will be able to continue every year with the concerts
which I started last April in New York; concerts with chorus
and orchestra, or orchestral concerts (without choir), or
large chamber music concerts, which will serve the purpose
of introducing the lesser-known works of my favourite
composers (Grieg, Frederick Delius, Cyril Scott, Herman
Sandby, etc.). I will probably also give concerts of this sort in
other American cities, as well as in Australia, and maybe in
due course in Germany, Holland and Scandinavia.

My address is *always* as below, in White Plains.

Yours sincerely,

Percy Grainger

Henri Hinrichsen was thrilled about Grainger's enthusiasm for
performing Grieg's lesser-known works and wrote to him on 31st
January saying that he would gladly publish Grainger's revised version
of the Piano Concerto and also an edition of the translated *Psalms*.
However, he pointed out that it had always been a policy of C F
Peters to pay for any works published and offered Grainger $500.00.
He also hoped to meet Grainger in person if he ever came to Leipzig.
In his reply of 25th February Grainger wrote that he would undertake
the translations of the *Psalms* and the choral works for male voices as
soon as possible; however, in view of the 100 concerts he was giving
that season, his time was limited. He felt that $500.00 was far too
much for such a little piece of work, which he would gladly do for
nothing.

By 5th June, 1925 Grainger had finished the translations of the
Psalms which he sent to Leipzig. He wrote of a successful
performance which he had given of *Den Bergtegne* in New York. Letters
followed frequently, discussing various aspects of the work, concerts,
proposed performances and other matters. Henri Hinrichsen was
delighted that a musician of the calibre of Percy Grainger, should
take such an interest in promoting the works of Edvard Grieg.

In spite of Grainger's gruelling schedule, when he was also teaching
for eight hours a day, he had the translations of Grieg's Op 30, together
with a foreword and the texts entered on the vocal score, ready to
send to Leipzig on 16th July. He felt that it was important to print the
foreword to explain and emphasise the deeper creative meaning and

the modern importance of the choral works. He had written copious programme notes explaining the significance of the music, for his concerts. Grainger was staying with Delius in Grez-sur-Loing in France until 28th August and received the proofs there. By October 1925 Henri Hinrichsen could send Grainger all the copies he needed of the newly published Edvard Grieg works in his editions: Op 30 *Album for Male Choir*, the *Psalms* and also the new edition of the Piano Concerto. He pointed out that copies of all of these would be available from the New York house: C F Peters (Enoch & Sons), 9 East 45th Street, which office was being run at this time by his son, Max Hinrichsen.

Percy Grainger travelled widely in the USA, Canada and Australia during 1926 and performed Grieg's works frequently, with great success. He also encouraged other musicians to follow his lead. Hinrichsen sent free copies of the works to various musicians at his request. However, in spite of all these performances, there was little tangible result in the form of sales.

Percy Grainger continued to promote Grieg's works and ask for copies to be sent to various musicians who might be interested in performing them. By August 1932, copies of the first printing of Grainger's English translation of the Op 30 *Album for Male Choir* were finally exhausted. Sales had been sluggish, business was poor and a reprint was not considered worthwhile. But Grainger wrote that he would be making great efforts to introduce the volume in Australia. Thus encouraged, C F Peters ordered an immediate re-print. Grainger's English translation of the *Psalms* was reprinted in October 1933. However, despite all his efforts, he had to write on 20th January, 1935: 'Up to now I have not been able to organise any performances of the Grieg *Album for Male Choir*, but I am still hoping to be able to...' So the reprinting of Op 30 was after all an unnecessary expense.

Max Hinrichsen, who had taken over the correspondence with Grainger wrote on 9th March, 1935 expressing appreciation of Grainger's efforts to introduce Grieg's music in Australia adding:

> ...Why the *Album for Male Choir* has been relegated into the background, I really don't understand; in response to your suggestions, I sent approval copies of a variety of works to the music dealers there with whom we deal; they were virtually all returned to me. If anything at all is to be done with the Choruses over there, then it will be only through your own efforts...

Grainger wrote of more successful broadcasts and performances of Grieg's works which he had instigated in Australia and he was sent a number of works from C F Peters to introduce in Australia. He was tireless in his promotion of the music in which he believed and wrote a long letter on 1st September, 1935:

Dear Mr Geheimrat Hinrichsen,

Many thanks for your friendly letter of 17.8.35 and for the two very welcome scores of *Landerkennung*. I will immediately recommend the arrangements for mixed choir and chamber orchestra to Mr J Post, the excellent conductor of the 'Wireless Chorus' of the Australian Broadcasting Commission (Radio) in Sydney, in the hope that he will order the choir parts (etc.) and organise a performance. If my efforts with him should prove to be of no avail, I will try elsewhere. As I will be leaving Australia in a few weeks, it is too late for a performance under my direction. By the time I leave Australia and New Zealand, I will have some 158 radio broadcasts and 56 public concerts behind me. I have given or organised several performances of Grieg works in every State and in every larger city. The radio programmes which I sent you are typical of my programmes *everywhere*. As you can see, I have instigated a performance of Grieg's *The Great White Host* (*Album for Male Choir*) on 8th August in Sydney, on the radio.

Now (in Oct-Nov) there will be twenty concerts and broadcasts in New Zealand. Grieg will be frequently represented in these twenty programmes (as well as in Australia) – in Christchurch in fact, there will be a complete concert of Grieg's piano works. I will play the Grieg Piano Concerto with orchestra (on 5th Dec.) in Auckland...

Grainger proceeded to list a number of Grieg works he would be performing in his broadcasts, and then continued: 'Seen as a whole, it would be fair to say that I have thoroughly **drenched** Australia and New Zealand with Grieg over the past one and a half years.'

Percy Grainger was in a unique position to recognise budding talent. In London, he had a Norwegian student, Sparre Olsen, who he felt was a worthy follower of Grieg. He now introduced this young genius to Henri Hinrichsen:

Sparre Olsen, a young Norwegian composer, born in 1903 in whom I am very interested. In my opinion he is the most talented of **all** of the young Norwegian composers known to me. Apart from which, I see in his music (as in no other) the development of Grieg's spirit and musical legacy. I am so excited by Sparre Olsen that (apart from playing his *Six Old Peasant Songs from Lorn* all over the place) I have arranged his song, 'Fjell-Norig' (Mountain Norway) for mixed choir and chamber orchestra (even though I had so little free time) and have performed it far and wide in Australia. This little work (duration three minutes) aroused incredible excitement wherever it was performed in Australia – in Hobart, Melbourne, Adelaide, Brisbane, etc.

He then went on to describe the various arrangements he had made of the work and urged the publisher to contact the composer; he himself offered to send a copy of the score of his own orchestral arrangement. Grainger was full of praise for 'Mountain Norway' and was planning to perform and broadcast the work several more times in Australia and New Zealand. So keen was he to see the work published, that he also offered his various arrangements free of charge.

Grainger next wrote on board the RMS *Niagara*, on 25th December, 1935, having completed his tour of New Zealand and being bound for the USA. He listed the many performances of Grieg's works he had given in New Zealand and mentioned that he had endowed four new music libraries, in order to facilitate the study of Grieg's lesser-known works. Another long list of names of people who should receive free copies of Grieg's music was appended, in hope of performances during his absence.

Grainger wrote on 6th June, 1936, from England, saying how pleased he had been to meet Walter Hinrichsen, then working at the C F Peters' agent, Summy, in Chicago. Still promoting his translations of Grieg's works, he wrote again two weeks later with news about 'America's biggest Music Camp', which had been organised every year since 1928 by Joseph E Maddy, in Interlocken, Michigan. He urged Hinrichsen to send twenty free copies of his *Album for Male Choir* and thirty free copies of his *Psalms* and some other works.

Sparre Olsen visited Percy Grainger in Pevensey Bay in July which spurred Grainger on to promote his young protégé. He sent the score and material of *Mountain Norway* and expressed his enthusiasm for Olsen's *Norwegian Folk Melodies from Gudrandsdal* arranged for piano, at great length, in his letters of 14th and 24th July, 1936, likening the compositions to Grieg.

Both of Sparre Olsen's works thus introduced were very carefully considered by C F Peters reader Wilhelm Weismann, who wrote a report on them. Max Hinrichsen wrote to Percy Grainger on 30th July, 1936 kindly, regretting that the works would not be suitable and suggesting possible alternative publishers. Percy Grainger wrote on 7th August, 1936, shortly before his return to New York, expressing his warm gratitude for the consideration and for the further suggestions and was in agreement with everything Max Hinrichsen had written. That was the last communication from Grainger, preserved in the archives of C F Peters, Leipzig. However, the association continued with Max Hinrichsen, after the latter's emigration to England in 1937.

Concurrently with those composers already discussed, the association between C F Peters and Hans Pfitzner had been in effect since early in the century.

Hans Pfitzner

Pfitzner received many honours and Pfitzner Societies were organised in several German cities. He had a post 'for life' in Munich, where the city authorities decided to celebrate his sixtieth birthday in 1929, lavishly. Henri Hinrichsen, who had plans for a personal presentation to the composer, responded with his customary generosity to the Mayor of Munich's appeal dated 27th March, 1929, for a contribution of at least 500M towards a gift for Pfitzner's sixtieth birthday. Hinrichsen sent 1,000M. A small Mercedes car was bought for Pfitzner with the 13,000M donated.

Pfitzner, a family friend, was a frequent guest at the Hinrichsens' home in 10 Talstrasse. Martha Hinrichsen attended his concerts and events whenever possible and one or other of her three eldest sons often represented their father. Hans-Joachim, just twenty and studying law, attended Hans Pfitzner's sixtieth birthday celebrations in Munich.

His brother Walter, aged twenty-two, was at the time serving an apprenticeship in Lausanne. When Martha, who kept him up to date with home news, wrote to him on 6th May, 1929[9] she mentioned the honours bestowed on Pfitzner. She also referred to his opera: '…His *Palestrina*[10] will surely one day be recognised as something important; I really wish I could have the chance of hearing it more often. I was so pleased that Hanns could attend the celebration…' She wrote to Walter again a few days later, on 13th May, when she enthused to him at greater length about Pfitzner who had invited her to come to Chemnitz to attend the final rehearsal of his Cantata composed in 1921, to words by Eichendorf, 'Von deutscher Seele' (Of the German Soul). She continued her letter:

> …Pfitzner received enormous honours in Munich, such as no other composer or musician has received for a long time, only Furtwängler is celebrated in such a manner these days, his journey is like a triumphal march. Pfitzner got a master class in Munich including a certain number of opera performances as conductor and medals, golden medal of the

city of Munich, honorary membership of the university there. His followers throughout Germany gave him a car with paid chauffeur for a year. For a whole week there were festive Pfitzner performances, the most important being a celebration when a choir of 1,000 sang his choral works. There were 6,000 people invited to witness the bestowing of all the honours on him and all the speeches; at the end all participants and audience sang the 'Deutschlandlied' which made a powerful impression on everybody. And that such an admired individual took pleasure in spending an evening alone with me, just chatting, really makes me very happy...

Fourteen years had passed since the last time that C F Peters had published a work by Pfitzner (in 1918), and before Henri Hinrichsen was able to persuade the composer to send him further works for publication: though, once sent, the composer was impatient for their speedy publication. In 1932 C F Peters published his *Six Lieder,* Op 40 and *Three Sonnets,* Op 41. He displayed no understanding for the intricacies of music publishing, when he wrote arrogantly on 15th January, 1932:

...I am of course disappointed to hear that the songs will not be ready until the middle of February. I had encouraged the Pfitzner Society in Munich to include them in a concert on 15th February. I have to go to Austria in the second half of February; so the concert cannot take place later than the middle of February. It would really be very desirable that the first performance should take place with myself at the piano and first-class performers like Paul Bender and Luise Willer. I could let them sing Op 40 and 41 from the manuscript; but that would not be in *your* interest, because there should be an opportunity for the public to buy the songs on the next day. On the other hand, I don't like the idea of having to delay the concert until March. So I would ask you to try your hardest to get my new work published by the latest during the first week in February and to see that the singers can at least get proofs by the end of January. It is surely possible to print nine songs in four weeks...

Hans Pfitzner was known to be a somewhat cantankerous person and Henri Hinrichsen always made allowances for artistic temperament.

Pfitzner was never afraid of asking for something and, thanking Henri Hinrichsen for a score which he had sent, asked for something else. He needed money. On 14th February, 1933 he wrote offering some early songs, which he had composed before the age of seventeen and before and during his student years at the Conservatory and also asked Hinrichsen to publish a series of compositions for piano by a student at the Academy. Henri Hinrichsen knew there was no commercial sense in publishing any of these works, as he explained on 18th February, 1933:

> ...As much as it was a pleasure to me, to present the *Heiling* score to you by return of post, it is my regret that I will not be able to accept the works offered to me in your letter of 14th inst for publication. Since I published three books of songs by you last year, which will naturally take a considerable time to achieve popularity, I see no possibility that six youthful songs – in which you have apparently not had any confidence up to now – can be issued with any success at this time. I must concentrate on trying to introduce those of your songs which I published recently. As my new issues list for September has already gone over budget, whilst the purchasing power of the public has unfortunately shrunk, I would not like to hold anything back; least of all to introduce piano pieces by a 'talented student of the Academy' into my catalogue, which in any case goes against the traditions which I have followed these past forty years. The Edition Peters has always sought to publish works of a classical nature, which is why the business is still relatively successful.

> With Very Kindest Regards,

> Henri Hinrichsen

Pfitzner appears to have chosen to misunderstand this reply and expressed his anger in a very bitter, lengthy letter two days later. The hiatus was resolved and the relationship remained cordial. Hinrichsen continued to support Pfitzner financially, even though the composer's political convictions made this difficult.

Hans Pfitzner supported and admired Adolf Hitler long before he came to power in 1933. Hitler had long been an admirer of Pfitzner's music and had visited the composer in hospital, in 1921. The friendship between Pfitzner and Henri Hinrichsen did not suffer as a result.

Pfitzner became disillusioned with the Nazi cause and in 1934 lost his 'for life' teaching post in Munich, when he said that anti-Semitism was stupid. His income plummeted. When Henri Hinrichsen heard in mid-1935 that his friend was in severe financial straits he wanted to help him. He wrote on 11th July, 1935 expressing his pride at having some of Pfitzner's best works in the C F Peters' catalogue, in recognition of which he was sending him an honorary fee of 2,000M, hoping he would accept it in the same spirit of friendship in which it was sent. Pfitzner's rejection on 17th July, of his friend's generosity, was an indication of his political conviction, over his own needs:

> Your offer of an honorary fee was indeed a welcome surprise and I thank you sincerely for the good intention and for your generosity. However, I beg you to understand that, in the Germany of today, it could be wrongly interpreted and could have serious consequences for both of us, if I were to accept an honorary fee from a non-Aryan publisher.
>
> As hard as it is for me, both personally and economically, I have had to decide to return the cheque to you with a renewed expression of my thanks. I hope you will respect my standpoint and, along with your dear wife, continue to think kindly of me...

Hinrichsen did continue to think kindly of him and wrote to him sympathetically on 12th February, 1936 after Pfitzner had been involved in a motor accident. In his reply of 15th March Pfitzner gave him a graphic account of the accident. When he wrote again on 8th October, 1936 asking if he could purchase a score of Haydn's Symphony in D-maj, EP No 5, Hinrichsen responded by return on 9th October, sending him the score free of charge and adding: 'Your friendly lines of yesterday gave me an especial pleasure as they must, in view of our friendship over so many years, to know that you use material from the Edition Peters in your concerts...' Hinrichsen was especially moved, in view of the general anti-Semitic embargo against using music published by C F Peters and Pfitzner's previous rejection of his financial help.

Hinrichsen commissioned Pfitzner to make some arrangements. However, his previous generosity encouraged Pfitzner to make unreasonable demands. On 10th November, 1936 he wrote that 75M was unacceptable for preparing the instrumentation of 'Wanderers Nachtlied' (Wanderer's Night Song) and added: ' Some time ago you offered me 2,000M for much less. If you would willingly pay me 150M for the instrumentation, I will accept this...' The sum was sent and in spite of one or two misunderstandings on Pfitzner's part, relations remained cordial.

Though Pfitzner fell on hard times, such appeal as his music had, was not lost. Christian Sinding and Walter Niemann were two amongst many whose music fell from popularity after World War I. Another was Sigfrid Karg-Elert [Fig 29], whose memory was to suffer a similar fate.

Sigfrid Karg-Elert

C F Peters had been publishing organ works and arrangements for the harmonium by Karg-Elert since 1910. He was acclaimed world-wide as a composer for organ and a Karg-Elert Festival was planned in London. He wrote enthusiastically to Henri Hinrichsen on 22nd February, 1930:

> ...The most important organ authorities in England are planning to form a Karg-Elert Society. Mr Chisholm gave a series of Organ Evenings in Glasgow in November during which Op 65 (66 Symphonic Choral works) received a private, sensational first performance. He was asked to repeat these three recitals in London. A plan was launched by the Royal College of Organists (of which I am an honorary member), to organise a major Karg-Elert Festival, during which, in a series of ten recitals, my complete organ works should be performed in chronological order. These are to be supplemented by analytical lectures.
>
> Godfrey Sceats, who has worked tremendously hard to make my works known in England and the Colonies, including Australia, has arranged several larger harmonium works for his own use, for the modern English and American organs. He has been booked by the London consortium to give the first performance of my 2nd Harmonium Sonata, Op 46 (*Fantasie und Doppelfuge über BACH, Canzona, Tokkata und Epilog*) in his own grandiose arrangement. He has asked me for my, and the original publisher's agreement...

Mr Chisholm was Erik Chisholm, Scottish conductor, composer, organist, administrator and writer on music. He was an ardent promoter of new music, forming the Active Society for the Propagation of Contemporary Music in 1929, for which he organised over 200 first performances in Britain. As conductor of the Glasgow Grand Opera Society (1930-39) he presented many first British performances.

Karg-Elert had been elected an honorary member of the Royal College of Organists in London in 1914. He subsequently used the title of Dr h c, though it was doubtful whether this was in fact legitimate.

The Karg-Elert Festival of 1930 was the only time the composer visited Great Britain. Organised by Godfrey William Sceats, it was a resounding success. Sceats had first contacted Karg-Elert in 1922, when he had sent the composer a copy of his article: 'The Liturgical Use of the Organ', which had been published in the magazine, *Musical Opinion*. They did not however start corresponding on a regular basis until 1926.

This one visit of the composer to Great Britain was the only occasion on which the two met. Godfrey Sceats continued to promote Karg-Elert's music and in 1940 he compiled a booklet: *The Organ Works of Karg-Elert*, which was reprinted in a revised and enlarged edition in 1950. These booklets were published by Max Hinrichsen, who emigrated to England in 1937. He collaborated further with Godfrey Sceats, publishing several of Karg-Elert's works during the 1950s.

Karg-Elert was already seriously ill, when he offered Henri Hinrichsen some works for publication in March 1933, which were rejected. He died two weeks later, at the age of fifty-six.

It was left to his daughter, Käthchen Karg-Elert, a music student, to organise her late father's manuscripts. She found a drawerful of manuscripts which she catalogued and sent the list to Henri Hinrichsen on 8th November, 1935[11], offering them for publication. Henri Hinrichsen had his difficulties in 1935 and few people were interested in buying Karg-Elert's works, so his reply of 11th November[12] was negative:

> ...I am indeed sorry, as I am sure are many of Karg-Elert's admirers, that so many of his manuscripts have not yet been made available to all. I would very much have liked to have accepted one or two of the works for publication in the Edition Peters, if the works which I have already published were in greater demand. But because these edition numbers are so rarely asked for, I have to assume that the works of Sigfrid Karg-Elert are not sought in my publishing house. I have in fact still got an Organ Symphony of your father's here, which, for the above reasons, I have not yet dared to publish.
>
> In expressing to you my regret that I cannot accede to your wishes, I remain...

Interest for the compositions of Karg-Elert was not sustained. It was revived in 1984 when the *Karg-Elert Gesellschaft* was founded in Germany. The Karg-Elert Society was founded in Great Britain in 1987; the President, Nicholas Choveaux was one of the organisers of the 1930 Festival.

Publishing music, social involvement and education were only part of the activities occupying Henri Hinrichsen during the 1920s. The Peters Music Library made considerable demands on his time and finances. To this was added a new and major benefaction, the Music Instruments Museum, which earned him enormous prestige.

1 StAL Bestand, C F Peters, No 2531.

2 StAL Bestand, C F Peters, No 4560.

3 StAL Bestand, C F Peters, No 2152.

4 *Ibid.*

5 StAL Bestand, C F Peters, No 2129

6 *Ibid.*

7 Letter from Grieg to Henri Hinrichsen dated 29th June 1906, in Bergen
   Library, Norway.

8 All correspondence quoted in StAL Bestand, C F Peters, No 1137.

9 Martha Hinrichsen to Walter Hinrichsen. Both letters in the author's archive.

10 *Palestrina* received its première in Munich on 12th June, 1917 and has been
   performed regularly in Germany since then. It was given its first fully
   professional staging in Great Britain at the Royal Opera House, Covent Garden
   on 28th January, 1997.

11 StAL Bestand, C F Peters, No 1749

12 *Ibid.*

CHAPTER TWELVE

The Peters Music Library 1919 to 1933
The Music Instruments Museum 1926 to 1929

Development of the Peters Music Library

The first quarter-century of the existence of the Peters Music Library since its foundation by Dr Max Abraham in 1894 had seen a huge growth in its content and hence its value as one of the finest music libraries in Germany. Users had increased steadily. The war years, 1914-1918, saw a natural drop in visitors, but pre-war borrowers would arrive in grey military uniform, when they were on leave. The scores which were most often borrowed reflected a certain historicism, people were more interested in Bach and the classical composers than in Richard Strauss. 1919 saw a gradual return to pre-war interest, with 3,516 users compared with only 1,678 during 1918, in spite of fewer working days. The Library was closed from 28th February to 11th March during the general strike and during Christmas week to conserve coal stocks. Prices of books and music had risen, meaning that instead of 200 to 300 new additions annually, only about 100 items were purchased in 1919.

Communist inspired street brawls lead to the closure of the library from 5th to 11th March, 1920. Still the year saw almost 4,000 visitors; these included members of an international delegation taking part in 'Leipzig University Week' given a tour of the Peters Music Library. New purchases included eighteenth century books on musical theory, and several full orchestral scores. Until the war, the Peters Music Library *Yearbook* had listed a complete bibliography of music literature issued in Germany for the year as well as all items published in the USA, France and Holland. Inevitably, this was not possible during the war, but was started again in the 1921 *Yearbook* when also, for the first time, a complete bibliography of all those books published in Great Britain was included.

The inflation years were disastrous for the Peters Music library. When Dr Max Abraham had presented the Library to the City of Leipzig, he also bequeathed a capital sum of 400,000M, the interest on which was to finance the library, the upkeep of the house, the head librarian's salary and new purchases. The Leipzig finance department, responsible for the capital, had made some unwise investments resulting in an almost total loss, the original sum being reduced to 10,000M. 1921 to 1923 saw severe economies in terms of purchases and the production of the *Yearbook*, whilst the library was open only four days a week. However, its future was assured with Henri Hinrichsen's willingness to take over the entire financial responsibility for the upkeep, new acquisitions and employees' salaries from 1922 onwards. He also donated a further capital sum of 100,000M.

There came the moment, however, when he felt that the city authorities were expecting too much of him. He drew the line when they demanded a totally unjustifiable tax from him. Desperately seeking new ways of raising money, they demanded a new Residential Accommodation Tax. He responded angrily on 16th March, 1923:[1]

> I regret to advise you that I strongly object to the demand of a Residential Accommodation Tax for the premises of the Peters Music Library at 26 Königstrasse. These rooms have been available free of charge for almost thirty years, to music students, and can be regarded as class-rooms, which have also drawn many students to Leipzig over the course of the years. This is a Trust which Dr Max Abraham set up in 1900 and which is supervised by the city authorities. There is no way that the interest, which comes to approximately 14,000M every year even begins to cover the costs. Up to now I have never asked for a grant from the city and I do not have the intention of doing so, even though I have this year spent several million marks on the upkeep of the library. I would regard it as unreasonable if I were also expected to pay a Residential Accommodation Tax for these premises.

The Peters Music Library was a focal point for music students from Leipzig, the neighbouring town of Halle and from all over Saxony. To make it a more welcoming and comfortable place for them to carry out their researches, Henri Hinrichsen had the entire premises re-decorated and newly furnished in 1924. The refurbishment was celebrated with a visit from the Mayor of Leipzig, Dr Rothe, and the Director of the Conservatory of Music, Professor Max Pauer. Some 150 new acquisitions were added to the library that year and each of the following years. Opening hours were extended.

1927 was a golden year for acquisitions of very early books on music. Henri Hinrichsen presented a valuable library of music and books published during the sixteenth and seventeenth centuries, which he had purchased as part of the Heyer collection of 2,600 musical instruments for the University of Leipzig. More very early books were purchased for the library in the following two years, when the collection formed by the music collector and critic Werner Wolffheim was auctioned in Berlin; this was considered to be the most important auction of its kind in the twentieth century.

Professor Rudolf Schwartz, who had been head librarian of the Peters Music Library since 1900, retired at the age of seventy-one in 1930, having guided the library and edited the *Jahrbuch der Musikbibliothek Peters* (Peters Music Library *Yearbook*) from 1902 to 1929. The bibliographies of books and articles on music which he compiled and published in the *Yearbooks* are still referred to, more than sixty years later. His expertise on Renaissance secular music enhanced the academic value of the collection of early music and books. His work as head librarian was of immense importance, not only to the library, but, through his researches and the editing of the *Yearbook*, to the musical world at large. Henri Hinrichsen paid a pension to Professor Schwartz, until his death in 1935, and thereafter to his widow. Schwartz was succeeded by Dr Kurt Taut as head librarian.

The Peters Music Library grew to about 30,000 items by 1930: some 15,000 were books and an equal number were manuscripts, sheet music and scores. Almost all were purchased through funds provided by Henri Hinrichsen. It was the largest privately funded library of this sort in the world.

Almost 1,000 books were added to the library between 1930 and 1933, including many priceless items from the eighteenth century. As one of the finest music libraries in Germany, it saw 3,636 visitors in 1932. Kurt Taut oversaw the creation of an entirely new section. Recognising the value of up-to-date musicological research, an offer was made to all universities in Germany, inviting them to provide the Peters Music Library with a copy of each thesis on musicology written by their students, in exchange for a copy of the Peters Library *Yearbook*. The first thirty theses were catalogued in 1932.

There were several original portraits of composers in the Peters Music Library which were available on loan to publishers wishing to reproduce them. A popular, frequently reproduced one, was a portrait of J S Bach, allegedly by the painter E G Haussmann. C F Peters also produced a poster using this portrait in 1931. Strictly speaking, the attribute is misleading and not entirely accurate, as the portrait which hangs in the Peters Music Library is not the original Haussmann picture; it is a copy by an unknown painter of around the beginning of the nineteenth century.[2]

June 1931 saw the centenary of the birth of Dr Max Abraham with celebrations in his honour in the offices of C F Peters. The Mayor of

Leipzig, Dr Carl Goerdeler and the President of the German Supreme Court, Dr Erwin Bumke, visited the Peters Music Library.

The Peters Music Library and the Henriette Goldschmidt School, causes which Henri Hinrichsen supported with such enthusiasm and generosity, were close to his heart. They were at one and the same time educational and also designed to benefit people who would not otherwise have the opportunities which were offered by these institutes. They were also centres which contributed greatly to Leipzig's reputation as a focal point of culture and study. 1926 brought the opportunity for Henri Hinrichsen's third major sponsorship to benefit his adopted City of Leipzig: the purchase of the Heyer collection of 2,600 musical instruments to form the Music Instruments Museum and Music Research Institute of the University of Leipzig. This became the second largest museum of this sort in Europe.

The Musical Instruments Collections of Wilhelm Heyer comprising those of Baron Alessandro Kraus, Paul de Wit and Ibach

The Heyer collection incorporated three older collections of musical instruments and its genesis is worth recording. The oldest collection is that of Baron Alessandro Kraus Jun. of Florence, who, in 1875 planned to write a complete history of all musical instruments of the world; not just European instruments, but also ethnic and folk instruments. He never actually wrote the book, but from that date onwards he collected the instruments. A catalogue of the collection appeared in French in 1878, listing 516 instruments, including several extremely rare and valuable pieces. By the time the second catalogue was published in 1901, the collection had doubled and comprised 1076 instruments with several more unique items having been added.

Other collectors were becoming interested in the historical significance and cultural relevance of old instruments around that time. Probably the most dedicated and certainly the luckiest in terms of finding priceless pieces was Paul de Wit, a Dutchman who lived in Leipzig. He sold two of his collections to Berlin in 1888 and 1890. A third collection, which he was already forming by 1892, grew substantially over the coming years. These instruments were on display and could be viewed by anybody, in the Bose-Haus at 16 Thomaskirchhof, which today houses the Bach Museum. Paul de Wit wanted his collection to remain in Leipzig and made every effort to sell it to the Leipzig authorities. He tried to encourage them to enlarge the old Grassi Museum in order to contain this very valuable collection. However, the city declined and de Wit had to find another buyer.

Figure 15, above – c 1900: The Bindery of Emil Alexander Enders. Binders to C F Peters for over half a century.

Figure 16, below left – Ludwig van Beethoven, portrait by Joseph Carl Stieler. Purchased by Henri Hinrichsen in 1909.

Figure 17, below right – 1910: Max Reger (1873-1916) and his wife Elsa with their two adopted daughters: Lotti and Christa.

Edition Peters Nr. 3272

9451

Figure 18, opposite below – 1907: Max Reger's *Wiegenlied.* Dedicated to Martha Hinrichsen on the birth of her second son, Walter.

Figure 19, right – 1909: Publication of Max Reger's *Symphonic Prologue to a Tragedy* op 108. Inside title page showing the famous C F Peters engraving designed by F Baumgarten.

Figure 20 , above – c 1900: Office of C F Peters. Paul Ollendorff, General Manager on the left.

Figure 23, opposite above – Ludwig van Beethoven Death Mask. Issued as a poster and book cover by C F Peters in 1927.

Arthur Nikisch
zugeeignet.

Symphonischer Prolog
zu einer Tragödie
für
großes Orchester
von
Max Reger.
Opus 108.
PARTITUR.

Aufführungsrecht vorbehalten.
Eigentum des Verlegers.

LEIPZIG
C. F. PETERS.

Figure 24, above – c 1935: Martha (born Bendix) Hinrichsen (1879-1941).

Figure 21, below – 1919: The Hinrichsen Family in Leipzig. Back row: Hans-Joachim (ten), Paul (seven). Left to right: Geheimrat Henri Hinrichsen, Ilse (fifteen), Martha Hinrichsen with Robert (one), Max (eighteen), Charlotte (twenty), Walter (twelve).

Figure 25, above – c 1935: Dr Henri Hinrichsen (1868-1942).

Figure 26, below left – 1927: Visiting Nina Grieg in Loftus, Hardanger, Norway. anding: Hans-Joachim Hinrichsen (eighteen), Nina Grieg. Seated: Tonny Hagerup (Nina's sister), Geheimrat Henri Hinrichsen.

Figure 22, below right – 1931: The Five Hinrichsen Sons (aged thirteen to thirty): standing: Robert, Paul, Hans-Joachim. Seated: Walter and Max.

Figure 27, above left – 1938: Christian Sinding (1856-1941). Composer of *Rustle of Spring*. Phot dedicated to Hans-Joachim Hinrichsen.

Figure 28, above right – 1938: Walte Niemann (1876-1953). Pianist and composer. Photo dedicated to Hans-Joachim Hinrichsen.

Figure 29, opposite above – 1930: Sigfrid Karg-Elert (1877-1933). In London for the Karg-Elert Festival

Figure 31, opposite below – 1936: Obligatory march past for all the staff of all the Leipzig publishers, showing the C. F. Peters continger in the Parade of May 1936.

Figure 32, below left – 1934: Richard Strauss (1864-1949). Photo dedicated to Hans-Joachim Hinrichsen.

Die Philosophische Fakultät der Universität Leipzig

ernennt durch diese Urkunde den Inhaber des Leipziger Verlagshauses C. F. Peters, Herrn Geheimen Kommerzienrat Henri Hinrichsen, der das Leipziger Erziehungswesen tatkräftig gefördert, vor allem aber um die Pflege der deutschen Musikwissenschaft sich unvergängliche Verdienste erworben hat und durch den verantwortungsbewußten Ausbau der altberühmten „Edition Peters" die Weltgeltung deutscher Musik unablässig befestigt und verbreitet, ehrenhalber zum Doktor der Philosophie.

Leipzig, den 27. Februar 1929.

Der Dekan

Dr. L. Lichtenstein

Figure 30 – 1929: Certificate of Award of Honorary Doctorate to Henri Hinrichser from the Philosophical Faculty of the University of Leipzig.

Another avid collector of musical instruments who started his collection around the turn of the century, was Wilhelm Heyer, a paper manufacturer in Cologne. Heyer was an obsessive and very rich collector who originally specialised in numismatics and philately. His interests expanded to music autographs, music portraits, interesting pictures of music historical significance and books. Not only did he buy the collection of musical instruments formed by Paul de Wit, in 1905, but in 1908 he added the collection formed by Baron Alessandro Kraus. To enlarge his collection still further, he purchased a large collection of keyboard instruments made by the firm of Ibach in Barmen.

Wilhelm Heyer built a house to accommodate this huge collection which, apart from 2,600 instruments included some 20,000 letters written by musicians, 1,700 autographs, 3,700 pictures and a huge library. He employed an instrument restorer and, in 1909 took the twenty-seven-year-old Georg Kinsky onto the payroll as music historian. Kinsky expanded the collection and organised popular lectures and concerts with historical instruments. He compiled and issued two catalogues, each comprising more than 700 pages. *Volume I: Keyboard Instruments*, in 1910 and *Volume II: Stringed and Plucked Instruments* in 1912, both published by Breitkopf & Härtel. They formed an example which later compilers of such catalogues have sought to emulate and are still highly prized. He followed this up in 1913 with a smaller catalogue, a kind of guide to the collection. In 1916 he issued a catalogue of the music autographs. Kinsky was a lecturer in musicology at the University of Cologne from 1921-32, where he took his doctorate, and author of several books. (In 1944 his home and his private library were confiscated and he was sentenced to a year of hard labour under the Nazi regime. His health broken, he moved to Berlin in 1945 where he worked on a thematic catalogue of Beethoven's works until his death.)

Purchase of the Heyer Collection for Leipzig and Inauguration of the Music Instruments Museum

Wilhelm Heyer died in 1913 and after long drawn-out negotiations his heirs sold the entire collection of musical instruments to the University of Leipzig in 1926. The other parts of the collection were sold at auction and widely dispersed. Several important items and books were bought by Henri Hinrichsen for the Peters Music Library.

The person responsible for persuading the Leipzig authorities and the Rector of the University, Dr Le Blanc, to secure this valuable collection for Leipzig and to buy it for the Musicological Institute in 1926, was the musicologist Theodor Kroyer. After studies in Munich he become a reader in 1907, his speciality was sixteenth century vocal music. A professor in Heidelberg in 1920, he moved to Leipzig as

Professor of Musicology at the University of Leipzig in 1923, where he edited publications on early music. He emphasised that this purchase would further enhance Leipzig's reputation as a major centre of music in Germany.

However, the current financial situation meant that the Leipzig authorities could not find the money within their budget. After the heirs of Wilhelm Heyer had agreed to remove the autograph collection (valued at 1,000,000M) from the deal, the protracted negotiations resulted in an agreement between them and the State of Saxony. The price of the collection of instruments was set at 800,000M of which one quarter (200,000M) had to be paid immediately; the rest was payable in instalments of 70,000M per annum over ten years. Leipzig did not have the 200,000M. The story is taken up by Henri Hinrichsen who wrote in his *Chronik*:

> Having been interested in everything large and valuable for along time, I offered to provide this sum of money. After Professor Straube had expressed his great enthusiasm for the purchase, the then Mayor of Leipzig, Dr Rothe, summoned me to visit him to hear my ideas on the subject. I was fire and flame for the acquisition, especially in view of the fact that a large part of the collection had been in Leipzig when it had belonged to Paul de Wit. It had been offered to the city authorities about twenty years earlier for the sum of 400,000M, but without success. If I had not offered to put up the money then, the collection would never have come to Leipzig.

The city authorities agreed to provide sufficient accommodation for the collection and also for the Musicological Institute, which was to be founded at the same time; so that, the two connected together would elevate Leipzig to a historical research centre of style and culture of the highest standard.

The collection of 2,600 instruments comprised 300 keyboard instruments, 700 stringed and plucking instruments, 800 wind instruments and a number of exotic instruments. They covered the whole historical range and were in excellent condition. Most of them could be played satisfactorily.

The City of Leipzig made the North Wing of the new Grassi Museum available for the Music Instruments Museum and so Paul de Wit's dream finally became reality.

In gratitude for his sponsorship, the main exhibition hall on the first floor of the Music Instruments Museum, which contained the rarest items in the collection, was named after the benefactor: 'The Henri Hinrichsen Hall'.

On 31st December, 1926, Professor Theodor Kroyer wrote to Henri Hinrichsen from the Musicological Institute of the University of Leipzig, expressing his gratitude and appreciation for the publisher's sponsorship and adding:[3]

> ...We can sing our praises that within a short time we will have the best Instruments Museum and the best research establishment that any musicological institute could wish for today. And so we recall with heartfelt gratitude, your magnificent help which provided the rootstock for the extraordinarily difficult negotiations, on which the new establishment could finally be built for the honour of our city...

Over the course of the next few years Henri Hinrichsen purchased about 100 further instruments for the Music Instrument Museum and made several generous financial donations for various purchases, such as the lighting installation, pictures and general running costs.

The grand inauguration of the Musicological Institute and the Music Instruments Museum of the University of Leipzig took place on 30th May, 1929. A report by the chorus master and musicologist Barnet Licht appeared in the *Leipzig Illustrierte Monatschrift für Kultur*[4] issue of July 1929, included the following paragraph:

> The celebration was opened by the present Director of the Institute, Prof. Theodor Kroyer. The Collegium Musicum played Monteverdi's *Moresca*, the final dance from *Orfeo*, under his baton. In his speech which followed, Professor Kroyer especially emphasised the importance of sound, for the academic study of musicology today, and that it was only through direct utilisation of the old instruments that the style of playing could be studied and understood. Several addresses followed this, as well as the inauguration of the Straube Organ, which had been presented by a group of Leipzig patrons. Professor Karl Straube, the sponsor of this organ introduced it with works by Buxtehude, Pachelbel and Muffat. The celebration closed with a further performance by the Collegium Musicum, conducted by Professor Kroyer, of a Concerto Grosso by Handel. Afterwards there was a conducted tour through the collection, which has well over 2,000 items and excited so much interest and material for a more detailed description, that a special discourse will follow here shortly.

Barely a week before the official opening of the Music Instruments Museum, another, almost equally important event had taken place

there. Leipzig, as the centre of the music trade in Germany, was the
venue for the Jubilee celebrations marking the centenary of the *Verband
der Deutschen Musikalienhändler* (VDM) (The Association of German
Music Dealers), which had been founded in 1829.

Association of German Music Dealers Centenary Celebration

As a leading member of the Association, Henri Hinrichsen had
suggested that the opening ceremony of this long weekend should take
place in the new Music Instruments Museum. The Association welcomed
this suggestion, which offered an added attraction to the participants.
After the speeches there was a guided tour through the exhibition,
which was introduced by Professor Kroyer. So many participants wanted
to join, that several groups had to be formed. A report in the *Leipziger
Abendpost* of 25th May, 1929[5] tells us that:

> ...In his words of welcome, Professor Kroyer said that the
> Museum would be officially opened the following Thursday,
> and that there were still some things to be organised; all hands
> had been fully occupied making things ready for this guided
> tour. The Leipzig Music Instruments Museum, whose purchase
> had been made possible through the generous sponsorship
> of Henri Hinrichsen, and which had subsequently been added
> to, was now the third largest such institute in Europe. Whilst
> Brussels and Berlin were larger, the development of the
> various sections in Leipzig put it on the same level as the
> two larger museums. On viewing the collection it was apparent
> that this was so. Everything seems to be represented in its various
> forms and developments. Not only is the comprehensiveness
> to be admired, but there are many beautiful and valuable
> pieces in the collection. For Leipzig, the acquisition of this
> museum is incredibly important and of inestimable value. The
> appearance and arrangement of the collection have been
> carefully thought out to make the whole even more attractive.
> Just one example: right at the front of the downstairs hall,
> there is a Silbermann organ standing as it would have done
> in Bach's day; all the instruments of a Bach orchestra have
> been grouped around it, thus immediately giving a realistic
> picture of the same. Indescribably impressive is the Hinrichsen
> Hall on the first floor in which the most valuable pieces of
> the collection are displayed...

Then followed a description of the beautiful concert hall with its
remarkable acoustic. The report closed with the words:

Anyway, the Association could not have found a better way of introducing its Jubilee celebrations.

Several events were held over the course of the last weekend in May. An extract from the same report gives us a brief insight into the organisation of the VDM and some of its current concerns:

...The last hundred years have seen an unprecedented increase in German intellectual and economic culture and have accorded a special place in this to music. As a result of this, German music publishing, printing and dealing have developed into some of the finest in the world. The effect is twofold. Most importantly, German philosophy and life as shown in the works of German heroes has been made known throughout the world. This cultural mission was made easier through its presentation, the internationally comprehensible language of musical notes. Then, economically seen, the production of music and its trade has been an activity of considerable importance. After a pyramid like upswing, however, there was an equally sudden fall, through the World War and its consequences. But German music has been able to hold its place in the world. Economically though, the home market has become narrowed owing to the general lack of demand, brought about through gramophone records and radio, and the overseas market has, for the most part completely disappeared. Hence the problems of music dealing today, are not insignificant, and it is understandable that the jubilee should bear a serious note...

The serious note did not, however, detract from the three-day festivities, which attracted virtually all the music publishers in Germany, as well as the major music dealers and many book publishers and dealers together with some of their employees. Apart from the conference, Saturday evening saw a reception in the concert hall of the Central Theatre. The Sunday morning ceremony which comprised a concert and many speeches, including a greeting from the Mayor of Leipzig, Dr Rothe, took place in the large hall of the House of the Book Dealers.

At the gala luncheon the President of the VDM, Dr Helmut von Hase, proprietor of Breitkopf & Härtel, referred in his speech to the serious economic crisis since 1918 which was affecting the music industry. Several speeches acknowledged various aspects of the music trade and different personalities. Prof Dr Johannes Wolf, a specialist in Renaissance music and contributor to the Peters Music Library *Yearbook*, gave a glowing tribute to Dr Max Abraham, proprietor of C F Peters until his death in 1900.

A major event of the weekend was the dinner for more than 100 guests, hosted by Martha and Henri Hinrichsen in their home at 10 Talstrasse on the first evening. We owe this report to Martha Hinrichsen who wrote to three of her children on 28th May, 1929:[6]

> ...The success of the prelude to the Jubilee in the Talstrasse wildly exceeded our expectations. We received everybody on the roof garden – the music dealers were of course mostly total strangers to me – I welcomed them each in a friendly manner, told them my name, they told me theirs and the name of their firm and the town as well, and the ice was broken. It was really quite amazing, the entire evening became like a huge family party in spite of the fact that the most divers elements were present: music publishers like Tonger, Lienau, Fischer etc. and also the music retailers whose lower middle-class aspect is stamped all over their person, then again the wholesalers – a unity and joyfulness such as one rarely finds. As those taking part in the guided tours in the Music Instruments Museum were divided into groups, people were arriving from 6.45 to 8.15. Only then was the buffet, which had been laid in the corridor, served. They all launched themselves on it as, after a whole day of meetings with only little time to eat, they were starving. I had ordered enough for 130 people; 105 came and all that was left were a few rolls, some cutlets in aspic and a wild boar's head which nobody wanted to touch because of its tough skin. Everything else, and there was lots, disappeared as though by magic. There was white wine and Pilsner beer to drink; I had planned so well that there was enough wine and only some beer left, which I could return – that is why I ordered bottles and not siphons. The dining room, the study, the salon and the living room were filled with tables for six people each, and my room too, where, after everybody had left, I found some poems which I am enclosing and which I would like back...

The overwhelming success of the dinner, like other similar events held in 10 Talstrasse, can be attributed to Martha Hinrichsen's gracious personality and the way she had of always making everybody feel that they were a special person, to be welcomed and treated with respect. It is interesting to note that in spite of the Hinrichsen's lavish hospitality, Martha Hinrichsen had an eye to the budget and was concerned to buy the sort of beer which could be returned if it was not required.

1929 was a memorable year for Henri Hinrichsen. It saw the recognition of his thirty years of major sponsorship towards education in Leipzig, in the form of an honorary doctorate, which was awarded to him by the Philosophical Faculty of Leipzig University.

The Educational Sponsor awarded an Honorary Doctorate

The application for the grant of an Honorary Doctorate originated from seven professors of the University of Leipzig who wrote a justification for their application, which they all signed on 15th December, 1928.[7] It referred to Henri Hinrichsen's achievements as a music publisher and how he had added considerably to the good reputation of the world famous firm of C F Peters and had promoted German music through the excellence of his publications. It went on to praise his promotion of new music and continued:

> ...So it is as a result of his efforts, that the sphere of activity of the 'Edition' has continued in the spirit of its founders and has even been increased during the most difficult times. It should not be overlooked that he has promoted contemporary music at a time when others did not dare. This is shown by a whole series of names which have now become established, starting with Brahms and Hugo Wolf (whose Lieder he took up in his Edition), via Grieg (practically all of whose works have been published by C F Peters) to Pfitzner, Mahler, Arnold Mendelssohn and Schönberg. Especially Reger, when this artist was still fighting for his existence in Munich. It has always been Hinrichsen's pleasure to help rising musicians...

The application went on to praise Henri Hinrichsen's contribution to musicology in the form of his publications, his support of the Peters Music Library and his sponsorship of the Music Instruments Museum. It continued with mention of his support of the Peters Music Library *Yearbook* and, through his financial contributions, his support for research in various faculties of Leipzig University, including the Psychological Institute. It also mentioned his founding of the *Sozialpädagogisches Frauenseminar* – the Henriette Goldschmidt School, in 1911. It ended:

> ...Henri Hinrichsen has this year received many honours from the City of Leipzig and its citizens on the occasion of the celebration of his sixtieth birthday, for his contributions as a benefactor to the spiritual well-being of Leipzig and as a promoter of its educational establishments.

Henri Hinrichsen was awarded an Honorary Doctorate of the Faculty of Philosophy of the University of Leipzig on 27th February, 1929. [Fig 30] The citation reads:

> With this certificate, the Faculty of Philosophy of the University of Leipzig names the proprietor of the Leipzig publishing house of C F Peters, Mr Geheimer Kommerzienrat Henri Hinrichsen, who has contributed so energetically to the improvement of education in Leipzig and who has done so much to further the development of musicology in Germany; who has earned himself untold recognition for the conscientious development of the famous 'Edition Peters', promoting German music throughout the world, an Honorary Doctor of Philosophy.
>
> Leipzig, 27th February, 1929
> The Dean,
> Dr L Lichtenstein[8]

The new Dr h c Henri Hinrichsen was well aware of the great honour which had been bestowed upon him. He was the first German music publisher ever to have received this recognition. In his lengthy speech of acceptance[9] he referred to this and added:

> …My connections with the Leipzig Alma Mater are not new. It is almost forty years since I, having been born in Hamburg, arrived in Leipzig. The day on which I became partner in the firm of C F Peters in 1894, was the day on which the then proprietor, Dr Max Abraham opened the doors of the Peters Music Library, through which since then there has been a constant traffic of students of musicology. I have been watching over them for twenty-eight years and delight in the lively participation of the students.
>
> This, my tie with the University, will from now on be an even stronger one, when the Music Instruments Museum – obtained from Cologne through the active participation of Professor Kroyer – names the *Cimeliensaal* [the hall containing the finest pieces] in my honour for all time. I will not refrain from expressing my most appreciative thanks also for this honour…

The euphoria of the new Music Instruments Museum was to be short-lived. Professor Kroyer left Leipzig in 1932 to take up the newly created chair of musicology at Cologne, where he remained until retirement in 1938. His vacant chair at Leipzig University became the subject of economies in the university budget. He was to be replaced by an associate professor, whose salary would be considerably less. In order to avoid this diminution in the status of the position, the then Dean of the Faculty of Philosophy, the Professor of Geophysics, Ludwig Wiekmann, asked Henri Hinrichsen on 4th January, 1933 whether he would send 20,000M to the Ministry of Culture to cover the difference in salary between that of a full professor and of an assistant professor for at least two years. Hinrichsen declared himself willing to provide this as an endowment for the payment of a Professor of Musicology for Leipzig. However on 25th March, the ministry turned down his offer, without giving any reason. Adolf Hitler had come to power.

---

1   StAL Bestand, C F Peters, No 4553.
2   It was copied from an engraving of 1774 by Kütner. He made his engraving from the Haussmann Bach portrait II, which was itself a copy of around 1748 of the original Bach portrait (I) painted by Haussmann in 1747. Haussmann II used to belong to Carl Philipp Emanuel Bach. (It is now owned by William H Scheide in Princeton.) Haussmann I used to belong to the *Thomasschule* (St Thomas School in Leipzig) and now hangs in the Council Chamber of the Leipzig *Stadtgeschichtliches Museum* (History Museum) in the Old Town Hall. Full details of the Bach Haussmann portraits can be found in: Conrad Freyse, *Bach Antlitz, Betrachtungen und Erkenntnisse zur Bach-Ikonographie* published by Bachhaus, Eisenach 1964. See also *The Newly discovered Bach Portraits* by Stanley Godman, in *Music Book, Vol VII* pp 341-353, Hinrichsen, London 1952.
3   Kroyer's letter in the author's archive.
4   VI Jahrgang, Nr 2, 'Zur Eröffnung des Musikwissenschaftlichen Instituts und Instrumenten-museums im Grassimuseum,' in the Deutsche Bücherei. Barnet Licht wrote regular music reviews until 1933.
5   Stadtarchiv Leipzig, Kap 35, Nr 1521.
6   Martha Hinrichsen's letter in the author's archive.
7   Leipzig University Archive, Phil Fak, Ehrenprom, No 156.
8   *Ibid,* Doktor-Diplome 1928/9, Dr Leon Lichtenstein (1878-1933) professor of mathematical physics.
9   See the *Chronik.*

CHAPTER THIRTEEN

The Family Business: 1920s-30s

Henri Hinrichsen followed in his uncles' footsteps in his attitude towards publishing and in his patronage of musicians. With his charitable donations and interest in the welfare of others, he was expressing his beliefs that the money which he earned from publishing music was not there merely to enhance his own, and his family's standard of living. However, his strong sense of duty did not dominate his life. He also had wide-ranging cultural interests, and the comradeship and friendship of others was an important aspects of his life. His son Max really summed up his father's philosophy on life and duty in an article published in the *Börsenverein* journal of 1st December, 1961:[1]

> When anyone used to ask my father what business he was in, he used to answer: 'I am no businessman, my profession is Music Publisher.' And it has become apparent to me over the years that not only music publishers, but also book publishers, generally consider themselves to be 'professionals' rather than businessmen. The profession of a 'Professional' is duty towards the public at large, whilst a businessman's first and foremost concern is for himself and his own enrichment. He therefore sees only competitors in those who have the same type of business as he, rarely colleagues who share the same interests.

Max, the eldest son, who became Henri Hinrichsen's partner in 1931, had a school-friend, Martin. The two boys shared their parents' sense of duty towards the community and Max used to recall their experiences during the First World War when they volunteered together for the *Hilfsdienst* (Emergency Relief Service).

Max and Martin also had a common destiny, both being sons of the two most important music publishers in Leipzig. Martin von Hase was the younger brother of Dr Helmuth von Hase; their father, Oskar von Hase, was the proprietor of Breitkopf & Härtel. Max and Martin were the third generation of the owners of their firms sharing a close friendship. Competitors as music publishers, the proprietors of each,

Henri Hinrichsen and Oskar von Hase were colleagues on various committees and shared many social occasions.

The business and the family were closely intertwined – in the same house, living by the same moral code, and presided over by the same authority. The hub of the home and family was Martha Hinrichsen, mother of seven children, a gracious hostess to her husband's many guests, a tireless worker for social causes and devoted wife and adviser to her husband. Henri Hinrichsen was a man who enjoyed a well-ordered routine and precise rituals.

Playing his Steinway grand piano (No 206098) which he bought in 1921 was a passion and he got great pleasure from playing chamber music with his musical visitors and his children. He also enjoyed his Skat evenings, when card tables were set up in his office and in the music room; drinks and snacks were served before the game, which was then followed by an exquisite supper. Women and children were excluded from these totally masculine evenings.

The elegant and spacious family apartments were on the second and third floors over the business premises. The children grew up within the lively atmosphere of their father's business circle and of their mother's social concerns. The servants in the household were regarded as part of the family and the children were brought up to respect all people as equals.

In 1917 Henri Hinrichsen's father Robert Hinrichsen, owner of a corset factory in Hamburg died. His mother Betty, the vivacious and cultured lady who had given her son his love of art and music died in 1919. Barely a year later Martha Hinrichsen's mother Bertha died, leaving her blind father, Waldemar Bendix in Berlin. He was seventy-one and came to live with the family in Leipzig. When he died in 1924 his ashes, combined with his wife's, were buried in the Christian South Cemetery in Leipzig. Henri Hinrichsen had purchased a family burial plot in 1909 for the new Hinrichsen dynasty he had founded in Leipzig. Within the space of seven years, the older generation had gone, and Martha and Henri Hinrichsen took their place, as their own children grew to adulthood.

When Dr Max Abraham died in 1900, the church had objected to burying a man who had died by his own hand, in consecrated ground, in the cemetery which had been founded four years previously. These objections were subsequently set aside and Dr Max Abraham's ashes could finally be laid to rest in the family burial site.

The 1920s were also a time of celebration. The Hinrichsens' celebration of their Silver Wedding anniversary on 6th March, 1923 was shared by relatives, and friends from their Leipzig social and musical circle. Henri Hinrichsen was well aware of his good fortune and of the advantages and privileges he was able to provide for his children. In a typical gesture of his generosity, he marked this family celebration by sharing some of this with poor and disadvantaged children. Sending 500,000M to the Mayor of Leipzig, he suggested that this could be spent on sending poor children to holiday colonies during the long holidays, or providing milk for them.

The Hinrichsens' two daughters married during the 1920s.

Charlotte (called Lotte) Hinrichsen, the eldest child, born on 27th December, 1898, had enjoyed a conventional upbringing and at the age of eighteen attended the Henriette Goldschmidt School, where she stayed for two years. She then went on an extended visit to her Bendix grandparents in Berlin, where she met Dr Otto Sobernheim, who was destined to become her husband.

Otto Sobernheim was born in Berlin on 3rd March, 1882 to Justizrat Dr Heinrich Sobernheim and his wife, Elise, née Bütow. He attended the *Französisches Gymnasium* (French Grammar School) in Berlin and was in the Imperial Army during the Great War, when his two younger brothers were killed on the Western Front in 1918. He studied in Freiburg, Baden and received his doctorate of law degree. He chose a government legal career and after a few years became *Landgerichtsdirektor* (Director of the District Court) in the Prussian Court System, serving in *Landgericht* I in Berlin as a County Court Judge.

The wedding took place in Leipzig on 5th September, 1920. The religious ceremony was interdenominational – Rabbi Goldmann, the Chief Rabbi of Leipzig and a Protestant Clergyman officiated. Lotte Hinrichsen said farewell to the parental home in Leipzig to create a new marital home with Dr Otto Sobernheim in Berlin. They had three children between 1921 and 1930.[2]

Ilse, the Hinrichsens' third child was born on 29th January, 1904. She also attended the Henriette Goldschmidt School, graduating as a qualified Kindergarten teacher. She often accompanied her father on trips abroad and to social occasions when her mother was unavailable. Ilse was one of those people whose company everybody enjoyed; she was always full of laughter and love for mankind. On 8th November, 1928 Ilse Hinrichsen married Dr Ludwig Frankenthal according to Jewish Law, in a ceremony presided over by Rabbi Goldmann. Ilse and Dr Ludwig Frankenthal, who lived in Leipzig, had two sons: Günther, born in 1929 and Wolfgang in 1931.

Ludwig Frankenthal, one of nine children, was born in Schwanfeld, Bavaria on 27th November, 1885. He studied medicine at the University of Munich from 1906-1911 and was qualified as a medical doctor in 1912. After working in Hamburg and Berlin he volunteered his services as a military surgeon and was posted to various military hospitals during the Great War, where he was regarded as a first-class surgeon and diagnostician. There he observed muscle stresses about which he wrote numerous papers which led to his wide recognition and assured him a place in medical history. He was awarded the Iron Cross 2nd Class for his war-time military service by the Kaiser in May 1915.

After the war Dr Frankenthal took up a post in the largest surgical university clinic in Germany, in Leipzig, under the direction of Erwin Payr. In 1928 he became the Medical Director of the new Jewish Hospital in Leipzig, founded by the Chaim Eitingon family, together with the internist, Pascal Deuel. Both had received international renown. Frankenthal had by that time published over twenty important papers, which increased to around fifty by 1937. The work for which he will be mainly remembered is his disclosure in 1916-1918 of what is now known as the 'Crush Syndrome', appertaining to burial alive, resulting in muscle and kidney damage. He is regarded as the pioneer in this field.

By 1928 the young adult Hinrichsens were no longer living at home. Martha wrote to all her absent children regularly telling each what was happening at home, about the plays and concerts she and their father had attended and her opinion of them, the books she had read and who came to visit. She also told each one what all the others were doing. In this way she laid the groundwork for sustaining a very close-knit family. They maintained this concern for each other for the rest of their lives; it offered them strength and it helped them to come to terms with the horrors which they were to experience within the next few years.

Henri Hinrichsen's health was not good; as was customary in Germany, he paid frequent visits to spa resorts where he received treatment for stress, for a delicate stomach condition and for his back problem. The responsibilities which he had taken on for many years were becoming too heavy, so he decided that his approaching sixtieth birthday was a suitable time to turn down further invitations to accept honorary duties, and to relieve himself of some of those which he held. He had been on the board of the Leipzig Conservatory of Music for several years and feeling that the board, in the capable hands of its chairman, the paper supplier, Gustav Flinsch, could well manage without him, he resigned. The Mayor, Kurt Rothe, in thanking him for his years of service added, in his letter of 28th February, 1927:[3]

> ...I hope that you, dear Mr Geheimrat...will continue the valued interest in the Conservatory which you have always held. We lay especial value on your continued contact with the institute...it is most important that the contact with men such as you, who have always promoted the interests of the Conservatory, should not be lost...

He did accept the invitation onto the board of the Friends and Promoters of the University of Leipzig, in May 1927, which he deemed a great honour and which would make no particular demands on his energies. As one of the foremost supporters, in 1930 he donated the money for the construction of a new *Mensa* (dining hall) at the university. When the *Verkehrs-Verein Leipzig* (the Tourist and Cultural Bureau) of which Henri Hinrichsen had been a leading member for many years, voted him onto the board of working governors during his absence, he turned them down. In his letter to the chairman, Justizrat Karl Lebrecht, dated 12th December, 1927,[4] which is typical of several he wrote at the time, he explained his reasons:

> ...The reasons for my refusal, which I can assure you I am doing with a very heavy heart, are that, on the threshold of my sixtieth birthday, I do not wish to add to my many sided honorary duties in Leipzig. I have, since 1894 – that is over thirty years – been occupied in a great variety of duties outside of my profession, with many of which I am still involved, in an honorary capacity. I now feel that I have fulfilled my duties in this respect and it would be of greater benefit to the organisation, if younger people were to be drawn in...

Henri Hinrichsen's Sixtieth Birthday

In Germany, a sixtieth birthday has great importance. Resulting from Henri Hinrichsen's prominent position in Leipzig, in the musical world and as the centre of a large extended family, the festivities for his sixtieth birthday on 5th February, 1928 were extended and multifaceted.

The Mayor of Leipzig sent a huge bouquet of flowers and a long letter of congratulation and appreciation, thanking Henri Hinrichsen for his many years of service to the City of Leipzig and for his foundation of the Henriette Goldschmidt School, his support of the Peters Music Library, his donation of the Music Instruments Museum, his work for the Conservatory of Music and much else. Several other members of the Council of the City of Leipzig also wrote fulsome letters of appreciation. The council commissioned an official portrait of Henri Hinrichsen from the well-known German portrait painter, Eduard Einschlag, born in Leipzig in 1879, for which the subject gave a number of sittings. In thanking Mayor Rothe for his congratulations on 9th February, Henri Hinrichsen assured him of his continued interest in Leipzig:[5]

> ...If I have contributed towards the City in various ways during the past thirty years, it is because I feel a strong sense of duty towards our beautiful Leipzig. I assure you, Dear Mr Mayor that, as long as you shall remain at the helm of our

community this, my fundamental attitude, will remain
unchanged...

There was a concert and speech day in his honour at the Henriette
Goldschmidt School, which delighted him. Unhappily, when the portrait
was finished he disliked it intensely and stayed away from the unveiling
ceremony on 10th May, when the modernistic portrait was hung in
the main hall. He subsequently had it moved out of sight and
commissioned a further portrait at his own expense, by Willy Geiger,
to replace it.

The staff at C F Peters laid on a celebration and produced a little
illustrated booklet entitled *Henri Hinrichsen. Ein Gedenkblatt zu seinem
60. Geburtstag* (Henri Hinrichsen a Souvenir Booklet for his Sixtieth
Birthday).[6] A peon of praise, it details his achievements as proprietor
of C F Peters, his contacts with the composers and musicians,
publications, acquisitions and more. The section of photographs starts
with photos of his five young sons, with the caption: 'Why the Birthday
Child need have no worries about the future of the house of C F Peters.'

The birthday celebrations lasted for three days. There were big
formal gala dinners with speeches in Henri Hinrichsen's honour. The
family celebrations included a performance by three of his nieces of
dances to Edvard Grieg's *Norwegian Dances*.

Martha and Henri Hinrichsen shared a fascinating hobby; they
collected autographed letters of composers. They each had their own
collection and often Henri would give his wife prize pieces in celebration
of birthdays and special occasions.

The Autograph Collection

C F Peters – owned by Henri Hinrichsen – already had 19 letters from
Beethoven, approximately 60 from Forkel, 30 from Czerny, 156 from
Spohr (which belonged to Martha Hinrichsen), 20 from Brahms, 406
from Grieg and 420 from Reger (these last three included some
postcards): also, many letters each from Reichardt, Dotzauer,
Meyerbeer, A Streicher, Weber, Wagner, Liszt, Mahler, R Strauss,
Schönberg, Sinding and many more.

Martha and Henri Hinrichsen started their collections with about
100 of the letters which had been addressed to C F Peters, in 1902.
These were added to over the years by the purchase of rare and original
letters and documents, until the collection numbered about 370 pieces
by 1933. Some of the more choice items were from Gluck, Monteverdi,
Gombart, Frescobaldi and Tartini amongst others. These would be
proudly and carefully shown to anybody who shared their owners'
interest and enthusiasm in trying to read them.

In 1926 Henri Hinrichsen bought the entire collection of correspondence between the violinist Joseph Joachim and Brahms, from Joachim's son (Dr Joachim of Göttingen), which he gave to his wife as a souvenir of the Handel Festival in Göttingen. An admirer of Hugo Wolf, in 1926 Henri Hinrichsen was delighted to be able to buy the complete collection of 230 letters from Hugo Wolf to Heinrich Potpeschnigg. A competent accompanist on the piano and also a composer, Potpeschnigg was an Austrian dentist and close friend of Wolf's.[7] When the opportunity arose in 1932 to buy a collection of about forty letters from Hugo Wolf to Paul Müller, he bought that too. Müller was a grammar school teacher in Berlin, where he met Wolf in 1892. In 1895 he founded the first Hugo Wolf Society, in Berlin.[8] Occasionally Henri Hinrichsen would delight in making a present of one of these letters and in this way gave away about ten of them.

Some of the Hinrichsens' children shared their parents' passion, forming their own collections.

1929 saw Martha Hinrichsen's fiftieth birthday. With only the two youngest children, Paul and Robert still living at home, she had more freedom to follow her own interests, reading and photography and she assembled an impressive archive of photographs of musicians and composers. She could now also look forward to travelling with her husband more often. To celebrate his wife's birthday, Henri Hinrichsen took her to Paris in April 1929. In March 1930 they went on the only cruise of their lives, to Rio, which they loved. And in May 1931 they went to London for a holiday.

Henri Hinrichsen made his eldest son, Max, a partner in 1931. These later years of less responsibility for the elderly couple, and more time for relaxation together, when Max was running the business, were to be of all too short duration.

Looking to the Future of the Business and Upholding its Principles

A new employee, Wilhelm Weismann, was engaged by C F Peters on 20th September, 1929, to assist the ageing manager and editor-in-chief, Paul Ollendorff. Weismann was to become a stabilising factor over the course of the next discordant years and to remain with the company, apart from a few short breaks, until 1966. A composer and musicologist, his talents were many and he became indispensable as adviser, editor, writer and public relations officer. He was amongst the most loyal, responsible and hardworking employees in the company and in due course replaced Paul Ollendorff, as reader-in-chief.[9]

The company celebrated the centenary of the birth of Dr Max Abraham, on 3rd June, 1931. This was followed closely by the death, ostensibly from a stroke but actually by his own hand, of Paul Ollendorff, on 25th June, 1931. Ollendorff had been Henri Hinrichsen's school friend and faithful employee for thirty-five years, since March 1896, when Hinrichsen had invited him to Leipzig to work with him. He had always been a depressive and the world situation gave him the feeling that there was no hope for the future. Ollendorff was a perfectionist and conscientious to the last detail about everything and so Henri Hinrichsen had entrusted a great deal of the work, not only the editing, to him. He was also a staunch supporter of the staff and always represented their best interests; it was he whom the staff could thank for their higher than average wages, their Christmas bonus and extra holiday pay, as well as extra payments for coal and potatoes. As Weismann said of him many years later:[10] 'Ollendorf was everything in everything. He oversaw everything. He oversaw the stock room and he oversaw the despatch department; he reorganised where necessary and was responsible for the editing and publication of New Issues lists.'

Paul Ollendorf's last job at C F Peters was the preparation of the parts for Verdi's *Requiem* which, until the expiry of the copyright in 1932, had only been available for hire from the original publisher, Ricordi of Milan. Now they were to be available on sale from C F Peters; their issue, six months after his death, marked a kind of memorial to Paul Ollendorff.

Ollendorf's understanding of the profession of music publisher and of the most important principles according to which a music publishing business should be conducted, were written down by him in a kind of *Vademecum*, which he presented to Henri Hinrichsen on his sixty-third birthday, 5th February, 1931. The following entry is perhaps most characteristic of its writer and his idealism:

> To be a good businessman and never to forget that one is not dealing with cheap consumer goods, but with works of the spirit – to be an accountant with foresight but still, full of idealism, to devote oneself truly to the service of the cultural task – what a wonderful responsibility.[11]

Together with Henri Hinrichsen, Paul Ollendorf had instilled his high principles on the business of music publishing into the three eldest sons of Henri Hinrichsen, Max, Walter and Hans-Joachim who were relieving their father of much work.

Gentilität or courtesy was a maxim of the company handed down from Dr Abraham and one which Henri Hinrichsen had always followed. Maintaining the good reputation of the firm and the respect in which it was held were for him of paramount importance. The consequences of following through the principle of *Gentilität* in every situation was what gave C F Peters, in the words of Paul Ollendorff, 'its aristocratic atmosphere'. The five Hinrichsen sons had grown up with the high principles set by their elders and were to continue to maintain the same standards throughout their lives, though two of whose were to be all too short.

Henri Hinrichsen had always, since 1891, kept the main accounts himself and prepared the annual accounts himself, as well as preparing the tax returns together with his bookkeeper. He settled all accounts immediately in order to avoid any future problems. Another main business principle was to insist on prompt payment from his customers – those who paid cash got higher discounts. He would never accept credit and never borrow money, limiting his publications to what he could afford from current resources. Hence he was never in debt and never had to pay extortionate interest; rather, he would from time to time be in a position to lend money to relatives and those he could trust.

It was also part of the C F Peters tradition to select employees and suppliers who would remain with the company. This practice saved time, money and problems and thus conserved energy. Since the inception of the Editions Peters in 1867, the company had kept the same firms for engraving, printing, supplying paper and book binding. Even though Henri Hinrichsen had cut down on his working hours he continued to be kept fully informed about every aspect of the business in daily conferences with Paul Ollendorff until his death, and with his own three sons.

His sons had grown up aware of these principles, along with the prime one of 'quality and not quantity'. This was why only a limited number of works were accepted for publication. In this way the purchasing public could safely buy works unseen, knowing that the quality would be of a standard which they had grown to expect. C F Peters also avoided publishing avant garde music and jazz which during financially difficult times would have made commercial sense. The company was renowned for its publications of classical music and, with the exception of Grieg, Reger, Mahler, Schönberg, Pfitzner, Richard Strauss and a few others, published little contemporary music and was often criticised for taking this stance. Hinrichsen accepted that his heirs might well take a different view.

Wilhelm Weismann, speaking in 1973,[12] repeated what he had been told by either Paul Ollendorff or by Carl Martienssen, one of the editors, when he had joined the firm:

>...With regard to new music, this is completely unknown territory. Of course a publisher must occasionally take a risk, but Peters is a world publishing company and when Peters sends out its list of publications, its order forms, then every

music retailer knows that he can order those works in the secure knowledge that he can rely on selling them. People believe in Peters as they do in the Bible so to speak. And if we include uncertain works, then we ruin the whole market for ourselves. They will say that Peters is just like all the others – in short, the trust will be lost. Occasionally we do of course issue a modern work, but that has to have a certain prestige for the company. Even though we know that modern music is no sort of business at all. Then it doesn't matter whether the sales are large or small, what is important is that people will think: Aha, Peters published that!

Business fluctuated. In 1930 there were thirty-five employees, but this dropped to thirty-two in 1932; the reduction in the number of staff reflecting the decline in turnover. From a sales' high point for two years following the stabilisation of the currency after the inflation, there was a gradual decline from 1926 onwards resulting from the economic crisis, which more than halved the turnover by 1932. That this drop in sales was once again turned round, can be partly attributed to a new policy in the company which Max Hinrichsen introduced on his return from the USA. There he had learnt the art, and the value of publicity and advertising. C F Peters had never advertised, having always relied on the quality of the product and the high reputation of the company, to sell its music. The informative catalogues which were sent out regularly were the only form of publicity used. Now Henri Hinrichsen was forced through circumstances, into a more aggressive and up-to-date mode of salesmanship.

Employees of C F Peters enjoyed good working conditions and tended to remain with the company for most of their working lives. As a mark of appreciation for their loyalty, the management arranged occasional celebrations. There was a May Celebration on 2nd May, 1936 organised by Max Hinrichsen which lasted all day. A limited, numbered edition of sixty copies of the programme,[13] edited by Max, was sponsored and printed by the printers, Poeschel & Trepte, with whom the company had enjoyed a good working relationship for many years. Max had planned his programme with panache and a great sense of humour and it included, in one way or another, all the members of the staff and their wives. (The ladies on the staff were unmarried.)

By 1933 the secretary Fräulein Hopfe had been with the company for thirteen years and was well versed in its history. An entry from her diary dated 2nd October, 1933, enthusiastically reports on a long-awaited event:

Yesterday Mr Hinrichsen gave us a talk in praise of Max Abraham. At the same time he presented the *Chronik* of the history of our publishing house which CK and I had been permitted to type. A wonderful chronicle of German musical history. Interested employees will be allowed to look at a copy.

The *Chronik*

For many years, people had been urging Henri Hinrichsen to compile a history of C F Peters and this task had been occupying him for some time. Research was carried out not only by himself but also by Paul Ollendorff, Elsa v Zschinsky-Troxler, who had compiled the book of Letters from Edvard Grieg, and Max and Walter Hinrichsen. Martha Hinrichsen had, with great diligence found pictures and photographs of often long-dead musicians and others with which to illustrate this splendid tome. Entitled *Chronik des Hauses C F Peters. Geschichte des Verlagshauses C F Peters von seiner Gründung am 1. Dezember 1800 an bis zum 1. Oktober 1933* (History of the Music Publishing House of C F Peters from its Foundation on 1st December, 1800 till 1st October, 1933), it was prepared ostensibly for his family and completed on 1st July, 1933. With the anti-Semitic changes which were taking place during 1933 since the National Socialists had come to power, which will be elaborated upon in Part IV of this book, Henri Hinrichsen felt the need to add some closing words, which he did on 1st October, 1933:

> ...Recently I had the pleasure of seeing my eldest son, Max's, name enrolled in the Register of Companies as Partner in the company. Though I have entrusted to him the daily running of the business more and more over the last few years I see myself as fortunate, during these commercially catastrophic years, in being able to continue to participate through daily conferences, contributing my many years of experience.

> Until my recent retirement from office I have always promoted the interests of the Association of German Music Dealers and the German Music Publishers' Association in an honorary capacity to the best of my ability, so that I carry the certainty that the old, good relations which the firm of C F Peters has enjoyed with its friends, will be maintained in the future, whereby the firm will hopefully be successful in surviving the current general crisis...

> It is my heartfelt wish that my son Max and later collaborating sons will:

continue to run our German business in the spirit of its predecessors, because the publishing house **has always specialised in German music from its beginnings** and has been **directed towards** this end during its **entire existence!**

This depiction of the true German patriot which the sixty-five-year-old Henri Hinrichsen had always been, never ever reached those whom it was meant to assure, because the volume was never published. Beautifully leather-bound, typewritten copies, fully illustrated with photographs were prepared for his sons, whilst the correction typescript remained in the archives of C F Peters.

We will let Martha Hinrichsen have the last word on the *Chronik*, in a letter to her son Walter, who was in the USA at the time, dated 7th October, 1932:[14]

...I constantly see how useful such a chronicle is, because it is through the chronicle that tradition is maintained. And even if Gustav Mahler, frustrated at the somnolent tradition at the Vienna Opera, shouts out loud 'Tradition is sloppiness', used in sensible measure with respect, it leads to blessing. Tradition means not blindly following in the footsteps of your predecessors. Approximately every thirty years there should be a shift in the business to let in new blood and to adopt modern ways of conducting business, which should be combined with the experiences of the past. And not to smash up everything which is there, but to continue that which is good – that is tradition. More than a lifetime ago, your father was the youngster who, in his apprentice years rebelled against the ideas of Uncle Max Abraham, but he had the good luck to work with him for many years before taking on the full responsibility of the business...

Your father changed many things, but he retained the tradition, that which was worthwhile and which Max Abraham constantly emphasised. This was why he maintained the publishing house as a small entity, to concentrate on the publishing, leaving the problems of printing, engraving and binding to others. Many of the larger firms who did not do this, have now collapsed.

She went on to point out that Henri Hinrichsen had never speculated on the stock exchange and was thus able to save the firm through the war – and worse, inflation years. She said that he was now in a position to support himself during his retirement years and that he had made provision to support the firm for his heirs through the purchase of the rights to the Bruch Violin Concerto and the Richard Strauss works from Universal Edition. When Max Abraham had died, the obligations in his will were so high, that not a penny remained for Henri Hinrichsen and meant the latter even accepted responsibility for supporting several members of Max Abraham's family for many years. She concluded her letter with her wishes for the future of the firm in the hands of her sons:

> But it is my fervent wish that Max, you and Hanns should be as successful in being able to pass on the business to your heirs in as honourable and secure a position as it holds today…

Martha presented a beautifully leather bound copy of the *Chronik* to her eldest son, Max. She enclosed a brief note dated 2nd April, 1935, which can be seen as a reflection of the times:[15]

> Dear Max,
>
> I am delighted at last to be able to hand you the copy of the *Chronik*; it should serve you as a reference work. I hope with all my heart that the rumours which you hear whilst carrying out your duties, melt away to nothing, and that you can work with pleasure to maintain the position of the business, which is more difficult (especially these days) than to build it up.
>
> With Love, Mother

Fervent and heartfelt wishes are not always granted and these were to be denied in the most terrible manner. The rumours did not melt away. They materialised into the most tragic, gruesome, state-inspired, organised persecution and murder of the Jews – the Holocaust.

---

1 Written on the occasion of the sixtieth birthday of Max Hinrichsen's school-friend, Dr Martin von Hase, one of the directors of the music publisher, Breitkopf & Härtel.

2 Their names are withheld at their request.

3 StAL Bestand, C F Peters, No 4571.

4 *Ibid.*

5 Stadtarchiv Leipzig, Schulamt, Kap VIII, No 228, Bd IV.

6 In the author's archive.

7 The correspondence between Wolf and Potpeschnigg was edited by Heinz Nonveiller and published by the Union, Deutsche Verlagsgesellschaft, Stuttgart in 1923, before Henri Hinrichsen bought it.

8 Paul Müller published *Erinnerungen an Hugo Wolf* (Memories of Hugo Wolf),
   which included extracts of some of the letters, in *Die Musik* Year 2 (1902/3), Vol
   12, pp 428-440. He published a booklet, mainly about the Lieder : *Hugo Wolf,* in
   Berlin, 1904. *Ungedruckte Briefe von Hugo Wolf an Paul Müller aus den Jahren 1896-
   1898* (Unpublished letters from Hugo Wolf to Paul Müller from 1896-1898) was
   published in the Peters Music Library *Yearbook,* Year 11, Leipzig, 1904.

9 Wilhelm Weismann eventually received the State Prize for *Künstlerisches
   Volksschaffen* (Artistic Peoples Creativity) in 1959; in 1961, the *Kunstpreis der
   Stadt Leipzig* (Artistic Prize of the City of Leipzig); and in 1964 the National
   Prize of the DDR.

10 From transcript of interview with Weismann recorded by Bernd Pachnicke,
   then manager of C F Peters, Leipzig, on 3rd February, 1973.

11 Quoted in the *Chronik*.

12 Interview as above.

13 *Programm Mai-Feier 1936,* edited by Max Hinrichsen, C F Peters, Leipzig 1936, in
   Musik Bibliothek Leipzig, Wilhelm Weismann Nachlass.

14 In the author's archive.

15 Martha Hinrichsen's note in the author's archive.

PART IV

The Holocaust

CHAPTER FOURTEEN

Anti-Jewish Legislation after 1933 and its Effects on C F Peters, Henri Hinrichsen's three Eldest Sons and his Trusts

Some of the New Laws

With their state-inspired anti-Semitism, the Nazis were adopting a return to the attitudes prevalent towards the Jews in the Middle Ages. With one difference. Then, the motive was of a religious nature; with the Nazis it was 'Racial Purity'. From March 1933 onwards, one piece of anti-Semitic legislation followed another, with the aim of eliminating all aspects of Jewish influence from German life and of economically crippling the Jews and driving them from Germany. The first general manifestation of this was the officially sanctioned, organised, wild and excessive 'Boycott' on 1st April, 1933 which was intended: '...for practical, planned implementation of the boycott of Jewish businesses, Jewish products, Jewish doctors and Jewish lawyers...'[1] Jews, and other critics of the regime were sent to the concentration camp of Dachau in their thousands from March 1933 onwards. The persecution of the Jews by the Nazis which was already under way before 1933, rapidly escalated after the accession of the National Socialist Party. At that time there were around 600,000 Jews in Germany (less than one per cent of the population). Of these, 15,000 lived in Leipzig.

A new concept entered the German vocabulary as a term used to define the difference between a Jew and a Gentile: 'Aryan'. Originally a linguistic term referring to the Indo-European group of languages, the concept had been distorted since the late nineteenth century, to denote racial superiority over the Semitic races. 'Semitic' was itself originally a linguistic term referring to a language group which included Hebrew and Arabic. Hitler re-defined the term to fit his new racialism. 'Aryan' became synonymous with 'pure' and 'Semitic' with 'Jew', hence 'impure'.[2]

Germans were henceforth registered as either 'Aryan' (denoting German) or 'non-Aryan' (denoting Jew). People with one Aryan and one Jewish parent, were classified as *Mischling ersten Grades* (First degree mixed race) and so on.

An early piece of legislation, introduced on 7th April, 1933, dismissed all Jewish judges from their state appointments, this included Dr Otto Sobernheim, husband of the Hinrichsens' eldest daughter.

Jewish professors were sacked from the universities. Doctors' practices were limited by a decree of 2nd April, 1933 barring all non-Aryan doctors from work at state-supported health clinics and hospitals. This affected the Hinrichsens' other son-in-law, Dr Ludwig Frankenthal. Lawyers' practices were limited. The visiting of museums was forbidden, Jews were banned from using swimming pools, or sitting on park benches, from going to concerts, the theatre or the cinema. They had to forfeit their driving licences and were forbidden from using public transport except to go to work – but they were only permitted to do menial work, until that too was forbidden to them. They had to give up their bicycles. They were not permitted to go to the hairdresser or to have their shoes mended by the cobbler. Many more such new laws made life progressively more difficult for the Jews.

Jewish children were barred from attending non-Jewish schools. This affected two of the Hinrichsens' grandchildren, Günther and Wolfgang Frankenthal who attended the small Carlebach School, with under 100 children. In 1933 it was suddenly forced to accommodate over 1,000 children.

In 1934 a decree was issued forbidding Jews from marrying Aryans, which affected Max Hinrichsen. On 1st January, 1935 a decree was issued obliging all Jews to be officially identified, if their names did not appear on a list of 'typically Jewish' names issued by the Interior Minister. They had to re-register their birth certificates adding the middle name 'Israel' for a man and 'Sarah' for a woman. Martha and Henri Hinrichsen had to apply – and pay – for their re-registered birth certificates in the names of Henri Israel Hinrichsen and Martha Sarah Hinrichsen.

Jewish shops and businesses were gradually closed down and 'aryanized' – forcibly bought by people classified as Aryans (and generally members of the Nazi Party) for a fraction of their value; a concept which will be explained in the next chapter, in terms of how the firm of C F Peters and Henri Hinrichsen were affected. Large numbers of Jews began to emigrate in 1933, by which time a Reich's Refugee Tax was already in operation. This tax, which was supplemented by other taxes, increased over the years to a crippling extent, leaving emigrants who could not get out until 1939, penniless. Those emigrating after 13th May, 1938 were not permitted to take any valuables with them and had to provide a complete list of all personal property which they wanted to take with them, for the imposition of an export tax. We will see how these measures affected the Hinrichsen family.

Jews were forced to sew large yellow star-shaped patches on their clothes; punishment for failure to wear the star in a public place could mean death or immediate transportation to the concentration camps. Henri Hinrichsen steadfastly refused to wear the star and hence, for his own safety, he did not go out of the house. Many Jews left Germany, but many stayed on, thinking it could not get worse and for some time, Henri Hinrichsen believed that he would be exempt from the excesses of the persecution, because of his position. After the mid-1930s when larger numbers of Jews wanted to emigrate, visas for admittance to another country became difficult to obtain. Penalising taxes were inflicted on Jews and they had to register all their assets and property. In the summer of 1938 all Jewish owners of shops and other business premises were ordered to paint a Star of David, as well as their names in large white letters across their windows.

Every kind of activity was affected, including key musical organisations with which Henri Hinrichsen was involved, such as the German Music Publishers' Association and the German Music Dealers' Association, as well as the German Book Traders' Association.

The Börsenverein (The German Book Traders Association)

The *Börsenverein der Deutschen Buchhändler* (The German Book Traders' Association) was founded in Leipzig, in 1825. Respected for its integrity, its weekly circular the *Börsenblatt* (Book Trades Newsletter) had always given reliable, factual and up-to-the-minute information. This remarkable, and up to 1933 independent organisation, was one of the first to embrace the new political era. Even before the 'Book Burning' event in Berlin on 10th May, 1933, the *Börsenblatt* of 3rd May announced its *Sofortprogramm* (Immediate programme).

It starts as follows:

> The German Book Trade greets the National Uprising. It has immediately declared its willingness to collaborate in its goals. In the meantime cultural and economic guidelines have been set out. They facilitate the German Book Traders' Association in preparing a programme in complete agreement with the principles.

In trying to ingratiate itself with the new powers, the Börsenverein could assure the government that it had not had *Rassenfremde* (racial foreigners) on its committee for the past fifty years and that the official posts had always been held by 'Men of a Nationalistic outlook'.

Membership had never been compulsory, but now all publishers and writers were forced to join and to adhere to the new rules, which included the banning of all books by Jewish writers. As a prominent publisher, Henri Hinrichsen had been a member and supporter of the *Börsenverein* for over forty years. Now, Jews were banned from membership. Only publishers or writers who were members, were permitted to publish anything. So the *Börsenverein* effectively became an arm of the National Socialist government and was in control of virtually all printed matter.

To effect the legislation, an official specialist department was created within a government ministry. The architect for this was Dr Joseph Goebbels, the Minister for Propaganda and Popular Enlightenment. He created the *Reichskulturkammer* (State Chamber of Culture) with himself as President with absolute power. This was divided into separate chambers for the various arts. The *Reichsschrifttumskammer* (The State Literature Chamber) worked to devastating effect and immediately produced a *Black List* of banned authors.

The Parade of May 1936

The annual meeting of the *Börsenverein* in Leipzig, was the occasion for a grand parade. Parades and mass gatherings were an important feature of life during the Third Reich; they were intended to glorify the collective of the state, over the individuality of the citizen.

The Minister of Propaganda, Josef Goebbels ordered a parade in Leipzig on 10th May, 1936. He was the guest of honour and speaker and a grand propaganda exhibition was staged for him in the *Haus des Buches* (the House of Books). There was an obligatory march past through the streets of Leipzig for all the staff of all the Leipzig publishers, each group carrying a placard showing its publisher's name [Fig 31]. Armed soldiers controlled the procession. The buildings were hung with huge swastika banners. In spite of his non-Aryan status, at that date Henri Hinrichsen was still held in some slight official respect; he was the only person permitted to observe the procession from inside the *Haus des Buches*, with Goebbels and the officials.

The Reichsmusikkammer (State Music Chamber) 1933

Music was an important propaganda weapon in the National Socialist armoury of persuasion. It was intended forcibly to guide the taste of the population away from all 'foreign' influences such as avant-garde music and jazz, and back to a 'heroic' national music, such as that of Beethoven and Wagner. As much of the reviled new music was by Jewish composers such as Kurt Weill, Arnold Schönberg and Anton Webern, this led to restraints on performances of all music by all Jewish composers, living or dead – including Felix Mendelssohn-Bartholdy and Gustav Mahler, and the banning of Jewish musicians and conductors. It also led to restrictions on Jewish music publishers and music sellers.

The section of the *Reichskulturkammer* which controlled music, was the *Reichsmusikkammer* (State Music Chamber). Many influential German musicians welcomed the creation of this ministry as they felt that they had become alienated to much of the music being composed and performed during the Weimar Republic, and that this was a way of preserving what they perceived as the true national values of music. Henri Hinrichsen, who avoided publishing much avant-garde music and was especially keen to promote German classical music in the Editions Peters, was one who initially applauded the creation of this department; he was a member of the *Reichsmusikkammer* who was tolerated because of his international standing, until 1938.

The *Reichsmusikkammer* was inaugurated on 15th November, 1933. Richard Strauss was the first President with Wilhelm Furtwängler as his deputy. However, differences of opinion with the authorities caused their resignation after two years. They were replaced by two respected musicians, both members of the Nazi Party: Prof Dr Dr e h Peter Raabe and Henri Hinrichsen's long-time friend Prof Dr e h Paul Graener. By 1937 seven separate sections evolved which legally controlled all aspects of music making in Germany:

Functionaries were appointed in the thirty-one districts of Germany to administer the policies formulated by Goebbels. They tended to favour popular over serious music; the people could be more easily influenced through marches, politically inspired cantatas and patriotically inspired music.[3]

A thorough and ruthless policy of anti-Semitism was pursued, aiming to eliminate every possible Jewish element from German musical life. One of Goebbels' first decrees was the dismissal from their posts of all Jews holding important positions in any aspect of music making in Germany. Amongst these were Otto Klemperer and Henri Hinrichsen's friend, the Gewandhaus conductor, Bruno Walter, who was summarily told not to come for his rehearsal on 16th March, 1933. The *Reichsmusikkammer* issued a decree on 29th September, 1934 prohibiting performing artists using foreign sounding names. Its decree issued on 30th August, 1935 forbade Jews and any other non-Aryans from playing in German orchestras. Another forbade Jews from teaching at Music Conservatories.

Jewish musicians such as Yehudi Menuhin and Artur Schnabel were not allowed to perform in Germany. Music magazines such as the *Zeitschrift für Musik* (Journal of Music) and *Die Musik* (The Music) were taken over to promote the party message of purification of music from alien influences. *Die Musik* issued a special anti-Semitic number on 1st March, 1936 including such articles as 'The Jew as Musical Manufacturer' and distorted, caricatured photographs of Mendelssohn, Mahler, Weill and Klemperer. A directive from the *Reichsmusikkammer,* dated 21st December, 1937, banned the distribution of records featuring Jewish or Negro musicians. Another one, of 1st May, 1938 prohibited Aryans from teaching music to Jews. Whilst genuine music criticism was disapproved during the Third Reich, an organisation, *Institut zur Erforschung der Judenfrage* (Institute for Research into the Jewish Question) was officially sanctioned. It compiled a scurrilous *Lexicon of Jews in Music,* which was first published in 1940.[4]

The *Reichsmusikkammer* issued a regular fortnightly bulletin – *Amtliche Mitteilungen* (Ministerial Information). The six page issue of 1st July, 1938 (Year 5 No. 12/13)[5] is worth noting. Between an item on the inauguration of a national music prize and one on the enlargement of the department for choirs and folk music, is a long item entitled '*Kennzeichnung jüdischer Betriebe*' (Characteristics of Jewish Businesses). It demonstrates in minute detail how thorough and precise the Germans were in their legal justification for the persecution of the Jews. It started:

> The *Law Gazette of the Reich* (Part I, p 627/8) of 14 June, 1938, announces the third decree referring to the Citizenship Law. The decree reads: It has been decreed that, further to Point 3 of the Citizenship Law of 15th September, 1935 (*Law Gazette* I, p 1146):
>
> > Article I
> > Point 1
> >
> > (1) A commercial enterprise is considered to be Jewish if the proprietor is Jewish (Point 5 of the first decree of the Citizenship Law of 14 November, 1935 – *Law Gazette,* I p 1333).
> > (2) The commercial enterprise of an open commercial company or a limited partnership is considered to be Jewish, if one or more of the partners are Jewish...

And so on, covering many points. Article II goes from Point 7 to Point 16 describing how a register of all such companies is to be compiled. It defines precisely who may decide in cases of doubt as to whether a person or business is Jewish – the *Gauleiter* (head of the Nazi administrative district), amongst other officials. Subsection 15 states that all who wish may look at the register. Article III Point 17 states:

> The Reich Minister of Trade is empowered, in conjunction with the Reich Minister of the Interior and the representative of the Führer, to decree that the commercial businesses which are entered in the register of Jewish commercial businesses should be identified with a distinctive mark as from a date to be determined.

After five years of increasing regulation and persecution, it marked the final nail in the coffin for businesses owned by people who happened to be of Jewish descent and paved the way for the terrible *Reichskristallnacht* (State Night of the Broken Glass) a few months later.

The marginalisation of publishers who were Jewish, also reflected on the composers with whom they were associated. The appointment of Richard Strauss [Fig 32] as President of the *Reichsmusikkammer* in 1933 was to cause him some embarrassment, in that he was associated with a Jewish music publisher.

Richard Strauss

Strauss had offered his *Alpen Symphonie* to C F Peters in 1914 for a very high fee and Henri Hinrichsen had since regretted having rejected it. The publisher had wanted to acquire more orchestral works by Strauss, who was amongst the foremost contemporary composers and entered into negotiations with Strauss's Viennese publisher, Universal Edition. Since 1908 the director had been Emil Herzka. The negotiations were somewhat protracted and the deal was not completed until after Herzka's death in 1932, when C F Peters was finally able to purchase six of the seven *Symphonic Tone Poems*, composed in the 1880s and '90s. Thus, with a contract dated 7th October, 1932, at a price of 225,000M – which covered the rights and engraved plates as well as all stocks, the catalogue of C F Peters was enriched by *Don Juan, Macbeth, Tod und Verklärung* (Death and Transfiguration) *Till Eulenspiegel, Also Sprach Zarathustra* (Thus Spake Zarathustra) and *Don Quixote*, as well as the four movement programme symphony, *From Italy*, Op 16.

An agreement was reached at the same time that both Universal Edition and C F Peters would supply the orchestral material for Strauss's Symphony in F minor, Op 12. After four years, at the latest by March 1937, C F Peters would acquire the complete rights to the symphony for two and a half times the amount of the entire income which both companies had received from this symphony between 1st October, 1932 and 31st December, 1936.

Henri Hinrichsen was delighted finally to purchase six of Strauss's *Symphonic Tone Poems* from Universal Edition in 1932. Now Strauss resented this representation of his music by a Jewish publisher. He also knew that the new regulations discouraged performances of music published by a Jew. In 1934, he asked for the return of the copyright to his six *Symphonic Tone Poems*. Henri Hinrichsen felt obliged to comply, which Strauss acknowledged on 10th April, 1935. The rights and complete material to Strauss's *Tone Poems* were repurchased by C F Peters in 1938 for 250,000M at the time when both C F Peters and Universal Edition were being 'aryanized' by the Nazis.[6]

The second Director of the *Reichsmusikkammer,* Paul Graener, was happy that Henri Hinrichsen was permitted, uniquely for a Jew, to be a member until 1938.

Paul Graener

C F Peters had published Graener's A-minor Trio, Op 61 and, in 1929, his setting of the 'Drinking Song of the Leipzig Bibliophiles'. In recognition of many years of friendship, Henri Hinrichsen congratulated Paul Graener on his sixtieth birthday in 1932 with a cheque.[7] Five years later, his sixty-fifth birthday in 1937, he presented his friend with a special item out of his own autograph collection – an original letter from Richard Wagner. This was the two page letter of 15th March, 1871 from Richard Wagner to Dr Max Abraham, about *The Emperor's March* which Abraham had commissioned from Wagner. It is interesting to note, that for all Wagner's anti-Semitism, he had not been averse to accepting a commission to compose a work for a publisher who was Jewish. This generous gift was an acknowledgement of Wagner's status in Nazi Germany.

Henri Hinrichsen, whose family had held German citizenship for almost 300 years, became a victim of all the anti-Semitic persecution which the new Third Reich could devise; though, with his international standing in mind, certain concessions were made in his favour during the early stages. This lead him to the false belief that he would be spared the excesses of the regime. He was able to retain his membership of the *Reichsmusikkammer* until 1938 because Goebbels wanted to make a good impression on the world during the 1936 Berlin Olympics, indicating that German cultural institutions were being respected. However, Henri Hinrichsen was dismissed from other associations long before then. The Association of German Music Dealers and the German Music Publishers' Association, which he had always worked hard to promote, were forced to dismiss him.

Whilst the political climate made business and life ever more difficult for the Hinrichsen family, and Henri Hinrichsen was forbidden to participate in almost all honorary, social and business functions, many of his friends remained loyal. Composers, editors and musicians whose collaboration he had enjoyed for up to forty years, remained his friends. This heartened him and helped to confirm in him the mistaken belief that everything would turn out all right.

Elsa Reger

That Max Reger's widow Elsa and others continued to maintain cordial relations with the Jewish publisher, indicates that personal relationships were held higher than political decrees.

Since Reger's death in 1916, Henri Hinrichsen had been supporting the widow of the composer whom he had helped so generously. When Elsa Reger wrote to him on 12th April, 1935[8] he took her letter not only as a mark of her appreciation, but also as a sign of friendship and support in recognition for the persecution he was suffering. She wrote:

> Dear, Honoured Mr Geheimrat,
>
> Whilst looking for a contract in Reger's document case, I found your letter of 18th December, 1906. I cannot begin to tell you how shaken I was.
>
> Even though I had read the letter at the time, I had forgotten the wording during the intervening twenty-eight years, and the fact that it had been kept: I can do nothing else, dear Mr Geheimrat as to thank you from the depths of my heart for your understanding and your deep feeling for my husband. May God reward you for it, I can only and for always think of you with deepest thanks.
>
> Your true
> Elsa Reger

The letter to which Elsa Reger was referring, and which is quoted in Chapter Seven, was the one in which Henri Hinrichsen offered to support Reger financially for a whole year, so that he could devote himself to composing. Henri Hinrichsen's reply, dated 13th April, 1935[9] expresses his continued faith in the music of Max Reger and his appreciation for her thoughts:

> My Dear Mrs Reger,
>
> You gave me an especial pleasure with your letter of yesterday – a pleasure which, as you can will understand, I really need

in today's circumstances. By the way, I would like to mention, that the letter to your husband, of 18th December, 1906, gave me great pleasure and I never had any reason to regret the suggestion it contained. Anyway it is so very kind of you to have written to me about this quite out of the blue and I really appreciate your thoughts...

Elsa Reger was constantly promoting her late husband's music with annual Reger Festivals. When she wrote to Hinrichsen in May 1938 announcing a performance of Reger's *Psalm 100* which he had published in 1909, the publisher was delighted to hear from her and replied on 10th May, 1938:

> I was very happy to hear from you again; I hope you are well rested after your sojourn in Wiesbaden and will be able to attend the Reger Festival in Berlin, which will be very strenuous for you. My wife, who sends you her kindest regards, is planning to attend the performance of the *Psalm 100* in Berlin on 28th May, whilst I, on account of my age and the current situation, will refrain. If my way should take me to Munich during the coming year, it will be my pleasure to pay you a visit. It is indeed wonderful how Reger becomes ever more popular, year by year, and I am convinced that this is largely due to your promotion of his music. In this respect I am indeed indebted to you dear Frau Doctor.
>
> With friendliest Greetings,
>
> Your faithful
> Henri Hinrichsen
>
> Tomorrow it will be exactly twenty-two years since you lost the great master. I can hardly believe that it is already such a long time ago since we saw him for the last time in the Hotel Hentschel, an unforgettable, tragic memory.

Henri Hinrichsen had so many friendships, so many achievements and a lifetime of generous sponsorship to look back on, that he found the current political trends incomprehensible in the light of the respect and admiration which he had enjoyed for so long.

As the incessant implementation of new laws restricting their lives became ever more threatening, Jews had been leaving Germany in increasing numbers.

The Three Eldest Sons

To the great distress of Martha and Henri Hinrichsen, both their eldest son Max and their second son Walter decided to emigrate. Walter had for a long time been planning his emigration to the USA, where he would represent C F Peters and eventually form his own company.

Walter Hinrichsen was twenty-nine when he left Germany on 3rd March, 1936, separating himself from the situation which would destroy his family. He never saw his parents or two of his brothers again. The fact that he managed to get to the USA, where he eventually obtained citizenship, was ultimately to the best advantage of his remaining family and to the eventual restitution of C F Peters.

After Walter's departure, Henri Hinrichsen promoted his third son, the twenty-seven-year-old Dr Hans-Joachim, as partner in C F Peters and wrote to him on 24th December, 1936:[10]

Dear Hans!

After having worked for more than four decades in the promotion of the Edition Peters, it is time for me to limit my duty more to one of consultancy. I have formed the impression over the course of the last few years that you are following Max's example and are in full agreement, sharing the understanding that our unique publishing house can only continue to maintain its high reputation in the world, if the same general principles which have been in operation since the foundation of the Edition Peters by Uncle Max Abraham, continue to be followed. That is: that the ideals always go hand in hand with the material substance.

It is therefore not only a wish, but also a great pleasure, to name you, my dear son, as partner in the two firms: C F Peters and J. Rieter-Biedermann [Henri Hinrichsen had purchased J Rieter-Biedermann in 1917], as from 1st January, 1937, with a share of ten per cent, which will be increased by five per cent per year up to a total of thirty-three-and-a-third per cent.

The official entry in the Register of Companies should follow during January and at the same time we will inform our friendly colleagues in the trade, banks and personal friends. It would be best to avoid sending out a printed circular.

In the firm belief that the Edition Peters will enjoy the same high reputation throughout the world under my sons Max

and Hans-Joachim, as it has so far enjoyed, I lay the future
fate of the company in your hands.

With Love and fidelity, Your Father,
Henri Hinrichsen

Max's promotion to a partnership in 1931 had been proudly
announced with printed circulars throughout the music trade and
announcements in the musical and trade presses; Henri Hinrichsen's
reticence to do the same for Hans-Joachim was due to his desire not to
draw anti-Semitic attention to C F Peters.

Max Hinrichsen

Unlike his two sisters, who had both married Jews, Max chose to marry
a woman who, in Nazi terminology, was of pure Aryan descent.

Max, Henri Hinrichsen's partner since 1931, was thirty-three when
he met the twenty-four-year-old Marie-Luise von Siegroth und Slawikau
on 27th February, 1934; they married on 28th June that same year,
both having been baptised Evangelical (Protestant) a few days earlier.
The hasty marriage was necessary in order to circumvent the new 'Racial
Purity' laws soon to take effect, forbidding intermarriage between Jews
and Aryans. Both families warned against this ill-conceived match. The
young couple would not be deterred, even though a special court in
Nuremberg had sentenced the Aryan wife of a Jew to four months in
prison as a 'race-defiling female' on 14th June.[11]

Born in Silesia, into an aristocratic Roman Catholic family, Marie-
Luise had three older brothers. Her eldest brother Hanns was killed at
the age of nineteen as a lieutenant in the trenches in France in 1915,
having been awarded the Iron Cross. Joachim was a major general in
the *Wehrmacht* (the German army) in 1934. Fearing that his sister's
marriage would jeopardise his promising military career, he disowned
her completely. He refused to attend the wedding and he never spoke
to her or had any contact with her again.[12] Eberhard, her youngest
brother, had no such qualms. The widowed Baroness Elisabeth von
Siegroth und Slawikau divided her time between her home in Berlin
and her daughter's new home in Leipzig.

Max and Marie-Luise enjoyed a comfortable lifestyle and Max
worked hard alongside his father. On 8th April, 1935 a baby was
born, whom they named Irene.[13] When her birth was registered,
the racial terminology described her as *Mischling ersten Grades* (First
degree mixed breed). Life was embarrassing for the young couple. In
August 1935 a newspaper campaign began throughout Germany

demanding legislation to prevent sexual relations between Jews and non-Jews.[14]

Max Hinrichsen felt a tremendous sense of responsibility to his father and to the family business with which he had grown up. He was joint Managing Director of C F Peters and Administrator of the Peters Music Library, involved in the editing of its famous *Yearbook*. Marie-Luise, who could foresee a worsening situation, urged him to emigrate. Max would have liked to have gone to the USA, but he joked that the country was not large enough for both him and Walter. In reality, the brothers felt that C F Peters would be better served if they each founded a company on opposite sides of the Atlantic. He opted to emigrate to Great Britain.

On 27th October, 1937 business formalities were officially completed, when Max Hinrichsen resigned as joint managing director of C F Peters, Leipzig and his place was taken by his younger brother, Dr Hans-Joachim Hinrichsen. The details were recorded in the *Handelsregister* (Register of Companies). Whilst rejoicing at the fact that his third son was now officially his partner, Henri Hinrichsen was devastated at Max's decision to leave.

The bureaucratic formalities required of Jews wishing to emigrate from Nazi Germany took several months to complete. On 12th November, 1937 Max, Marie-Luise and Irene Hinrichsen left Leipzig for England, where Max Hinrichsen founded Hinrichsen Edition Ltd in March 1938 and eventually Peters Edition, London. Henri Hinrichsen never forgave his eldest son for leaving and refused to communicate with him from that moment onwards – a heartbreaking tragedy which was to haunt Max for the rest of his life. Contact was maintained with Hans-Joachim and in her letters, Marie-Luise urged him to leave Germany and to persuade his parents to do likewise. The now seventy-year-old Henri Hinrichsen refused even to consider leaving, saying that he owed it to his uncle, Dr Max Abraham, from whom he had inherited the business in 1900, to remain, with the business, in Leipzig.

With the advent of National Socialism in 1933, the esteem in which Henri Hinrichsen had been held in the college for which he had been the founding benefactor in 1911, was replaced by a policy of humiliation and vilification. His name and very existence were to be expunged. This was also the stance adopted against the memory of Henriette Goldschmidt.

The Henriette Goldschmidt School

The college became subordinate to a new educational policy. Children's first obligation was no longer to their parents, but to the state. Parents were told: 'Your child belongs to us now! You will pass, but your descendants are already in the new camp. Very shortly they will only recognise the new community.'[15] Henceforth '…students would be educated towards duty to the people and the family in professions promoting the spirit of National Socialism.'[16] Those entitled to apply for a place in the college were girls who had completed high school education, were of pure Aryan descent and had proved their worthiness in the *Bund Deutscher Mädchen* (Association of German Girls) [a Nazi propaganda and fitness organisation], preferably as leaders.[17] The director of the college, Frau Dr Meister-Trescher was removed from her post and sent to a village to work on the land.

On the second-floor landing there was a bronze plaque set into the wall with a dedication from the patron, commemorating the inauguration of the house on 29th October, 1911; this was now covered with a picture which showed the quotation: 'You are nothing, your Nation is all.'[18]

Henriette Goldschmidt's birthday, which had been regularly commemorated on 23rd November, was to be replaced with an outing for the students, without reference to her name.

Starting in August 1933, the Education Department, the Mayor, the Leipzig Town Council and the governing body of the *Sozialpädagogisches Frauenseminar* (cleansed of its founder's name) expended a great deal of time in discussion and in correspondence, about what was to be done with the sculpture bust of Henriette Goldschmidt, the large portrait of her and the portrait of Henri Hinrichsen. It was no longer seen as fit that the participation of Jews in the founding of the first college for women in Germany, should be acknowledged to the students. The correspondence points to innumerable moves of all three items, between the director's room, the library, the cleaners' store room and another house. (The students had been so indoctrinated that it was reported that one refused to take part in a discussion in a room where there was a portrait of a Jew.)[19]

Henri Hinrichsen expressed his distress, when he wrote to the Mayor on 21st November, 1933:

> …The city *Sozialpädagogisches Frauenseminar*, Königstrasse 18/ 20 has for over twenty years invited me, as the creator of its house and donor of the one-time *Hochschule für Frauen* which was founded there, to all its events. For the first time ever, I was not sent invitations to the two events held yesterday, the 20th, and Thursday the 23rd, presumably because it was not thought possible to protect me from the aggression of Aryan employees. You will surely be able to understand my feelings, Mr Mayor, at not being permitted to enter this city

building. I presented the house at that time with the
dedication:

THE NOBLE STRIVING OF GERMAN WOMEN

and fought hard to ensure that it should promote those
branches of education which were specifically appropriate
for women and which are still acknowledged to this day.

The fact that my portrait has been hung in the director's room
and has been replaced by a portrait of the Führer, is totally
appropriate, as a portrait of Adolf Hitler should be in the
main hall of every school. But, in the same position as my
picture has hung for the past five years a saying has been
painted on Hitler's picture, which, whilst I do not take this as
a reference to myself, I nonetheless find extremely hurtful.
Apparently this saying has been applied by somebody who
has no idea that my wife's and my forebears have held German
citizenship for over 250 years, and that I am every bit as good
a German as millions of others of a different faith. It is precisely
the Führer's watchword: 'The common good before the self',
which not many German citizens have followed in such a
convincing manner as my late uncle Dr Max Abraham and
I have done over the course of the last seventy years, as
citizens of Leipzig, proprietors of C F Peters and in private
life.

I regret having to write these lines to you, Mr Mayor...

The quotation which had replaced Henri Hinrichsen's portrait read:

When the best fell at the front, one could at least exterminate
the vermin at home, flush the perfidious lads out of their
hiding places and hang them from the highest gallows.

The letter caused a further flurry of communications between the
various authorities. On Henri Hinrichsen' insistence, it was agreed that
for the sake of formality, he was in future to be sent invitations to all
events at the college, on the understanding that he would decline.
The authorities gave in to him on certain points because he was the
trustee of the Henri Hinrichsen Trust for the college. The formulation
of the trust meant that he could at any time withdraw his huge
investment; the authorities relied on the income from this to support
the college.

The warped educational outlook was exemplified in the selection of reading materials available to the students. The library of educational books which Henri Hinrichsen had donated became 'cleansed' in 1936. Books by such authors as Freud, Horden and Fischhard were destroyed. The director, Frau Dr Braune, wrote to the Department of Education on 30th August, 1937, asking for permission to remove the ex-libris label with the portrait of Henriette Goldschmidt from all the books. She received the following reply:

> I just cannot understand how a school in this National Socialist State could still possess a Trust which carries the name of a Jew. I regard it as intolerable that books in the Social Pedagogical Women's College, which originate from the Henri Hinrichsen Trust, should carry an ex-libris label with the portrait of Henriette Goldschmidt.[20]

It took four years for the authorities to reach a final decision about the portraits, which by then had been completely removed, whilst the correspondence as to their disposal continued. Their fate, and that of the other offending items, is given in a letter from the college director to the mayor, dated 10th November, 1937: 'The oil painting by Geiger and the bronze plaque have been sent to Dr Hinrichsen today. The Ex-libris labels will be removed and the painting by Einschlag will be destroyed.'

The painting by Eduard Einschlag, a Jew, had been commissioned by the Leipzig Town Council in honour of Henri Hinrichsen's sixtieth birthday, in 1928. The huge portrait of Henriette Goldschmidt was kept safely in store. Many years later it was re-hung. The sculpture bust of Henriette Goldschmidt was destroyed. The marble pedestal, too heavy to be moved, remained. It still stands, empty, as a memorial to those times.

The authorities also had to dispose of a huge collection of educational material which the sponsor had given the school, which carried the name Henri Hinrichsen Educational Materials Trust. He agreed to allow it to be incorporated into the general holdings of the school. The authorities also needed to rename a number of houses, including a kindergarten and a student's home, carrying the name of Henriette Goldschmidt, which had been provided by Henri Hinrichsen and were supported through the Henri Hinrichsen Trust. They just dropped her name. The houses were eventually taken into DDR State ownership and allowed to fall into decay.

The Henri Hinrichsen Trust posed a larger problem for the authorities, who desperately needed to hold on to this substantial capital. Eventually, political decrees and the Leipzig authorities caused the Trust to be renamed 'Trust for the *Sozialpädagogisches*

Frauenseminar' which was accepted by the Saxony Ministry of National Education in Dresden, on 19th April, 1941, by which time Henri Hinrichsen had long ceased to have any influence on anything in Leipzig any more. When a school inspection was carried out in February 1942, his name was not mentioned in the report, which described the foundation of the college: 'In the year 1911 a benefactor donated the building which was named *Hochschule für Frauen* (High School for Women).'[21] After some years even the new name of the Trust disappeared. Placed in a general trust incorporating several redundant trusts, the funds were frittered away by the DDR authorities, to become untraceable.

The acknowledgement of Henri Hinrichsen as the benefactor of another major institution, was similarly erased.

The Music Instruments Museum

Henri Hinrichsen had been the sponsor behind the purchase of the Heyer collection of musical instruments in 1926, which formed the Musical Instruments Museum in Leipzig. When the original curator, Professor Kroyer, left in 1933 the Ministry of Culture in Dresden wanted to appoint an academic of lower standing, in order to save money. Henri Hinrichsen was prepared to pay the additional salary for a full Professor of Musicology, but his offer was turned down by the Ministry on 25th March, 1933. The Dean of the Faculty of Philosophy of the University of Leipzig, Professor Ludwig Wiekmann, who had asked Henri Hinrichsen for his support, was extremely disappointed at the anti-Semitic decision made by the ministry. He wrote to the Assistant Secretary of the Ministry of Culture, Ministerialrat von Seydewitz, on 27th March, 1933:[22]

> I acknowledge your letter -A:2 f L 2- of 25th March, 1933, regarding the professorship of musicology at the University of Leipzig, with thanks. I deeply regret the revocation of the decision of the Finance Ministry regarding the acceptance of the endowment of 20,000M from the hand of Geheimrat Dr h c Hinrichsen. This endowment was meant as a totally selfless gift in the interests of promoting the work of the University and developing his generous endowment for the Music Instruments Museum.
>
> Professor Gurlitt, whom you suggested, is specifically rejected by the Faculty. Your information that 'he would be the first choice' is completely wrong. I will present the list of those proposed by the Faculty shortly...

Dean Wiekmann also wrote to Henri Hinrichsen on 27th March:[23]

> One of the last dispositions of the Finance Minister of the dismissed Government of Saxony, was the acceptance of your endowment for the maintenance of the Professorship for Musicology.

> The order confirming this was shown to me by *Ministerialrat* Dr Ulrich, on 10th March. Today I have received the notification from the new Government, that the acceptance of the endowment is being rejected, and that the post will be that of an Assistant Professor.

> Whilst informing you of this decision by the Ministry, I would like you to accept my warmest thanks for your promotion of the work of our University, which you intended to consolidate with your selfless endowment...

Whilst the University of Leipzig valued Henri Hinrichsen's support of the Music Instruments Museum, the government ministry controlled policy. Only four years after the grand inauguration of this fine museum which, without Henri Hinrichsen's generous financial contribution would not have existed, the sponsor was banned from further involvement in any aspect of the institution. In 1929, when the large notice reading: 'Henri Hinrichsen Hall' in large, solid bronze letters on each side, was hung in the centre of the hall holding the finest pieces, it was expected to hang there 'for all time'. Now it was thrown on a heap of rubbish in the cellar.

Much worse was to happen in the aftermath of the state-inspired Kristallnacht (Night of Broken Glass) on the night of 9th-10th November, 1938.

---

1   Order of the direction of the NSDAP, dated 28th March, 1933. Quoted in Barkai.
2   Gilbert, p 26.
3   *Musik im Dritten Reich,* Joseph Wulf, Sigbert Mohn Verlag, 1963.
    Deutscher Musiker-Kalender, 1943, Erster band, Max Hesse Verlag, Berlin, 1943.
4   *Lexikon der Juden in der Musik* edited by Dr Theo Stengel and Dr habil. Herbert Gerigk, published 1940 by Hahnefeld Verlag, Berlin.
5   StAL Bestand, C F Peters, No 4410.
6   All Strauss letters and contracts, in StAL Bestand, C F Peters.
7   9th January, 1932, StAL Bestand, C F Peters, No 1132.
8   All Elsa Reger correspondence in StAL Bestand, C F Peters, 671.
9   *Ibid.*

10 Letter in the author's archive.
11 Gilbert, p 44.
12 Major General Joachim von Siegroth und Slawikau was awarded the Iron Cross for distinguished military service. Taken prisoner by the Russians, he was killed in Siberia, probably in 1945. The sister whom he had spurned helped support his four little daughters for many years.
13 The author.
14 Gilbert, p 46.
15 *Unser Jahrhundert im Bild*, Gütersloh 1964, p 452.
16 Stadtarchiv Leipzig: Akten des Schulamts No 4/101/9, p 283.
17 *Ibid,* 4/101/9/7, p 23.
18 *Ibid,* 4/409/4, p 41 *ff.*
19 *Ibid.*
20 *Ibid,* 4/409/4, p 35.
21 Report dated 11th February, 1942, signed by Ruth Kresse, a copy of which was given to the growing collection of archive material in the Henriette Goldschmidt Schule.
22 Universitätsarchiv Leipzig: UAL, B1/14 27 1Bd, 1, Bl 19.
23 *Ibid.*

CHAPTER FIFTEEN

1938: Kristallnacht, The Peters Music Library and the 'Aryanization' of C F Peters

Kristallnacht

The first mass deportations from Germany of 18,000 Polish Jews took place on 28th-29th October, 1938. The German Jews, like the Hinrichsens, comforted themselves thinking that they were not involved. Up to November 1938 Henri Hinrichsen still pursued his belief that things would not get worse for him and his family and that they would be spared the ultimate excesses of the measures against Jews. He felt that his prominent position and his many fine and generous gifts to benefit Leipzig institutions would stand to his credit. But most of those city officials and bureaucrats who had known him for many years, had been replaced by Nazis, intent on carrying out every new law and stricture against the Jews, with fanatical obedience. The event which signalled the desecration of everything he had believed in and everything he had worked for over the course of more than forty years, was the *Reichskristallnacht Pogrom*, the Nazi State sponsored Night of Broken Glass, on the night of 9th-10th November, 1938.

The shattering of glass, of the windows of shops belonging to Jews, the looting of their homes, the desecration of synagogues, the brutality directed at innocent Jews and the ferocity unleashed by the Nazis throughout Germany, commenced at exactly three a.m. on 10th November, 1938. All Leipzig synagogues, Jewish shops, offices, businesses and institutes were vandalised and looted, many being completely destroyed. Jews were fined a billion marks for the destruction the Nazis had wrought on their property, which was levied by the compulsory confiscation of twenty per cent of the property of every Jew.[1] They were ordered to clear up the mess immediately at their own cost. The insurance companies refused to pay any compensation.

Through some fortuitous stroke of luck, Martha and Henri Hinrichsen were in Vienna on the fatal night. Returning on 10th

November they found that the Nazi thugs had entered the premises at 10 Talstrasse and ransacked their apartment, vandalising and looting their possessions; smashing what they could not remove, or did not want. They had broken into the offices of C F Peters and smashed everything they could lay their hands on. They had thrown furniture, books, files and sheet music out of the window and had made a bonfire in the courtyard. They had ransacked the huge stock room and thrown all the music by Felix Mendelssohn-Bartholdy onto the bonfire – in this they were helped by a Nazi member of the staff.

Jewish men were rounded up. Dr Henri Hinrichsen and his son, Dr Hans-Joachim Hinrichsen, were arrested. Henri Hinrichsen was soon released, but Hans-Joachim disappeared for several weeks – to a concentration camp. His name was entered in the Prisoners' Book of the Leipzig Police Department, 1938 Vol II, as Prisoner No 75, registered on 13th November at 11.30 a.m.[2]

Confiscation of C F Peters

Martha Hinrichsen, in understandable panic, wrote to her son Walter in the USA on 20th November:

> The dice have fallen. The business was confiscated from us on Thursday afternoon, with immediate effect. None of us may enter the office...I would have written it to you immediately, but I wanted to wait until Hans returned. That seems to be taking a longer time, we have no idea where he has been taken, we only know that he is no longer in Leipzig, it is eight days since they came to fetch him. Ilse and Lotte are in the same state of ignorance about their husbands. Father is finding it terribly difficult to make the decision to emigrate, but it will be impossible to remain here, even he said that this morning. The whole affair is terribly difficult for Father, who sees his life's work collapse like this – through no fault of his own...I cannot write in greater detail, I have to be careful because Hans is being held as a sort of hostage, that is why none of you must take any action on account of C F Peters...

During his absence, Hans-Joachim was sent a letter, dated 15th November, 1938, from the *Reichsminister für Volksaufklärung und Propaganda*, Goebbels Propaganda Ministry, informing him that he was forbidden to practise his profession:

> As from today, I exclude you from membership of the State Culture Chamber and also from the State Music Chamber.

> This decision is irrevocable. Through this decree you lose
> the right to exercise any activity in the sphere of the State
> Culture Chamber and at the same time lose the possibility of
> exercising all rights which as partner in the music publishing
> company of C F Peters you have exercised.
>
> I have engaged a consultant of Department II of my house,
> SS-Standartenführer G Noatzke of Berlin to take over the
> custodial direction of C F Peters. You are ordered to make
> yourself available to him in Leipzig.

Noatzke's job was to confiscate the company; he was to be an interim
custodian until the firm could be 'sold' to a suitably qualified Aryan
person, who understood music publishing. Many companies owned by
Jews and taken over were to be liquidated. The ministry had no intention
of liquidating C F Peters, rather to continue to benefit from it as a
profitable source of foreign revenue for the Nazi state. They did not
want to run it as a state-owned business, which might not attract foreign
trade, but wanted it to be 'legitimately' sold. There were several
opportunists wishing to 'buy' what was arguably the finest music
publishing business in Germany. It was Noatzke's job to weigh up the
merits of the various applicants and to make his recommendations.
The selling of the business to an Aryan would then constitute its
'aryanization'.

Henri Hinrichsen did not feel himself to be capable of handling
this grotesque situation on his own. With immense courage and in
danger of himself being arrested again, he demanded that Hans-
Joachim be released, so that they could together oversee the
compulsory hand-over of the business to Noatzke, who knew nothing
about music publishing whatsoever. He said that unless his son were
released, he would not co-operate. It must be credited to his determined
stand, that the twenty-nine-year-old Hans-Joachim was released from
his incarceration.

At that time his two younger brothers were still in Leipzig: Paul,
aged twenty-six, had been in Brazil on a six months' visitor's visa and
was still trying to get a visa to return to Brazil and Robert, aged twenty,
who had returned from school in England. The Hinrichsen family was
desperately trying to get out of Germany. Walter tried to obtain visas
and guarantees from the USA and Max was trying to facilitate
arrangements in England.

The visa application process was complicated and by that time,
required a guarantor from a host country to make an application. The
American Consulate was so inundated with applications that they could
not easily trace one before it came to the top of the pile.

Martha wrote to Walter on 13th December about the difficulty of obtaining visas and the various plans which his three younger brothers were pursuing to get out of Germany:

> ...This should be the Christmas letter...Father puts a brave face on things, at least in public, but the thought that he has to give his whole life's work away, just like that, has depressed him terribly. Above all, the uncertainty as to how he will lose the business. He has not been permitted to enter the business premises since the 12th November, and has been forbidden to say anything about the running of the business...

> We want to make sure that Hans and Robert get out of German territory as soon as possible, and until then we will not know what remains to us from the business, and they must have something to live on. We and Hans cannot get at our money, and Robert hasn't any. We have enough to live on here...Max moved heaven and earth to try and get Hans out for us. He sent a Peruvian visa for him, which made no impression, because it has no value without the various papers which are demanded to accompany it and which take a long time to procure. He also sent an invitation for Hans from a friend in England, which also had no effect with the authorities, because he had to have an entry visa to London...Robert has written to Sydney, Melbourne and New Zealand offering himself and Hans and has a tiny ray of hope...Paul is now also here, he is helping Robert with the organisation of our emigration so that everything is running smoothly by the time they leave. Paul is still hoping to be able to leave on 29th December; they hand out the first visas on the 22nd and he is planning to stand in the queue in Berlin all night. Then I will take him to the ship in Hamburg...

None of Martha's hopes or her sons' plans were realised. Paul was not able to leave on 29th December and neither Hans-Joachim nor Robert were able to leave. Martha was right to worry about whether any part of the considerable Hinrichsen fortune would be left to herself and her husband.

On 3rd December, 1938 a new decree was issued referring to the *Planned de-Judaising of our Economy*. It concerned the deployment of Jewish wealth, a ban on the purchase of property and land by Jews, compulsory deposit of stocks and shares, official sales' places for valuable metals and jewellery in Jewish ownership. Jews were forbidden to purchase valuables or to pawn or sell those which they possessed, except to the government-controlled depots.

Henri Hinrichsen had written to SS Standartenführer G Noatzke, the custodian for C F Peters, asking what his position was. Noatzke's reply of 30th December from the Propaganda Ministry in Berlin informed him that neither he nor his son Hans-Joachim were permitted to be in any way involved with the day-to-day running of C F Peters. They were not to exercise any influence concerning the sale of the business and if any prospective buyers approached them, they were to refer them to Noatzke immediately. He ended the letter with a veiled threat: 'I am convinced that your interests will be best served, if you refrain from interfering in any way with the transfer of the business into German hands.' As a Jew, Henri Hinrichsen was no longer considered to be a German.

In the meantime, the staff of C F Peters carried out their normal duties, without anybody at the helm. The secretary, Fräulein Hopfe, noted in her diary on 17th January, 1939:

> Today with Mr Günther at C G Röder and Oskar Brandstetter, comparing the inventory of the engraved music plates with the Plate Control Book. According to our Plate Book 2,242 plates out of the 249,663 are with Brandstetter, the rest with Röder.

C G Röder were the company's printers. The publisher had been using Oscar Brandstetter initially for storing some of the plates, but then also for printing. This quantity of engraved metal plates represented a massive investment over the years and an enormous stock in terms of weight. It constituted a large part of the capital of C F Peters.

With the changing conditions Wilhelm Weismann, who had been with the company since 1929, took on more responsibility and acted, to the best of his ability, in the way Henri Hinrichsen would have done.

Wilhelm Weismann

As early as 1933 Aryans were being discouraged from working for Jews. Weismann was summoned by the leader of the Cultural Department in Leipzig, Stadtrat Hauptmann, around 1933, with whom he recalled having something like the following conversation:[3]

> But Mr Weismann, we don't understand why you are still working for this Jewish publisher. You must become one of *us*. I must say...all your compositions, yes everything...You are a German and you must come to us. If you come, you will immediately be given an important position. Would you like

to be musical director of the Leipzig Radio? So I said: 'Do you mean I can do whatever I like?' And he replied: 'Yes, you are of course answerable to the Propaganda Ministry, Minister Goebbels.' To which I answered: 'No, thank you, there is no question of that for me!' He continued: 'Yes, but why are you in this publishing house?' My reply was to the effect: 'Whilst I am aware of the well-known fact that the Hinrichsen family is Jewish, there has never been any point at which I have had to tell myself that I must not stay in this publishing house. It is a highly reputable publishing company. Geheimrat Hinrichsen is a man of the highest moral calibre, I can only hold him in the highest respect. I have no reason. Why on earth should I leave? Just because they are Jews? These Jews...we are serving a common goal, to continue to develop and promote good editions of music.'

In his own words he then became 'the stained sheep – sometimes seen as black, sometimes as white'. But otherwise he was left unmolested by the authorities and remained with the company.

Wisemann expressed his support and friendship for Henri Hinrichsen when he wrote on 24th January, 1938, congratulating the publisher on his seventieth birthday – a dismal occasion, compared with the civic honours bestowed on him for his sixtieth birthday. Such a letter was valued as a moral booster to Henri Hinrichsen, whose whole world and lifetime's achievement were crumbling about him in 1938:

...I write this in the knowledge that your life's work is not to be regarded as finished. I most sincerely hope that, in the interests of the publishing house, this will long continue to be the case...

Another wish is that you can be strengthened from far away, by the thought that your life's work, irrespective of outside evaluation can, especially today, be seen to have realised its goals in its breadth and cultural significance. It is on this that the impression rests, of the firm of C F Peters as one of the leading German cultural publishers and it shows clearly which direction the goals of the future should take...

Of the aryanization period Weismann recalled:

Yes, much of the time I ran things alone, as it was all rather dramatic in those chaotic years after the retirement of Geheimrat Hinrichsen. I was called out one day into the main office, and there he was, and next to him stood a high Standartenführer, sent by Goebbels. It was explained to me, that as from this day, the Hinrichsen family were retired from the business and that the management would be in the hands of the Propaganda Ministry, represented by Noatzke. I still remember what I said then: 'I don't understand! I would have wished that the government could have conducted itself in a more loyal manner.' Whereupon Noatzke answered; 'Oh, please, loyal…' Whereupon Geheimrat Hinrichsen said: 'I would like you to stay with the company! The work stands higher than the person!' That was well said.

Coincidentally, on the same day Dr Ludwig Landshoff called and said: 'I am coming to you, as I am not able to speak to the Geheimrat. What's happening here?' I explained to him. He said he had come to say goodbye, he couldn't stand living in Germany any more and was leaving for Paris.

Wilhelm Weismann added that Landshoff eventually went to America, where he died of a heart attack in 1941 on landing on American soil. He continued with an explanation of how he ignored the order not to communicate with the Hinrichsen family, who were permitted to go on living in their apartment upstairs:

I couldn't care less. I went upstairs every day to visit the Geheimrat, because the old man was still very attached to the business and wanted to know what was happening. There was a sort of interregnum; Noatzke was clever enough to say that he didn't understand much about these things and said to me: 'You run things, I'll come every three weeks and have a look at how things are going. There will be things for me to sign. Otherwise, do as you like. If there are any problems, etc.' That was the interim time [whilst the business was being aryanized].'

And all the time the Hinrichsens were making every effort to obtain entry visas to another country – any country – which would enable them to leave Germany.

Visas Unavailable

Max Hinrichsen had placed applications with the British authorities on 17th November in respect of the Hinrichsens and their three sons for leave to take up residence in the United Kingdom. A letter to Henri

Hinrichsen from the solicitor R Shapiro & Co of London, dated 18th January adds: 'Such application was supported by a very strong guarantee, and there is every reason to believe that there will be a favourable decision…Unfortunately there are so many cases under consideration that some time must elapse before your case receives approval.'

Every country sent the same message to the Jews wishing to get out of Germany after Kristallnacht: 'So many applications…some time must elapse…'

The 5th February, 1939 saw Henri Hinrichsen's seventy-first birthday. What was keeping him from total depression were letters from his son Walter in the USA whose sense of humour and efforts to try and secure entry into the USA for his parents gave them constant jolts of optimism. Responding to his son's cheerful birthday letter on 10th February, Hinrichsen also outlined some of his current concerns:

> …Until we have an entry permit to the USA, as a mature man I will set aside all other plans. I am sure that this permit will be a long time coming…So, in the meantime we are trying with London, but that will also take a long time. But first the business has to be aryanized, which will take place in a few weeks. We don't know who will get it…I am attempting through tax, atonement fines, emigration tax and the like to reduce the fortune acquired through half a century of hard work. Hopefully there will be some left at the end. It really is a difficult time for an old man…Looking forward to receiving another sunny letter from you soon…

Henri Hinrichsen had heard nothing from Noatzke, though he had repeatedly tried to get an appointment to see him; but after ten weeks he felt he had to take some action. On 26th February, 1939, he wrote to Staatsrat Hans Hinkel, Noatzke's superior, at the Propaganda Ministry:[4]

> At the end of last year the custodian of my publishing company informed me that my interests would best be served if I refrained from trying to have any influence on the transfer of my business into German hands. I followed this suggestion, even though – as I have recently discovered – originally, the opportunity was to be granted to the owner of a company to come to some agreement with a prospective purchaser. In the meantime the accounts for 1938 have been approved. I was promised an interview with the custodian which has now, after ten weeks, been refused. I am approaching you today

with the request that you inform me of the current situation. I can only successfully pursue my preparations for emigration if I know what will remain to me abroad from the sale of my publishing business. To what extent may I take my collections with me abroad, bearing in mind my decades of work promoting German music to the world, my Trusts for the general good such as the Music Instruments Museum, the Peters Music Library and the *Sozialpädagogisches Frauenseminar* [the Henriette Goldschmidt School]. I have no means to call on abroad and after fifty years in the music trade and at the age of seventy-one, I am not in a position to earn a living and support my wife.

It can only be to the disadvantage of C F Peters, whose export business under my direction during the years 1932-1937, brought approximately three million marks in foreign currency into Germany, if it lacks a director for very much longer.

Henri Israel Hinrichsen

As a Jew, Henri Hinrichsen had been obliged to add the name 'Israel' to his name. This he did on 25th January, 1939, a copy of his birth certificate being stamped and dated 7th April when an entry was made in the Archive of the Hansa City of Hamburg, where he had been born in 1868.[5]

As a Jew, Henri Hinrichsen was stripped, too, of all responsibility for the Peters Music Library. The fortieth anniversary of the foundation of the Library on 2nd January, 1934 saw continuity of musicological work being maintained, but supervisory control gradually devolved into Nazi hands.

The Peters Music Library

The Max Abraham Trust was responsible for the Peters Music Library. It had three trustees: the head of the Cultural Department of Leipzig, the head librarian of the Peters Music Library and the proprietor of C F Peters – Henri Hinrichsen. On the retirement of the head of the Cultural Department, Professor Dr Alfred Jeremias, at the beginning of 1933 his place as a trustee had been taken by Councillor F A Hauptmann, leader of the Cultural and Educational Department of the NSDAP, the Nazi Party, in Leipzig.

Since Professor Schwartz's retirement, Henri Hinrichsen had been paying him a pension. He died on 20th April, 1935, and the Leipzig authorities asked Hinrichsen to continue to pay the pension to Schwartz's widow. The authorities expected his continued financial contributions to various causes, but denied him any autonomy.

A copious correspondence between various members of the Leipzig Town Council, leading towards Henri Hinrichsen's complete marginalisation as overall director of the trustees of the Max Abraham Trust was started by Councillor Richard Falb, with a letter dated 4th November, 1936.[6] Writing to Senior Councillor Otto Wolf, he pointed out that the proprietor of C F Peters and of the Peters Music Library was the non-Aryan Hinrichsen and added that: 'Should the Peters Music Library ever be moved to another town, or even sold abroad, which could easily happen with a non-Aryan, it would be an inestimable loss to the city of Leipzig.' He went on to suggest that it would be ideal for the music and book city of Leipzig if this library were eventually to be incorporated into the City Library. Wolf sent the letter to Councillor Hauptmann of the Cultural Department; one of his staff clarified the situation in a confidential letter addressed to Wolf, dated 17th November, 1936, explaining that the Peters Music Library had been secured for the City of Leipzig for many years. The one-time proprietor of C F Peters, Dr Max Abraham, had made the library which he had founded freely available for musicians and music students. He had left instructions in his will in 1897, to ensure the continuity of the library. The library was governed by a board of three trustees, one of whom should be a member of the town council – Councillor Hauptmann had been a member of this board since 1933. He added further that Dr Abraham had also left 400,000M in his will to be invested by the city authorities decreeing that the interest from this sum should be used for the running costs and new acquisitions for the library. In the eventuality that the firm of C F Peters should be wound up, or moved to another place, he had decreed that the ownership of the library and the building, Königstrasse 26, in which it was housed, as well as the capital sum, should devolve to the City of Leipzig. His letter continued:

Abraham's heir, Dr Henri Hinrichsen, followed these instructions with a contract between himself and the city authorities in 1901, this was certified by a notary in 1929. The relevant details have been entered in the Land Registry.

It is further decreed in the bequest that the city should pay the accruing interest to the firm of C F Peters who would determine how the money was to be spent. Neither the firm of C F Peters nor its proprietor are obliged to provide financial support for the running of the library, this is supposed to be covered by the accrued interest. However, as arranged in May

1935, Hinrichsen does not claim any of the interest for the support of the library, having asked that it be paid to the widow of the previous librarian, Schwartz, to supplement her pension.

The city authority has the right to examine the accounts, which are kept by the company, in order to be certain of the running costs and costs of acquisition of the library. No use has so far been made of this right, as the company has never asked for the interest and supports the library entirely at its own cost. The interest, which is variable, amounts to between 600-700M per year and is in no way sufficient to meet the costs, so that the company undertook to accept the full responsibility for all costs.

Councillor Falb is therefore under a misapprehension about the company. This is an incredibly generous trust, and the conduct up to the present gives absolutely no cause to doubt that the conditions will be fulfilled.

The letter, written by somebody who valued Henri Hinrichsen's generous support of the Peters Music Library over the years, should have assured a continuity of confidence in a situation which was all to the advantage of the City of Leipzig. But it was not the end of the matter.

The new mayor of Leipzig, who had succeeded Dr Goerdeler at the end of 1937, was Kurt Walter Dönicke, the local NSDAP leader. He wrote a four-page report on the constitution of the Max Abraham Trust on 23rd June, 1938, which echoes what the above writer noted so succinctly. However, he noted that: 'a legally constituted trust has not been formed.' He continued with the remarks:

The first trustee, Henri Hinrichsen who, according to the book edited by Christa Maria Bock and Hans Brückner, *Judentum und Music* (Jews and Music), is a Jew, has, as he also selects the second trustee, the deciding influence on the supervision of the trust. It is therefore two-thirds under Jewish supervision.

The second trustee was always the Head Librarian, who was selected by Henri Hinrichsen after consultation with others.

Henri Hinrichsen's trusteeship of the Peters Music Library was brutally terminated. On 21st November, the director of the Ministry of Culture in Leipzig wrote to the Legal Department of the city asking what action he should take in view of the new regulations forbidding the acceptance of any Jewish Trust Funds. Because the Peters Music Library was an exceptionally valuable piece of property, it was important to handle the matter with complete correctness and ensure that it remained in Leipzig, whilst also maintaining its income. A lengthy reply quoting many different new laws, was sent on 24th November. It pointed out that whilst the current owner of C F Peters was a Jew, this would not be the case for much longer, as the company was in the process of being 'aryanized' and that the new owner would then be expected to take on the trusteeship.

The work of the Peters Music Library continued and the *Yearbook* No 45 for 1938, which appeared in 1939 reports its activity as being on a par with previous years. The elderly Christian Sinding, much of whose music had been published by C F Peters, was one of a host of celebrities who came to visit. The library lent many valuable items to an exhibition entitled *Leipzig als Musikstadt* (Leipzig as City of Music). 224 new acquisitions (purchased by Henri Hinrichsen) were added to the library. It was also noted that a collection of valuable early music was put at the disposal of the library by a private collector – without mentioning that this was Henri Hinrichsen.

Dr Kurt Taut died quite suddenly, at the age of fifty-one, on 19th January, 1939. A replacement for the head librarian had to be found. For the first time since 1900, Henri Hinrichsen was allowed no say in the selection of the man who was to head the Peters Music Library.

No time was lost, and a memo dated 25th January, 1939 shows that the candidate favoured by the Ministry of Culture was Prof Dr Eugen Schmitz, a music critic from Dresden, whilst Stadtrat Hauptmann favoured Dr Rubarth of Leipzig, who would also have been Wilhelm Weismann's choice. A series of lengthy official memos detailing all the conversations and communications which took place at that time, were signed by 'Klinnz'. They would appear to be from the cultural ministry to the legal department of the Leipzig City Council, though the paper is unheaded. Though a decision had apparently already been made, the post was advertised and seven people with excellent references were recommended to C F Peters; the applications were dealt with by Wilhelm Weismann. One of the most persuasive advocates for Dr Schmitz, in a letter dated 2nd February, 1939, was Winifred Wagner, the virulently anti-Semitic, staunch Nazi supporter, daughter-in-law of Richard Wagner. On 29th March SS Standartenführer Noatzke, the custodian for C F Peters informed the Mayor of Leipzig that Schmitz had been appointed.

A lengthy article by Dr Eugen Schmitz entitled *Das Judentum – Eine Gefahr für die deutsche Musik* (The Jews – A Danger for German Music) may well have influenced his selection.[7] A few extracts will give some insight into his views:

The Jews a danger to music? One immediately thinks back to
the glorious days of atonality which are really not so long
ago. That was then, when Jews and Jewish sympathisers
created operas whose heroes were black jazz band violinists
and gangsters, or nuns who made love in unspeakable ways,
with a crucifix...

He elaborated his thesis by saying that the Jews wanted to throw out
all that was true and noble in German music of the Classical and
Romantic periods; not to replace it with anything new but in order to
wreak pointless destruction. He wrote that all that Jewish musicologists
did was to praise all this atonality and to revile the great master, Wagner;
that they would like to pile all his operas onto a huge bonfire, sit Cosima
Wagner on top and set light to the whole heap. Jewish influence, going
back as far as 1220 when a Jewish *Minnesänger* (Minstrel Knight) called
Süsskind was performing, had been to the disadvantage of German
music. He continued:

However, it is enough to look back only as far as the nineteenth
century for a clarification of the Jewish problem. Because it
was only then that the Jews appeared as a closed force to make
an impression on European music, especially on German
music...Four names of Jewish musicians can be seen as an
example of this incurable progression. They are: Schönberg,
Mahler, Mendelssohn and Meyerbeer. These four are to
be judged not only as individual personalities but as
representatives of a direction or a principle of the
machinations of Jewish music...

He followed this with a lengthy denigration of the music of these four
composers, and gave a totally false impression of the thoughts of Jews
about the music of Wagner. He continued in the same vein and concluded:

With the smile of one who has become wise, but also with fist
clenched in anger we can look back on this game. It has been
lost for the Jews. But we must and want to be on our guard, to
ensure that it remains forever lost to them.

These were the opinions of the man, a respected music critic, who
became the new Head Librarian of the Peters Music Library. His
promotion was thanks to the considerable influence which Winifred
Wagner wielded in the highest quarters in Berlin.[8] The preference in
Leipzig was for other candidates. The views of Henri Hinrichsen were
not required.

Professor Dr Eugen Schmitz had excellent references to his credit and, coincidentally, two historical points of contact with C F Peters. He was a great-great-grandson of Louis Spohr, whose association with the company had spanned the first fifty years of its existence; and he had been a student of Professor Theodor Kroyer. The leading German music dictionary wrote of Schmitz in 1963:[9] '...The work he developed as Head of the Peters Music Library in Leipzig was of immense value to musicology.'

When C F Peters was forcibly sold on 22nd July, 1939, the new owners questioned their obligation to continue to support the Peters Music Library and to pay a pension to the widow of the deceased head librarian. There was a concern that this responsibility would fall to the City of Leipzig. With the 'de-Judaising' of C F Peters the problem of its Jewish ownership was solved. Carl Friedrich Peters, after whom the firm was named, had not been Jewish, so there was no need to change either the name of the firm or the name of the Peters Music Library. However, the Trust supplying the money, was named 'The Max Abraham Trust'. A new law passed on 8th May, 1939 barred all Jewish trusts. The solution found by the Leipzig authorities was to rename the trust as 'The Trust for the Peters Music Library', which new name took effect on 22nd January, 1940.

Between the death of Taut and the appointment of Schmitz, the library was closed for almost half the time. The *Yearbook No 46*, for 1939, which appeared in 1940, also points to the restrictions brought about by the onset of the war. All the same, some 220 items were added to the stock. In 1940, the library was open for 222 days, the work continued and some choice items were lent for an exhibition *entitled Gutenberg and the Printing of Music*. The Peters Library *Yearbook* appeared for the last time in 1941, with issue No 47, for 1940. Publication ceased due to paper shortages and the expense, and was not started again for some years. The position of the Peters Music Library as an independent unit, finally came to an end when it was taken over at the time of the DDR, in 1954, and became incorporated into the Music Library of the City of Leipzig. Dr Eugen Schmitz, at the age of seventy-two, retired that year as head librarian.

Meanwhile, the aryanization of C F Peters dragged on for over a year.

The 'Aryanization' – Sale of C F Peters[10]

SS Standartenführer G Noatzke arrived in Leipzig on 19th April, 1939 with two accountants who, in the course of two weeks had to approve the accounts of five publishing companies, including C F Peters. He returned to Leipzig again on 21st April for a progress report and to settle the price and future profitability of the companies. This was finished by the end of the month and he aimed to have all the business sold by 15th May; though this was not achieved in the case of C F Peters. The most suitable, and politically correct person for the job had still to be found.

Another music publisher due to be aryanized was Universal Edition of Vienna. The publisher B Schott Söhne of Mainz had put in a bid and sent a senior manager, Dr Johannes Petschull, to Berlin to the Propaganda Ministry to discuss the purchase with Staatskommissar Hinkel and SS Standartenführer Noatzke. Petschull noted that C F Peters was also to be aryanized and that no buyer had yet been found. He sent in his notice to his employer, to take immediate effect. He required capital and chose as his prospective partner Dr Kurt Herrmann, a book dealer. Herrmann's connections were most advantageous, he was a friend and hunting partner of Reichsmarschall Goering, and had been awarded the title of Staatsrat (Councillor of State) sometime after 1934. Together Petschull and Herrmann put in a bid for C F Peters.

Dr Johannes Petschull[11], born in 1901, had studied economics and musicology, gaining his doctorate in 1923. He worked in music publishing and joined B Schott Söhne in Mainz in 1927 where he held a managerial position with power-of-attorney, until leaving in 1939. Dr Kurt Herrmann[12] born in 1888, the son of a labourer, trained as a building engineer and married the daughter of a rich industrialist, Bernhard Meyer in 1914. From his father-in-law he inherited three aeroplane factories, a motor factory, a publishing house and a printing works and maintained a lavish lifestyle, also owning hunting estates. He became the owner of several Jewish businesses, including jewellers and substantial properties which he 'bought' at extremely advantageous prices and aryanized.

Both men were full card-carrying members of the NSDAP (the Nazi Party). (There were approximately ten million members of the Party – one fifth of the adult population of the German State.) Certain definite obligations were entailed in membership, not the least of which was the swearing of an oath of allegiance to the Führer, Adolf Hitler.

The transfer of ownership, called *Arisierung* (Aryanization), as well as *Entjüdung* (de-Judaising) was a special, complicated process completely outside of normal market practice. Neither sales nor purchases could be freely entered into; the dispossessed owners were not allowed any influence and were not allowed to recommend any particularly suitable Aryans to become their heirs; in the same way, the buyers were reduced only to announcing their desire to purchase the company. Everything else was regulated by the Propaganda Ministry and the Ministry for Trade and Industry. Every purchase was subject to the personal approval of Dr Goebbels. He had the prospective

purchasers thoroughly investigated from the point of view of political
loyalty and professional competence.

Dr Petschull and Dr Herrmann had two contracts drawn up in Berlin
through the well-known notary, Dr Philipp Möhring, on 22nd July,
1939; a contract founding a commercial company for the continued
management of C F Peters and a contract for the purchase of the entire
business and property of the firm. Ostensibly this was the date of sale,
however, the contracts had to be ratified by the Propaganda Ministry, with
reference to the Ministry of Trade and Industry, which took some months.
Approval of their suitability, both politically and professionally, was
necessary in the case of Herrmann and Petschull, before the contract
could be signed. In order to hasten the process, the notary, Dr Möhring,
wrote to the Ministry of Trade and Industry on 28th July, 1939:

> I would like to point out that both prospective purchasers are
> Party members. Staatsrat Dr Kurt Herrmann is a member of
> the Prussian Council of State. The music publisher Dr
> Johannes Petschull is a recognised successful music publisher
> having carried power of attorney at Schott Söhne, Mainz
> successfully for some years. The connection between the two
> prospective buyers is therefore a particularly happy
> partnership between professionally qualified and politically
> reliable personalities.

In this way, the notary attempted to avoid long drawn-out
investigations by the Ministry of Trade. His very plausible reason was
that C F Peters earned approximately 500,000RM per year in foreign
currency and that this high income of foreign currency should be
maintained under all circumstance.

The ministry took some time longer to reach its decision, so that by
mid-September the contract was still not ratified. The registration was
eventually dated 28th December, 1939. The contract was inevitably
affected by the fact that Germany had been at war for four months.
The various clauses of the contract laid especial emphasis on
maintaining the flow of foreign currency.

There is no evidence that either Dr Petschull or Dr Herrmann
discussed their take-over of C F Peters with Henri Hinrichsen before
they entered into the aryanization procedure. Henri Hinrichsen was
never given the opportunity to express his views on who was to become
the new 'owner' of his business. When the contract was entered into in
1939 it was on the understanding that it would be maintained in
perpetuity.

The partnership agreement between the two buyers which was
certified by Dr Möhring on 22nd July, 1939, along with the purchase

agreement, holds an unusual clause which documents Dr Petschull's autonomy from the beginning: 'The partner, Staatsrat Dr Kurt Herrmann, is only entitled to represent the company and to conduct the business of the company. He is not obliged to undertake any work for the company.' Whilst Dr Johannes Petschull: 'is bound to devote his entire working energy to the company.' From this somewhat one-sided division of labour it is apparent that Herrmann saw himself primarily as a provider of capital, whilst Petschull welcomed the full responsibility of the working publisher.

The contract overlooked the fact that the partnership between Dr Henri Hinrichsen and Dr Hans-Joachim Hinrichsen had not been dissolved and that they were still named in the Register of Companies as the owners of C F Peters. In spite of this, the custodian, Noatzke, was registered as owner on 19th April, 1939. This was in order to facilitate the sale, because it was forbidden to have business dealings with Jews. Hence the participants in the agreement were all Aryans.

Noatzke ceded to the purchasers, Herrmann and Petschull 'the entire commercial business of the firm of C F Peters and transfers to the purchasers all current activities and liabilities, especially all mature outstanding debts, the rights, especially the copyrights belonging to C F Peters, the complete stocks, engraved plates and manuscripts as well as the complete office inventory.' This included the two large business properties.

In return, a purchase price of one million Reichsmark was provided, of this sum 550,000RM was to be immediately payable to Henri Hinrichsen. This sum, as Clause Four of the contract emphasises, should serve to 'cover the requisite amounts due in taxes, deposits and personal debts to be paid by the emigrating partners.'

It is apparent through these very specific conditions, that the buyers knew the precise demands of the currency laws relevant to the 'Jewish Laws'. Hinrichsen should not be in a position to have obtained money through Aryan middlemen, with which he could buy valuables to take out of Germany or to give away. He should leave Germany with nothing but a single suitcase and the clothes in which he stood. The buyers will have known that the Finance Ministry would demand a high percentage of this 550,000RM as *Reichsfluchtsteuer* (Refugee Tax). This was an additional tax levied on Jews moving abroad.

The sale's agreement demanded a further indirect act of collaboration to something which had been confiscated from the Hinrichsens. Clause Three of the agreement bound the former owners, 'after transfer of their domicile to England, they should commit themselves to furthering the export of C F Peters sheet music through the firm of Novello [C F Peters agents in England] in the British Dominions and in China.' Hence the robbed Hinrichsens were to be used to bring money into the treasury of the National Socialist State, to finance the war which Hitler created. In order to assure the submission of the dispossessed, the buyers offered them £12,000, payable in London, from a half of the Peters' income generated by their London agent, Novello. By the outbreak of the war, all enemy credits were frozen and confiscated in Great Britain. The Hinrichsens never received a penny of even this small sum. And they never had the opportunity of being called upon to fulfil Clause Three of the contract.

The buyers would have been well aware that the Propaganda Ministry had no choice but to work with them as there were no other suitably qualified bidders. However, it was possibly Clause Nine which caused the Ministry of Trade and Industry to delay giving consent to the contract for so long. This clause decrees: 'The parties are in agreement that consent subject to a condition, does not bind the buyers to fulfil this condition.' Then, more precisely defined: 'If the consent is granted under a condition, the buyers have the right to refuse the execution of the contract.'

This was an extremely unusual type of deal. Not only did Noatzke grant Dr Petschull permission to start familiarising himself with the business and taking part in its organisation before the ministry granted its consent, but the costs and taxes generated by the contract to purchase were not to be charged to the instigator, the buyers, but, according to Clause Ten, were to be charged to the firm of C F Peters, whose owners they had not yet become. The outcome was so secure, that the contract in fact took effect before the Ministry of Trade and Industry gave its consent on 28th December, 1939.[13]

There were nine clauses in the contract,[14] which also included J Rieter-Biedermann. The properties of 10 Talstrasse and 26 Königstrasse, in which latter the Peters Music Library was housed, were also part of the deal. The whole price offered was merely a fraction of the value of the business, its stocks and the properties. Ultimately nothing at all was left for Henri Hinrichsen. The only small concession allowed the Hinrichsens, under Clause Four, was permission to continue to live, rent-free, in their apartment in 10 Talstrasse until such time as they left Germany. This was a remarkable concession at a time when those Jews remaining in Leipzig were being herded into 'Jewish houses' in ghettos; but it also had its reason.

Business continued after the take-over, much as it had done for the past year, under the interim management of Wilhelm Weismann. As he said in his taped interview many years later:

> At first nothing much changed and Petschull's direction of the company was quite light, but he did follow some principles which a real Peters director would not have allowed, things

which one wouldn't do even against the competitors. He was merely thoughtless. In general, though, he followed the traditional line. Before he came I was in charge of the production and I was very proud to have been able to increase the turnover by a third. So, nothing much changed and we continued to follow much the same thematic development of the business.

The Secretary, Fräulein Gertrud Hopfe wrote the following comment in her diary for Christmas 1939:

> The new publisher [Dr Petschull] is a correct man. Friendly and circumspect with everybody. But a charmer towards women; even so, Charlotte isn't fooled. We hardly ever see the Herr Geheimrat any more. The mistress told me that he and Dr Petschull meet late at night in the office. The Herr Geheimrat uses the back staircase when the staff have left. Martha Hinrichsen is very confused about what is happening in Germany lately. Herr Geheimrat sees it as the act of an uncouth rabble such as happens in every revolution. One can see it in our Mr L in the office. He was the one, said by CK, who threw the Mendelssohn music out into the courtyard to be burnt on the treacherous night in '38. It is right that our Führer should protect our economy from corrupt Jews, who live at the expense of the state. But our Geheimrat has done so much for Leipzig. Surely our new manager Dr P will respect that. I have never seen the second boss, Herrn Staatsrat [Herrmann].

Charlotte Kretschmar was Dr Petschull's preferred secretary, whilst Gertrude Hopfe, who had been Henri Hinrichsen's loyal secretary since 1915 was not entrusted with confidential material any more.

Though Henri Hinrichsen was no longer permitted to have any say in the running of C F Peters, Dr Petschull sensibly took advantage of the previous owner's forty years' experience. There was an internal staircase linking the private apartment with the office and the two men would use this, after the staff had left in the evening, to meet and discuss problems.

The former owner had to be extremely careful not to be seen by anybody; had he been caught, it would have meant immediate transportation to a concentration camp for him.

1 Gilbert, p 73.
2 Stadtarchiv Leipzig, PP-S Nr 8513.
3 Taped interview with Bernd Pachnike, the then managing director of C F Peters, Leipzig, in 1973.
4 Berlin Document Center.
5 Copy in the author's archive.
6 All letters, documents and memos quoted referring to the Peters Music Library, in the Stadtarchiv Leipzig. Kap 36, P No 10 and No 30.
7 The article by Schmitz which is in the Music Library in Leipzig shows no source. Research has placed it as 'probably from the *Dresdener Nachrichten* (Dresden News) between November 1938 and March 1939'. The Sächsische Landesbibliothek Dresden was unwilling to make the necessary searches when approached by the Music Library in Leipzig. (Letter to the author from the Music Library, 26th March, 1996.)
8 Memo of 17th March 1939.
9 *Die Musik in Geschichte und Gegenwart,* Vol 11, published by Bärenreiter, Kassel in 1963.
10 Details about the 'Aryanization' process abstracted from: *Fred K Prieberg, Historisches Gutachten, MDR, Leipzig, 1994,* reproduced with kind permission of Fred K Prieberg.
11 Information on Dr Johannes Petschull in *Zeittafeln.*
12 Information on Dr Kurt Herrmann from *Diamanten für den Reichsmarchschall* (Diamonds for the Field Marschall) by Henryk M Broder, *Der Spiegel* magazine, 17th February 1997.
13 End of Prieberg abstract.
14 The contract is in the StAL Bestand, C F Peters, No 4100.

CHAPTER SIXTEEN

The Struggle to Leave Germany

Kristallnacht and the aryanization of C F Peters, the culmination of six years of Nazi persecution of the Jews, spelled disaster for the entire Hinrichsen family.

Max Hinrichsen had felt guilty, in November 1937, at leaving his elderly father and younger brother to cope. But his decision and that of their brother Walter who had left in 1936, had been wise. They had been able to emigrate officially; paying a substantial emigration tax, they could take all their personal possessions – though little money with them. However, their three brothers and two sisters were still in Germany in November 1938 and were to experience far greater difficulties.

The demand for passports and entry visas to other countries escalated, and the problems faced in getting out of Germany attained horrific proportions. All the Hinrichsens had applied for visas to the USA, but would settle for any country granting them interim visas. The embassies and ministries providing the various documents were mostly in Berlin. So the home of the Hinrichsens' eldest daughter, Lotte, and her husband, Dr Otto Sobernheim, became a family meeting point. The first to leave was Lotte's younger sister, Ilse Frankenthal, with her husband and two young sons.

The Frankenthals

Dr Ludwig Frankenthal, director and chief surgeon of the Jewish Hospital in Leipzig, was arrested by the Gestapo on arrival at his hospital early on 10th November, 1938. He was sent to Buchenwalde concentration camp. Ilse and the two children – Günther, nine and Wolfgang, seven – hid for several days. Then Ilse went to the Gestapo, daily, to negotiate her husband's release. His release on 27th November was under the condition that the family left Germany within two weeks. Seventeen days in Buchenwalde had a terrible effect on Dr Ludwig Frankenthal's health and mental condition.

The energetic Ilse had to make all the arrangements for their departure, forever, from Germany, within two weeks. The Frankenthals had to sacrifice all their life insurance policies and all their valuables. They were allowed to send their household possessions to the USA, on payment of 100 per cent duty. Before they were permitted to leave, they were forced to pay their entire fortune to cover the various taxes: Refugee Tax, Jewish Wealth Tax, Emigration Tax, Religious Community Tax, Income Tax, Higher Income Tax and other taxes. They left Leipzig on 14th December, 1938, arriving in Holland on 15th December.

Robert Hinrichsen

Robert Hinrichsen, the seventh and last child of Martha and Henri Hinrichsen, was born on 8th February, 1918. When the Nazis came to power in 1933 he was fifteen; as a Jew, the school doors were soon closed to him. Not wanting to send their youngest son to a Jewish school, his parents sent him to Scotland, to complete his education at Gordonstoun School, founded in 1934 by Kurt Hahn. Returning to Leipzig; he was somewhat startled at an abrupt entry to adulthood.

Robert went to Berlin in March 1939 to attend to official business before he would be permitted to leave Germany. The formalities regarding currency and possessions were considerable and the complex bureaucracy delayed the issue of a passport several times. To the great relief of the family, he was finally granted a passport and visa and emigrated to England in July 1939. Had his papers been delayed by a further six weeks, when war broke out on 3rd September, he would not have been permitted entry to Great Britain. His luggage never left Germany and he never saw his possessions again.

The Sobernheims

Lotte Sobernheim had a similar struggle to get entry visas for herself and her family to emigrate to another country. In spite of contacts abroad, all her efforts to keep her family intact were in vain.

An entry visa to the USA for her seventeen-year-old son was granted in early November 1938. He was due to leave by train for Holland on the evening of 10th November – the day after Kristallnacht. After a traumatic day spent in hiding from the mob and the Gestapo he managed his escape. The next day Dr Otto Sobernheim was arrested and sent to Sachsenhausen concentration camp, where he remained for six agonising weeks. On 12th November the boy sailed to the USA and freedom. His passport was stamped with the obligatory large red 'J'. At the instigation of the Swiss Justice and Police Department, and as negotiated by the Foreign Section of the Swiss Federal Political Department (*Abteilung für Auswärtiges des Eidgenössischen Politischen Departementes*), German authorities issued a decree on 5th October, 1938, directing that passports of all Jews be marked with a large red 'J'.[1]

Resulting from his schoolboy friendship with an English boy, Kent Nowell, his two young sisters were able to escape to England with the help of the boy's Methodist parents. They arranged for the girls to be brought to England on the *Kinder Transport* in July 1939, and guaranteed to provide their maintenance. The *Kinder Transport* was a scheme organised by the British Jewish Refugee Children's Movement in conjunction with the Red Cross, which saved the lives of 10,000 children up to the age of sixteen, ninety per cent of them Jewish, in 1938-9.

It was not until 25th August, 1939, just a week before the outbreak of World War II, that Lotte and Dr Otto Sobernheim could themselves leave for England. Had it not been for the Nowell family's vigorous efforts and guarantees on their behalf, they would not have survived. After war broke out, the British Home Office banned virtually all immigration from Germany and declared all previously issued visas to be invalid.

Dr Hans-Joachim Hinrichsen

Hans-Joachim Hinrichsen, could not get permission to leave Leipzig until the aryanization of C F Peters was complete; he had to register regularly with the police department. Well-known throughout the relevant circles in Europe for his doctoral thesis on *The Transfer of Musical Copyright to Music Publishers and Authors and Composers' Societies,* he tried to find himself a job, and hence an entry permit, in another country. In April 1939 he wrote to some of his contacts in legal and copyright associations throughout Europe, offering his services and asking for references and introductions.

He received many glowing testimonials and letters of admiration and appreciation. They all recommended him, not only for the excellence of his thesis, but also for his thorough practical grounding in all aspects of his subject, and suggested that he would be a great asset to a future employer. Hans-Joachim had all these testimonials translated into English by an official translator in Leipzig – Justizrat (judicial adviser) Dr Walter Müller and set about applying for jobs abroad.

Paul Hinrichsen

Paul Hinrichsen, Martha and Henri Hinrichsen's sixth child, born on 20th December, 1912, had attended an agricultural college in Denmark, as university study was banned to Jews in Nazi Germany. His ambition was to study at a colonial college in the USA and then to buy a farm in Brazil, where he would settle and raise a family. In the spring of 1937, at the age of twenty-five, he went to Brazil on a six-months study visit.

Unable to extend his visitor's visa, Paul returned home to his family for Christmas 1937, hoping to emigrate to Brazil in March 1938. He tried unsuccessfully over the course of the next three years to acquire the necessary papers and visas. A realist, he tried to cover his emigration for all eventualities and so applied for a transit visa to other countries, but all without success.

Martha and Dr Henri Hinrichsen and the confiscation of their Collections

The elderly Martha and Henri Hinrichsen found it terribly hard to comprehend what was happening to them and why. After forty years of having lived in comfort and having been respected citizens of Leipzig, they were being stripped of everything and were frightened of facing their old age without any money, in a strange country and of being dependant upon their children. They kept in constant touch with all of their seven adult children.

On 12th July, 1939 Professor Dr Schmitz, the new head librarian of the Peters Music Library was ordered by the Foreign Exchange Office of Leipzig, to present himself for consultation in connection with the application of Dr Henri Israel Hinrichsen and his son Dr Hans-Joachim Israel Hinrichsen to take 'cultural goods' out of the country. He was asked to prepare a valuation (at the expense of the applicants, the Hinrichsens) of all the autographs, and especially the scores in their possession, in accordance with Regulation A v E No 58/39 Clause Six of the RWM dated 17th April, 1939. He should apply to the Customs Investigations Department in the Adolf Hitler Strasse who had placed the items in safe custody in the Hinrichsens' home. By 18th July, Prof Schmitz had completed his valuation which he presented to the Foreign Exchange Office. The report was three pages long and presented an analysis of the value of the items. It was divided into several sections.

1)   Since 1935 Henri Hinrichsen had loaned a number of music items to the Peters Music Library which he had taken back in view of the aryanization of C F Peters.

2)   A collection of 350 musicians' letters including some from Bach, Gluck, Mozart, Weber and others.

3)   A collection of letters from Hugo Wolf.

4)   The correspondence between Brahms and Joachim.

5)   A group of Mozart manuscripts.

6)   A Beethoven String Quartet manuscript.

7)   The manuscript of a Bach Cantata.

8)   The first edition of a Piano Work by Bach.

9)   Dr Hinrichsen Jr's collection of autographs including letters from Beethoven, Wagner, Wolf and others.

10)   Letters from Beethoven, Schumann and Spohr, not directly owned by Hinrichsen, but actually belonging to C F Peters.

11)   Collections of the letters from Edvard Grieg and Max Reger.

A comment in Prof Schmitz' report is very relevant to the time, and to the article by him previously quoted: 'It is debatable whether one should consider the letters of Jewish musicians (Meyerbeer, Mendelssohn, Joachim etc.) which are in the collection, as 'cultural goods'. But on balance perhaps one should. Because such Jewish writings have some relevance as source documents to researchers who want to study the effects which Jewish musicians had on the development of German music.'[2]

Henri Hinrichsen wrote to Robert in London on 22nd August, 1939, telling of some of their worries and problems:

> ...We haven't got much further with our emigration plans, even though Hans is going to an enormous amount of trouble and we are greatly helped by your excellent preparatory work. Dr Frey is on holiday until the beginning of September, which naturally delays our departure. The authorisation for the contract [the aryanization] which was completed four weeks ago has still not been given. At the moment, the pictures and photographs are causing us a lot of difficulty; so, the whole thing can drag on for weeks. Yesterday Paul and I collected all the prints and engravings from the whole apartment and put them together in the dining room with the earlier ones which have not yet been sold and hung them so that we could enjoy them...Hans' friend Herr Weg is leaving today after

great difficulties! All the rest of us publishers and book dealers are still here...

Ration cards were issued on 27th August, 1939 and Hitler announced the annihilation of the Jewish race if war were to break out. In October and November, Leipzig Jews were moved out of their homes and herded into forty-seven 'Jewish houses'. The Nazis would thus have better control over them and could easily round them up for deportation.

Henri Hinrichsen was arrested on 8th November, 1939. He was incarcerated in the Leipzig Police Prison, in cell no II, with several others, for six weeks until he was released on 19th December. The reason for his imprisonment was given as 'political'.

Dr Hans-Joachim Hinrichsen was arrested on 10th November for the same reason as his father, and placed in the same cell. He was also released on 19th December.[3]

The authorities wanted to strip Henri Hinrichsen not only of all he possessed, but also of his honorary doctorate from the University of Leipzig. In order to emigrate, it was necessary to apply for a *Heimatschein* (a certificate of domicile), which he had done. In respect of this, the director of the Electoral Register department of the City of Leipzig wrote to the university on 28th November, 1939 pointing out that Henri Hinrichsen was a Jew and asking whether he was still entitled to use the title of Doctor. The Dean of the Faculty of Philosophy of the University of Leipzig, Bräunlich, bravely replied on 1st December, stating:

> In reply to your enquiry of 28th November, 1939, I inform you that the Geheime Kommerzienrat Dr phil. h c Henri Israel Hinrichsen, born in Hamburg on 5th April, 1868, [the writer had written April in error – Henri Hinrichsen was born on 5th February, 1868] is still entitled to use the title of Doctor of Philosophy awarded to him by our Faculty. According to the regulations in force, the fact of his Jewish descent does not justify the withdrawal of his doctorate.
>
> Heil Hitler![4]

Henri Hinrichsen had a splendid collection of German paintings, which he was obliged to sell before being granted permission to leave Germany. He wanted the paintings to go to the *Museum der bildenden Künste* (the Museum of Art) in Leipzig, where they would be available to the art loving public of Leipzig. Negotiations had been taking place with the museum since the beginning of 1939, because the City of Leipzig was keen to acquire this collection. Problems had arisen in the early stages, when the custodian overseeing the aryanization of C F

Peters, Noatzke, had ordered Henri Hinrichsen to sell his paintings within two days, to a dealer in Berlin, which Hinrichsen had steadfastly refused to do. He was supported by the director of the museum, who even wrote to Hitler personally, stating the case for retaining the paintings in Leipzig. The matter was sorted out after much negotiation between ministries. The Director of Finance had written to the Museum of Art on 20th July, 1939[5] concerning: 'The Protection of German cultural goods against removal – the removal of property by Jews emigrating', informing them that he had no objection to their arranging to purchase paintings from Henri Hinrichsen's collection. He wanted to be informed of the titles and the prices agreed. (This was in order to establish the precise amount which could then be demanded against the various taxes payable on emigration.)

Henri Hinrichsen agreed, albeit under duress, to sell his pictures, which were all by eminent nineteenth century German painters, to the Museum of Art on 18th September, 1939, at a price well below the current market value. This was one of the most important collections of German paintings ever to come on the market and, seeing a considerable profit to be made, several dealers had been trying to purchase it. By way of acknowledgement of its priceless acquisition of fine German paintings, the museum was planning a celebration on 2nd October, in conjunction with the centenary of the birth of Thoma, one of the painters represented.

On 16th November, 1939, the Director of Finance of the Foreign Exchange Bureau in Leipzig used Henri Hinrichsen's absence in prison to justify the removal, from 10 Talstrasse, of those items from his collection of paintings which still remained to him, and his collection of autographs, as detailed above. Martha Hinrichsen and her son Paul were faced with a recorded delivery epistle, addressed to her husband, Hans-Joachim and herself:

Safeguard Order according to Rule 59 DevG. v. 12.12.1938:

It has been established that the music publisher, Dr Henri Hinrichsen, of 10 Talstrasse, Leipzig C1, named in my Safeguard Order of 23.1.1939, is in protective custody.

In order to avoid the possibility that the following valuable listed art works which are easily transportable and are still in the apartment, should be removed, which could easily happen through a third hand wishing to undermine the authority of the Currency Exchange Department, the following has been decreed according to the order of 13th November, 1939.

> The listed art works and hand-written items should, in the case of the paintings, be transferred to the Museum der bildenden Künste (Museum of Art) in Leipzig; the remainder should be transferred to the Stadtbibliothek (City Library) for safety, until the release of Hinrichsen…

There followed a list of all the paintings, engravings and autographed letters and manuscripts in the collection. The communication concluded with the words:

> The costs of this order are to be met by the person affected.

> The right to complain to me against this Safeguard Order is given, but it will have no effect.

> Any contravention of this Safeguard Order will be punishable by arrest and in particularly difficult cases by long-term imprisonment.

Against such an order, there is no resistance for an old lady. Not only were Henri Hinrichsen's collections being confiscated, but he was also expected to pay the costs of such action.

After his release from prison, Henri Hinrichsen negotiated the sale of two of the paintings thus taken to the dealer Gurlitt in Hamburg and on 11th January, 1940, the Finance Department gave the Museum of Art permission to release them. He was also permitted to arrange the sale of two further works to Gurlitt. On 23rd January a further sale – Lucas Cranach's *Lucretia* was sanctioned by the Finance Department, to the Galerie Combé in Berlin. He was informed that the money would be paid into his blocked account at the Deutsche Bank in Leipzig. All the contracts were handled by Henri Hinrichsen's lawyer, Dr Franz in Leipzig.

Henri Hinrichsen received nothing of the money which was due to him from the compulsory sale of his entire valuable collection. The Finance Department did not sanction the release of his money to him. As a Jew, he had no form of redress.

Deployment of parts of the collection continued after the Hinrichsens had left Leipzig. Permission for the sale was granted by the Finance Department on 21st January, 1941. Negotiation for the sale of the *Relief* by Thorwaldsen, which took equally long, were conducted between the Museum of Art, the Finance Department and the dealer, Lange, in Berlin. He was upset to learn after a year, that the National Gallery of Art in Berlin was entitled to have first refusal of items confiscated from Jews. And so the *Relief*, which had belonged to

Henri Hinrichsen, was acquired by Germany's most important art gallery. Again, for all of this, the owner received nothing, though the Finance Department insisted that the money be paid into Henri Hinrichsen's blocked bank account.

The Leipzig City Library was delighted with its acquisition of a unique autograph collection. An article was published in *Philoblon* in 1940[6] entitled '*Musikautographen aus fünf Jahrhunderten*' (Music Autographs of Five Centuries) and subtitled: 'An Important Acquisition of the Leipzig City Library'. The name of the original (Jewish) owner, Henri Hinrichsen, was not mentioned. The introductory paragraph reads:

> The Director of the City Library Dr Johannes Hofmann, with the support of the Minister of State Freyberg,[7] the new Mayor of Leipzig, took the initiative over the last few months, during the reorganisation of a world-famous music publishing house, to secure for the City Library an important part of the music autograph collection. This includes sixteen unpublished letters from Richard Wagner to his Leipzig publisher, E W Fritsch, an important autograph of Bach, Mozart manuscripts, the correspondence between Brahms and Joachim and that between Hugo Wolf and Potpeschnigg and a box containing 267 letters from important musicians of the sixteenth to the nineteenth centuries. We thank the Director, Dr J Hofmann, that he has made it possible for us to reproduce these valuable acquisitions here for the first time.

Dispossessed Departure

The Hinrichsens had already been denied one entry permit, which they had not been able to claim in time because of all the bureaucratic delays. The aryanization process of C F Peters and arrangements for the compulsory sale of his paintings and autographs were complete, so Henri Hinrichsen wanted to hasten his departure from Germany. He had a fight against time, exacerbated by a sense of being harassed by bureaucracy. It would mean certain death for himself and his wife if they were unable to use the visas which they had been granted for entry to Belgium by the due date. He wrote to the Director of finance in Leipzig on 7th January, 1940 detailing the arrangements he had completed, enclosing a copy of a letter from the Consulate of Belgium in Leipzig and wrote: 'From this you will see that the right to a visa for Belgium will be lost to my wife and I and to our son, if we are not able to present our passports to the Consul in Berlin by 19th January. I would respectfully request you to treat our affair with urgency, in order to avoid our losing an entry permit for the second time.'

The letter from the Embassy of Belgium in Berlin, to the Belgian Consulate in Leipzig was dated 3rd January, 1940:[8]

> The Belgian Ambassador in Berlin has the honour to inform the Belgian Consulate in Leipzig, in reply to his letter of 29th December, 1939, B.13, No. 7237/650, that the transit visa for Belgium must be collected by the beneficiaries within thirty days of their being informed by the diplomatic representative.
>
> In this case the couple Hinrichsen and their son must collect the visa before 20th January, 1940...

On 8th January[9] Dr Hans-Joachim Hinrichsen wrote to C F Peters along the same lines and enclosing a copy of the letter from the Belgian Ambassador. He begged Dr Petschull to help expedite matters:

> As you well know, we lost the opportunity of an entry visa abroad which we had obtained with the greatest difficulty, because our passports were withheld owing to the business. Now, after great effort, we once again have the possibility of an entry visa, this time to Belgium. We have no hope of receiving another offer of an entry visa if we cannot make use of this one in time.
>
> Therefore I ask you to expedite the processing of our affairs. Without the acknowledgement of the various authorities that my parents will be able to receive the sum promised to them abroad, they do not dare leave. Apart from that, they will not be given their passports until the Finance Ministry and the Religious Community have issued the document certifying that they have no taxes, loans, etc. outstanding. This is on the assumption that you have transferred the sum of RM550,000 to pay for the *Reichsfluchtsteuer* (Refugee Tax), *Judenvermögensabgabe* (Jewish Wealth Tax), *Auswander-Abgabe* (Emigration Tax), *Gemeinde-Anlage* (Religious Community Tax), etc.
>
> Please will you effect the transfer without delay and impress upon all the authorities the necessity for immediate settlement of the arrangements made with Dr Franz...

Hans-Joachim asked Fräulen Hopfe to give the letter to Dr Petschull, who replied the same day,[10] pointing out that the delay was caused by the judicious absence of the person whose signature was required:

I have received your letter of 8th January and have to inform you that on the very day of the handing over of the publishing business to me, I contacted the Finance Ministry. I was told that the official in charge, Assessor Blumenau, would be away until today and I was asked to delay the matter until his return. As I told Dr Franz today, I will make contact with the official tomorrow morning. I will not delay in seeing the matter to as speedy a conclusion as possible. The agreed purchase price was forwarded to Mr Noatzke last week...

Enough papers were gathered together for the passports to be issued to Martha and Henri Hinrichsen and for them to be able to claim their visas for Belgium. But their financial security was not assured and there was still a great deal to be organised in connection with their departure. Before leaving, Henri Hinrichsen wrote a letter to the staff of C F Peters on 27th January[11] taking his leave of them:

Dear Ladies and Gentlemen!

Before we leave Leipzig, I would like to say goodbye to you in the name of my wife and son. As much as it was always my pleasure to work with you in the steady growth of the Edition Peters, in which we enjoyed considerable success, it is my pain that the conditions now prevailing have caused a sudden severance.

I wish you all that you are able to enjoy many years under the new management in the old established company and thank each one of you for your faithful collaboration.

With Kind Regards,

Henri Hinrichsen

A letter of farewell from Wilhelm Weismann, who had enjoyed Henri Hinrichsen's confidence and trust for ten years, also dated 27th January, was found in Weismann's papers after his death. It is uncertain whether this was a draft, or whether the letter was never sent:

Dear Mr Geheimrat,

I heard today that you would be leaving Germany tomorrow evening with your wife and your son. I must tell you that I and my wife send our friendliest regards to accompany you. I would really have liked to have shaken hands in farewell with you, but it would have been difficult for me, and so I must limit myself to a written greeting. Your wife wronged me when she said some time ago that I did not visit you because I was afraid. I was so exhausted that I really could not cope with any more stress. Though I managed to take a two week break in the new year. Please forgive this truly human failing, which you should not misinterpret.

In grateful memory of ten years' mutual work I wish you and your wife and son all the very best, from the depths of my heart.

Wilhelm Weismann and wife.

The next night, Henri and Martha Hinrichsen crept quietly out of their house, 10 Talstrasse, Leipzig. Shutting the door behind them for the last time, they put their keys through the letter box. Without money and with nothing but hand luggage, they made their way towards the railway station with their son Paul to see them off.

Paul, who was twenty-eight by then and no nearer obtaining a visa for anywhere, was living in the *Isrealitisches Kinderheim* (the Jewish Children's' Home) in the Jewish ghetto in Leipzig, where he helped with the children and drove the horse-drawn cart. Hans-Joachim remained in Leipzig for a further six weeks, in hiding, alone in 10 Talstrasse, trying to organise his parents financial affairs and make some sort of provision for his and his parents' future. Paul brought him food.

Paul helped Hans-Joachim pack their parents' household goods and personal possessions – other than their valuables, which they had had to forfeit – for despatch to the USA. They worked from five o'clock in the afternoon, right through the night, preparing the obligatory list. The customs official came at eight o'clock the next morning to check everything as it went into the ten packing cases. The list was four pages long and included every single item from table linen, dish cloths and egg cups to pictures (of little value), sheet music and 'about 100 books'. It was in German and English, to be acceptable to the US customs. The cases were despatched by the Leipzig company of Lieberoth, via the port of Bremen. They never left Germany.

The different officials who were supposed to give acknowledgements that the various taxes demanded of Henri Hinrichsen had been paid, were singularly disinclined to make themselves available. Time was running out for Hans-Joachim whose entry visa to Belgium would expire for a second time, if he did not leave Germany soon. He had to appeal to Dr Petschull to try and expedite matters and wrote to him covering all the points, on 12th February, 1940:[12]

> Following our discussion of last week, I sent a detailed petition to the Finance Department. I was once again given the reply, that an assessment could only be undertaken when the amounts in question had been settled. As I have already told you, the amount of the refugee tax cannot be established until receipt of the tax assessment.

He went on to explain that he had not accompanied his parents when they had left, even though they had needed his help, but had remained in Leipzig in order to clarify the tax matters. He now realised that his presence has been entirely useless, unless Dr Petschull immediately declared his agreement to transfer the amount in question for the Ollendorff pension and the taxes paid on his own behalf by the company, to his father's blocked account number 17039 at the Leipzig branch of the Deutsche Bank. He continued:

> My father undertook to commit his entire private fortune to cover the taxes and officially required payments. Alone for the publishing company he has paid RM650,000, irrespective of Refugee Tax, Jewish Wealth Tax, Emigration Tax, Religious Community Tax and other taxes. Clause Two stated that RM550,000 was to be paid to my father immediately on completion. It was specifically agreed that only the compensation requirements of the custodian had to be met by my father. If only for this, my father cannot be held responsible for the Ollendorff pension or for the taxes paid on my behalf. Apart from the fact that the business was taken over with 'all existing active and passive assets' except for the personal accounts of the partners. There is therefore no doubt at all that my father is not responsible for the Ollendorff pension.

> The same is also true of the taxes paid by the business on my behalf. Apart from the reasons detailed, my father can really not be held responsible for this, because the purchase price of RM550,000 is to be paid exclusively to my father and not to my father and I. In addition, I could not possibly have been in a position to pay the taxes, because my capital and net profit were paid to the business to cover my taxes (Income Tax RM12,127; Higher Income Tax RM2,676; Jewish Wealth Tax RM4,800). For this reason I could not have been held

responsible for the amounts, unless I had known that the
custodian had agreed the settlement of my tax debts through
the business, with Dr Franz. Apart from this, the contract states
specifically; 'Any payments made to the partners after 17th
November, 1938, need not be refunded.' Finally, the taxes
were paid from the business on someone's own initiative,
against my wishes, whilst I was in prison. I myself only asked
that an appeal should be registered against the taxes which I
was required to pay – Income Tax, Higher Income Tax and
Wealth Tax.

As more than six weeks have passed since the day the company
was transferred, I would like to ask you to undertake the
necessary steps. You know that a great deal depends upon
this for us, quite apart from the fact that I am very much
afraid that I will lose my entry permit for the second time.

Please, Dear Dr Petschull, do not again say that you can
make no decisions or that the whole matter will be cleared
up within a few days. Please give the bank instructions
immediately, so that I can at last reach a conclusion with the
Finance Department. Please accept my grateful thanks for
your efforts...

Dr Petschull did not react to this plea of desperation. Hans-
Joachim wrote to him again three days later, on 15th February,
emphasising the urgency of the matter and pointing out that he had to
leave Germany very shortly. It was a further six days before Dr Petschull
spoke to him, on 21st February, as noted by hand on both the letters.
There were further procrastinations and nothing was settled.
Dr Hans-Joachim Hinrichsen left for Brussels on 6th March, 1940.
Dr Petschull wrote to him on 9th March telling him that Noatzke had
not appeared for an appointment and that therefore the matter was
still not settled. He was going to Berlin the following Tuesday to meet
Dr Möhring, the lawyer and Noatzke. In the meantime Dr Möhring
had written to Hans-Joachim who wrote to Dr Petschull on 18th March
pointing out that Möhring had been available for discussions at any
time and that the whole matter could have been settled. Hans-Joachim
regretted that he had risked his life pointlessly by staying in Leipzig to
be able to sort everything out personally and to be available for personal
discussions. He was, however, still willing to make himself available
through correspondence.
Dr Petschull replied on 28th March saying that everything possible
had been done from his side to settle things before Hans-Joachim's

departure; it had not been possible to see Noatzke and Möhring before 12th March. In order not to complicate anything further, he would not write any more about the matter, but would leave the correspondence to Dr Möhring and Dr Franz.

There were now no Hinrichsens left at 10 Talstrasse, their house in which the family had lived for forty years and which had been confiscated from them. Paul was the last of the family living in Leipzig, in the Jewish Children's Home, in the Jewish ghetto. Dr Petschull wrote to him there, on 1st April, 1940, asking him to return the keys to the house, which were still in his possession. He also wanted to be informed when the cupboard, which was standing on the first floor, would be collected.

A hand-written note on the copy letter says; 'settled.'

With this last act, the Hinrichsen family had been deprived of absolutely everything except for the clothes which they were wearing.

---

1 Häsler, Alfred A, *Das Boot ist voll...Die Schweiz und die Flüchtlinge 1933-1945* (The Boat is full...Switzerland and the Refugees 1933-1945), Zürich, Ex Libris Verlag, 1985, pp 41-61; 90-115.
2 Correspondence in the Music Library, Leipzig.
3 Details of both arrests from Stadtarchiv Leipzig, Polizeipräsidium Leipzig, PP-S Nr 8514 (1939), Gefangenentagebücher (Daily Record Book of Prisoners).
4 Both letters in the Leipzig University Archive: Phil Fak, Ehrenprom, Nr 156.
5 All correspondence concerning Henri Hinrichsen's collection of paintings and the Museum of Art is in the archive of the Museum der bildenden Künste, Leipzig.
6 *Philoblon,* Jg 12 (1940), pp 52-57.
7 Alfred Freyberg, SS Group Leader, Mayor of Leipzig 1939-1945. Committed suicide in 1945.
8 StAL Bestand, C F Peters, No 1381.
9 *Ibid.*
10 *Ibid.*
11 StAL Bestand, C F Peters, No 5016.
12 All following letters quoted: StAL Bestand, C F Peters, No 1381.

CHAPTER SEVENTEEN

The Final Solution

The Hinrichsens arrive in Brussels

Martha and Henri Hinrichsen arrived in Brussels on 30th January, 1940 after a traumatic two day journey. New regulations regarding luggage were imposed at the last minute. They were made to change trains several times and suffered interminable delays. As Jews, they had to queue for hours whilst their luggage was searched and examined several times and they also suffered the indignity of having to submit to body searches. When they finally arrived, exhausted, Martha did not break the habit of a lifetime and wrote to her children the next day, detailing the trials of their awful journey.[1]

They found accommodation in the front room of a small boarding house at 42 Rue de la Loi, a busy main road. The noise of the trams thundering past every few minutes made sleeping difficult. But they were alive, and they were safe, and for that they were grateful. They lived in extremely straitened circumstances, somewhat eased by money which Walter sent them from the USA. Their three trunks, to their great amazement were delivered three weeks after their arrival.

Martha had been unwell and very weak for some time, partly due to her diabetes, for which, as a Jew, she was forbidden insulin. Getting away from the terrible stresses and responsibilities of their life in Leipzig over the previous few years, they were able to relax a little. Henri Hinrichsen was in fact feeling remarkably well for his seventy-two years.

Death of Dr Hans-Joachim Hinrichsen

The Hinrichsens were delighted when their son, Hans-Joachim, finally arrived from Leipzig on 7th March, having been sadly unsuccessful in sorting out the paperwork concerning his parents' money. Whilst still in Leipzig he had not only been working on their behalf, but had been helping all those Jews who sought his assistance with the legal requirements of their departure from Germany. He was able to bring all his luggage with him, and many files and documents about the business, the disposal of the art and autograph collections and the aryanization of C F Peters. He found a room about fifteen minutes' walk from his parents, at 9 Rue de Toulouse, in a quiet side street, in which he settled happily. However, within a month the house was sold and on 15th April he moved to 33 Rue Marie Thèrese, a quiet street just around the corner from his parents.

On 10th May, 1940, German forces attacked Belgium, France and the Netherlands. Within days the Germans were in full occupation of Belgium and the Netherlands. Those Jews who had fled to these safe havens were now at risk.

Hans-Joachim Hinrichsen disappeared. His parents paid for his room for a further two weeks, but when they had heard nothing from him by 1st June, they packed all his trunks and files and moved them with the help of the local coal merchant, in his lorry, to the friends who were storing some of their own luggage. At the end of June, they moved to another boarding house, at 21 Rue de Suisse, hoping to remain there until their departure for the USA.

Just ahead of the Gestapo who had entered Brussels, Hans-Joachim had made his escape to France. Heading for the Pyrenees, he was arrested by the French police who interned him in the camp of St Cyprien in Perpignan, which was soon taken over by the Germans. He contracted typhoid fever. Without proper medical care this industrious and intelligent young man, beloved by so many people, died, just six months after leaving Leipzig, on 27th September, 1940. Dr Hans-Joachim Hinrichsen, Martha and Henri Hinrichsen's fifth child, was thirty-one years old. He was buried in the Jewish corner of the Haut Vernet Cemetery in Perpignan. His parents and his brothers and sisters, separated by the circumstances forced upon them, in Germany, Holland, Belgium, the USA and England, were devastated. None could attend his funeral.

Death of Martha Hinrichsen

After her son's untimely death, Martha's health deteriorated. She and her husband continued to live extremely modestly in Brussels and were grateful for the food parcels which their daughter, Ilse, sent from Holland and the money which Walter sent. They were sustained by letters from their children and with the memories of forty years of stimulating life in Leipzig to look back on.

Anti-Jewish laws were introduced by the German authorities in Belgium on 28th October, 1940. Many Jews who had fled from Germany, now tried to flee Belgium. Martha and Henri Hinrichsen could only wait for their American visa.

It was on 20th May, 1941 that Goering first referred to the 'Final Solution' of the 'Jewish Question'.

On 31st July, 1941 Goering instructed Heydrich 'to carry out all the necessary preparations with regard to organisational and financial matters for bringing about a complete solution of the Jewish Question in the German sphere of influence in Europe'.[2]

As the war progressed, communication became extremely difficult and it was not possible to correspond by letter with Great Britain. So it was through the Red Cross Message Bureau, part of the war organisation of the British Red Cross and Order of St John, that Robert Hinrichsen was able to keep contact with his parents. The department which dealt with this type of communication was the 'Prisoner of War, Wounded and Missing Department'. Only twenty-five words were permitted on a printed form from an 'Enquirer', who had to be related to the Addressee and was obliged to state his relationship. These brief communications took well over a month to reach their destination and a twenty-five word reply was permitted. The forms went through censors and via the Red Cross in Geneva and had to be collected by the addressee. So, for example the 'Enquiry' dated 13th February, 1941 from the 'Son' in England, was despatched on 1st April with the number 2466 and date stamped again on 2nd May. It was some considerable time before the addressee received it and was able to reply on 18th July. It is not clear when the reply was finally received.

Martha and Henri Hinrichsen continued to hope for the miracle of their American visa. But they also realised that they might not live to receive it and made new wills. Martha wrote to her children on 2nd August, 1941: '...We are now standing in the dark forest whose path is rugged and it is time to concern ourselves with our lives after our deaths...' and then she outlined what should be done with the contents of all of their trunks and with their possessions.

Martha's health was deteriorating, and she was suffering from heart disease, diabetes and lung problems. On 27th September, the anniversary of the death of her son, Hans-Joachim, she suffered a thrombosis from which she did not recover. She died on the night of 7th October and was buried three days later in the Cemetery of Saint Gilles, in the village of Calevoet in the southern suburbs of Brussels. Henri Hinrichsen had to attend the funeral alone – his six remaining children being scattered throughout a war-torn world. When Walter Hinrichsen received the news of his beloved mother's death, he organised a memorial service for her at the Reform Synagogue in Chicago. Apart from the traditional Jewish memorial service, the *Cradle Song* which Max Reger had composed in 1907, in celebration of Walter's birth and which he had dedicated to Martha Hinrichsen, was performed.

Henri Hinrichsen took over the correspondence with his children which his wife had so assiduously conducted over many years. In one letter Walter had asked him about the portrait of Beethoven by Stieler and he replied on 25th November: 'There is only one Beethoven-Stieler portrait. That was mine. Stieler wrote on the back: "Painted from nature." All others are copies.'

Friends in Brussels took care of him and Walter still sent money. After Martha's death Henri Hinrichsen moved into lodgings in 109 Rue St Georges with a Jewish lady, Mrs Wolf, until she went to a convent to hide from the Gestapo, when he moved to a boarding house at 176 Avenue Hippodrome.

On 25th November, 1941 the Eleventh Ordinance of the Reich Citizenship Law was issued in Germany stipulating that the property belonging to Jews 'whose usual place of residence is abroad...should pass to the ownership of the Reich upon loss of citizenship.'[3] The Hinrichsens' ten packing cases had never left Germany and had been in the dock sheds in Bremen for almost two years; these were now confiscated by the Gestapo. A so-called *Juden Auktion* (Jewish Auction) was held in Bremen on 19th June, 1942, when all their possessions – clothes, linen, household goods, books, music, etc. – were auctioned off. The sum realised, 18,315.20RM, was paid into the German State Treasury.[4] Robert Hinrichsen's trunks were similarly disposed of.[5]

The Final Solution

Heydrich announced plans for the 'Final Solution' at the Wannsee Conference, on 20th January, 1942. These were to be carried out by Adolf Eichmann, who would organise all the trains to be used in the transportation or 'resettlement' as it was euphemistically called, to the concentration camps.

With her death, Martha Hinrichsen (born Bendix) was spared the terrible events which were to follow. In 1942 two of her brothers, with their wives, were killed in the concentration camps; their four children had managed to escape from Germany. Her third brother, who was married to a gentile, committed suicide in order to avoid the fate of his brothers.

Death of Paul Hinrichsen

Paul Hinrichsen had remained in Leipzig. Not only had the visa for his emigration to Brazil, which he had striven so hard to acquire, not been issued, he had not been able to obtain any other visa either.

On 15th January, 1941 he was transported to Neuendorf, Fürstenwalde, to work as a slave farm labourer. He was fit and healthy and loved the outdoor life, so this did not distress him too much. His last letter, still full of optimism for the future, was written to his 'adopted' uncle and aunt, Barnet Licht, a Jew, and his non-Jewish wife who were still in Leipzig. It was written on 5th April, 1943, shortly before his transportation to the East.

No further word was ever received from Paul Hinrichsen. Following sworn statements made by the businessman Salo Looser of Leipzig on 5th June, 1946 and 7th April, 1948 the Berlin *Landgericht* (County Court) issued a death certificate on 13th April, 1948. Paul Hinrichsen was in the concentration camp of Auschwitz at the beginning of September 1943, where he met his death through gassing. He had survived the horrors of concentration camps for just over five months. The date of his death was established as 15th September, 1943. Like his brother, Hans-Joachim, who had pre-deceased him in the internment camp in Perpignan by three years, he was thirty-one years old.

Ilse Frankenthal-Hinrichsen and the Deaths of her Husband and Children

Ilse Frankenthal-Hinrichsen, the Hinrichsen's third child, with her husband, the surgeon Dr Ludwig Frankenthal and their two young sons, Günther and Wolfgang, arrived in the Netherlands on 15th December, 1939. They had obtained visas because three of Dr Frankenthal's brothers had already been granted refuge in Holland. The Frankenthals settled in S'Gravenhage, the Hague, where they existed on what little money Dr Frankenthal's brothers were able to spare them. Those three brothers, as well as two further brothers and a sister were subsequently transported to concentration camps, all to meet their deaths through gassing. (From a family of nine siblings, only two survived.)

When the Germans took possession of Holland in May 1940 many Jews fled or committed suicide. The Frankenthals considered this latter option but discarded it on religious grounds. At the beginning of September the Germans ordered them to leave the Hague. They found an apartment in Bennekom, Gelderland at 42 Veenderweg, where they survived under very difficult conditions from 6th September, 1940 until 8th April, 1943.

Their constant efforts to obtain visas for the USA were finally rewarded; they had all their necessary papers by May 1941 and were due to leave on the next transport – to safety – and freedom. Then came the biggest blow, the United States of America entered the war and all the Frankenthals' expectations were dashed, and the large sum of money which they had had to lay out was gone.

They were sent to the concentration camp at Westerbork, where a doctor was required. Each was allowed to take only one large rucksack and a blanket. This meant leaving behind their entire household and possessions which they had brought with them in thirteen trunks, over four years earlier. After their departure the Germans blew up the house and destroyed or stole everything.

The Frankenthals were in the Westerbork concentration camp from 8th April, 1943 until 4th September, 1944. He worked seven days a week in a well-equipped modern surgery, operating on and curing hundreds of people who would subsequently be transported to the gas chambers. Ilse worked from morning to night cleaning the hospital wards and surgery. Günther, who was fifteen then, had to work as a metalworker.

One day, thirteen women arrived. Dr Frankenthal was ordered to sterilise them. He refused, as it was against his religious principles. His refusal amounted to a death sentence for himself and his family. At five o'clock in the morning of 4th September, 1944, Dr Ludwig Frankenthal, Ilse, Günther and Wolfgang were amongst 3,000 Jews herded into cattle trucks at Westerbork concentration camp for an unknown destination. After two days in the train they arrived in Theresienstadt concentration camp on 6th September. The report Ilse wrote of her terrible ordeal in the concentration camps was used in the Nuremberg Trials after the war.

On 12th October, 1944 they were transported by train for two days and two nights with nothing to drink!! Ilse and her family had arrived in Auschwitz, where she remained from 14th October until 1st November, 1944. In her report she wrote:

My husband immediately saw what our lot was and took his leave of me for life. Order: Nothing to be taken from the train, no rucksack, no food, men and women were separated. That was the last time I saw my two boys and my husband. A doctor stood there and selected the people. Boys had to go with the father and girls with the mother. Then the young and the old were selected. From one transport of about 2,000 people, only 200 remained. We, the remaining ones, were driven into the bath halls. We had to stand there naked for hours. Everything was taken from us, we were not allowed to take anything with us. I had to give up my wedding ring and my spectacles and all my things. All the hair on our heads and bodies was shaved off, and after showers and selection we received very little to wear and it was very thin. It was most probable that one would be gassed if one's body did not look perfect. My body was covered in bites from the bugs in Theresienstadt. The man who selected me kicked me with his heavy boots through the entire bath hall, which meant

that I had not passed the selection. He said that I had syphilis.
The others who were selected as good, were put on a work
transport to go to work in factories.

Ilse survived the horrors of Auschwitz. What she could not find out
definitively until 1948, was that her husband, Dr Ludwig Frankenthal,
at the age of fifty-eight and her two sons, Günther aged fifteen and
Wolfgang who was only twelve, were gassed in Auschwitz; the date was
presumed to have been 15th October, 1944, the day after their arrival.[6]
On 1st November, 1944 she left Auschwitz in a sealed, ice cold cattle
truck which travelled for days and nights to Bergen-Belsen
concentration camp. The conditions there were horrific and she could
never forget the lashings with the whips which she received.

Ilse survived Bergen-Belsen concentration camp from 3rd November
to 15th December, 1944. Then she was transported to Salzwede
concentration camp where she arrived on 18th December. She worked
and suffered terribly. When the Americans liberated the camp on 14th
April, 1945 she was taken straight into hospital on account of starvation
and mental breakdown.[7]

Henri Hinrichsen

On 4th August, 1942 the first 998 Jews were deported from Belgium,
via the Dossin camp in Malines to Auschwitz. Deportations continued
until 31st July, 1944. A total of 23,838 Jewish men, women and children
never returned. Their names are inscribed on a Monument to the Jewish
Martyrs of Belgium in the Rue Carpentier in Brussels.

There was no further news of Henri Hinrichsen from August 1942
onwards. It was not until April 1945, after the war was over, that Walter
Hinrichsen could go to Brussels and find out for himself the terrible
fate of his father. This is perhaps best described in the original words
in English, of Berthold Kirstein, an old friend of Henri Hinrichsen's
who, at Walter Hinrichsen's request addressed a letter to him with which
he could pursue official confirmation of his father's death.

Brussels, April 15th, 1946.

Dear Mr Hinrichsen!

I confirm to you that after the death of your mother your
father, Mr Henri Hinrichsen, changed his lodgings and took
a furnished room at the residence of Mrs Wolf until this lady
went into a convent in order to escape the grip of the Gestapo.
Then Mr Hinrichsen moved to a boarding house. I was told

that early one morning in September 1942 officials of the
Gestapo came to this boarding house in order to search for a
man who had left several months previously. The officials then
asked whether there were any Jewish residents in the house,
and got the answer in the affirmative. These, six, amongst
which our friend Mr Hinrichsen, were at once arrested and
sent to the Jewish camp at Malines. In September 1942 a
transport was put together in Malines and your poor father
was on it. I do not know where the sealed vans were sent to.
But I was told that this transport had the number 10, and
your father the number 901. I might add that on arriving at
the Jewish camp in Malines everyone was deprived of his card
of identity so that these persons lost in all future their names
and became mere numbers.

Yours very truly,

Berthold Kirstein

The *Aide Aux Israélites Victimes de la Guerre* (Aid for Jewish War Victims)
bureau in Brussels confirmed on 20th June, 1947 that Henri Hinrichsen
was deported to the Jewish camp at Malines on 15th September, 1942
on the transport No X and that he was given the number 901.
   A letter of further confirmation, from Antwerp, dated 20th January,
1948, was written by a man who was on the same transport and survived,
N Jakubowitz:

> ...I can inform you that your father was deported with the
> same transport as I was, I even looked after him in the train,
> in my capacity as medical orderly. We arrived in Auschwitz on
> 17th September, 1942 and all those who were over fifty years
> old, as was your father, were loaded onto lorries and driven
> to Birkenau, where they were killed by gas on the same day...

The fresh heady smell of printer's ink, which Henri Hinrichsen had
inhaled with so much pleasure on his arrival as a young man in Leipzig
fifty-five years earlier, had been supplanted by the acrid fumes of the
Zyklon B, as he took his final choking breath in the gas chambers of
Auschwitz concentration camp in Poland, on 17th September, 1942.

1 Martha Hinrichsen to her daughter, Ilse Frankenthal in Holland, 31st January, 1940, and all letters quoted in this chapter either in the author's archive or in the family archive.
2 Letter of 31st July 1941: International Military Tribunal, Nuremberg, document PS-710.
3 Walk, IV, p 272.
4 Stadtarchiv Bremen, Landesamt für Wiedergutmachung, Akte Henri Hinrichsen Erben, Rü 5827.
5 *Ibid.*
6 Notification from the Amtsgericht Berlin-Zehlendorf dated 31st March, 1948 to Ilse Frankenthal. However, Peter Voswinckel, writing in *Judaica Lipsiensia*, p 291 received information from the Arolsen International Search Service dated 16th February, 1988, that Günther was not gassed with his father and brother. His date of death was given as 28th February, 1945 'in the area of Auschwitz'. There were many satellite camps around Auschwitz to house inmates working in local factories. Günther, by then a metal worker, would have been employed in a factory and would have died in one of those camps.
7 Ilse Frankenthal-Hinrichsen's report is in the author's archive.

Afterword

Whilst everything, including his life, was taken from him in such a terrible manner, what Henri Hinrichsen and his uncle, Dr Max Abraham gave away in the form of sponsorships and artefacts and the institutes which they founded and supported, remain as a living tribute to two remarkable men. The music which they published, often as an act of faith in a composer, lives on in recognition of their belief in the pursuit of excellence. And the company to which they devoted their lives, lives on.

The Hinrichsen family had been torn apart and many members murdered, through the Nazi regime in Germany. Those still alive were dispersed in a world thrown into chaos by war.

Max, the eldest son of Martha and Henri Hinrichsen had gone to London in 1937 with his wife and baby. In 1938 he founded Hinrichsen Edition Ltd. Walter, the second son was in the US Army. Robert, the youngest son was in England, in the British Army. Charlotte Sobernheim was in England with her husband and two daughters; their son in the USA. Ilse Frankenthal was in Holland, coming to terms with life after her horrendous ordeal in the concentration camps, where her husband and two sons were killed. She was the only member of the Hinrichsen-Bendix families who entered a concentration camp to have survived. Fourteen members of the family fell victim to the 'final solution', dying in the most horrible circumstances.

C F Peters, Leipzig had survived. Its survival was due to its immense prestige as a publishing business of world stature and its ability to earn substantial sums of foreign currency for the German government. Its importance was underlined by a directive from Goebbels himself, the head of the Propaganda Ministry, dated Berlin, 29th May, 1941:[1]

Declaration

It is herewith certified that the maintenance of the world famous Edition C F Peters, Leipzig C 1, 10 Talstrasse, lies in the cultural and export political interest of the Reich throughout the duration of the war and that the supplies required necessary to the music publishing business should be given the highest priority.

The firm was managed throughout the war by Dr Johannes Petschull, as his own business, acquired by aryanization in 1939. A number of new works were published and the firm was expanded with the purchase in 1940 of the music publishing firm of Henry Litolff's Verlag of Brunswick.[2] In 1941 Petschull took over the majority share holding of Universal Edition, Vienna, (which was returned to the original owners in the 1950s).

All the necessary records and archives and a part of the Peters Music Library were moved to Eisenhammer, about forty kilometres from Leipzig, in the summer of 1943. Special metal boxes were constructed in which the most valuable documents and manuscripts were stored; Dr Petschull and one colleague secretly buried these one night on farm land, informing nobody of their action.

During the bombing raids on Leipzig in December 1943 the printing works of both C G Röder and Poeschel & Trepte, the C F Peters' printers, as well as the book bindery, E A Enders, binders for the company for over fifty years, were completely destroyed. 10 Talstrasse suffered little damage during the war and the premises of C F Peters served as temporary offices for various publishers and printers who had been bombed out and living accommodation for a few musical associates, including Professor Karl Straube.

At the end of the war in April 1945 Dr Petschull's partner, Kurt Herrmann, escaped to Liechtenstein. With Germany divided up into allied zones, Leipzig was in the American zone until June, when it became part of the Russian zone.

The first member of the Hinrichsen family to return to Leipzig, was Walter Hinrichsen. His German background and experience in music publishing was the reason for his presence in Germany at the end of the war. He had joined the US army in 1942, becoming a US citizen in 1943. A master sergeant when the war ended, he became the US Music Officer, in the Control Commission and was stationed in Berlin. It was in this role and wearing his US army uniform, that he came to Leipzig.

Walter's first aim was to retrieve the firm of C F Peters for the Hinrichsen family. The current state of the law made it necessary for his four remaining brothers and sisters legally to relinquish their inheritance in his favour. He wanted to replace Dr Petschull with Wilhelm Weismann as general manager. However, Weismann, though loyal to the Hinrichsen family, insisted that he was a musicologist and editor and had no desire to be business manager. Many important items being hidden where only Dr Petschull could locate them, Walter entered into an agreement with him, in order to reclaim what belonged to the family. That was how Dr Petschull became an equal partner with Walter and Max Hinrichsen, as owners of C F Peters in Germany. On 21st June, shortly before the withdrawal of American troops from Leipzig,

Dr Petschull transferred the ownership of C F Peters, Leipzig to Walter Hinrichsen, at the Leipzig District Court. In exchange, Petschull was granted power of attorney and a partnership and was to manage C F Peters, Leipzig.

Walter also negotiated the return of a quantity of manuscripts and autographed letters which had belonged to his parents and the return of some of the paintings which his father had been forced to relinquish to the Museum der bildenden Künste (Art Gallery); though only after donating some of the paintings and a considerable sum of money to the museum. When the Russians took over Leipzig, all bank accounts were confiscated, so it was only with difficulty that business could be conducted.

More speedily achieved than this, was the re-naming of the Abrahamstrasse. Named after Dr Max Abraham in 1910, the Nazis had changed the name to Robert Naumann Strasse in 1935. It was officially re-named Abrahamstrasse on 19th May, 1945.

In 1945 Dr Petschull had to go through a de-Nazification process. According to Fred K Prieberg, whose research into the aryanization of C F Peters was quoted in Chapter Fifteen, Petschull at first insisted that he had never joined the Nazi Party, then, on 16th July, 1945 he allegedly signed a form saying that he had joined on 1st January, 1939. However, Prieberg says there is evidence in the Berlin Document Centre that he had a Nazi Party membership card dated 6th July, 1937. Following his de-Nazification, on 22nd August, 1946, Dr Petschull was removed from his managerial position at C F Peters by the Soviet authorities, who replaced him with a 'custodian' approved of by them. After considerable negotiation he was eventually reinstated. In January 1947, 'as an act of humane and legal duty'[3] Walter Hinrichsen was once again recognised as the proprietor of C F Peters by the government of Saxony. Petschull received a licence from the Soviet military authority in Leipzig on 17th March, 1947 to continue publishing. But he and the Hinrichsen brothers realised that business under Soviet occupation would be unsatisfactory.

Secretly, Petschull negotiated the transfer of about 100 cases of the most valuable C F Peters documents to Switzerland and thence to Frankfurt, in the American zone. At the end of 1948, C F Peters, Leipzig was once again confiscated from the Hinrichsen family. The fact that the Hinrichsen family was hence unjustly robbed of its ownership of C F Peters for the second time, was conveniently veiled by a legal manoeuvre which stated that 'the transfer of the business to Walter Hinrichsen was declared as unlawful and therefore annulled'. Thus Herrmann and Petschull were once again the legal owners; as one-time members of the Nazi Party, the business was then confiscated from them. In November 1948 Petschull was arrested and imprisoned in

Dresden. Another custodian was installed at C F Peters, the position of manager being given to a music dealer, Georg Hillner.

Through the intervention of Walter Hinrichsen, Dr Petschull was released from prison after fourteen months and went to Frankfurt in the spring of 1950. On 28th August 1950, C F Peters, Leipzig was officially taken over by the newly formed DDR (German Democratic Republic) and recognised as a *Volks Eigener Betrieb* (State-owned Business), under the control of the government. The company was re-named VEB C F Peters, Leipzig. Neither Walter nor Max Hinrichsen nor Dr Petschull were involved in its management or ownership any more; they had been totally dispossessed. All profits from the business henceforth devolved to the German Democratic Republic.

Dr Petschull, together with Max Hinrichsen in London and Walter Hinrichsen who had by then founded C F Peters Corporation in New York, founded the parallel music publishing company of C F Peters GmbH Frankfurt/London/New York in 1950. Despite the enormous difficulties of the post-war years and the fact that all the printing plates had remained in Leipzig, the first major catalogue of works, published by the three companies, appeared in 1953 and comprised some 900 titles. The three partners complemented each other by publishing different works from the huge catalogue, the sooner to be able to supply the whole of the Western world with most of the music published in the Edition Peters. Later, commercial links were also forged with the DDR State-owned C F Peters in Leipzig.

The legal declaration of the nullification of the aryanization contract and the world-wide legal fight for recognition of the Hinrichsen family as owners of C F Peters took many years. The establishment of the new company, the continuation of C F Peters, Leipzig, as well as the lengthy negotiations, contracts, copyrights and legal arrangements between the four different C F Peters companies are beyond the scope of this book. Legal processes for the reclamation of much of the Hinrichsen property dragged on for over fifty-five years, way beyond the lifespan of any of the surviving five children of Henri and Martha Hinrichsen.

Meanwhile Max and Walter Hinrichsen were extending the interests of C F Peters in Great Britain and the USA.

Walter Hinrichsen

Walter Hinrichsen married Evelyn Merrell in New York City in 1946 and after completing his tour of duty in Germany they returned to the USA at the end of 1947. Their two children, whom they named after Walter's parents, Martha and Henry, were born in 1948 and 1949. Together with his cousin, Walter Bendix (the son of one of his mother's brothers who had been gassed in the concentration camps), Walter

Hinrichsen founded C F Peters Corporation in New York City on 1st September, 1948.

He set about reprinting the main works in the Edition Peters and soon started publishing the works of contemporary American composers such as John Cage, George Crumb, Alan Hovhaness, Ned Rorem, Charles Wuorinen and others. His attitudes towards publishing reflected those of his father, Henri Hinrichsen.

In 1963 C F Peters Corporation, New York received a citation from the National Association for American Composers and Conductors. The American Composers Alliance Laurel Leaf Award 1964 was given to Walter Hinrichsen 'For distinguished Achievement in Fostering and Encouraging American Music'. He was a member of the board of directors of the Music Publishers Association, a member of the Music Library Association and the American Musicological Society.

Walter Hinrichsen died suddenly, at the age of almost sixty-two, from a heart attack on 21st July, 1969. His widow, Evelyn Hinrichsen took his place as President of C F Peters Corporation, New York. His brother Max's career as an independent music publisher started earlier, but also ended earlier.

Max Hinrichsen

Arriving in November, 1937, Max Hinrichsen founded his own music publishing company, Hinrichsen Edition Ltd. in London, on 10th March, 1938. He had two main objectives:

> To re-issue in up-to-date editions forgotten works of the past, especially those by British composers such as Arne, Blow, Boyce, Greene, Thomas Roseingrave, Stanley, Tallis and Wesley; and to issue new compositions by our living composers.[4]

His first publications were a series of easy original compositions for piano, by classical composers. HE numbers 1-7 covered respectively: Beethoven, Chopin, Haydn, Mozart, Schubert and Schumann. In publishing this series he was acknowledging the pioneering achievements of Dr Max Abraham, whose 'Edition Peters' classics were launched some seventy years earlier.

The outbreak of war in 1939 brought difficulties for publishing, as paper was rationed; so Max published booklets and small scale works. He became involved in entertainment for the troops. From 1942-1948 he was the Honorary Editor of a weekly newsletter, *On Leave in London*, issued for the troops by the London Regional Committee for Education among HM forces. He also ran a successful concert agency.

Max Hinrichsen had become stateless with the issuance of the 'Eleventh Ordinance' regarding the Law of Reich Citizenship, promulgated on 25th November, 1941, which deprived non-resident Jews of citizenship of the German Reich. He was granted all privileges of British citizens except the right of free travel, but his naturalisation was held up owing to the war, when his official status was that of an 'enemy alien'. Granted British citizenship by naturalisation, on 1st May, 1947 he could then travel to Germany to continue to disentangle the affairs of C F Peters.

On his arrival in Great Britain, Max Hinrichsen had been working with Novello and Co Ltd, as the personal representative of the Edition Peters. Frustrated at not being permitted to publish the music himself which was his birthright, after the war ended in 1945 he did eventually publish the all-time C F Peters best-seller, Sinding's *Rustle of Spring* and some other works. Thereupon Novello and Co, claiming that he had no right to do so, took legal action against Hinrichsen Edition Ltd for infringement of their copyright. They argued that Max Hinrichsen was not the owner of the copyright because his father had lost it, and that they, as licensees under the emergency legislation, were the sole persons entitled to publish the works in England. The judgements are fully re-printed in the Chancery Division records.[5]

Bridging the years 1950 and 1951, the case lasted nineteen days before Justice Wynn Parry in the Chancery Division of the High Court. Max Hinrichsen won. Novello appealed against the judgement. The appeal occupied four days in the Court of Appeal in June 1951; it was dismissed. Again Max Hinrichsen was successful. In his summing up of the first case on 21st February, 1950, Mr Justice Wynn Parry made it clear that Nazi decrees did not make law in England. The English copyright was never lost by Henri Hinrichsen, and his son Max was now the true owner:

> The courts of this country will not give effect, so far as regards assets within their jurisdiction, to the law of a foreign country which is confiscatory in policy…Novello and Co have no merits in this case. I would have been quite unwilling in the interests of justice to allow the plaintiffs to succeed in depriving the Hinrichsen family, who have already suffered enough, of their inheritance.

The publication of Edition Peters' music in England, by its rightful owners, could now go ahead without further hindrance. Max Hinrichsen then founded Peters Edition, London, to publish in parallel with his own Hinrichsen Edition Ltd. In 1954, after a traditional apprenticeship, Max's daughter, Irene Hinrichsen (the author) joined her father's business; she left in 1960.

A major, lasting achievement, was his series of *Hinrichsen's Musical Year Book*, which first appeared in 1944. In the compilation of these books he was emulating the Peters Music Library Year Books which he had helped edit. They were meticulously compiled reference works listing many aspects of musical life and containing a wealth of information. Nine books were issued, though the title was changed to *The Music Book;* Volume X, *Organ and Choral Aspects and Prospects,* comprised the Papers read at the first International Organ Congress, held in London in 1957 and Volume XI, the Proceedings of the 1959 Congress of the Association of Music Libraries, was entitled *Music Libraries and Instruments.*

Hinrichsen Edition Ltd published music by contemporary British composers such as Richard Arnell, Elizabeth Maconchy, Thomas B Pitfield, William S Lloyd Webber and Peter Wishart, and foreign composers. Much organ music was published and the series, *From Tallis to Wesley,* comprising several volumes of early English music, was welcomed by keyboard players everywhere. Max Hinrichsen also commissioned and published new works for brass bands. The firm also made available modern music, which was not initially published, through CELL (Composers' and Editors' Lending Library), a service to composers and ensembles, providing a substantial library of works, largely in manuscript.

Involved in every aspect of music publishing, Max Hinrichsen took an active lead in various associations including the Mechanical Copyright Protection Societies, the Music Trades Association, the National Book League, the Performing Rights Society, the Publishers' Association. He belonged to the Incorporated Association of Organists and other organ societies, the International Association of Music Libraries, the Royal Musical Association, the Dolmetsch Foundation, the Galpin Society, Holy Trinity Choral Society – of which he was the Vice President, the Hymn Society of Great Britain, the Viola da Gamba Society – as Vice President, the Society of Authors, the American Musicological Society, the *Internationale Gesellschaft für Musikwissenschaft* and more. He was a Council Member of the Arts Committee of the London Council of Social Service, Vice President of the National School Brass Band Association, Vice President of the British Copyright Protection Association, London and a Deputy Member of the *Conseil d'Administration du Bureau de l'Edition Mecanique, BIEM,* Paris.

Max Hinrichsen was elected an Honorary Fellow of Trinity College of Music, London (Hon FTCL), in July 1965, the first music publisher to be so honoured in the ninety-two years that the awards had been made. The citation, read by Dr Greenhouse Allt, former Principal of Trinity College of Music and Past President of the Royal College of

Organists, in terms similar to those used by the University of Leipzig in
honouring his father in 1929 read:

> In recognition of his scholarship in music, especially
> distinguished in the field of Bach research, the Board seeks
> to honour Max Hinrichsen. He is an outstanding progressive
> publisher of music and books of world-wide fame, mainly
> through the great Hinrichsen and Peters editions, and he is
> an educationist in the most practical sense of the word,
> through and by the provision of up-to-date training material,
> and other facilities, for the use of students of music.

That was his proudest moment; it marked the recognition of twenty-
seven years of achievement, as a foreigner who had been accepted by
the British musical establishment. Five months later he suffered a heart
attack and died, at the age of sixty-four, on 17th December, 1965.

The direction of the company which he had founded, was taken
over by his widow (his second wife), Carla Eddy Hinrichsen. In 1975,
the company was re-named Peters Edition, Ltd, London.

Meanwhile VEB C F Peters, Leipzig continued as a state-owned business.
With the re-unification of Germany in 1990, protracted legal
negotiations led to the return of the business to its rightful owners –
the widows of Max and Walter Hinrichsen and Dr Johannes Petschull.

The music publishing firm of C F Peters, founded as Bureau de
Musique Hoffmeister & Kühnel in 1800 in Leipzig, has been all but
liquidated in Leipzig. It will remain a memory, with a small office and
a memorial plaque. The descendants of the shattered and dispersed
Hinrichsen family will never return to live in the city to which Henri
Hinrichsen contributed so much.

The bicentenary of the company is being celebrated as the new
millennium commences, by the three sister firms: Peters Edition Ltd,
London with Hinrichsen Edition Ltd, headed by Carla Hinrichsen and
managed by Nicholas Riddle; C F Peters Corporation New York, headed
by Evelyn Hinrichsen with her daughter, Martha Hinrichsen, and
Nicholas Riddle as CEO; and C F Peters Frankfurt, in 1999 headed by
the ninety-eight-year-old Dr Johannes Petschull and managed by Karl
Rarichs. They bear one of the foremost names in music publishing
into the twenty-first century.

1   Reference number M 10039-06/, StAL Bestand, C F Peters (file number unknown).
2   Purchased from Hanna Litolff, a Jewess (d 1957), the widow of Richard Litolff (1868-1937).
3   *Börsenblatt (Frankfurt)* 48/15.6.1990, p 1958ff.
4   Quoted from *Max Hinrichsen,* Notes prepared for his round-the-world trip, 1955, Peters Edition, London.
5   *All England Law Reports* (1951, pp 44-61 and, pp 770-772), *Law Report, Chancery Division* (1951 pp 595-611 and 1026-1038). Also, several legal, musical and literary journals in Great Britain and abroad, as well as British newspapers including *The Times* (22nd February, 1951), *The Evening Standard* (23rd February, 1951).

THE END

Source Material

C F Peters Documentation

The history of C F Peters is well documented by an immense amount of archival material. Undamaged during the Second World War, the archive goes back to the foundation of the company in 1800. The documents appertaining to the first 126 years were transferred from the basement of 10 Talstrasse (the business premises of C F Peters) to the *Sächsische Staatsarchiv Leipzig* (the Archive of the State of Saxony, in Leipzig) in 1966. The transfer was overseen by Dr phil. Hans-Martin Plesske who wrote a booklet covering the scope of this remarkable collection: *Der Bestand Musikverlag C F Peters im Staatsarchiv Leipzig* (The Archive of the Music Publisher C F Peters in the State Archive Leipzig), subtitled *Business Letters from the years 1800 to 1926 as Source Material for Musical Research and the History of the Book Trade.* It is a reprint from the *Jahrbuch der Deutschen Bücherei* (Year Book of the German Library) Year 6 – 1970. (Leipzig 1970). A further part of the archive was transferred in 1981 and the remainder, including that of the DDR years, was transferred during the 1990s.

All this material, which encompasses more than a million items, is stored in the new, modern premises of the *Sächsische Staatsarchiv Leipzig* and takes up over 150 meters of shelf space; it is catalogued on card indexes, though not in detail and has all been transferred to microfiche. In August 1997 C F Peters signed an agreement consigning the archive to the *Sächsische Staatsarchiv Leipzig* on free loan for twenty-five years, thus enabling access for research. Most of this material had remained untouched since it was wrapped in brown paper to lie unattended in the basement of 10 Talstrasse over a hundred years ago. There is a veritable treasure-trove for the dedicated researcher.

There are letters from over 300 important musical personalities including Clara Schumann, Hugo Wolf, Max Reger, Richard Strauss, and hundreds of others – for example there are over 300 letters from Moritz Moszkowski dating from 1886-1914; 38 each from Eugen d'Albert and Ferruccio Benvenuto Busoni; 83 from Arnold Mendelssohn; 100 from Emil Mattiesen; 200 from Christian Sinding; hundreds each from Gustav Kogel, Karl Straube, Hans Pfitzner, Max Friedländer, Gustav

Brecher, Walter Niemann and many more, including letters from conductors and performing artists. They cover many aspects of musicology and musical opinion, as well as progress of music in hand.

Added to this is the correspondence from the company in the form of Copy Books, which contain over 250,000 letters. In the days before the invention of the typewriter and carbon copies, it was the custom at C F Peters for a clerk to copy the business details, though not generally any personal observations, of every letter to be sent out, into a *Kopierbuch* (Copy book). This was done each day; so that these copies are not filed in alphabetical order together with the incoming correspondence, but are bound in order, according to the date on which they were written in the books. Hence, following through the replies to any correspondence is a time-consuming occupation. C F Peters had several series of Copy books, which are now housed in the *Sächsische Staatsarchiv Leipzig*. Details appear in the Bibliography.

Apart from the correspondence there are many original manuscripts of works by well-known composers, published by C F Peters. There are also many documents pertaining to the work of publishing such as catalogues of plate numbers, records of print orders, details of proofs of individual works. There are thousands of documents about the personal professional involvement of the owners, such as Carl Friedrich Peters, Dr Max Abraham and Geheimrat Dr Henri Hinrichsen, in the spheres of the Börsenverein (the Book Trades Association), the printing industry, copyright protection, musical research and so on, which are intrinsic to the development of the cultural history of Leipzig.

There are many documents and letters concerning aspects pertaining to the Leipzig City Council in the *Stadt Archiv Leipzig* (Leipzig City Archive) where there are also many items covering the Nazi period. The archives of the University of Leipzig, the *Stadt Geschichtliches Museum* (Leipzig City Museum) and the *Galerie der bildenden Künste* (Leipzig Art Gallery) all have documents. There is information housed in the Berlin Document Center and in the *Staatsarchiv Bremen* (The Bremen City Archive).

Bibliography

Leipzig History:

Baedekers Leipzig, Karl Baedeker, Freiburg, 1973.
Leipzig Stadt der Musik, VEB Edition Peters, Leipzig, 1990.
Leipzig – The little blue-yellow city guide, Fackelträger-Verlag GmbH, Hannover, 1990.
Literarische Leipzig, Das, edited by Andreas Herzog, Edition Leipzig, 1995.
Musical Events in Leipzig, an information leaflet issued by the Gewandhaus zu Leipzig, 1994.
Neues Forum Leipzig, Jetzt oder nie – Demokratie! Leipziger Herbst '89, Forum Verlag, Leipzig, 1989.
Neues Leipzigisches Geschicht-Buch, commissioned by the Council of the City of Leipzig, edited by Dr phil. Klaus Sohl, Fachbuchverlag, Leipzig, 1990.
Thomaskirche zu Leipzig, Die, Kunstverlag H C Schmiedicke, Leipzig, 1988.
Völkerschlacht-Denkmal, Das, edited by Dr phil. Klaus Sohl, Sachsenbuch Verlagsgesellschaft, Leipzig, 1993.

C F Peters History:

Chronik des Hauses C F Peters – *'Geschichte des Verlagshauses C F PETERS von seiner Gründung am 1. Dezember 1800 an bis zum 1. Oktober, 1933',* by Dr hc Henri Hinrichsen, unpublished, 1933. [Referred to as *Chronik*]
C F Peters Musikverlag, Zeittafeln zur Verlagsgeschichte 1800-1867-1967, by Heinrich Lindlar, C F Peters Frankfurt, 1967. [Referred to as *Zeittafeln*]
1880-1975 Edition Peters, Erschienen anlässlich des 175 jährigen Bestehens des Musikverlages Peters am 1 Dezember, 1975, edited by Bernd Pachnicke, C F Peters, Leipzig. [Referred to as *1880-1975 Edition Peters.*]

Kopierbuch:

C F Peters had several series of *Kopierbücher* (Copy books), which are now housed in the Staatsarchiv Leipzig (the titles were accorded by the Staatsarchiv not by the publisher):

Internationale Autorenkorrespondenz (International Authors'
  Correspondence), Copybooks with index, 26 volumes, 1801-1940;
  StAL 5021-5042.
Internationale Geschäftskorrespondenz (International Business
  Correspondence), Copybooks with index, 129 volumes, 1892-1940;
  StAL 5047-5155, 5160-5179.
Allgemeine Geschäftskorrespondenz (General Business Correspondence),
  Copybooks with index, 1800-1949, each year from A-Z; StAL 2588-
  3690.

Hinrichsen Family History:

Information from family documents in the author's archive and:

*Die Hoffinanz und der moderne Staat, Geschichte und System der Hoffaktoren
  an Deutschen Fürstenhöfen im Zeitalter des Absolutismus,* Heinrich Schnee,
  (3 Vols) Berlin, 1953, Vol 2, pp 293-308.
*Henri Hinrichsen, Ein Gedenkblatt zu seinem 60 Geburtstag, Gewidmet von
  den Angestellten der Firma C F Peters,* C F Peters, Leipzig, 1928.

Peters Music Library:

Musikbibliothek der Stadt Leipzig, leaflet, 1972.
'Die Musikbibliothek der Stadt Leipzig', by Ellen Roeser and Peter Krause,
  reprint from *Jahrbuch zur Geschichte der Stadt Leipzig,* 1979.
*'Die Musikbibliothek Peters in Leipzig, Zur Erinnerung an ihre Eröffnung
  vor einhundert Jahren',* by Peter Krause, reprint from *Forum
  Musikbibliothek,* 2/1994.
'Auch Londons "Standard" schwärmte' (Also London's "Standard" went
  into raptures) by Werner Wolf, *Leipziger Volkszeitung,* 13th January,
  1994.
'Was geschieht mit Leipzigs Schatztruhe' by Walter Vorwerk, *Neue Musik
  Zeitung* p 10, Feb/March 1994.
'Die musikalische Bibliothek', by Peter Krause, *Leipziger Amts-Blatt,* 7th
  February, 1994.
Jahrbuch der Musikbibliothek Peters, Preface to each volume 1895-1941.
  Issued annually from 1895, C F Peters Leipzig.

Other:

'Abraham, Max', by Paul Ollendorff, *Jahrbuch der Musikbibliothek Peters
  für 1931,* C F Peters, 1932. (Reprint of the obituary written in 1902.)
Archivmitteilungen, 2/1984.
Bach-Jahrbuch 1904, p 35, Breitkopf & Härtel, Leipzig.

Bach Jahrbuch 1906, p 140, Breitkopf & Härtel, Leipzig.

Bachhaus Eisenach, Fünfzig Jahre, Conrad Freyse, 1950.

Beethoven, L, van, Seine an den Verlag von Hoffmeister und Kühnel, später C F Peters, Leipzig gerichteten Briefe, Verzeichnis seiner in der Edition Peters erschienen Werke, C F Peters, Leipzig, 1927.

Börsenblatt für den Deutschen Buchhandel, No 148, 30th June, 1931.

Deutsche Buchhändler-Lehranstalt Leipzig gegründet 1853, Private print, Leipzig, 1995 and 1997.

Fraungewerbeverein, from Leipzig newspapers, 1902, 1907, 1909, 1910, 1911, 1913.

Führer durch das Musikwissenschaftliche Instrumenten Museum der Universität Leipzig, edited by Helmut Schultz, Breitkopf & Härtel, Leipzig, 1929.

Grieg, Edvard, Briefe an die Verleger der Edition Peters 1866-1907, edited by Elsa v Zschinsky-Troxler, C F Peters Leipzig, 1932.

Grieg, Edvard, Briefwechsel mit dem Verlag C F Peters 1863-1907, edited by Finn Benestad & Hella Brock, C F Peters, Frankfurt, 1997.

Grieg, Edvard, by Hella Brock, Reclam Verlag, Leipzig, 1990.

Grieg, Edvard, Verzeichnis seiner Werke mit Einleitung: Mein erster Erfolg, C F Peters, Leipzig, 1910.

450 Jahre Gelehrtenschule des Johanneums zu Hamburg 1979, Hamburg, 1979.

Judaica Lipsiensia, Zur Geschichte der Juden in Leipzig, edited by Dr Manfred Unger, Ephraim Carlebach Stiftung, Leipzig, 1994.

Kemp, Annerose, *Henriette Goldschmidt – Vom Frauenrecht zur Kindererziehung,* Private print, Horst Kemp, Leipzig, 1993.

Kemp, Annerose and Nimschowski, Ilse, *Henriette-Goldschmidt-Schule 1911-1991,* Fachschule für Sozialpädagogik Henriette-Goldschmidt-Schule Leipzig, 1991.

Leipziger Neunundneunzig, Die, Leipzier Bibliophilen Abend, Leipzig, 1929.

Klemm, Eberhardt, editor: *Gustav Mahler, 'Zur Geschichte der Fünften Sinfonie',* in *Aufsätze zur Musik,* Jahrbuch Peters 1979, C F Peters Leipzig, 1979.

Lieberwirth, Steffen, *Bruckner und Leipzig,* Edition Peters, Leipzig, 1990.

Max Hesses Deutscher Musikerkalender für das Jahr 1919, Max Hesse Verlag, Berlin, 1919.

Musik in Geschichte und Gegenwart, Vol 5, 1956.

'Musikinstrumenten-Museum', extract from *Kunstschätze der Karl-Marx-Universität-Leipzig,* published for the Chancellor, E A Seemann Verlag, Leipzig, 1981.

Rektorwechsel an der Universität Leipzig am 31 Oktober, 1929, Leipzig, 1929.

Reger, Max, Briefwechsel mit dem Verlag C F Peters, edited by Susanne Popp and Susanne Shigihara, Dümmlers Verlag, Bonn, 1995.

Reger, Max, Briefe an Karl Straube, edited by Susanne Popp, Dümmlers Verlag, Bonn, 1986.

Riemann Musiklexikon, Vol 12, Mainz, 1959.

Sauerlandt, Max, *Ausgewählte Schriften*, Vol I, Verlag Hans Christian, Hamburg, 1971.

Schebera, Jürgen, *Gustav Brecher und die Leipziger Oper 1923-1933*, Edition Peters, Leipzig, 1990.

Schönberg, Arnold, *Der Briefwechsel zwischen, und dem Verlag C F Peters'*, Eberhardt Klemm, Deutsches Jahrbuch der Musikwissenschaft, 1970.

Volksliederbuch für Männerchor, Vol I, C F Peters, Leipzig, 1907.

Volksliederbuch für Gemischten Chor, Vol I, C F Peters, Leipzig, 1915.

Part IV, The Holocaust:

Deutscher Musiker-Kalender, 1943, Vol I, Max Hesse Verlag, Berlin, 1943.

Diamant, Adolf: *Chronik der Juden in Leipzig, Aufstieg, Vernichtung und Neuanfang*, Verlag Heimatland Sachsen, 1993.

Festliche Gründungsveranstaltung am 14. Dezember 1991, Freundes- und Förderkreis Musikinstrumenten Museum der Universität Leipzig eV, University of Leipzig 1992.

Lexikon Leipziger Strassennamen, edited by the Stadtarchiv Leipzig, Verlag im Wissenschaftszentrum, Leipzig, 1995.

Prieberg, Fred K, *Historisches Gutachten, MDR Leipzig, 1994*. (Unpublished, for inclusion in *Deutsche Musiker 1933-1945*, in preparation.)

Schinköth, Thomas, *Jüdische Musiker in Leipzig 1855-1945*, Verlag Klaus-Jürgen Kamprad, Altenburg, 1994.

Schinköth, Thomas, editor: *Musikstadt Leipzig im NS-Staat, Beiträge zu einem verdrängten Thema*, Verlag Klaus-Jürgen Kamprad, 1997.

Unger, Manfred, *Die Juden in Leipzig unter der Herrschaft des Nationalsozialismus*, in *Verdrängung und Vernichtung der Juden unter dem Nationalsozialismus*, Hans Christian Verlag, Hamburg, 1992.

Unger, Manfred and Lang, Hubert, editors: *Juden in Leipzig, Eine Dokumentation*, Rat des Bezirkes Leipzig, Abteilung Kultur, 1989.

Walk, J, ed, *Das Sonderrecht für die Juden im NS-Staat: Eine Sammlung der gesetzlichen Massnahmen und Richtlinien – Inhalt und Bedeutung*, Karlruhe, 1981.

Wilke, Martina and Winter, Albrecht, editors, *Dokumente, Programe, Biografien Zur Arbeit des Jüdischen Kulturbundes Leipzig e V*, Ephraim Carlebach Stiftung, Leipzig, 1994.

Wulf, Joseph, *Musik im Dritten Reich*, Sigbert Mohn Verlag, 1963.

Books in English:

The Cambridge Encyclopaedia, edited by David Crystal, Cambridge
    University Press, Cambridge, 1990.
The New Grove Dictionary of Music and Musicians, edited by Stanley Sadie,
    Macmillan Publishers Ltd, London, 1980, paperback reprint, 1995.
The Oxford Dictionary of Music, edited by Michael Kennedy, Oxford
    University Press, 1994.
Composers Since 1900, compiled and edited by David Ewen, The H W
    Wilson Company, New York, 1969.
Barkai, Avram, *From Boycott to Annihilation, The Economic Struggle of
    German Jews 1933-1943,* translated by William Templer, Published
    for Brandeis University Press by University Press of New England,
    USA, 1989.
Gilbert, Martin, *The Holocaust: The Jewish Tragedy,* Fontana Press, 1987
    (Collins, 1986), London.
Grünberger, Richard, *A Social History of the Third Reich,* Penguin Books,
    1991 (Weidenfeld & Nicholson, 1971), London.
Hinrichsen, Max, editor: *Music Book Volume VII,* Hinrichsen Edition
    Ltd, London, 1952.
Hinrichsen, Max, editor: *Music Book Volume VIII (2nd edition),* Hinrichsen
    Edition Ltd, London, 1966.
Hinrichsen, Max, *Peters Edition and Max Hinrichsen,* Hinrichsen Edition
    Ltd, London, 1955.
Hinrichsen, Walter, A Tribute, C F Peters Corporation, New York, 1969.
Horton, Paul, *Grieg* (The Master Musicians Series), J M Dent & Sons
    Ltd, London, 1974.
Levi, Erik, *Music and National Socialism: The Politicisation of Criticism,
    Composition and Performance,* in *The Nazification of Art,* edited by
    Brandon Taylor and Wilfred van der Will, The Winchester Press,
    1990.
Lyth, Peter J, *Inflation and the Merchant Economy – The Hamburg
    Mittelstand, 1914-1924,* Berg Publishers Inc, Providence, RI, USA
    and Oxford, England, 1990.
Monrad-Johansen, David, *Edvard Grieg,* translated from Norwegian by
    Madge Robertson, Princeton University Press – American-
    Scandinavian Foundation, New York, Princeton, 1938.
Noakes, J, and Pridham, G, editors, *Nazism 1919-1945,* Volume 2, *State,
    Economy and Society 1933-39,* University of Exeter Press, 1984.

Index